GREAT POWER DISCORD IN PALESTINE

GREAT POWER
DISCORD IN PALESTINE

The Anglo-American Committee of
Inquiry into the Problems of
European Jewry and Palestine,
1945–1946

AMIKAM NACHMANI

Department of International Relations,
The Hebrew University of Jerusalem

Routledge
Taylor & Francis Group

LONDON AND NEW YORK

First published 1987 by
FRANK CASS AND COMPANY LIMITED

Published 2004 by Routledge
2 Park Square, Milton Park, Abingdon, Oxfordshire OX14 4RN
711 Third Avenue, New York, NY 10017

First issued in paperback 2016

*Routledge is an imprint of the Taylor and Francis Group,
an informa business*

Copyright © 1987 Amikam Nachmani

British Library Cataloguing in Publication Data

Nachmani, Amikam
    Great power discord in Palestine : the Anglo-
    American Committee of Inquiry into the problems
    of European Jewry and Palestine, 1945-1946.
    1. World politics—1945-1855 2. Palestine—
    Politics and government—1929-1948
    I. Title
    956.94'04   126.4

Library of Congress Cataloging-in-Publication Data

Nachmani, Amikam.
    Great power discord in Palestine.

    Bibliography: p.
    Includes index.
    1. Anglo-American Committee of Inquiry on Jewish
Problems in Palestine and Europe.   2. Holocaust
survivors.   3. Great Britain–Foreign relations–United
States.   4. United States–Foreign relations–Great
Britain.   5. Palestine–Emigration and immigration.
6. United States–Foreign relations–1945-1953.
I. Title.
DS126.4.N23   1986   327.73041   86-6107
ISBN 0-7146-3298-8

ISBN 13: 978-1-138-99204-7 (pbk)
ISBN 13: 978-0-7146-3298-8 (hbk)

Contents

List of Illustrations

between pages 166 and 167

Map

ACKNOWLEDGMENTS

Pictures 1, 2 and 4 are published by courtesy of the Central Zionist Archives, Jerusalem. Pictures 3, 4, 6, 7 and 8, and the Provincial Autonomy Plan, are published by courtesy of the Middle East Centre, St Antony's College, Oxford.

Quotations from Richard Crossman, *Palestine Mission*, are reprinted by permission of A.D. Peters & Co. Ltd.

Acknowledgements

Many individuals and institutes helped me in writing this book. Some gave good advice; some gave access to documents; some financial support. Without their help, this research would not have been completed.

The Truman Institute at the Hebrew University of Jerusalem; the Friends of the Hebrew University in Britain; the Oxford Centre for Post Graduate Hebrew Studies; the Avi Foundation, Geneva; the Wolfson Trust, London; St. Antony's College, Oxford; the Truman Institute, Independence, Missouri; the Oriental Institute at the University of Oxford; the Bryce and Read, the Beit and the Arnold Funds of the University of Oxford, all generously lent their financial support for which I am deeply grateful.

The librarians and archivists of many institutions assisted me far beyond my expectations, and to them I owe a great debt of gratitude. My very special thanks are extended to the staff of the Public Record Office, Kew, and of the Middle East Centre of St. Antony's College.

Mrs Haya Amir has painstakingly and skilfully edited my manuscript. Professor Stuart Cohen also made helpful editorial contributions.

Mr Albert Hourani of St. Antony's College, Oxford, allowed me access to documents in his possession, and was always ready with good advice and encouragement. I owe him a great deal.

My deepest gratitude is to Lord Bullock of St. Catherine's College, Oxford. Working with him has been an exciting intellectual experience. His patience and persistent encouragement, both academically and personally, extended beyond the usual relationship between mentor and student. I can only hope that the book fulfils some of his expectations.

And perhaps everything is due to Nitza, Amos, and Hagai, who, with admirable fortitude, endured – and survived – the years of spiritual, almost physical presence in our home of the twelve members ("the twelve apostles") of the Anglo-American Committee.

List of Abbreviations

AAC	Anglo-American Committee
ACPC	American Christian Palestine Committee
ACS	Army Council Secretariat
AJC	American Jewish Committee
AJDC	American Joint Distribution Committee
AZEC	American Zionist Emergency Council
CID	Criminal Investigation Department
C in C	Commander(s) in Chief
CIGS	Chief of Imperial General Staff
CM	Cabinet Meeting
Cmd	Command Paper
COS	Chiefs of Staff
CP	Cabinet Paper
CZA	Central Zionist Archives
DNB	Dictionary of National Biography
DPs	Displaced Persons
FRUS	Foreign Relations United States
GOC	General Officer Commanding
HMG	His Majesty's Government
HQ	Headquarters
IGCR	Inter-Governmental Committee on Refugees
MP	Member of Parliament
NRC	National Record Centre
OSS	Office of Strategic Services
PA	Provincial Autonomy
PMM	Prime Minister's Meeting
Pt	Part
RG	Record Group
RIIA	Royal Institute of International Affairs
SACMEC	St. Antony's College, Middle East Centre
SOS	Secretary of State
TJFF	Trans-Jordan Frontier Force
UN, UNO	United Nations Organization
UNRRA	United Nations Relief and Rehabilitation Agency
UNSCOP	United Nations Special Committee on Palestine
USNA	United States National Archives
ZANY	Zionist Archives, New York

Preface

On 22 March 1946 Sir John Shaw, the Chief Secretary of the Palestine Government, appeared before the Anglo-American Committee of Inquiry into the Problems of European Jewry and Palestine (AAC) in Jerusalem. He told them,

There have been commissions and commissions and they recommended this and that and there have been debates in all the Parliaments of the world and everything else, and it has never been clear where we really are heading ...

There had indeed been "commissions and commissions" since Britain received the Mandate for Palestine in 1920 – seventeen according to one count. And the AAC was not the last. Less than a year after the British Government rejected the recommendations of the AAC, it was instrumental in establishing yet another commission, the United Nations Special Commission on Palestine. It was this last committee that finally succeeded in giving the quietus to commissions on Palestine. Its deliberations and recommendations resulted in the United Nations partition resolution of 29 November 1947, a resolution supported by the United States while Britain, which objected to partition on principle, abstained from the vote. Thus began Britain's imperial retreat from the Middle East.

Sir John's lament that "it had never been clear where we really are heading" is a fairly exact appraisal of the situation. British policy in Palestine was a patchwork quilt of conflicting interests and capabilities – political, military, and imperial. Moreover, if Britain was not entirely sure where it was going, it was, in retrospect, even less sure of who would replace it.

The AAC was Britain's last attempt to stave off the inevitable, to safeguard its position in Palestine, by inviting controlled American cooperation. Its failure was not the failure of a commission: it was the failure of a tired Britain unable to compete on equal terms with a more powerful rival. This rivalry, resulting in the fruitless attempt to realize a joint accord over Palestine, became a turning point in the history of this much disputed land. For scholars, therefore, the AAC and the diplomacy surrounding it constituted a conundrum to be unravelled, a challenge that intrigued me. And this volume seeks to tell the story of how an apparently colourless committee turned out to be a crossroad in the history of Palestine, perhaps even in the Middle East.

Amikam Nachmani
The Hebrew University, Jerusalem
St. Antony's College, Oxford

1

Palestine and the Problem of European Jewry, 1945

With the termination of hostilities in Europe in the spring of 1945, United States President, Harry S. Truman, sent Earl G. Harrison as special envoy to the Continent to report on the refugee situation. He was to give special attention to the plight of the Jewish refugees. Harrison, who was Dean of the University of Pennsylvania Law School, had been Roosevelt's representative to the Intergovernmental Committee on Refugees (I.G.C.R.), which met at Evian in 1938, and was thus conversant with the subject. Harrison's report to Truman was shocking, especially with regard to the treatment of the DPs (displaced persons) by American troops. His conclusion that "we appear to be treating the Jews as the Nazis treated them except that we do not exterminate them," appalled America.[1] Consequently, insensitive American commanders like General Patton were relieved of their commands and replaced by more considerate officers and Jewish advisors were appointed by the American HQ.[2] Strong measures were taken to curb anti-Semitic feeling among U.S. troops since an inquiry among them had revealed that a high proportion believed that "Hitler was partly right" in his treatment of Jews. The Army Information Branch published material on the DPs to explain to the soldiers the particular situation of the survivors of the concentration camps. Yet the GIs

found it difficult to understand and like people who pushed, screamed, clawed for food, smelled bad, who couldn't and didn't want to obey orders, who sat with dull faces and vacant staring eyes in a cellar or concentration camp barrack, or within a primitive cave, and refused to come out at their command.[3]

Harrison's recommendations for alleviating the conditions of the

Jewish DPs included segregating them and discriminating in their favour.[4]

But his most crucial recommendation was that 100,000 Jewish DPs be admitted into Palestine.

The call for the admission of 100,000, which became official U.S. policy soon after, had a number of radical consequences. First of all, it linked the Jewish refugee problem inexorably with Palestine.[5] Secondly, it intimated that Britain was no longer the only arbiter of Middle Eastern affairs. Thirdly, it signalled official American retreat from the wartime Bermuda accords with Britain on refugees and immigration. The Bermuda Convention of 1943 had placed stateless Jews under the jurisdiction of the I.G.C.R. and stipulated that Jewish refugees were to be considered part of the overall refugee problem after the war, their problems solved within their native countries rather than through emigration. In addition, Britain agreed not to question U.S. immigration quotas, in return for which the Americans would not challenge Britain's immigration policy in Palestine.[6] Now, apparently, Anglo-American relations, which had flourished during the war, were to be put to the test.

BRITAIN, AMERICA AND PALESTINE: BACKGROUND

From the end of the First World War up to, and in fact through, the Second it was generally assumed in Whitehall that Anglo-American relations over Palestine rested on British responsibility for the country and American concurrence in whatever policy Britain chose to pursue there.

The United States had, indeed, followed a policy of political isolationism after the first war and insofar as it did concern itself with Palestine, it was to secure its non-political interests there. The Anglo-American Convention on Palestine of 2 December 1924 covered business matters, the legal status of American citizens, educational institutions, missionary affairs, etc; and since the Mandate for Palestine, including the Balfour Declaration, was appended to it, it served as American recognition of the British Mandate.[7]

For two decades, the American administration adhered to its non-political interpretation of the 1924 Convention. It even regarded the 1939 White Paper, which was an overt retreat from the Balfour Declaration and its Zionist promises, as purely British business. As a matter of fact, the State Department considered the plan to be a realistic compromise and fully concurred with the British reasoning behind it.[8] In 1943, Anthony Eden, the British Foreign Secretary, was able to state with apparent certainty that while U.S. attitudes towards Afghanistan, Persia, Saudi Arabia and Bahrein do not "entirely take into account the special interests of HMG", as far as Palestine was concerned the United States acted "only . . . after consultation with HMG and in agreement with their wishes."[9]

The American public did not necessarily see eye to eye with the Administration and during the war Jewish and, more vociferously, Zionist circles were at the head of an anti-British campaign vis-à-vis Palestine, into which a growing number of political and public figures were drawn. Whitehall and, to a lesser extent, Washington considered the campaign harmful to the Allied war effort, and HMG contemplated asking the U.S. Government's cooperation in silencing it. Such U.S. involvement in Palestine affairs was regarded as politically harmless:

If you ask your neighbour not to light a bonfire which may catch onto your house, you are not usually regarded as inviting him to discuss structural alterations in the latter.[10]

Throughout the war, Britian adhered to this view and regarded the United States as having no political interest in Palestine, other than that created by the Zionist campaign.[11] This rather short-sighted evaluation of the American position vis-à-vis Palestine circumscribed British thinking on the subject. Thus, for example, Britain had no qualms about not revealing her partition plan of 1943 to the Americans, whose political indifference on the subject was assumed to be axiomatic.[12] Neither the Foreign Office nor the State Department had difficulty in isolating the Palestine problem when discussing Anglo-American policies in the Middle East (winter 1944), though the British did not think the Americans would be "so foolish as to believe that we really have no policy in regard to Palestine."[13]

The Bermuda Convention of April 1943 strengthened British belief that the United States would not challenge their Palestine policy. Furthermore, they considered that America's war-time involvement in the Middle East through Lend-Lease and the Anglo-American Middle East Supply Center, as well as the

presence of U.S. troops in North Africa, and the growing importance of Arab oil, etc., would bring America to adopt, if at all, a
pro-Arab policy in the area in general, Palestine included.[14]

In short, insofar as the British were concerned, the global relations of the two powers regarding Palestine during the war could
be emblemized by President Roosevelt's support for Churchill in
whatever policy the latter chose to pursue there, and Churchill's
firm belief that such support would indeed be forthcoming.[15] Such a
situation could exist only if America took no political interest in the
country's future.

Once the war was over, U.S. interest in the Palestine issue
continued to be seen by the British as stemming largely from the
need to take the Zionist vote into consideration. Britain still
believed that America had no political interest of her own in
Palestine and even, as will be seen, saw no harm in inviting the
United States to discuss structural alterations there.

British conceptions of American interests stemmed from two
sources: the pre-war situation, on the one hand, and a rather
supercilious view of the Americans, on the other. The British, in
general, transferred American pre-war indifference to the post-
war period. Since the United States' lack of interest posed no
threat there was no reason why Britain should not invite her to
support British hegemony there. This indifference was further
compounded by inability. According to Lord Moyne, the highest
British authority in the Middle East during the war:

Whatever their intentions, Americans here do not seem capable of taking
advantage of the situation to any extent that need alarm us.[16]

If the Americans were to play any role in Palestine, and it was
conceivable that they would, it would be under British guidance
and leadership.

Truman's proposal to the British Government in the summer of
1945 that they admit 100,000 Jews into Palestine sounded the alarm
and called for British reappraisal of its major ally's priorities.
Truman's first overture on the matter was made to Churchill at
Potsdam, but at the end of July 1945 a Labour Government was
swept into power in Britain by a landslide, and the problem fell
squarely into the lap of Ernest Bevin, the new Secretary for Foreign
Affairs of HMG. Both the new government and its Foreign Secretary were confident of their ability to solve the Palestine problem

and in the course of late summer and early fall, no fewer than *eight plans* were submitted to the Cabinet and, for one reason or another, rejected (see Chapter 3). By the end of September, the dilemma which faced Britain was tersely summed up by an official of the Foreign Office: "The Arabs would do nothing provided HMG did nothing while the Jews are threatening to do something unless HMG did something."[17] "Something", apparently, had to be done, to placate the Zionists and tone down American criticism. On the other hand, "nothing" really could be done that would disrupt Britain's relations with the Arab Middle East. The situation had to be placed on "hold" until a new policy could be articulated, something that would take about six months.[18]

The precarious balance between "something" and "nothing" was maintained by two parallel decisions adopted by the Cabinet at the initiative of the Foreign Secretary. One was the proposal for the establishment of an Anglo-American Committee of Inquiry. The second was a reaffirmation – with certain adjustments – of the 1939 White Paper.

The primary aim of the 1939 statement, issued by the Chamberlain Government shortly before the outbreak of the war, was to prevent the Palestine conflict from adversely affecting Britain's position in the Arab world as a whole.[19] It had precious little relevance to the situation in Palestine itself.

The 1939 White Paper envisaged the creation of an independent Palestinian state within ten years, with a predominantly Arab population, and strong commercial and strategic ties to Britain. Jewish immigration was to be restricted to 75,000 persons for the period of 1939–1944, and made thereafter conditional upon both Arab consent and the economic absorptive capacity of the country; it was not to exceed one-third of the population. Jewish land purchase was to be strictly controlled and the subsequent Land Transfer Regulations of February 1940 permitted Jews to buy land in no more than about 5 per cent of the country.[20]

With the outbreak of the war, shortly after the statement was issued, the pro-Zionist Churchill replaced Chamberlain and inroads into the White Paper ensued. When the Jews of Palestine insisted in 1940 upon fighting Hitler under their own flag, albeit within the British Army, Churchill apparently made a deal with the Zionists whereby the establishment of a Jewish Brigade would be postponed and the constitutional provisions of the White Paper, that is, the eventual emergence of an Arab Palestine, would be suspended.[21] By 1942, when Anglo-German hostilities in the Middle East had subsided, the Arabs declared themselves no longer satisfied with previous British promises. Similarly, when the defeat of Hitler seemed probable, the Jews of Palestine decided to abandon their self-imposed policy of restraint in fighting against the White Paper – and against the British soldiers who were ostensibly implementing it.

Consequently, by the middle of 1943, the Cabinet began to plan a new policy for Palestine and in November of that year even revived and approved a plan for partition, based on the recommendations of the 1937 Peel Commission.

As could be expected, the idea met with strong opposition from the Foreign Office, from the Chiefs of Staff (C.O.S.) and from British officials in the Middle East. It was their common and traditional belief that partition would be detrimental to Britain's position in the Arab world. Thus, as the war ended, British policy for Palestine was nothing more than a truncated version of the 1939 White Paper: except for its regulations concerning immigration and land transfer, nothing remained. And now, with the cessation of hostilities in Europe and the liberation of the concentration camps, the appalling situation of the Jewish survivors was threatening to make a mockery of more than British immigration quotas. And, indeed, neither the Bermuda Accords nor the White Paper proved a barrier to Jewish immigration to Palestine. They were both expiring on paper, as was American passive concurrence in British policy. And if there were any doubts remaining, Truman's call for the admission of 100,000 Jewish DPs into Palestine gave all three the *coup de grâce*.

DESTINATION: PALESTINE

There is little doubt that Jewish immigration into Palestine was recognized by all the commissions that ever visited the country as the main reason for Arab hostility and intransigence: immigration brought in its wake settlement and more settlement – increasing Jewish dominion. And, indeed, immigration quotas were always among the recommendations designed to ease political tensions in the country.

Up to 1924, HMG had reason to be optimistic about the Mandate since most Jews emigrating from Europe preferred the United States to Palestine. However, the imposition of a quota system for immigration into the United States changed this pattern, and the growing number of Jewish immigrants entering Palestine resulted in increased political tension.[22] The Royal Commission (Peel) sent to Palestine in 1937 to investigate the cause of the Arab uprising recommended restrictions on immigration to 12,000 a year, pending the partition of the country.[23]

With the spread of Nazi control over Europe and the growing probability of war, the problem became even more acute. First of all, alternate ports of entry for the Jews were shrinking rapidly. Neither Great Britain nor the United States was prepared to adjust its own immigration quotas, and their records are common knowledge: the United States admitted some 70,000 Jews into the country during the war, 50,000 of them in the years 1940–41, before America joined the belligerents.[24] Britain admitted 10,000 during the same period. No wonder Palestine appeared a natural haven for Jewish refugees. But because Palestine offered an answer to the Jews, this did not necessarily mean that Britain was prepared to alienate the Arab world on that account. Thus, from 1939 on, Britain's immigration policy and its plans for saving Jews from Nazi extermination became dependent upon their compatibility with the White Paper figure of 75,000 for five years, with a certain measure of flexiblity exercised in application.

The Bermuda Accords of 1943 were more or less an attempt to extend Anglo-American understanding on this issue to the post-war perod. Britain would not press America to accept Jewish refugees and the Americans would not press Britain to change her Palestine quotas.[25] But, as noted, these best-laid schemes went a-gley, leaving the British, at least, with nought but grief an' pain.

Prior to the Second World War, there had been about ten million Jews in Europe. At the end of the war, there were some four million left. The table below shows the distributional changes.[26] One should keep in mind that in the confusion and general homelessness which pervaded Europe after the war, the accuracy of all statistics must be somewhat suspect. It was not uncommon to discover statistical errors to the order of 100,000 persons, and there were known to be Displaced Persons Centres of which even the local military authorities had never heard.[27]

Country	Jewish Population in 1939	Jewish Population in 1946
Poland	3,250,000	120,000
Soviet Union	3,020,000	2,000,000
Rumania	900,000	300,000
Hungary	403,000	200,000
Britain	340,000	350,000
Czechoslovakia	360,000	55,000
France	320,000	180,000
Germany	240,000	85,000
Benelux	253,500	60,500
Bulgaria, Greece, Turkey, Yugoslavia	280,000	153,000
Austria	60,000	16,000
Scandinavia/Finland	19,255	30,300
Italy	51,000	52,000
Switzerland	25,000	35,000

The above notwithstanding, it is estimated that six million Jews were slaughtered by the Nazis, almost half of them Polish Jews.

Of the Jews who remained in Europe after the war, some 10 per cent of them, or around 400,000 were either displaced persons (DPs) or refugees. "Refugees" was the term applied to homeless people who remained within the borders of their native countries; "DPs" were homeless people who, during the war, had been forcibly evicted from their homes.[28] The term "stateless" was too general and subject to too many interpretations. The term "infiltrees" was applied to those homeless people who had voluntarily moved into the Allied Zones after V-E Day.

Attempts to fit the Jews into these categories created numerous problems and were finally abandoned. Many Jews had initially gone back to their homes looking for relatives or hoping to recover their property. When they were confronted with the extent of the destruction which had taken place, they returned to the DP camps in Germany and Austria. Were they then "infiltrees" and "should a Jew who suffered outside Germany ... be differentiated from one who was 'lucky' enough to suffer in Germany?"[29] At all events, the original Jewish population of Germany and Austria had been largely replaced after the war by Jews from other countries, mainly from Poland (50 per cent in Austria and 80 per cent in Germany).[30]

While Jews constituted no more than 1 per cent of the ten and a half million Europeans classified as DPs in 1945, their plight attracted particular attention and seemed to epitomize the problem in its entirety.[31] There were a number of reasons for this misconception, among them the particular horror of the Jewish experience in the war, the successful efforts of the Zionists to promote this image, and the stubborn fact that the Jewish DP problem persisted and relatively increased. By the end of 1945, some eight and a half million non-Jewish DPs had been repatriated.[32] But among the Jews, there appeared to be little prospect of reintegration into their countries of origin, and by 1947, Jews constituted 20 per cent of all DPs.

The DP camps, it should be remembered, were at best part of an emergency welfare operation being carried out in areas devastated by the war for people devastated by the war. Accommodation was minimal, food adequate but far from nutritious, employment scarce and not always acceptable; and there was a flourishing black market with all that that implied. In addition, most of the inmates were suffering from severe social and psychological problems, attendant upon the war, and the breakdown of all normal community and family life, not to speak of the harrowing memories of the extermination.

Insofar as the Jews were concerned, their problems were compounded by additional difficulties, most notably the question of whether they were to be considered as Germans, Poles, Austrians, etc., or as Jews – and consequently segregated as a separate entity. Their tendency to congregate together and the strong group consciousness which developed among them made the question academic. The almost total absence of normal family units contributed to a desire among them even to remain together in the future. Thus, for instance, plans for transferring orphans to happier surroundings were strongly resisted.[33] The inmates of the camps formed organizational frameworks and committees, and by the summer of 1945 the Central Committee of Liberated Jews came into existence with headquarters in the former concentration camp of Bergen–Belsen.[34]

With the passage of time, some of the physical conditions improved, although housing remained extremely short and many remained in the camps. The food ration was increased to 2000 calories (although more than 50 per cent was bread).[35] But the social and psychological problems were becoming more acute. Jewish DPs were repeatedly described as the black market elements, and camp authorities complained of

depredation and banditry ... more than 2,000 died from drinking methylated alcohol and other types of poisonous liquor. Many others died by violence or were injured while circulating outside our assembly centres, perhaps then we were overzealous in our surveillance.[36]

Laconic reports, such as the following one, often described the displaced Jews as troublemakers:

On Swallow train that arrived to British Zones, 28.2.1946, from Poland: about 1550 passengers. Of this 480 Jews. These were the only ones to cause any trouble. All the German Jews demanded, repeat demanded that they should be sent to Frankfurt. Found necessary to turn out a few soldiers to make them leave.[37]

Displaced Jews refused to do any work, particularly for the Germans, and when they wanted to work, opportunities were few. Their employment opportunities were limited to working for the Army or for themselves, which was more of an "economic sport."[38] Idleness, which often turned into unrest, became prevalent and they even refused to spread out gravel to improve their own living conditions.[39]

All the difficulties notwithstanding, the DP camps became the lodestone for the Jews of Eastern and Central Europe, producing a steady mass migration. British representatives reported that

it is not difficult to sense the pathological emotions,[and] the memory of a persecution may be as bitter as the persecution itself ... no imaginative Jew could be blamed for refusing to ever feel safe in Europe again.[40]

Zionism and Palestine now appeared to offer the DPs a new beginning and it soon became obvious that the preference of many Jews for one centre over another depended on the facilities it offered for immigration to Palestine. They moved westward in the hope of reaching the DP camps in Bavaria, and south to Italy, where Jews accounted for 60 per cent of all DPs.[41]

The largest numbers came from Poland where from the end of the German occupation until January 1946, some 300 Jews had been killed.[42] Polish Jewry was in a state of perpetual motion, many returning from their war-time stay in Russia and moving through the country and out. Hopes for a renewal of Jewish life in Poland were regarded by the British embassy in Warsaw as "nonsense," and a mass exodus was predicted – "whatever His Majesty's Government or anyone else may say ... A Pole can cross most frontiers. A Jew is also skilful at this."[43] The inability of the Jews to cope with the hardships of life in Poland, including resurgent anti-Semitism, stemmed from the almost total destruction of the pre-war community and the concomitant destruction of their charitable and religious organizations. Restitution of property became a dangerous demand since it aroused the hostility of the population, as did the presence of a number of Jews in the unpopular Provisional Polish Government. Above all, as the British Embassy in Warsaw noted, "they do not wish to continue residence in what is for them one huge cemetery."[44] The combination of these factors, which "you cannot put in order of priority, they react differently on different people," caused a mass migration of Polish Jewry.[45]

This migration was in fact welcomed by the Polish and Soviet governments. Although Polish Jews were promised rehabilitation by the authorities, steps were taken to induce them to leave. They received passports which permitted them to leave Poland but not to return. Without a passport, "only a bottle of vodka is needed at the Polish frontier."[46] The Poles were washing their hands of the whole business:

[they] say that it is the business of their neighbors to keep out of their territory persons who seek to enter it without visas ... the grant of the passport itself only shows that the Polish government have no objections to the person concerned leaving Poland.[47]

Britain threatened to exclude the German population of Poland from her zones (in accordance with the Potsdam Agreement) if Warsaw continued increasing the "chaos" over the situation of DPs in Germany.[48] But she could not make it hold since Jewish determination to leave was so strong. The Soviets, while advocating repatriation for the 150,000 Polish Jews within their borders, did, in fact, press the Polish Government to let them go to Palestine, since "it would facilitate Communist penetration there." Accordingly, Russian lorries helped in the transfer of Jews westwards.[49]

The Jewish Agency for Palestine, the Zionists' official representative leadership, was naturally in the forefront of organizational efforts to get the Jews out of Europe and to Palestine. It established an organization called *Bricha* (Hebrew for "flight" or "escape"), which directed the Jews westwards to the U.S. Zone in Germany, and their very presence there created pressure for immigration to Palestine. The would-be immigrants were then directed to the French, Italian and Black Sea ports where Agency ships waited to carry them to Palestine.[50] Several relief organizations, such as the American Joint Distribution Committee, financed and furnished Bricha with food, medicine and motor vehicles.[51] Jewish Brigade units (of the British army) stationed in Italy and northwestern Europe also took an active part in this clandestine movement which spread all over Europe, evading travel controls and making nonsense of the laws of half a dozen countries and of the edicts of great armies.[52]

While all this movement was going on, the British Foreign Office maintained a different position, namely that the Jewish migration was not a necessary component of the rehabilitation of European Jewry. Conditions within the Jewish communities were depicted as similar to those of the non-Jewish population.[53] According to reports, there was no discrimination or expression of anti-Semitism, and little interest in emigration to Palestine.[54] Even in Poland, despite reports to the contrary, the situation "offers no cause for panic or mass exodus."[55] If Jews suffered from hostile comments, these stemmed from their activities in "more or less illegal channels [and] employment of Jews ... in the secret police," and from the resentment caused by their migration from one country to another.[56] The Head of the Refugee Department of the Foreign Office, G. Randall, concluded that:

there is little or no evidence of actual persecution and it would be a lamentable situation indeed if it had to be admitted that the new governments of Poland and other East and Central European countries which have been brought to power as a result of our victory over Nazi principles, were now tolerating an anti-Jewish policy on Nazi lines.[57]

Accordingly, some Cabinet members "did not accept the view that as a whole, the European problem of Jews is over a period fundamentally less tractable than it was before the German persecution."[58] Jews, therefore, were to be treated like others and not as "a special category at the head of the queue."[59] This was for their own sake, in order not to provoke other groups of DPs. As to their segregation, the Foreign Office flatly stated that "above all, Jews should never be referred to as possessing a separate nationality" since they will be encouraged to regard themselves as belonging to "a specific Jewish nationality with Palestine as its country." And "any discriminatory treatment on behalf of Jews runs counter to the fundamental principle of the Foreign Office policy."[60]

Attempts, however, to apply these principles to Jewish DPs and to repatriate them failed. The Control Authorities were then forced to declare the displaced Jews as non-repatriables, thus causing non-Jews – sometimes from the same country – to demand this status as well.[61] The need to segregate Jews, which had earlier been seen as tantamount to "Nazi attempts to regard Jews as possessing a separate and overriding Jewish nationality as distinct from their political nationality," stemmed from the Jews' refusal to live together with the Poles and Slovaks who had persecuted them in the past, and from their "legitimate grievance [that they are] given treatment no more favourable than that accorded to the defeated enemy."[62] It was, therefore, necessary to accommodate them in separate premises and "to recognize that they represent a special kind of DP and . . . they are treated as if they were a separate nationality."[63]

In addition to making decisions about existing Jewish DPs in the various zones, London had to determine its policy towards the new arrivals – the "Infiltrees." The conclusion was that this migration resulted from "the natural nervousness of the Jews [which] had been unscrupulously exploited by the Zionists."[64] Explanations which pointed to economic hardship as the root cause were ruled out by the reported appearance of these Jews in Germany, "well fed, well heeled, pockets lined with money, well clothed."[65] The Jews' claim that they had fled for their lives was refuted since "always the stories [are] that it occurred in the next town." The conclusion was that some force was deliberately influencing Jews to give up "comfortable" living in Poland.[66] Accordingly, the Cabinet Office ordered the Control Authorities not to admit Jewish migrants into the British Zones and to treat them "on the same lines as German, repeat, German refugees. They are Not, repeat Not, to be accorded the status of Displaced Persons or stateless persons."[67] This was expected to be embarrassing, "but it would be . . . most effective deterrent to further unauthorized movements."[68] The fact that the United States, the French, and the Russians were all admitting Jews into their zones caused a British official to ask: "How can we accept the invidious position of being the only Ally to refuse admittance?"[69] Nonetheless, this did not move the Foreign Office. Nor was the comparatively favourable status of statelessness to be given to these Jews, even in the face of the anticipated agitation of world Jewry "who are very much on the look out for any alleged anti-Jewish action on the part of HMG."[70]

Accordingly, migrant Jews were left to merge into the hostile German population to help them to "rebuild a sane and free Central Europe [where] the Jews may be able ... to return willingly to play a most valuable part in its moral and physical reconstruction."[71] Only by sitting in London and not sensing the reluctance of both sides could one arrive at such a philosophy. It accorded, however, with a broader scheme which aimed to deter Jews from migrating westwards, and which included the cessation of DP care after a certain date; complete closure of camps as soon as the Jewish inmates had been cleared; the granting of immigration certificates to Palestine only to DPs registered before a certain date, with "wide publicity to this ruling"; reduction of the living standards of displaced Jews who were to be compelled to work; acceleration of the demobilization of Jewish units; and registration of all Jews in British Zones.[72]

Soon, however, the Control Authorities on the Continent alarmed London with requests to dispose of those Jews who

represent at present about one-twentieth of the DP population ... but the problem ... cannot be interpreted on a purely arithemetical basis ... their past lack of discipline and black market records does not dispose us to regard them as desirable ... and the morale of our camps as a whole would benefit by their departure.[73]

Resettlement outside Europe, i.e., in Palestine, appeared to be the remedy, and the Control Office asked for priority in allocation of Palestinian certificates, concluding that:

because many of them wish to go to Palestine, their treatment must be related generally to our policy towards Palestine.[74]

This was a major deviation from views held till then by any department of the British Government. In addition, the Refugee Department at the British Foreign Office strongly objected to any notion which might prevent a Palestinian solution for the Jewish DPs, like the emptying of the DP centres in summer 1946. They recommended that Jewish camps, unlike others, should continue to function pending such a solution. The protest of the Eastern Department was equally sturdy:

We dislike all proposals such as made ... for isolating the Jewish DPs. The implication of keeping them in centres in a time when all other DPs were being dispersed ... that they were being held in readiness for transfer to Palestine.[75]

Another call for exceptions in the treatment of Jews – in comparison to others which stressed "that in the midst of the universal suffering of Europe this winter, they at least have shelter, clothing and food" – came from the British Embassy in Washington.[76] It seems that beyond the walls of the Eastern Department of the Foreign Office, a more humane view prevailed.

One war-time policy, however, was preserved: HMG was not ready to admit Jewish refugees into Britain and "so far he [the Home Secretary] and his predecessors had been able to resist pressure of this kind." Bevin suggested that those Jews who were, after all, admitted should be trained in agriculture, in order to prevent too many of them from "seeking openings in commerce."[77] This remained the only war-time policy which Britain retained after the war. In 1939, 340,000 Jews lived in Britain. By 1946, the number was 350,000.[78]

With the publication of Truman's call for the admission of 100,000 Jews into Palestine in the fall of 1945, a new chapter began in the relations between the American military authorities in the European theatre and between the Jewish refugees and DPs, and the Zionist representatives as well. The Army started to furnish the Jews migrating from Poland with transportation, and American B-17s flew between Frankfurt and Lydda in Palestine, carrying Jewish Agency staff and materials for the DPs. Landings in Palestine were made without prior arrangements with the British authorities there or with American Air Force H.Q., or even the control tower at the airport. Again, without consulting the British, U.S. medical officers examined the possibility of setting up a 1,000-bed hospital in Palestine for Jewish refugees, a plan which caused R.A.F. personnel to comment: "There is more in it than meets the eye."[79]

In the camps themselves, the U.S. Army granted equal treatment to all Jews, not bothering to distinguish between refugees, DPs, or infiltrees. By June 1946, there were 87,000 Jews in 433 American-run DP camps in Germany and Austria. There were, at the same time, 21,200 Jewish DPs in the British Zone.[80]

Washington saw this as a heavy financial burden,[81] which could only be alleviated by emptying the camps as quickly as possible. The distinctions between the categories of homelessness were not only linguistic: they were also financial, with DPs receiving larger allocations of funds. With the Americans treating all applicants as DPs, they had to be granted the right to be housed in a camp as against being out-centre DPs. In comparison, the majority of inmates of British DP centres in Austria were not, in fact, DPs, but "refugees in different categories."[82]

Zionist circles did not fail to realize the effects of this situation and pushed as many would-be immigrants as possible into the U.S. Zones "creating a political fact which presses on the Americans and can be of importance to us for the continuation of our struggle after we will get the 100,000."[83] The urgent need to ease this burden became further complicated due to the growing U.S. interest in the strategic position of West Germany: they wanted to transfer the DPs out of the country, the Jews among them to Palestine.[84] This resulted, inter alia, in collaboration between the United States and the Jewish Agency.

So, within six months of the end of the war in Europe, pressure on Palestine was reaching unprecedented proportions. Tens of thousands of Jews were wending their way down to the Mediterranean ports, aided and abetted by highly efficient Zionist organizations, both on the ground and in their councils of state, and financially assisted and politically encouraged by the United States of America, and to a lesser extent, by the Soviet Union. There were even a few small voices in the British political establishment calling for a revision of policy. But Whitehall remained adamant, and immigration quotas to Palestine remained close to their 1939 level – 1,500 a month. But the immovable object was no match for the irresistible force: illegal immigration began.

In order to grasp the significance of illegal immigration, it should be remembered that at the end of the war, the Jewish population of Palestine was under 600,000. Between the end of the war and the establishment of the State of Israel in May 1948, when the country became responsible for its own immigration policy, 120,000 people made their way to the country, 50,000 in accordance with the official quota and 70,000 by trying to enter illegally aboard sixty-five ships.[85] The relative weight of illegal immigration was, therefore, enormous.

Aside from wreaking havoc on the quota system, illegal immigration was seen by the British as the most serious threat to peace in Palestine. It would force Britain to fight a war on two fronts, against both Arabs and Jews. This was the worst possible prospect imaginable for Britain in the Middle East.[86] Accordingly, the prevention of illegal immigration was rated as the most important task the British forces in the Middle East had to perform, much more important than "fighting sabotage and preventing assassinations."[87]

As a result, every shipload of immigrants that reached Palestine brought in its wake ugly armed confrontations between British soldiers and the wretched human cargo of refugees, on the one hand, and between British soldiers and the Palestinian Jews who came to their aid, on the other. Needless to say, the effect on the British troops was not particularly salubrious, since among those resisting arrest – among the refugees and among the Palestinians – were large numbers of women and children.[88] Secondly, and no less pressing, was the fact that the illegals were considered to be the major source of reinforcements for the Palestinian Jewish underground movements.

The prevention of illegal immigration thus had to be tackled simultaneously at its source in Europe, on the high seas and at points of debarkation (which were not always easy to discover on the long coastline). In a Foreign Office directive to Belgrade, it was noted that:

It is almost impossible to prevent their entry into Palestine and once they have reached countries bordering on the Mediterranean, it is very difficult to prevent them embarking. It is accordingly important to stop this traffic at its source in Central Europe ... take this matter up with the Yugoslav Government.[89]

On the spot, the Royal Navy and the Royal Air Force operated along the 120 miles of Palestine coast, with one cruiser and up to six destroyers intermittently engaged in this problem, and in constant danger of running aground since the main chase took place within the shallow territorial waters of Palestine.[90]

Of those ships intercepted at sea, detention was carried out either at camps in Palestine – and the detainees released monthly in accordance with quotas – or, later, in Cyprus. One boat was returned to Germany, and the uproar against the British for this operation was heard round the world. While international public opinion could be roused against Jewish terrorist acts in Palestine, there was no chance of eliciting any kind of support for British action against illegal immigrants. But, again, as far as the British were concerned, the illegals, for the most part, were potential soldiers for the Jewish underground armies:

Among the Stern Group members captured after recent attacks on railway workshops in Haifa Bay on June 17, there were several recently arrived illegal immigrants who could not even speak Hebrew. Police investigation point to the large proportion of illegals recruited into the Jewish underground organizations ... former guerilla fighters in Europe are given priority in illegal immigration transport for the sake of the use of their experience against government and security forces in this country. On arrival, several have described themselves as "partisans."[91]

Ernest Bevin, the British Minister for Foreign Affairs, and his Middle East generals described them as "indoctrinated terrorists ... sent to Palestine to make a nuisance of themselves," "the flower of youth," "practically all between the ages of 18–30 ... no children ... no very old people at all."[92] All of them were considered fit for tough army service, a first-class military menace to the British.

At this point, the war against the illegals can only marginally be regarded as an attempt to placate the Arabs and thus avoid having to fight them as well. It was, first and foremost, an attempt to prevent reinforcements for the Jews in the already ongoing Anglo-Jewish war in Palestine.

JEWISH UNDERGROUNDS IN PALESTINE

Jewish underground activity against the British in Palestine began following the publication of the 1939 White Paper. With the German offensive in North Africa and Egypt in 1940–41, and the threat of a German invasion of Palestine, there was an almost complete cessation of this kind of activity. But after the battle of El Alamein in October 1942, and the turn of the war in the Allies' favour, resistance in Palestine was renewed and eventually reached almost war-like proportions.

There were three underground Jewish organizations operating in Palestine, with a total of some 56,000 members. The largest, the Hagana, with about 50,000, was the most representative and was, indeed, considered the quasi-official military arm of the Jewish community in Palestine (the *Yishuv*), responsible to the Jewish Agency. The other two, the National Military Organization, or Irgun, and the smaller Freedom Fighters for Israel, the Stern Group, numbered 6,000 and were not under Jewish Agency authority.

The Hagana was organized and administered territorially. The country was divided into commands and subdivided into districts, all under the authority of a GHQ. The Hagana underground was, in fact, so visible, that the C. in C. of the British forces was able to state that

The Palestine government is completely in control of those areas which are primarily Arab [and] the Agency [in] areas where the Jews predominate.[93]

The underground movements avoided direct military clashes with the British Army, employing guerrilla tactics instead. This meant that the British had to cope with scattered individual actions, performed by small units, or even single persons, such as the blowing up of various installations, the posting of placards or the harassment of British soldiers and policemen.

By the end of 1946, some 100,000 British troops, one tenth of the total British forces, were stationed in Palestine, engaged in action against the Jewish undergrounds. This was the equivalent of two and a half divisions, an air contingent equal to seven squadrons and naval forces of the order of one cruiser and four destroyers.[94] No wonder the military aspects of the Palestine problem received the widest publicity in Britain and became the key issue of its policy after the war.

During the war, certain repressive measures had been employed to keep trouble to a minimum but that had not been general policy. With the intensification of Jewish armed resistance after the war, in the autumn of 1945, it was clear that policy in this area had to be rethought. The military repeatedly advocated escalation, the disbanding of the Jewish Agency and the disarming of the Yishuv. The Cabinet, on the other hand, considered such extreme action less than helpful, seeking as they did some sort of political modus vivendi, even with American cooperation.[95] Even when large scale operations were finally approved, following the blowing up of all the bridges connecting Palestine with outside countries, and not long after the blowing up of the King David Hotel in Jerusalem, which housed the British Government offices, a myriad of provisos was attached. They limited action to "the actual perpetrators of the outrage and those who aid them locally," and while "the High Commissioner should be authorized ... to break up the illegal organizations ... there should not be any attempt to secure the wholesale disarming of individuals," etc.[96] In the row that later developed over who should be blamed for the inability to cope with the situation, the following comment by Sir Alan G. Cunningham, the last High Commissioner for Palestine, is significant:

The general conclusion that the army is not allowed to develop its full power ... is of course true, but ... it is equally true to say that were it allowed to do so, it would be ineffective against the type of terrorism we are now experiencing.[97]

Military measures alone could not solve the problems raised by Jewish armed struggle.

First of all, British troops in Palestine were not equipped to cope with urban guerilla warfare.[98] The use of the Royal Air Force and Royal Artillery, used against the rural Arab population during the 1930s, was out of the question. Nonetheless, the generals persisted in believing that success could be insured "if heavy weapons are used in full" against the Jews as they had been against the Arabs. General Ismay, the Chief of the Imperial General Staff (C.I.G.S.), was of the opinion that an increase in the calibre of the artillery and use of air force would prove efficacious against the urban resistance that Britain confronted then in Palestine.[99] In addition, while the army constantly refused to police the country and was reluctant to see Jewish resistance as a nuisance which it was necessary to live with, it repeatedly alarmed the Cabinet about the magnitude of the problem, causing London to regard them as "spineless and alarmists."[100] But the most significant failure was the failure of the British to assess the aims of Jewish resistance. When asked to specify whether it was aimed at the British, or at the Arabs, or employed merely in self-defence, the highest ranking officers in the Middle East had no answers.[101] Hand to mouth tactics were no substitute for an overall political-military strategy.

The entire situation was further exacerbated by a total lack of mutual confidence and perhaps understanding between all those involved in the resolution of the problem. The Cabinet's rather cautious instructions to the military were interpreted, for example, by General Montgomery, who succeeded Ismay as C.I.G.S., as follows:

This will lead to war with the Jews with all that implies ... they must be utterly and completely defeated and their illegal armed organization smashed forever.[102]

Further civil-military dissonance was reflected, for instance, in directives to the Army by Montgomery to see

that Cunningham does not begin to wobble or to try to sit on the fence ... I rely on you to let me know privately the moment the Palestine Government shows any signs of not wanting to face up to its responsiblities or to shirk the issue.[103]

Bevin, on the other hand, concluded that the Army had let him down over the Palestine issue, and Montgomery could add: "We have only ourselves to blame."[104]

There were 184 British soldiers killed and 371 wounded in Palestine in the year following the end of the war.[105] The British were finding it more and more difficult to rule the country. President Truman's call for the admission of 100,000 more Jews into the country could only aggravate the situation.

NOTES

1. Truman to Eisenhower, July 1945, President's Secretary file, Foreign Affairs, Box 184, Truman Library, Independence, Missouri.
2. Herbert Agar, *The Saving Remnant*, London, 1960, p. 181.
3. Quoted in Leon Dinnerstein, "The U.S. Army and the Jews: Policies towards the DPs After World War II," *American Jewish History*, vol. 68, no. 3, March 1979, p. 363.
4. See Report on improvement in living conditions of the Jewish DPs by James D. Rice, American Joint Distribution Committee, Austria, 15 March 1946, New York, AJDC Archives.
5. Washington to Foreign Office, 4 Oct. 1945, FO 371/45400/E7459; Yehuda Bauer, *Flight and Rescue: Bricha*, New York, 1970, p. 89.
6. Richard P. Stevens, *American Zionism and U.S. Foreign Policy: 1942-1947*, New York, 1962, p. 70; Bernard Wasserstein, *Britain and the Jews of Europe*, London, 1979, pp. 185, 196, 199-200, 217-218, 343.
7. Christopher Sykes, *Cross-Roads to Israel*, London, 1965, p. 323. Frank E. Manuel, *The Realities of American Palestine Relations*, Washington, 1949, p. 4.
8. Manuel, *Realities*, p. 310; Amitzur Ilan, *America, Britain and Palestine* (Hebrew), Jerusalem, 1979, p. 43.
9. Eden to Halifax, 8 Aug. 1943, CO 732/88 Pt. 4. Halifax was the British Ambassador to Washington.

10. Comment by Sir Maurice Peterson, Head of the Eastern Department, Foreign Office, 8 June 1943, FO 371/35035/E3295/G; Gavriel Cohen, *The British Cabinet and the Question of Palestine April–July 1943* (Hebrew), Tel Aviv, 1976, p. 70.
11. Cohen, *British Cabinet*, p. 32.
12. Adopted in the Cabinet Committee on Palestine, Nov. 1943–March 1944. See Ilan, *America, Britain*, pp. 138-142.
13. E.B. Boyd, Colonial Office, Palestine Currency Board, to C.W. Baxter, Head of Eastern Department, Foreign Office (1944), 21 Feb. 1944, CO 732/88 Pt. 4/79303/44.
14. Lord Gort, High Commissioner for Palestine, to British Middle East Ambassadors, London, 6 Sept. 1945; Bevin to the same forum, 10 Sept. 1945 FO 371/45379/E6954 and E6955/G.
15. Ilan, *America, Britain*, pp. 105, 145.
16. Lord Moyne, Minister Resident, Cairo, to Foreign Office, 29 March 1944, CO 732/88 Pt. 4/79303.
17. Summary of conversation between Sir Walter Smart, the Oriental Counsellor, Cairo Embassy and Azzam Pasha, Secretary General of the Arab League, Cairo to Foreign Office, 24 Sept. 1945, FO 371/45240/E7145. See also minutes of the Cabinet, 11 Sept. 1945: "Whatever action we took we were likely to find ourselves exposed to sharp criticism," FO 371/45379/E6956.
18. Memo of Cabinet Committee on Palestine, 8 Sept. 1945, CAB 129/2, C.P. (45) 156.
19. Wasserstein, *Britain and the Jews*, p. 28.
20. Government of Palestine, *A Survey of Palestine*, Jerusalem, 1946, Annexure 2; the White Paper of May 1939, Cmd. 6019, p. 96.
21. Ilan, *America, Britain*, pp. 57, 75.
22. Elizabeth Monroe, *Britain's Moment in the Middle East, 1914–1956*, London, 1963, p. 79.
23. Palestine Royal Commission Report, Cmd. 5479, London 1937, p. 306; AAC Report Cmd 6808, London, 1946, p. 6.
24. Wasserstein, *Britain and the Jews*, pp. 132, 140.
25. Ibid., pp. 186, 196.
26. Table is based on figures from the *American Jewish Yearbook, 1946/47*, p. 606.
27. U.S. Commanders in charge of DPs to AAC, Lausanne, 9 April 1946, p. 8; Hutcheson Papers, Houston, Texas; Dinnerstein, "U.S. Army and Jews," pp. 360-361.
28. Bauer, *Flight and Rescue*, p. 47; Monthly Reports, U.S. Zone, Military Governor, 20 Sept. 1945, U.S. National Archives (USNA), Record Group (RG), 43, AAC, Box 1.
29. Richard Crossman, *Palestine Mission*, London, 1947, pp. 91-92.
30. Figures from Appendix III of AAC Report, Cmd. 6808, London, April 1946, pp. 58-59.
31. M.J. Sage, "The Evolution of U.S. Policy towards Europe's DPs: World War II to 25 June 1948," M.A. Columbia University, New York, 1952, p. 68; Sister M.M. Lorimer, "America's Response to Europe's DPs, 1945-1952," Ph.D., St. Louis University, 1964, p. 64; Anglo-U.S. Study of AAC Report, note by Foreign Office. 15 June 1946, CO 537/2319.
32. E.B. Tripp, "DPs: the Legislative Controversy in the U.S., 1945–1950," M.A., Columbia University, p. 2. After repatriation efforts, by winter 1946 only 1,500,000 DPs remained. See also Lorimer, "America's Reponse," p. 28; Dinnerstein, "U.S. Army and Jews," p. 354.
33. Judge Simon H. Rifkind, advisor on Jewish Affairs, U.S. Theatre Commander, to AAC, 18 Feb. 1946, p. 2, with Judge Rifkind, New York; AAC Report, p. 14;

Crossman, *Palestine Mission*, p. 87.
34. Ibid.; Agar, *Saving Remnant*, p. 180; AAC visit to Austria, 25 Feb. 1946 USNA, RG 43, AAC Box 12; Eisenhower to Truman, in Washington to Foreign Office, 4 Oct. 1945, CO 733/463 Pt. 1/75872/134. Eisenhower's letter was later released to the press, see *New York Times*, 17 Oct. 1945.
35. Eisenhower to Truman, in Washington to Foreign Office, 18 Oct. 1945, CO 733/463 Pt 1/75872/134; Field Marshall Montgomery, *Memoirs*, London 1958 p. 381; findings of Harrison report: see in Washington to Foreign Office, 4 Oct. 1945, FO 371/45400/E7459.
36. Eisenhower to Truman, 18 Oct. 1945, CO 733/463 Pt. 1/75872/134; Anglo-U.S. Study of AAC Report, 21 June 1946, CO 537/1765.
37. DPs Assembly Camps Staff, No. 78, to Refugee Branch, War Office 5 March 1946 WO 171/10912, emphasis in original.
38. Rifkind to AAC, 18 Feb. 1946, p. 15, with Judge Rifkind, New York.
39. AAC visit to Austria, 15 Feb. 1946, p. 1, USNA, RG 43, AAC, Box 12.
40. Washington to Foreign Office, 12 March 1946, FO 371/52568/E2198.
41. Anglo-U.S. Study of AAC Report, June 1946, p. 3, PREM 8/627 Pt 2; Anglo-U.S. Study of AAC Report, 21 June 1946, CO 537/1765; Crossman to Mrs. Zita Crossman, 28 Feb. 1946, SACMEC, Crossman Papers. Jews were only 4% in British Zones of Germany and Austria.
42. Warsaw to Foreign Office, 9 Jan. 1946, CAB 134/595.
43. Warsaw to Foreign Office, 20 Feb. 1946, FO 371/57688/WR736.
44. Ibid.
45. Meeting between U.S. Commanders in charge of DPs and AAC, Lausanne, 9 April 1946, p. 46. Hutcheson Papers.
46. Warsaw to Foreign Office, 9 Jan. 1946, FO 371/57686/WR213; Overseas Reconstruction Committee, 25 Jan. 1946, p. 2, FO 371/57686/WR267.
47. Unsigned note, 5 Jan. 1946, FO 945/655.
48. Warsaw to Foreign Office, 9 Jan. 1946, FO 945/655.
49. Warsaw to Foreign Office, No. 54, 9 Jan. 1946, FO 945/655. See also Political Representative, Bucharest, to Foreign Office, 7 Nov. 1945, on Communist activity regarding immigration to Palestine.
50. Bauer, *Flight and Rescue*, p. 280; Agar, *Saving Remnant*, p. 200; also unsigned memo on illegal immigration, March 1946, p. 13, FO 945/655.
51. Lorimer, "America's Reponse," p. 79; Agar, *Saving Remnant*, pp. 199–200. $25,000,000 was given by the Joint to Bricha as well as vehicles bearing the protective Joint shield.
52. Unsigned memo on illegal immigration, March 1946, p. 13, FO 945/655; Agar, *Saving Remnant*, p. 199.
53. Communication to the U.S. Govt., 16 Oct 1945, FO 371/45381/E7757/G.
54. Report on Hungarian Jewry, Refugee Dept., 24 Feb. 1946, FO 371/57686/WR327.
55. Report on Polish Jewry, ibid.; Bevin to Overseas Reconstruction Committee, 20 Jan. 1946, CAB 134/595.
56. Refugee Dept., Foreign Office, 24 Feb. 1946, FO 371/57686/WR327; report on Jews in Czechoslovakia, reaction to arrival of Jews from Poland, Refugee Dept. memo, 24 Feb. 1946, ibid.
57. G. Randall, Head of Refugee Dept., 9 Jan. 1946, FO 371/57689/WR839.
58. Herbert Morrison, Lord President of the Council, Head of Cabinet Committee on Palestine, 10 Oct. 1945, CAB 95/14.
59. Attlee to Truman, 16 Sept. 1945, FO 371/45380/E7251; comment of Foreign Office officials on Harrison report, 2 Oct. 1945, FO 371/45380/E7459.
60. Refugee Dept. to Control Office, Germany and Austria, 2 Sept. 1946, FO 371/57767/WR2176, and 30 July 1946, FO 371/57767/WR2103.

61. Cabinet Offices to Joint Staff Mission, Washington, 28 Sept. 1945, CO 733/463 Pt. 1/75872/134; Overseas Reconstruction Committee, 25 Jan. 1946, p. 1, FO 371/57686/WR267.
62. Cabinet Office to Joint Staff Mission, Washington, 28 Sept. 1945, CO 733/463 Pt. 1/75872/134; Randall's Memo, 9 Jan. 1946, FO 371/57689/WR839 (hereafter Randall's Memo I).
63. Control Office, Berlin, to Foreign Office, undated, FO 945/731.
64. Randall's Memo I.
65. Warsaw Embassy to Foreign Office, 9 Jan. 1946, CAB 134/595; statement by General Frederick Morgan, Director of the United Nations Relief and Rehabilitation Administration (UNRRA) in Germany, Washington to Foreign Office, 2 Jan. 1946, FO 945/655; C. in C., Berlin to War Office, 8 Dec. 1945, CAB 134/595.
66. General Morgan's statement, Washington to Foreign Office, 2 Jan. 1946, FO 945/655.
67. Cabinet Office to British Element, Control Office, Berlin, 28 Jan. 1946, FO 371/57693/WR2162.
68. Randall's Memo I.
69. Comment by I. L. Henderson, North American Dept., Foreign Office, 11 Dec. 1945, FO 371/51128/WR3648.
70. Randall's Memo I.
71. See Control Office draft for Anglo-U.S. Study of AAC report, June 1946, on hostility of Germans to this act, FO 945/729; Randall's Memo, 4 May 1946, FO 371/57691/WR1275.
72. Anglo-U.S. Study of AAC report, 21 June 1946, CO 537/1765; Refugee Dept. comments on emptying of DP centres, July 1946, FO 371/57766/WR2018; War Office meeting to consider preventive measures against illegal immigration, 27 April 1946, FO 945/655. The suggestion of Major General Templer, Director of Military Intelligence, to register all Jews was rejected since "we might be accused of racial discrimination," ibid.
73. Control Office, Vienna, to London, 19 June 1946, FO 945/655.
74. Foreign Office to Control Office, 19 June 1946, FO 945/738; memo on Jewish DPs, June 1946, FO 945/700; Control Office, Berlin, undated, FO 945/731.
75. Harold Beeley's comments, Foreign Office, Eastern Dept., 24 June 1946, FO 371/57763/WR1655. In June–July 1946, Anglo-American talks were held over the recommendations of the AAC Report to admit 100,000 Jews into Palestine; see Chapter 13.
76. Halifax to Bevin, in Washington to Foreign Office, 21 Nov. 1945, FO 371/45402/E8995.
77. Minutes of the Cabinet, 11 Oct. 1945, CAB 128/1, C.M. (45)40; Martin Gilbert, *Exile and Return*, London, 1978, p. 275. Accordingly, the terms of reference of the AAC excluded any implication that Jews might immigrate into Britain.
78. AAC Report, p. 59.
79. U.S. Commanders in charge of DPs to AAC, Lausanne, 9 April 1946, p. 18, Hutcheson Papers; G.O.C. Palestine to AAC, Jerusalem, 14 March 1946, pp. 17–18, USNA, RG, 43, AAC, Box 11; RAF Mediterranean/Middle East to RAF Levant, 4 Jan. 1946, SACMEC, Cunningham Papers, Box 1 file 1.
80. Lorimer, "America's Reponse," p. 44; Anglo-U.S. Study of AAC Report, 21 June 1946, CO 537/1765. U.S. Zones, Germany: 392,000 non-Jews, 76,000 Jews; Austria: 32,000 non-Jews, 11,000 Jews; British Zones, Germany: 349,000 non-Jews, 19,500 Jews; Austria, 81,300 non-Jews, 1,700 Jews, ibid.
81. Truman to Senator George, 17 Oct. 1946, in Robert J. Donovan, *Conflict and Crisis: The Presidency of Harry S. Truman, 1945–1948*, New York, 1977, p. 322.
82. Control Commission, Austria (undated) enclosure No. 6, FO 945/655; Anglo-U.S.

Study of AAC Report, 21 June 1946, CO 537/1765.
83. H. Yahil to Jewish Agency Executive, Jerusalem, 5 May 1946, Central Zionist Archives (CZA), S 25/5232.
84. Bauer, *Flight and Rescue*, p. 320; also General Hilldring, U.S. Assistant S.O.S. (Secretary of State) for Occupied Areas, to Dean Acheson, the Under S.O.S., 3 May 1946, FRUS 1946, vol. 7, p. 591.
85. Bauer, *Flight and Rescue*, p. 281.
86. Memo to the Cabinet by the Colonial Secretary on illegal immigration, 5 Aug. 1946, CAB 129/12, C.P. (46)310; memo by British C. in C. Middle East, to AAC, Cairo, 1 Feb. 1946, p. 3, USNA, RG 43, AAC, Box 10.
87. C. in C. memo to AAC, p. 2, ibid.
88. "Clashes with population, particularly women," directive by Major General C.F. Loewen, Commander of the 1st Infantry Division, 28 Oct. 1945, WO 169/19658.
89. Foreign Office to Belgrade, 4 June 1946, FO 945/655.
90. C. in C. to AAC, Cairo, 5 March 1946, p. 21, USNA, RG 43, AAC, Box 10; Meeting in Colonial Office to discuss illegal immigration, London, 2 April 1946, FO 945/655.
91. M. Scott, Palestine Secretariat, to Colonial Secretary, 27 July 1946, SACMEC, Cunningham Papers, Box 1, file 1.
92. Bevin to Abba H. Silver, 14 Nov. 1946, CO 537/1787; C. in C. to AAC, Cairo, 5 March 1946, p. 16, USNA, RG, 43, AAC, Box 10; General Officer Commanding British Troops in Palestine (G.O.C.) to AAC, Jerusalem, 14 March 1946, p. 15, USNA, RG, 43, AAC, Box 11.
93. C. in C. to AAC, Cairo, 5 March 1946, p. 26, USNA, RG, 43, AAC, Box 10.
94. J.C. Hurewitz, *The Struggle for Palestine*, New York, 1950, p. 280; C.O.S. report on Maintenance of Law and Order in Palestine, SACMEC, Cunningham Papers, Box 5, file 2.
95. Attlee to General Ismay, the Chief of the Imperial General Staff (C.I.G.S.) 10 May 1946, Prime Minister's Minutes 1945–1946, D 10/46, CAB 21/2277.
96. Attlee to Ismay, ibid.; Cabinet decisions 20 June 1946, CAB 128/5, C.M. (46)60; Cabinet Minutes, 25 July 1946, CAB 128/6, C.M. (46) 73.
97. Cunningham to Colonial Secretary, 3 Dec. 1946, SACMEC, Cunningham Papers, Box 1, file 3.
98. See Montgomery's account of the late and inefficient handling of an attack on a police station in Jerusalem, Nov. 1946, Montgomery, *Memoirs*, pp. 468–469.
99. Ismay to Attlee, 29 Nov., CAB 120/625.
100. See impressions of John Shaw, Chief Secretary to the Palestine Government, in a letter to Lt. General D'Arcy, G.O.C. British troops, Palestine, 15 June 1946, SACMEC, D'Arcy Papers.
101. C. in C. Middle East and G.O.C. Palestine to AAC, March 1946, USNA, RG, 43. AAC, Box 10, pp. 25–27 and Box 11, pp. 25–28.
102. Montgomery to General Dempsey, C. in C. Middle East Land Forces, 27 June 1946, WO 216/194.
103. Montgomery to Dempsey, 5 Aug. 1946, ibid.
104. Montgomery to Dempsey, 30 Jan. 1947, ibid.; Montgomery, *Memoirs*, p. 474.
105. SACMEC, Cunningham Papers, Box 5, file 4.

2

Power Rivalry in the Middle East

> HMG wish and intend to maintain a predominant political (and for that matter commercial) position and predominant responsibility for defence in the Middle East. [At the same time, however,] HMG desire ... that the United States should interest themselves in the Middle East. The question is how to reconcile these two objects. It is a matter of getting the mixture right.
>
> Sir Ronald Campbell
> Foreign Office, Eastern Department[1]

> They found themselves hard pressed throughout the empire, unable to muster either the funds or the forces to take care of all their responsibilities, and yet anxious to relinquish as little of their standing as a world power as possible.
>
> Harry S. Truman
> President of the United States[2]

Post-war relations between the United States and Great Britain vis-à-vis the Middle East were very much based on "getting the mixture right" on both sides. Britain wanted America "in" to a certain extent; America wanted Britain "out", to an even greater extent. The fact that there was no possible mixture that could satisfy both at the same time is fairly clear in retrospect. At the time, however, the vicissitudes of U.S. policy making in the Middle East were staggeringly unclear to the British. John Bull had not yet digested the fact that Uncle Sam was now calling the moves. The result was that the two countries began to pursue separate – and conflicting – policies.

For Britain, V-E Day marked almost six full years of war, in which it lost about 300,000 members of its armed forces. Civilian casualties at home accounted for another 60,000 dead, and 86,000 severely wounded. The merchant marine lost 35,000 men and half of its tonnage. The war cost Britain one-quarter of its national wealth, and when it ended the national debt had risen to 23 billion pounds in comparison with 7 billion at the beginning of the war.[3] During the war, Britain borrowed heavily abroad, mainly from the United States, liquidated its foreign investments, and reduced its export level to about one-third of its pre-war level, often to the advantage of American competitors. Debts, principally in the sterling area, amounted to over 3.5 milliard and the war-time concentration on war goods rather than manufacture for export impeded quick recovery.[4]

For many months after the war, the provision of food and fuel, especially coal, was at the top of the British Government's priority list. Rehabilitation and modernization of the economy, together with major social reforms, involved greater national ownership, which in turn necessitated huge investments. British sources alone could not provide them.

Yet Britain still conceived of itself as a Great Power in world politics, which meant the expenditure of huge amounts of money in troops and weapons. It had problems to contend with in India, Egypt and Palestine, insofar as the Empire was at stake, and further problems of the growing power struggle in Europe and in Persia. In order to maintain all of its interests abroad, Britain found it was forced to spread itself rather thin. For special tasks like the garrisoning of Palestine, for example, its only possible recourse was the deferment of demobilization and the recall of men already released.[5]

In the dawn of the new post-war world, Britain was hard put to handle all its problems, not merely those in the Middle East. In the European theatre it became obvious that the Russians were pursuing an expansionist policy at the same time that the United States was withdrawing its troops from the Continent. And indeed, from the end of the war until 1946, the Americans did not consider that their national interests would be affected by any of the territorial settlements in Europe and they had no intention of committing themselves to a new balance of power there.

In December 1945, Bevin's greatest anxiety was that James Byrnes, the American Secretary of State, might conclude a deal with the Soviets over his head; although Truman was publicly warning the Russians about their expansion in Eastern Europe, Byrnes was seeking avenues of compromise and conciliation with them.[6] The Potsdam summit meeting of July 1945 and the Foreign Minister's Council meeting of September-October left it to Britain alone to resist Soviet demands in Germany, the Balkans, Tripolitania and Persia.

The Russians, for their part, did not fail to see the gaps among the Western powers, and tried to persuade the United States to return to its pre-war policy of isolationism. Soviet propaganda was reported to be concentrating "the main assault ... as usual ... against British imperialism." They were much less active against American interests.[7] Thus, facing the Soviet political and military build-up in Europe, Britain sought American cooperation in defending it. Accordingly, in the context of post-war Anglo-American relations, Europe became the first theatre where the British agreed to U.S. supremacy. In other areas, such as the Middle East, where the Soviet menace looked less substantial, Britain was reluctant to agree to Anglo-American cooperation, which would push it into a secondary position. What Britain wanted in the Middle East was impossible: it wanted America to pay the piper while it called the tune.

WANTED: A NEW POLICY

In the period between the two wars, Britain's policy in the Middle East was based on dealing individually with each of the countries in the area, through a special political relationship – mandate, protectorate, a mutual assistance treaty, etc. This policy was backed by the threat of military force in the form of small but effective garrisons maintained at bases in the area. During the early years of the war, Britain dealt fiercely with any attempt to challenge its position in the Middle East. Anti-British activity in Egypt, the Vichy Levant states, Iraq and Palestine were all crushed by the military, the most famous incident being the suppression of the Rashid Ali rebellion in Iraq in May of 1941.

The anticipated recrudescence of Arab nationalism, and the emergence of a strong Russia on Britain's Middle Eastern flank, convinced Britain that this policy had outlived its usefulness. It was apparent that any major change would have to be deferred until after the war, but in Cairo, in 1941, the British Middle East Supply Centre and the Office of the Minister Resident had already started to deal with the countries of the area on a regional, rather than an individual, basis. Cooperation, particularly in the economic sphere, was contemplated as an alternative to the use of force.[8]

When the United States entered the war and began to participate in the Supply Centre (from early 1942), this added a new dimension to Britain's policy in the area. The exclusive position she had enjoyed during the inter-war years now disappeared. The Joint Supply Centre, which to a large extent was using American money and materials, enabled Britain during the war years to check a "further degeneration into acute nationalism hostile to British influence."[9] On the other hand, it demonstrated U.S. power to the peoples of the Middle East and thus proved to be detrimental to the British cause there. The Americans realized, however, that the extension of Supply Centre activity beyond the war period might serve British interests rather than their own, and gradually cut down their participation in it until, by the end of 1944, they ceased to be involved in it altogether.[10]

During the summer of 1945, HMG was preoccupied with the question of whether Britain should stick to its "overriding responsibility" in the Middle East, or whether "on financial and manpower grounds we should decide to seek the extensive assistance of other Powers."[11] If it were to ask for assistance, should it also invite the Russians

at least . . . to take part in the arrangements concerning Syria and Lebanon . . . Russia already showed signs of an exaggerated sense of isolation and we should do nothing to aggravate this, [or] would it assist in meeting any objective to the exclusion of the Soviet government if we refrained from bringing the U.S. Government into the discussions?[12]

The containment of the then largely theoretical Soviet expansion in the Middle East, either by joint Anglo-American action or by stationing of British troops in the area, was, however, totally rejected by the countries themselves, on the grounds that the threat, in fact, came from the British presence.[13]

Apart from global considerations, Britain considered the Middle East to be of vital importance to its standard of living. The significance of the region even grew as post-war nationalism mounted in India. The area was no longer a British bridge to the Far East; it was simply that

without the Middle East and its oil . . . he [Bevin] saw no hope of our being able to achieve the standard of life at which we were aiming in Great Britain.[14]

Consequently, despite a shortage of manpower, the War Office gave top priority to the allocation of available reinforcements to the Middle East Land Forces, and the bulk of military expenditure was accounted for by the Middle East.[15] The post-war view that as Britain relinquished its possessions in India, its interest in the Middle East would diminish, proved to be wrong.[16] The threatened loss of India added to rather than reduced the importance of the Middle East to Britain.

Britain began to contemplate an Arab policy for the area, destined to preserve its supremacy in an era of rising nationalism and competition among the powers. The successful exclusion of France and the proposals for an Arab Palestine (along the lines of a Chatham House paper of February 1945) were the major components of the policy.[17] Britain, however, could not satisfy Arab demands. It could not supply the weapons, the money or the manpower the local leaders wanted, nor could it allay Arab feelings that its aim was to reduce their opposition to Britain's refusal to evacuate military bases.[18] Furthermore, the fact that Arab admission to the United Nations was no longer an asset to be granted to Arabs in return for their friendship (five Arab states were already in the organization) left Britain with very few bargaining counters.[19]

In order to cope successfully with the requirements posed for the application of its Arab policy, Britain embarked from autumn 1945, on a double-pronged offensive. On the one hand, it aimed at a partnership with the peoples of the area, in which Britain would exchange its position of overt dominance for one of benevolent senior partner in the development of the Middle East. On the other hand, it aimed at controlled American assistance to make this possible. Neither plan materialized as conceived.

BRITAIN AND THE ARABS

With regard to British-Arab partnership, nothing more concrete than a stated intention for the establishment of a British-Arab confederacy ever emerged.[20] There were too many urgent issues that had to be resolved first, among them the revision of the 1936 Anglo-Egyptian Treaty, which the Egyptians were demanding, and, of course, the Palestine question. The two issues were, it is clear, inexorably linked, since at the basis of British thinking was the conception of the Middle East as a regional area for which one overall policy had to be articulated, a policy which aimed at easing the military and political problems, including those of Palestine, by plans for social and economic development.[21] Unfortunately, no matter how often the principle of "one area, one policy" was repeated – and it was reasserted in September 1945 at the Conference of British Ambassadors to the Middle East which assembled to lay down the principles for Britain's post-war policy in the area – it never seemed applicable in the field.[22] For example, when the AAC sought to alleviate political tensions in Palestine by improving social and economic infrastructures, their recommendation was immediately rejected as the revival of the "old fallacy of the hope of settlement of communal strife by way of economic interest."[23] Similarly, principles accepted for the Anglo-Egyptian Treaty were totally rejected by the Chiefs of Staff (C.O.S.) when it was suggested that they could also be applied to Palestine. The C.O.S. "have been very unwilling to accept any arrangement which makes military facilities in Palestine dependent upon treaty."[24] Earlier, a confederacy plan for the Middle East had to exclude Palestine, since "we cannot 'have it both ways' if we retain our full mandatory position and military rights [there]."[25] In short, Britain blocked any suggested solution for Palestine which did not accord with its Middle East policy, but that policy was rejected when attempts were made to apply it to Palestine. Thus it would appear that despite all claims to the contrary, HMG pursued two policies in the Middle East: one for Palestine, the other – the Arab policy – for the rest. Palestine had become the fulcrum of Britain's position in the Middle East: only if it had the freedom which it enjoyed there, unhampered by any treaty restrictions, would it be free to contemplate the solution of its other problems – such as Egypt. "We cannot adopt a policy of force in Palestine and a policy of evacuation in Egypt" was the way one British official put it.[26] Only peace in Palestine and British success there could guarantee British success elsewhere in the area. To ensure this peace, Britain needed help – in the form of "controlled" American assistance.

THE AMERICAN OPTION: A DOUBLE BIND

For Britain to call upon America to help with troops and money in order to carry out British policy in Palestine must be considered extremely naive and, indeed, it was not universally advocated in the councils of British policy making. "The United States hasn't invited us to share her influence in Panama ... we are entitled to our Monroe Doctrine in the Arab countries," was the way one British soldier argued.[27] And Richard Crossman was to argue:

"All right," you say: "Let us have some American troops." But if American troops go to Palestine they must carry out an American policy. We cannot ask the Americans to lend us troops to carry out an exclusively British policy.[28]

Yet, it was the considered opinion of Ernest Bevin that such co-operation was to be sought, and he had numerous reasons for embarking upon such a road.

Aside from the obvious British need for financial and manpower assistance, Bevin believed that Anglo-American cooperation would serve to check the internationalization of Middle Eastern conflicts, which, for example, would "invite the Russians and others to get their fingers in the Palestine pie."[29] From 1944 on, Britain had been trying to bring the Americans down from the clouds of high principles and away from international organizations (the United Nations) into more realistic Anglo-American regional planning. Although Soviet expansion in the Middle East was then largely theoretical, joint Anglo-American action was seen by some as the best means for Britain "to buttress her policy there against the menace of Russian encroachment."[30]

Still, the wartime relations between the two powers did not really portend a post-war Middle Eastern understanding. In June 1945, Sir Ronald Campbell had noted:

For some years, the United States have been showing an increasing interest in the Middle East. They worried us by an obstructive and disapproving attitude, the basis and reason of which remained obscure ... On the American side there is the lively conviction that the U.S.A. have the right to go where they wish and to the extent that they wish ... A unilateral presumption by another country of prior or greater right in respect of any area will only intensify their determination to vindicate their right ... But we, on our side, feel that the Americans, irrespectively of any suspicion on their part that we are trying to exclude them, are trying by means that seem to us both aggressive and unfair to build up a position for themselves at our expense, or at any rate without regard to our established interests ... We resist and advance ad hoc reasons for our resisrance, which leads the United States Government to think we are really finding excuses for applying a general policy of exclusion and going back on the specific understanding reached in the Wallace Murray conversations, and our general profession of a wish for American participation in world affairs in all regions of the world. A vicious circle is thus set up.[31]

And in the fall of that year, the Conference of British Representatives in the Middle East recalled that the experience of the Joint Supply Centre did "not offer much encouragement for a continuance of cooperation in fields that are essentially competitive" and went on to note that:

The Americans are commercially on the offensive ... but their export drive has now been held up by the stringency of the dollar situation in the Middle East countries. This state of affairs has produced a degree of exasperation in American minds which is not likely to be removed unless some relief in the dollar situation is forthcoming. This circumstance (for which we are blamed, but not responsible) dominates our relationship with the Americans in the Middle East, but we cannot afford to make any concessions in view of our difficult foreign exchange situation ... With the lifting of wartime controls (for which in the Middle East the Americans have been vigorously and prematurely pressing for some time) we shall enter a period of commercial rivalry, and we should not make any concession that would assist American commercial penetration into a region which for generations has been a British market.[32]

Campbell was very astute in assessing the situation by calling it a "vicious circle," but it was also Campbell who suggested "getting the mixture right." Britain could not really ask for American philanthropy to support tottering British hegemony and in the same breath call for an economic jihad against the Americans.

By the summer of 1945, it was clear that the Open Door policy which the Americans were demanding in the Middle East – and which London interpreted to mean "that the firm already holding a monopoly should give up part of its business in favour of the American firm" – would endanger Britain's position; this was especially true since America had already captured some 50 to 60 percent of the area's trade through participation in the Joint Supply Center.[33] Unfettered American activity not bound by any arrangement with Britain was defined in Washington as free competition in trade and communications matters, complete liberty on the part of the independent countries ... to select advisors and experts and in general a friendly vying among the powers in the course of which each will put its best foot forward.[34]

This actually meant U.S. supremacy in the region. This demand for an Open Door policy or "friendly vying" meant for the British Inter-Departmental Working Party on U.K.–U.S. Relationships in the Middle East that London must come to terms with Washington or else lose the area.[35] A desperate British concession – to divide a traditionally British area into spheres of influence – was rejected by the Americans because "we could not agree that [others] should concentrate their efforts upon assisting this country and we that country."[36] In other words, the United States wanted "this country" too. Although the American pursuit of an Open Door policy and of free trade was justified as being necessary to give the Americans an equal chance, in fact it served to eliminate other competitors.

One feature of American activity left the British puzzled, if not helpless, and they only realized the truth rather late in the game. In spite of its active commercial and strategic moves in the area, the United States had repeatedly claimed that it was giving top priority to non-political aims such as the preservation of American missionary and educational institutions like the universities in Cairo and Beirut.[37] There is no evidence whatsoever that Britain had challenged, or in any way interfered with, these supposed American priorities, and London could not grasp the reason for the somewhat aggressive policy that America pursued in the Near East. Similarly, the Americans preferred to present their active Palestinian policy merely as the inevitable outcome of Zionist pressures at home. There were, however, enough anti-Zionist facets to the U.S. Palestine policy (which were also known to the British) to undermine the validity of this excuse. Indeed, it wasn't until the summer of 1947 that the British perceived the difference between America's ostensibly passive stand and its actual policies. As a result they rated missionary work and education far behind strategic, oil and commercial, and other US interests in the Middle East.[38] This new rating of priorities which developed during the war indicated that the U.S. Near Eastern aspiration was basically political, and strove to defeat the Axis, to remove the French from the area, to contain the Soviets and to reduce Britain's position to that of a junior partner.[39] And, in fact, the years 1945 and 1946 were characterized by tough commercial and political competition between Britain and the United States. "Vultures are gathering for the kill," Lord Halifax warned in the face of a U.S. offensive in Saudi Arabia.[40] Quite ironically, after having made painstaking efforts to establish the Arab League, Britain was not in a hurry to recognize the organization. America, however, was quick to see the League as an official Arab body, to the cheering reactions of the Arabs, and the annoyance, even anxiety, of the British.[41] But the "hottest" point in Anglo-American strife was the capture from Britain of the lead in civil aviation in the Middle East. Here Britain complained about American trade conditions, which greatly favoured local markets. Business proposals included offers to send large free samples for demonstration; credit was given for periods of up to ten years; in several cases the total value of imports was spent locally on advertisement alone.[42] "So much so that many regard Uncle Sam as Uncle Santa Claus."[43] On the other hand, America took a tough line on Lend-Lease articles; these were repossessed by the United States with a view to selling them to customers in the Middle East. During the war, certain goods such as rail wagons had already been declared by the Americans to be outside Lend-Lease arrangements, and were offered for sale on the free market. This soon developed into a major row between Britain and the United States when rolling stock of British origin was moved into Lebanon for sale to the Lebanese government, while that of Lend-Lease, i.e., American, was moved down to Palestine and declared surplus and free of charge. "This was not cricket," reacted angry Americans.[44]

An inherent hostility permeated the two powers' relations in the area. A "deep rooted belief in British wickedness" was said to be at the basis of American attitudes towards British policy, and American sources described British acts as "in the category of sharp practice, bad faith and low ethics."[45] This corroborated a general attitude which held that

seldom has Britain been a cockshy for so many epithets. Nearly every corner of the globe reveals some aspect of our villainy. In Washington, we are greedy; in Westminster ungrateful; in the skies – mercenary; in Batavia – bloodthirsty; in Persia – shiftless; in Delhi and Jerusalem – tyrannical. We sustain corrupt monarchs abroad, while at home we institute a Commune. To dwellers in the Great Plains, it must seem that no perfidy is too base for Albion.[46]

In the Middle East, British resistance to American commercial advancement developed into an all-out confrontation. Britain refused to unfreeze dollars for Middle East customers who wanted to buy American products. America retaliated by restricting Lend-Lease supplies to Britain. Britain countered by encouraging Arab customers to boycott U.S. goods because of America's ostensible Zionist proclivities, this to the vocal protests of the Americans and the denials of the British, who claimed that they were not the "niggers in the woodpile."[47]

Anglo-American difficulties were not however confined to the Middle East. American efforts in this area, which had been directed towards helping certain countries to "extricate themselves from commitments which they were forced to make before the war ... to various great powers" were, in fact, the counterparts of U.S. acts to eliminate British competition in the Far East and the Pacific area.[48] In China, India, Australia, New Zealand, and in other areas of traditional British political and commercial supremacy, the United States acquired trade and military concessions, mainly at British expense.[49]

Another factor in the Americans' determination to use their economic might against Britain was the election in July 1945 of the Labour Government in Britain, which espoused socialist principles at home and might even apply a socialist foreign policy abroad. Influential members of the Labour Party were urging the establishment of a Third Force which, with India and the socialist governments of New Zealand and Australia, would stand as a buffer between the Americans and the Russians.[50] In August 1945, Lend-Lease arrangements were abruptly cancelled by the United States and soon after, Anglo-American negotiations for a loan for Britain were loaded with "all the conditions the traffic would bear."[51]

The impracticality reflected in the British plans that sought U.S. troops and money to support British supremacy, was also found in American policy. Clearly the United States could advance its position in the Middle East only if a certain amount of stability were maintained and, thus, it was left to the British to do the ground-work here. The Americans had to practise some caution in their relations with Britain:

... It would be possible to describe the situation in terms of a simple bargain. If for political and strategic reasons we want them to hold a position of strength in the Middle East, then they must have from us economic concessions.[52]

Be that as it may, no one in Britain wanted to police the area for America, not even for the above concessions.

So somehow the Americans too had to get the mixture right. A major American offensive could deprive Britain of her economic assets and this would "seriously hamper the ability of the United Kingdom to pay its debt to us and would impair its position as the best customer of the United States."[53] This too was an attempt to achieve the impossible – "an effort to reach an understanding as to how far we may go towards achieving our objectives without impairing British chances for recovery."[54]

A serious question which was often asked in the corridors of British power, and seldom answered unambiguously, was "What exactly *is* American policy in the Middle East and Palestine?" or "Do they have a policy?" British attempts to assess America's Near East policy above and beyond what they considered to be general American political indifference, on the one hand, and, with regard to Palestine, Zionist pressures on the other, were confounded by the contradictory reports and expressions of the American organizations in the area. Reports on the growing American under-standing and interest in the Arab world "comparable *mutatis mutandis* to that of the Latin American countries" were cancelled out by the reservations that "this interest is not necessarily always sympathetic to the Arabs."[55] Contemptuous comments about native Arabs, similar to the feelings that Americans had had towards the native American Indians, were heard as well. The confusion enshrouding the activity of the Presidency, the State Department and the various services operating in the area caused London's evaluation of U.S. policy to be carried out either by a process of elimination or by resorting to induction – observing U.S. deeds and their effects and then inferring the policies behind them. Requests like, "Can you get from them what is their real position?" were not rare phenomena.[56] Neither were complaints that "we are expected to adjust our policy according to the whims of different Departments in the United States and often placed in embarrassing positions."[57] This labyrinthine situation was particularly evident in Britain's attempt to assess the U.S. attitude toward Palestine. The failure to do so can be deduced from a comment which Bevin made as late as May 1948. "Who is Niles?" he asked, following a reference to the latter, which spoke of an American "whose real name [Niles] and origin will be known to you [Bevin]."[58] David K. Niles, Truman's adviser on minorities, was in fact the man responsible for the President's Palestine policy from the summer of 1945. In particular, he dealt with the British initiative to find an Anglo-American settlement for the country.

The United States, like Great Britain, did have a Middle Eastern or Near Eastern policy. This does not mean that it was publicly articulated with precision, or that what was said was what was meant, or that what was meant was actually put into effect. It had, like Great Britain, general aims and aspirations and their execution depended on the successful jockeying between various pressure groups and interests. One such general aim was America's Open Door policy, already mentioned; another was the "sympathy" with which America viewed the attempts of certain countries to "extricate themselves" from previous commitments, also already mentioned. These and other general aims and aspirations were, in fact, articulated in a State Department paper and approved by President Truman on 10 November 1945. Their major import was summed up by the phrase: "We have no intention of becoming again a mere passive spectator" in the Near East.[59]

This paper enumerated other policy lines, among them a guide to U.S.–Soviet relations:

There need be no conflict between us and Russia in that area ... Russian policy has thus far closely paralleled our own. Like ourselves, the Kremlin has accorded unconditional recognition of the full independence of Syria and Lebanon and seeks equality of treatment, now denied us both, in Egypt and Iraq.[60]

As long as America perceived the Russians as harmless, the desire for understanding between the less-favoured powers proved to be stronger than the traditional Anglo-American alliance.

What was omitted from the State Department paper is also rather significant. There was no reference to future relations with Great Britain and Britain was mentioned only in connection with "imperialist interference" and the division of the Near East into spheres of influence "to suit themselves."[61]

BEVIN GOES AHEAD

As already noted, in the fall of 1945, Ernest Bevin embarked upon the road of Anglo-American cooperation, with all its pitfalls and uncertainties, and in the face of a great deal of opposition outside the Cabinet. Foreign Office officials questioned whether the search for such cooperation "does not overstate: a. the extent of the communist danger in the Middle East. b. the inadequacy of British resources," and concluded that "we must compete with them as efficiently as we can."[62] The only area considered to be open to possible cooperation was the development of cultural projects and

a general intention to try to avoid competing with them [in] schemes of social betterment ... We cannot find, having examined the possible field of cooperation, that in practice there is much more that we can do.[63]

Many in Britain regarded America as a greater threat than Russia and in a similar context the following evaluation was made as early as 1944:

There is one danger, however, of which we have so far remained almost entirely unconscious. The danger is just as threatening to our Imperial interests here and elsewhere in the Middle East as was the Nazi menace and is much more difficult to combat. The danger is the growing interest being taken in this part of the world by the U.S.A. The U.S.A. has almost everything to offer Iraq that we have, without the taint we carry of broken promises, procrastinating policies and with that the most fascinating of attractions – the untried devil.[64]

British officials tended to be annoyed, if not offended, by any implications of the United States' right to be involved in British Middle Eastern affairs. It was a loaded subject, emotionally coloured by feelings of frustration and injustice. Expressions like "America wept for the Jews, but we bled for them," or "What would have been the attitude of the United States if ... we had suddenly proposed to send 100,000 West Africans there" were not unusual.[65]

The often repeated reason to cooperate with the Americans was the need to contain the Russians. But here the opposition claimed that Russia would be agreeable to British influence in the Middle East so long as the United States did not become involved. Otherwise, Russia "might suspect that [this] is aimed against [her] and

she can act in a preemptive act."[66] An Anglo-American confrontation was also predicted since in the event of America pro-
voking the Arab world, Britain would then be compelled to protect
Arab interests and find itself in a clash with the United States.
"Such a situation could be provoked also by a third party that would
strive to harm Anglo-American relations" warned the Chiefs of
Staff, referring no doubt to Soviet provocation.[67]

These and other warnings all failed to change the decisive desire
of Bevin to enforce a settlement in Palestine through Anglo-
American cooperation. Thus, Palestine was to become the testing ground for further cooperation in the entire area. It was still
very remote from the centres of British thinking that the United
States might actually be using Palestine as a lever to reduce
Britain's influence throughout the Middle East. But, as far as the
Americans were concerned, to recapitulate, the Palestine policy of
the United States was rooted in two contexts in accordance with
its overall aims and aspirations: the Anglo-American and the Near
Eastern. And its overall aims and aspirations, when distilled from
the contradictory and befogged public pronouncements of its
numerous departments and organizations were two: the improvement of American commercial and strategic interests which, ipso
facto, implied the undermining of British supremacy in the area,
and the achievement of this through a form of "remote control,"
that is, not getting involved militarily. Because British success in
Palestine would have given Britain the advantage in the Middle
East, Palestine probably became a target at which the United
States aimed in order to end Britain's supremacy in the area. The
more America pursued an anti-British policy in Palestine, the less
Britain could guarantee there a settlement which would enhance
British status in the Arab Middle East. As a result, the Arabs
tended to place less reliance on Britain, while America became the
key to future development. Only this ironic explanation, which
actually says that the apparently pro-Zionist policy of the United
States in Palestine had brought it profits among the Arabs in the
context of the Anglo-American struggle in the Middle East, could
explain the sad British conclusion that "*the Americans must realize
that their continued support of Zionism has an extremely serious
effect on the readiness of the Arabs to cooperate with us.*"[68] This was
the outcome of the U.S. Near Eastern policy and was probably its
intention as well.

At first the Americans assumed that that the British would continue to police the area, and that Britain could be "trained" to operate in Palestine in accordance with American interests.[69] Palestine itself (and later Israel) was to become one of America's foremost non-Arab assets, which could be simultaneously manipulated with its Arab clients.[70] When U.S. policy in Palestine caused resentment among the Arabs, the United States managed to contain it through large sums of money and other forms of assistance, on the one hand, and by supporting Arab claims in the Middle Eastern conflicts, such as Egypt against Britain, on the other.[71] Britain soon came to realize that "opposition to the United States arising from its Palestine policy will not be effectively sustained in the face of her material strength." [72]

When during the course of 1946 and 1947 it became apparent that Britain might withdraw its troops from the Middle East, that Britain was reluctant to play the game according to the American rules, it is possible that U.S. support for Zionism was given a greater incentive. Then attention was given to a memorandum submitted by the Jewish Resistance Movement – an amalgamation of the three Palestinian undergrounds – which claimed that Jewish forces could police Palestine and "not a single American soldier will be necessary. A few squadrons of aircraft will suffice."[73] This may be the basis for what became American policy in the entire area for the next thirty-five years, with minor deviations.

It is then with the help of hindsight that one can see Bevin's historically ironic assumptions with regard to American involvement in Middle Eastern affairs. He sought American participation primarily in order to forestall Russian expansion, years before the Americans were aware that any such threat existed. When the threat materialized and Bevin's involvement of the Americans could be seen as justified, Britain could no longer reap any benefit from it. Bevin considered America motivated primarily by Zionist pressures at a time when the very opposite was true. When American support for Zionism materialized it was as a means and not as a cause or an end of American policy, and resulted from Britain's forced withdrawal from the Middle East. Bevin considered Palestine to be the key to Britain's position in the Middle East, and American involvement the means of maintaining it. Palestine, it turned out, was the key to Britain's position in the region and American involvement the means of undermining it.

This diametrical opposition of interests came clearly to light with American acceptance of Bevin's AAC initiative in the fall of 1945 and their complete reversal of his anticipated terms of reference.

NOTES

1. 9 June 1945, FO 371/45267/E6623. On Anglo-American relations in the Middle East see also Michael Cohen, *Palestine and the Great Powers, 1945–1948*, Princeton, 1982; Roger Louis, *The British Empire in the Middle East, 1945–1951*, Oxford, 1984.
2. *Years of Trial and Hope, 1946–1953*, New York, 1956, p. 163.
3. Figures from A.F. Havinghurst, *Twentieth-Century Britain*, New York, 1962 (second edition), pp. 360, 382.
4. W.N. Medlicott, *Contemporary England, 1914–1964*, London, 1967, p. 475.
5. C.O.S. memo, 9 July 1946, p. 2, FO 371/52538/E6528/G.
6. Donovan, *Truman's Presidency*, pp. 43, 137, 156.
7. Moscow to Foreign Office, 22 July 1946, FO 371/52543/E6962.
8. State Department, undated memo for the Anglo-American "Pentagon Talks" of 1947, FRUS 1947, vol. 5, p. 511. The reference is to a previous memo by R. Casey, British Minister Resident, Middle East, August 1943.
9. Ibid.
10. Philip J. Baram, *The Department of State in the Middle East, 1919–1945*, Pennsylvania, 1978, p. 166; George Kirk, *The Middle East in the War*, Oxford, 1952, p. 192; Board of Trade memo, 8 July 1947, BT 11/3481.
11. Bevin to the Cabinet, 30 Aug. 1945, CAB 128/1,C.M. (45) 26.
12. Minutes of the Cabinet, 23 Aug. 1945, CAB 128/1 C.M.(45) 25.
13. George Kirk, *The Middle East, 1945–1950*, London, 1954, p. 18.
14. Bevin to Cabinet Defence Committee, undated, No.DO(46) 45, CAB 21/1686.
15. Foreign Office report, 26 Feb. 1946, Lord Keynes's Personal Files, Political and Military Overseas Expenditures, T 247/71; Quarterly Historical Report, General H.Q., Middle East Land Forces, 31 Aug. 1946, WO 261/77.
16. David Horowitz, *State in the Making*, New York, 1953, p. 97.
17. Harry Sachar, *Israel: The Establishment of a State*, London, 1952, pp. 30-32. By the winter of 1946, France had withdrawn all their troops from the Levant.
18. Monroe, *Britain's Moment in the Middle East*, pp. 156, 161.
19. J.C. Hurewitz, *The Struggle for Palestine*, New York, 1950, p. 227.
20. Formation of a Middle East Confederacy, 12 Nov. 1945, AIR 20/4960.
21. Bevin to Cabinet, 4 Oct. 1945, CAB 128/1, CM(45) 38; minutes of the Cabinet, 11 Oct. 1945, CAB 128/1, CM(45)40.
22. Minutes of the Middle East Policy Conference, 19 Sept. 1945, FO 371/45379/E6954.
23. Grafftey-Smith, British Legation, Jeddah, to Foreign Office, 23 April 1946, FO371/52516/E3663/G.
24. Colonial Office memo by Sir Douglas Harris, 14 Aug. 1946, PREM 8/627 Pt.4.
25. Memo by GHQ Middle East Forces, 7 Nov. 1945, WO 106/2330.
26. Memo by Sir Walter Smart, Oriental Counsellor in Cairo, 29 April 1946, FO 141/1090, no. 101/1448/46.
27. Memo by John Glubb, British Commander of the Arab Legion, Jan. 1946, FO 371/52310/E3135.
28. Lecture before the Royal Institute of International Affairs, (R.I.I.A.) London, 13 June 1946, p. 9, SACMEC Crossman Papers.

29. Bevin to Foreign Office officials, 28 April 1946, FO 371/52521/E4098; see also Bevin in Cabinet Committee on Palestine, 10 Oct. 1945, CAB 95/14; minutes of the Cabinet, 25 July 1946, CAB 128/6 CM(46)73; Bevin comments, end of August 1946, FO 371/52550/E7691.
30. Roger Wm. Louis, *Imperialism at Bay: The United States and Decolonization of the British Empire, 1941–1945*. Oxford, 1977, p. 310. Suggestion of British Embassy, Washington, 7 March 1946, FO 371/52318/E2612.
31. Memo by Ronald Campbell, 9 June 1945, FO 371/45267/E6623. Wallace Murray, head of the Near East and African Division at the State Department held discussions with his British counterparts in London, April 1944, on commercial and political matters which interested the two powers.
32. Recommendations of Conference of British Middle East Representatives, approved by the Cabinet, in Bevin to British Representatives Middle East, 18 Oct. 1945, SACMEC, Cunningham Papers, box 6, file 1.
33. Campbell memo, 9 June 1945; Michael J. Cohen, *Palestine: Retreat from the Mandate*, London, 1978, p. 154.
34. Gordon Merriam, Chief of Division of Near East Affairs in the State Department, Washington, 4 Jan. 1946, FRUS, 1946, vol. 7, p. 6.
35. See reports on the Working Party meetings, 8 and 25 Aug. 1947, BT 11/3481 and CAB 134/500.
36. State Department memo for the "Pentagon Talks", undated, FRUS 1947, vol. 5, pp. 515, 518.
37. State Department memo: Considerations Bearing Upon Handling of the Palestine Question, State Department Correspondence 1946, USNA, Box 6756, No. 867N 01/6–1846; memo by U.S.Cabinet Committee on Palestine, June 1946, USNA, RG, 43, AAC, Box 13. Both documents were presented at the Anglo-American study of the AAC Report, June-July 1946.
38. British Working Party to Consider U.S.-U.K. Relations in the Middle East, 25 Aug. 1947, CAB 134/500.
39. Baram, *The Department of State in the Middle East*, p. 321.
40. Washington to Foreign Office, 1 Dec. 1945, T 236/502.
41. See in Cairo to Foreign Office, 22 May 1946, CO 537/1763.
42. British Middle East Officials Committee: Activities of Major Powers in Middle East Territories, Monthly Progress Report, March 1946, FO 371/52337/E3828.
43. Memo by A. Bland-Calder, formerly first secretary at U.S. Legations in Moscow and Cairo, 14 July 1945, Washington D.C., State Department Building, Lot 54, D403, Box 1812.
44. In Washington to Foreign Office, 26 June 1946, FO 371/52617/E6357.
45. Washington to Foreign Office, 29 Nov. 1946, FO 371/52571/E11651; Bland-Calder memo, see note 43.
46. British Consulate in Denver to Embassy in Washington, 18 Dec. 1945, FO 115/4206. The reference is to public opinion in the United States concerning Britain's policies.
47. Correspondence on U.S.-Iraqi civil aviation negotiations, in Washington to Foreign Office, 17 Oct. 1946, FO 371/54578/W10346.
48. Loy Henderson, Director of Office of Near East and African Affairs, State Department, 10 Nov. 1945, FRUS 1945, vol. 8, p. 11.
49. See Medlicott, *Contemporary England*, pp. 485-486.
50. Ibid.
51. Comment by William L. Clayton, Asst. Sec. of State for Economic Affairs, quoted in Donovan, *Truman's Presidency*, p. 186.
52. State Dept. memo for the "Pentagon Talks", undated, FRUS 1947, vol. 5, p. 516.
53. Bland-Calder memo, see note 43 above.
54. Ibid.

55. Halifax to Bevin, 1 July 1945, FO 371/45378/E4849.
56. Bevin to Halifax, 29 Oct. 1945, FO 371/45382/E8161.
57. Foreign Office to Washington, 2 Sept. 1947, T 236/1274.
58. Comment by Bevin, 2 May 1948, FO 371/68649/E5986. American policy making was seen by the British Foreign Office as an outcome of competition between departments, and "in the background is the White House, where pressure from party managers ... may cut across the advice of the State Department and the Service Departments," M.R. Wright, Eastern Department, Foreign Office, 14 Nov. 1947, FO 371/61559/E10019/G.
59. FRUS 1945, vol. 8, p. 11.
60. George Wadsworth, Minister to Syria and Lebanon, to President Truman, FRUS 1945, vol. 18, p. 14. Both in Egypt and Iraq British Ambassadors had precedence over the diplomatic representatives of other powers in accordance with the Anglo-Egyptian and Anglo-Iraqi treaties.
61. FRUS 1945, vol. 8, pp. 10, 13.
62. Comments on Washington Embassy's suggestion for Middle Eastern cooperation with the United States against the Soviets, 28 March 1946, FO 371/52318/E2612.
63. Ibid., 4 April 1946.
64. J.G. McDonald, Area Liaison Officer, Baghdad, in Baghdad to Foreign Office, 14 March 1944, FO 624/39/547.
65. Edward Grigg's memo, Cairo, 27 June 1945, CO 733/461 Pt. 2/75872 Pt.2. The reference was to American calls to admit 100,000 Jews into Palestine; Prime Minister Attlee to LaGuardia, Head of UNRRA, 5 Sept. 1946, FO 371/57769, WR2494.
66. C.O.S. memo, 10 July 1945, No: JP(45)167, FO 371/45378/E5141. See also memo by Harold Beeley, Eastern Department, Foreign Office, 10 July 1945, FO 371/45378/E4939/G.
67. C.O.S. memo, 10 July 1945.
68. Memo on Middle East Economic Policy, prepared for Pentagon Talks, 2 Oct. 1947, T 236/1274. Emphasis mine.
69. State Department memo for the "Pentagon Talks," FRUS 1947, vol. 5, p. 515.
70. "Object to ... designating Palestine as an Arab country." Comment from the Palestine Desk in the Near East Division, State Department, Washington, State Dept. Bldg., Lot 54, D403, Box 9.
71. Foreign Office memo, Oct. 1947, FO 371/61558/E9452/G; Foreign Office memo, 2 Oct. 1947, FO 371/61559/E9599/G.
72. British Inter-Departmental Working Party to Consider Anglo-American Relations in the Middle East, 12 Aug. 1947, BT 11/3481.
73. Memo submitted to the AAC by the Jewish Resistance Movement (amalgamation of the three undergrounds) March 1946, USNA, RG 43, AAC, Box 7.

3

Britain seeks a Policy for Palestine

Within three months of taking office as Foreign Secretary, Ernest Bevin had started the ball rolling in his Anglo-American initiative for Palestine. As a matter of fact, in Britain's post-war foreign affairs, there was no other area in which he was so closely involved. He himself regarded the Palestine conflict as the testing ground for his ability at the Foreign Office and even pledged to "eat his hat" if he wasn't successful.[1] One result was that the issue became identified more with Bevin than with Britain or HMG insofar as the other contenders were concerned – and not without good reason. It became a self-perpetuating obsession in which the Foreign Minister found himself stripped of the support of his own staff and colleagues, not to mention that of the intellectuals of the Labour Party, although on different grounds. The former objected to the whole idea of bringing the Americans in; the latter simply supported the idea of a Jewish Palestine, an idea to which Bevin was unalterably unsympathetic. And a combination of the two, American participation in a non-Zionist solution to the problem, was the infrastructure of Bevin's Palestine policy.

There was ostensibly no foreign policy issue – except perhaps independence for India – on which Labour had taken so firm and consistent a line as its support for the Jewish National Home in Palestine. From 1917 to May 1945, eleven national party conferences had reaffirmed this line.[2] Leaders of the party who had visited Palestine were greatly impressed by the "socialist colonists, dear comrades" there.[3] Labour's favourable view of Zionism had even culminated in a recommendation to encourage the Arabs to leave the country and Jews to enter it – which caused Richard Crossman to comment: "a criminal thing."[4]

In the Labour Cabinet of 1945, almost all the members had, at one time or another, expressed strong support for Zionism. Clement Attlee, the Prime Minister, for instance, was in favour of the Jews extending their settlement even into Transjordan.[5]

Herbert Morrison, Chairman of the Cabinet Committee on Palestine, was described by Sir Alan Cunningham as "wishing to hand it [Palestine] over lock, stock and barrel to the Jews."[6]

This again ostensibly pro-Zionist stand was even more pronounced in comparison with the Party's opinions of the Arabs. On the whole, Arab governments were considered to be as outmoded and corrupt as feudalism.[7] Supporting them was compared to protecting "ruthless exploitation of the African in the copper mines of Rhodesia."[8] Furthermore, Labour supporters of Zionism believed that the Arab–Jewish conflict had been artificially fomented by the effendi, and that, if left to themselves, Arab and Jewish workers would find common ground.[9]

But to view that Labour Party as a secure Zionist stronghold would be a grave misconception. These were the resolutions and effusions not only of a party out of power but of its more vocal intellectuals. With the ascension of the Labour Party to power, the internal and external constraints of governing diminished the role of the Party as a whole, and the intellectuals in particular, in the formulation of government policy. In many instances, HMG simply preferred to carry on as before rather than upsetting any global applecarts merely because they were planks in the party platform.

Bevin, it must be remembered, came from the trade union movement. The constant suspicions of and confrontations with Labour intellectuals caused him a great deal of annoyance. With regard to Richard Crossman, he told Attlee that "nothing I can say will make him alter his ideas about Palestine which derive from his lack of judgement and his intellectual arrogance."[10] The mere mention of Harold Laski was reported to have given him nightmares of thousands and thousands of Laskis pursuing him down the road.[11]

As for the pro-Zionist resolutions of eleven party conferences, it was the opinion of one Labour M.P. "that the average member who attended these conferences had about as much knowledge of the Palestine question as I have of the moon. These resolutions were accepted because nobody objected."[12]

Bevin, at any rate, had expressed reservations about Jewish statehood as early as 1937 when he questioned whether the partition of Palestine would

contribute towards the ending for all time of the persecution of the Jewish race? Will the fact that they are a state with ambassadors at the various

Chancelleries of the world assist them to a greater extent than the Mandate granted by the League?[13]

And at the first party conference following the elections of July 1945, Bevin declared that

I do not believe in absolutely exclusive racial states ... you might just as well try to do that in England with the Welshmen and the Scotsmen or, what is worse, try to make Glasgow completely Scotch and see how you get on, or Cardiff completely Welsh. It is impossible.[14]

Bevin was not an anti-Semite by any means. His attitude towards Zionism was political and he tried to distinguish between his attitude towards Zionism and towards the Jews, a distinction that was not always possible or easily grasped. The Balfour Declaration, he said, "was a unilateral declaration, did not take into account the Arabs, and was really a power politics declaration."[15] He also wondered whether "the Jews would always be Jews politically and not divided on other lines as the Jews were in this country, where some of them voted Conservative, Labour, Communist, etc."[16] At one point he noted to Truman: "I tell them ... I can no more fulfil all the prophecies of Ezekiel than I can those of that other great Jew, Karl Marx."[17]

Nahum Goldmann, who played a leading role in Zionist negotiations, found that Bevin was, on the whole

rather helpful and with a certain amount of good will ... but he has to overcome the hostility of his advisers ... whenever he was ready to accept a formula ... other elements in the London field interfered and made it impossible.

And:

We have good friends in the Cabinet. Mr. Attlee seems rather antagonistic to us, but Mr. Bevin is certainly the keyman in the Cabinet with regard to Palestine and he could probably swing the Cabinet to his position.[18]

The difference between the views of some Labour pundits and the Palestine policy of HMG were symptomatic of a greater gap between the Party and its Ministers. The Labour members who served in the war-time Coalition were prevented from reporting and sharing their information with the rank and file in the constituencies. With Labour in power, the majority of the Party were unaware of the anxiety with which its leaders regarded the international situation. Thus, for instance, Harold Laski, Chairman of the Party, could state that the Party regarded Palestine as a purely internal problem to be solved simply by having more police there, whereas HMG's starting point was the global and regional aspects of the conflict.[19] Gradually, the Party came to play a diminishing role in the formation of Britain's policies, and while the Labourites stressed that the new Government had been elected with a clear expectation of radical change in foreign as well as domestic policy, the Cabinet, as noted, preferred continuity to innovation.[20] The result was that in foreign affairs, the Government and some parts of the Party clashed over such questions as the solution for Palestine and relations with Russia. It was the Government, however, who won the day and within the Government, Bevin's initiative for an Anglo-American Committee.

Before, during and after the July elections, HMG had contemplated several options which envisaged cardinal changes in Britain's Palestine policy. The need to solve problems like the imminent exhaustion of the White Paper immigration quota and to articulate long term policy for Palestine pressured the various bodies involved in policy making for Palestine to submit their plans. They were of the opinion that "Nothing could be worse than to fall between two stools and to arrive in September with no decision on major policy and no agreement for the continuance of the immigration quota."[21] The Colonial Office had devised a broad policy framework according to which the ultimate objective of every plan was the termination of the Mandate and the handing over of the government to the people of the country. The plan had to be capable of implementation within the terms of the existing Mandate, without recourse to any international body. It would have to clearly define the obligations of Britain to the Jews and Arabs, satisfying them insofar as it was practicable. The plan should safeguard the integrity and religious status of Jerusalem, accept as a basis the impossibility of obtaining cooperation between the Arabs and the Jews, and turn over to each community the largest possible measure of control over its own affairs. Above all, only a *single* Mandate should apply these principles: no external body should have any say with regard to immigration and Britain alone should retain responsibility for the administration of the country.[22]

As much as these principles were to guide British planners, they even more succinctly pointed to the impediments standing in the way of an agreed policy in Palestine. But on top of all this, not all of them were, in fact, agreed upon by all those involved in establishing policy. The C.O.S. and Foreign Office took exception to the fact that these principles focussed on Palestine alone, with only marginal reference to regional and international affairs ("the plan should be one which HMG can defend before the world as doing the utmost ... to reconcile the conflicting claims").[23] In addition, the assumption that negative planning, i.e., negation of the demands of one side in the hope that this would satisfy and allay the hostility of the other, emasculated any attempt to arrive at a constructive policy.[24]

EIGHT PLANS FOR PALESTINE

When the new Labour Government first discussed its future Palestine policy, the atmosphere was one of hope and confidence in its ability to cope resolutely with the problem, and, as noted before, Bevin was prepared to stake his career on its resolution. British manpower and money would be applied to produce a solution and defiant demands resisted. "While full justice should be done to the Arab claims, it was possible to exaggerate their importance" – was one impression which epitomized this feeling.[25] This self-assurance soon faded, however, when the various policies were measured against the principles and needs set out above.

As mentioned before, no fewer than eight plans were tabled by the various British bodies which handled the question.[26] Partition – to which the Arabs vehemently objected – was almost unanimously rejected since it "would lose us the goodwill and friendship of the whole Moslem world." It was also considered "very likely [to] bring into existence a Jewish Nazi state [sic]."[27] Partition, which also meant the termination of the Mandate, was regarded with horror by those who stressed that in the interests of Imperial security, the country should continue to be administered by Britain as an undivided whole. "Palestine and Trans-Jordan," they argued, "will be reliable buttresses in all weathers, provided we administer the former and cement the friendship with the latter."[28]

Others advocated the continuation of the White Paper policy, asking "why it was necessary in 1945 to depart from the White Paper which had been regarded as satisfactory in 1939?"[29] Some of the more sensitive members of the Cabinet, however, objected to a settlement based on this plan (which also meant no more Jewish immigration to Palestine). Otherwise the "Government would have to face serious opposition in Parliament ... an outcry from America [and] serious trouble with the Jews in Palestine."[30]

There were two plans of a more constructive character which called for constitutional as well as structural changes in Palestine. The first had been worked out in the Colonial Office and sought the division of the country into autonomous Arab and Jewish provinces under a central British administration. And indeed, a year later provincial autonomy became the formal British plan.[31] But in August 1945, the Foreign Office warned that if it were tabled before the Cabinet, they "would submit their modifications as regards minimizing troubles in the international sphere" in order to block the introduction of "the thin end of the wedge of partition."[32] This was enough to deter further consideration of the plan.[33] The second plan, submitted by Bevin, envisaged a federal union, composed of three parts – a Jewish area, the remaining Arab area of Palestine, and Transjordan – to be ruled by an Arab king, preferably Abdullah of Jordan. One reason given for this solution was the hope that it would be attractive to public opinion in the United States which was familiar with this system and "thought instinctively in terms of federation."[34] Another was that "the two together would form a good training ground for British forces."[35] The main objective to this "monarchical solution" was the anticipated Arab opposition to any extension of Abdullah's Kingdom.[36] Furthermore, it was clear that "so long as the Amir ... is alive it would not be possible ... to put another Arab king over his head."[37] In the face of strong opposition from his representatives to the Arab countries, Bevin withdrew his suggestion. This left HMG in September 1945 still with no plan for Palestine and hence not much could be achieved then beyond agreement on what not to do there.

There was in addition the annual Mecca Pilgrimage, due to take place in mid-November 1945, and HMG preferred not to add more fire to Moslem religious feeling by publishing a new Palestine policy at that particular time.[38] The preparation of a new policy was expected to take at least six months.[39] Meanwhile, it was decided to reinforce the British garrison in the Middle East in order to meet any contingency which might arise from the adoption of a new policy. Accordingly, two divisions and 9,000 administrative troops were moved into the area.[40] With regard to Jewish immigration into the country, there was an urgent need to regulate policy since the White Paper quota was nearing exhaustion. HMG tended to concentrate more and more on this aspect of the conflict since

it would be advantageous to postpone a decision on long-term policy for as long as possible, because the pressure for Jewish immigration into Palestine was likely to diminish ... as the months went by and the settlement of Europe progressed.[41]

A decline in the number of would-be immigrants was seen as a guarantee for continuation of the status quo in Palestine. This corroborated an earlier view which suggested that "if Russia places obstacles in the way of intending emigrants from Russian controlled territory, there may be no call for any ... drastic changes of policy."[42] Consequently, on this issue it was decided to ease the pressure for immigration by settling on a quota of 1,500 per month, but otherwise adhering to the points set out in the 1939 White Paper.[43]

THE 100,000: THE THIN EDGE OF U.S. INVOLVEMENT

This could have remained the full extent of British policy-making for Palestine for the time being were it not for President Truman's vexatious call for the admission of 100,000, which foregrounded the entire question of American involvement in the matter, elevating it from an issue of Zionist protest to one of high politics. Earlier references to the United States having a say in Palestine or suggestions to share responsibility with America there had already met with the strong objections of the British administration. Edward Grigg, British Minister Resident in Cairo, had proposed that the rate and extent of Jewish immigration into Palestine be determined by an Anglo-American body, a proposal rejected by Anthony Eden on the grounds that:

HMG should avoid at all costs a set up in which a non-British body takes important decisions (perhaps against British advice) on immigration, whereas presumably, British troops alone will suffer casualties if this decision leads to disturbance and revolt.[44]

The opposition to a separation of responsibilities reflected broader objections to the whole idea of U.S. intervention. Only a negligible minority supported an initiative which sought to develop further American interest in a subdued Palestine, through the laying of oil pipelines from Saudi Arabia to the Mediterranean via Palestine.[45] Suggestions that the United States should share or relieve Britain of the Palestine Mandate drew angry reactions from the C.O.S. They warned against the collapse of Britain's position all over the Moslem world, which would view Britain's withdrawal "as an indication that we were no longer either prepared or able to accept our responsibility. The psychological effects of this are incalculable."[46] The British in the Middle East were contemptuous of the proposal to relinquish the Mandate which came from "international enthusiasts such as Noel-Baker ... the great British Public won't stomach anything amounting to the surrender of our rights in an area such as this."[47] And, as noted in the preceding chapter, there was the argument that Russia would be agreeable to British influence in the area as long as the United States was kept out of Palestine. Otherwise, they "might suspect that [it] is aimed against them and ... can act in a preemptive act."[48]

Later, when the United States had actually been introduced into the Palestine conflict, some British circles in the Middle East, which were partly responsible for the implementation of this policy, expressed the same view as General D'Arcy, the G.O.C. Palestine, and acted accordingly:

He regarded the Prime Minister's request for U.S. assistance as a useful propaganda weapon as long as we could be sure that they would not comply.[49]

There is at least circumstantial evidence that these circles tried to block the Cabinet initiative to involve the United States in Palestine by carrying out a unilateral disarmament of the Jewish underground movement. They thus took the wind out of the sails of the argument that Britain needed American troops to assist her in such an operation.[50]

It was against this background that Bevin pursued his policy of involving America in Palestine. He had to convince his Middle Eastern officials that this was not an anti-Arab step, since the United States already perceived the importance of Arab oil, and would inevitably change her so-called one-sided view of the conflict. In a private initiative, previously revealed only to the Embassy in Washington, which fully endorsed it, Bevin put before the Cabinet (4 October 1945) the idea of an Anglo-American Committee.[51] The Prime Minister noted that "the Cabinet was grateful to the Foreign Secretary for the time and energy which he had devoted to the formulation of this new approach to the question of Palestine," and for the idea of associating the United States with Britain in finding a solution to the conflict.[52] It would be true to say that the Cabinet, rather than giving wholehearted support to Bevin's plan, merely desisted from raising objections to it, leaving it, more or less, as Bevin's private initiative.

The endorsement of the AAC plan was not considered in Britain as a dramatic novelty. Neither the actual termination of the discussions on American involvement in Palestine, nor the relinquishment of Britain's exclusive position there, had been subjects for heated discussions, although the decision to involve America moulded the conflict more than any other force. The two Cabinet meetings and the conference of the Cabinet Committee on Palestine regarded the proposal as a sensible motion.[53] They gave greater attention, however, to the way in which the new Palestine policy should be announced, defining it as a subject of the "utmost importance."[54]

The somewhat complacent handling of the decision could be attributed to the fact that as far as Palestine was concerned, the United States, it will be recalled, was regarded as being "harmless," and no danger was seen in her being associated with Britain there. In addition, nothing was altered in Palestine, because committees of inquiry had long been known for their marginal effect. None of the dozen or so previous inquiries had produced more than minor changes. In the meantime, no change was expected since the whole question had been bureaucratically frozen and the "Jewish problem is in the melting pot at the moment; the whole ... is subjudice."[55] Should some change result from the inquiry, it was expected to take the form of America's realization of the difficulties Britain faced in Palestine and the Arab Middle East, and consequently, approval of the British method of handling the conflict.[56] In this context, there is at least some indirect evidence that the idea of having a joint inquiry in Palestine sprang, in part, from the earlier success of the Anglo-American Caribbean Commission, which was established in March 1942 to regulate shipping and food production. In the general colonial discussions, the Caribbean body acted as a model for future regional commissions which advocated no derogation of sovereignty and no accountability to an international organization.[57] "No doubt the Americans would be a great nuisance to us on the Caribbean Committee ... but they will do that in any case," wrote Lord Cranborne, implying that it was preferable to check this annoyance through joint Anglo-U.S. organs.[58]

But if the Cabinet was "complacent" about the AAC, the lower ranks of the administration were actively hostile, as one member of the Committee was to observe:

The Foreign Office official [who accompanied us] always stressed that it was not in British interests to work for a joint Anglo-American control of Palestine since this would inevitably lead to a Russian demand for participation.[59]

This lower rank opposition found expression in a variety of ways (see Chapter 4), but at this point it should be noted that Bevin was completely at odds with his officials in the Foreign Office over the implications of the AAC with regard to the Russians. Bevin saw it as a tool to deter the Russians, while they saw it as a sure-fire way of getting the Russians to demand "in." Furthermore, if this aspect of the AAC was not complicated enough, the Americans were simply as yet unconvinced that there was any Russian threat.

Apart from the global aspects, Britain expected the AAC to examine local factors in Palestine and "to establish what element of truth there may be in the many statements and claims made by the Zionist organizations."[60] And also:

... to ascertain what is the view of the Jews in Europe. Are they going to survive and under what conditions? [and] what can Palestine absorb? Figures have been submitted to me that seem just fantastic ... The south can be developed and that great opportunities out of that desert are possible ... also that there is the question of the Jordan scheme which has been advocated by Lowdermilk ... and I had a talk ... with Weizmann ... and he talked about a Swiss constitution with cantons ... I should be willing for consideration to be given to this as well.[61]

Whatever else might be the outcome of Bevin's AAC, it was sure to reduce America's nuisance value on the issue of Palestine, and Lord Halifax saw it as a politically prudent move from his vantage point in Washington:

The United States would not incline even to share responsibility in Palestine but asking her would get us to some extent from the uncomfortable position in which the Americans criticize us without sharing responsibility.[62]

AMERICA ACCEPTS THE AAC

For many in the British establishment, it came almost as a surprise when Washington accepted the idea of participation in an AAC. America was thus abandoning what could be considered an ideal position: freedom from responsibility in carrying out the terms of the Mandate, and freedom to criticize Britain for its inability to do so. So the question must be asked: why, indeed, did the United States agree?

On the face of it, America's reason was presented in moral terms. "We can't ask the British to do things for the Jews in Palestine without taking some responsibility ourselves," was the way U.S. Secretary of State Byrnes put it.[63] But behind this was something more akin to the general aims and aspirations approved by Truman at the meeting of 10 November 1945 with Near Eastern diplomatic representatives and the State Department: America must have a say in Palestine and be concerned with Britain's Imperial domains in general, in accordance with its active Near Eastern policy. So a good part of the reason for American acquiescence, at least, was a desire to encroach upon Britain's authority in Palestine and the Middle East. Another part was Truman's interest in curbing Zionism.

This latter motive was not only unknown in Britain: the very opposite was assumed. Britain believed that America's Palestine policy could be explained in terms of surrender to Zionist voting considerations and Bevin remarked at the time that:

to play on racial feeling for the purpose of winning an election is to make a farce of their insistence on free elections in other countries.[64]

The Americans were happy to let Britain assume this, and their subsequent insistence on the inclusion of Palestine in the terms of reference of the AAC was presented as being a result of these pressures. There could not, however, have been a more remote connection. First of all, the Zionists could best benefit from an inquiry which would *exclude* the Middle East and concentrate solely on the Jewish DPs in Europe, i.e., another Harrison report. Full support for Zionism was guaranteed as long as it was confined to theoretical policy making in the West. The experience of Great Britain had shown that as soon as the British came to Palestine, the

Balfour Declaration was devalued. When America revealed an interest in the Near East, political Zionism was seen as a refugee problem. But when, later, the AAC visited Palestine, they began to realize that "the Arabs are not all sheiks or fellahins." Against this background, one can explain why Abba Hillel Silver suspected a "trap" when he heard that America would be looking into the situation in Palestine at close hand, through the AAC. While there was some chance that the AAC would support the Zionist cause while in America and England, there was little chance of their maintaining that support once they reached Palestine. According to a Jewish Agency source, numerically "in America the Jews are strong, ... in Palestine, it's the other way round."[65]

There was also the evidence of the delegation of the Senate Committee on Foreign Affairs which had visited Palestine in October 1945 and concluded after a few interviews that

through refusal to face up to the basic facts in the perplexing Palestine problem, it would be unfair to all concerned – especially to the persecuted Jews ... to simply dump thousands of defenceless Jewish immigrants into Palestine ... to run the hazards of new abuses.[66]

And others voices in the Senate warned that "we do not have as much right to send the Jews to Palestine as we have to send them to South Carolina, or Maine, or California."[67]

Secondly, there had been a serious deterioration in the Administration's relations with the Zionists at that very time, and no one was more aware of this than the Zionists themselves:

America's agreement to participate in the Committee was undertaken in order to strip us of our main argument ... with which to appeal to the Americans against an English committee ... the introduction of America is tantamount to disarming us.[68]

This friction between the administration and the Jews culminated in the summer of 1946 with "Truman declaring that 'Jews are not going to write the history of the United States, nor my history' ... there are three groups in America who never leave him in peace ... the Italians, the Poles and the Jews."[69]

Thirdly, there is more than circumstantial evidence that America's agreement to participate in the inquiry, and to insist that the AAC investigate Palestine as well, sprang from a desire to clip the wings of political Zionism by treating the whole matter as a Jewish refugee problem.

In America as a whole, the Palestine question was seen largely as a refugee question and not a Zionist issue. The term "refugee" had become negatively synonomous with the Jew. Post-war arrivals in the United States were described as conducting "cut-throat competition with Gentiles and established Jews alike in almost every field of U.S. economic life."[70] Public opinion, therefore, resented the idea of a refugee invasion and demanded a reduction in immigration quotas. When an alternative such as Palestine was suggested support for it was massive, although U.S. opinions on Zionism itself were described as "largely indifferent and often anti-Semitic."[71] More than once, Truman was known to pour the strongest insults on Zionist circles: "These people are the usual European conspirators."[72] Or: "The Jews are like all the under-dogs. When they get on top they are just as intolerant and as cruel as the people were to them when they were underneath."[73] Or: "How difficult it had been with so many Jews in New York."[74] One should add to this the fact (very lucid to Britain's men in America, but not in Whitehall) that much of American feeling about Pales-tine stemmed *more from hostility to Great Britain* than it did from sympathy to Zionism.[75]

In all events, there is ample evidence that the United States, in accepting the idea of the AAC and then pressing for the inclusion of Palestine within its terms of reference, was not by any means succumbing to Zionist pressure, as Whitehall believed. Rather the opposite was true, they hoped for a pro-refugee, anti-Zionist report.

Apparently, this was clear to HMG's representatives in Washing-ton, but for a variety of reasons London saw things differently and remained convinced that the Zionist vote was the lever of Ameri-can policy in the Middle East.

NOTES

1. Michael Foot, *Aneurin Bevan: A Biography*, vol. 2, London, 1973, p. 89.
2. See also a motion by Richard Crossman, Michael Foot, Sidney Silverman and others to their fellow Labour Members of Parliament, June 1946, towards the Bourne-mouth Party Conference, Zionist Archives, New York, AAC Confidential file.
3. On visits of members of the Fabian Colonial Bureau to Palestine, Oct. 1936, see memo by Miss Susan Lawrence, Labour Party International Dept., Advisory Committee on Imperial Questions, Oxford, Rhodes House, Fabian Colonial

Bureau, Box 176, file 1.
4. Crossman's lecture to the Royal Institute of International Affairs, London, 13 June 1946, SACMEC, Crossman's Papers.
5. Weizmann to Attlee, 16 April 1946 (letter not sent) on meetings with Attlee and Churchill during the war, Weizmann Archives, Rehovot. It should be added that Attlee was not considered a supporter of Zionism.
6. Cunningham to Lord Killearn, Cairo, 19 Nov. 1945. Ms. of Lord Killearn Diaries, 19 Nov. 1945, SACMEC. On pro-Zionist pronouncements of Labour ministers, see "British Labour and Zionism," published by the American Jewish Trade Union Committee for Palestine, New York, 1946, Rhodes House, Arthur Creech Jones Papers, Box 32.
7. See note 2 above.
8. Harold Laski in Overseas News Agency, 12 July 1946, p. 4, University College, Oxford, Attlee Papers, Box 6.
9. Labour Party, International Dept. Advisory Committee on Imperial Questions, Oct. 1936, Rhodes House, Fabian Colonial Bureau, Box 176, file 1; Laski in Overseas News Agency, 12 July 1946, p. 3, University College, Attlee Papers, Box 6, Fabian Colonial Bureau, Minutes of International Colonial Bureau, 3 Dec. 1946, Oxford, Nuffield College, Fabian Society Papers, No. J. 52/4.
10. 27 Sept. 1946, PREM 8/302.
11. Shlaim, Jones, Sainsbury, *British Foreign Secretaries since 1945*, London, 1977, p. 61.
12. T. Reid, Labour M.P., former member of the 1938 Woodhead Commission which turned down the Peel partition recommendation, to AAC, London, 29 Jan. 1946, AAC London Public Hearings.
13. Bevin's presidential address to the British Trade Union Congress, 1937, in *British Labour and Zionism*, published by the American Jewish Trade Union Committee for Palestine, New York, 1946, p. 16, Rhodes House, Creech Jones Papers, Box 32.
14. Labour Party Conference, Bournemouth, 12 Jan. 1946, FO 371/52529/E5546.
15. Bevin on Field Marshal Smuts' evidence to AAC, Feb. 1946, FO 371/52509/E1413/G.
16. Speech by Bevin, Oct. 1946, p. 3 (probably at the London Conference which assembled at that time), SACMEC, Cunningham Papers, Box 5, file 2. On Bevin's favourable attitude (1930) towards Jewish immigration to Palestine, see Alan Bullock, *The Life and Times of Ernest Bevin*, vol. 1, London, 1960, pp. 456-457; Lord Morrison, *Herbert Morrison: An Autobiography*, London 1960, p. 272.
17. Bevin to Truman, Washington, 8 Dec. 1946, FO 371/61762/E221/G.
18. Goldmann to Judge Proskauer, President of the American Jewish Committee, 8 Sept. 1946, New York, American Jewish Committee (AJC) Archives, Proskauer Papers, Box 8; Goldmann to Byrnes, New York, 22 Nov. 1946, ISA 93/1. See also on Bevin, the Labour Party and the question of Palestine in Alan Bullock, *Ernest Bevin, Foreign Secretary 1945-1951*, London, 1983; Joseph Gorny, *The British Labour Movement and Zionism 1917-1948*, London, 1983.
19. Bartley Crum, *Behind the Silken Curtain*, New York, 1947, p. 73.
20. See also Joseph Frankel, *British Foreign Policy, 1945-1973*, Oxford 1975, p. 186.
21. Memo to the War Cabinet by Colonial Secretary, Oliver Stanley, 16 May 1945, No. W.P. (45) 306, FO 371/45377/3975/G. The immigration quota was expected to terminate in September.
22. Taken from an unsigned and undated memo on New Policy for Palestine, p. 13, CO 733/461 Pt. 2/75872, Pt. 3; on conditions to be satisfied regarding plans for Palestine, see also FO 371/52504/E389/G.
23. Colonial Office memo, p. 13, CO 733/461 Pt.2/75872, Pt.3, undated, unsigned.
24. Grafftey-Smith to Foreign Office, Jeddah, 23 April 1946, FO 371/52516/E3663/G;

Cabinet paper on reactions to AAC report, 27 April 1946, p. 1, CAB 129/9, CP(46) 173.

25. Cabinet minutes, 11 Sept. 1945, CAB 128/3, CM(45)30.
26. Partition; Grigg's plan on immigration under international auspices; White Paper; three versions of White Paper plus extension of immigration; Provincial Autonomy; Federation with Trans-Jordan. See references in this chapter and in memo on Palestine Policy, 11 June 1945, p. 4, FO 371/45377/E3975/G.
27. Memo on Palestine Policy, 11 June 1945, FO 371/45377/E3975/G; Edward Grigg, Minister Resident in the Middle East, to Eden, Cairo, 29 Jan. 1945, PREM 4/52-3.
28. Memo by the Minister Resident and Middle East Defence Committee, 2 July 1945, CAB 66/67 No. C.P.(45)55.
29. Grafftey-Smith, Minister in Jeddah, in Middle East Ambassadors Conference, London, 10 Sept. 1945, FO 371/45379/E6955/G.
30. Memo on Palestine Policy, 11 June 1945, FO 371/45377/E3975/G.
31. See Chapter 14.
32. Note on meeting between Foreign and Colonial Offices representatives, 23 Aug. 1945, CO 733/461 Pt. 2/75872 Pt.3.
33. There is little evidence for Ilan's version that HMG settled on it in summer 1945 but withdrew following Truman's demand to admit the 100,000. See Ilan, *America, Britain*, pp. 182, 185, 192-193.
34. Bevin to Hall, 1 Sept. 1945, FO 371/45379/E6622/G; Colonial Office memo, 7 Sept. 1945, FO 371/45380/E7407.
35. Bevin to Conference of British Ambassadors in Middle East, London, 10 Sept. 1945, FO 371/45379/E6955/G.
36. Ibid.
37. Memo by the Colonial Office, 7 Sept. 1945, FO 371/45380/E7407; comment by Harold Beeley, Foreign Office, 29 Aug. 1945, FO 371/45379/E6562.
38. Colonial Secretary memo, Sept. 1945, FO 371/45380/E6966. When the AAC was announced in the middle of the pilgrimage, the British legation in Jeddah replied to instructions to convey it to King Ibn Saud: "There is small hope of getting the King out of Mecca at such a time; one might as well try and whistle the Pope out of Rome on Easter Sunday morning." Grafftey-Smith to Foreign Office, 11 Nov. 1945, FO 921/318.
39. See note 18 in Chapter 1.
40. Memo by Colonial Secretary, 10 Sept. 1945, CAB 129/2, CP(45)165.
41. Bevin to Cabinet Committee on Palestine, 6 Sept. 1945, CAB 95/14; Bevin to Conference of British Ambassadors in Middle East, London, 10 Sept. 1945, FO 371/45379/E6955/G.
42. Oliver Stanley, Colonial Secretary, to Lord Gort, High Commissioner of Palestine, 11 June 1945, CO 733/461 Pt.2/75872 Pt.3.
43. Cabinet Committee on Palestine, memo to the Cabinet by Herbert Morrison, 8 Sept. 1945, CAB 129/2, CP(45) 156.
44. Eden in Foreign Office memo, 11 June 1945, FO 371/45377/E3975/G.
45. Minutes of Foreign Office officials, winter 1945, FO 371/45376/E1725/G. See also on U.S. pipeline from the Persian Gulf to the Mediterranean, 1946, FO 371/52598/E1873.
46. C.O.S. memo, 10 July 1945, No. J.P.(45) 167, FO 371/45378/E5141; see also comment by Beeley, 10 July 1945, FO 371/45378/E4939/G. However, on the military's war-time false alarms about Palestine and on Churchill's reaction "not a dog barked," see Wasserstein, *Britain and the Jews*, p. 280.
47. Ms. of Lord Killearn Diaries, 1 Jan. 1946, SACMEC. Philip Noel-Baker was Minister of State in the Foreign Office and greatly in favour of the United Nations and the devolution of powers to it.

48. C.O.S. memo, 10 July 1945, FO 371/45378/E5141.
49. C.O.S. meeting with D'Arcy, London, 15 May 1946, p. 2, FO 371/52525/E4774/G.
50. See Chapter 12 on Operation Agatha, below.
51. Halifax to Bevin, 3 Oct. 1945, FO 371/45400/E7449.
52. Attlee to the Cabinet, 11 October 1945, CAB 128/1, C.M.(45)40.
53. See Cabinet meetings of 4 and 11 Oct. 1945, CAB 128/1, No C.M.(45)38 and C.M.(45)40; meeting of the Cabinet Committee on Palestine, 10 Oct. 1945, CAB 94/14.
54. See note 52 above.
55. Refugee Dept. comments, 23 Oct. 1945, FO 371/51126/WR3209; comment on London U.S. Embassy memo, 25 Feb. 1946, FO 371/57759/WR552.
56. John Briance's note on Bevin's AAC statement and instructions to interpret it as an attempt to prove to the United States the inevitability of a White Paper solution in Palestine. Briance was Head of the Arab section, CID Palestine, Briance Papers, London.
57. Louis, *Imperialism at Bay*, pp. 181, 197.
58. Minutes of Lord Cranborne, Colonial Secretary, 9 Oct. 1942, quoted in Louis, *Imperialism at Bay*, p. 197.
59. Crossman to Attlee, 7 May 1946, SACMEC, Crossman Papers. The Foreign Office official was Harold Beeley, the British Secretary of the AAC!
60. Draft of an unsent telegram to East European governments, explaining the aims of the AAC, Jan. 1946, FO 371/52506/E560.
61. Bevin to Halifax, 12 Oct. 1945, FO 371/45381/E7757. On Lowdermilk's Jordan Valley Authority scheme see Chapter 6 below.
62. Halifax to Bevin, 3 Oct. 1945, FO 371/45380/E7599. On a similar pattern of shifting the responsibility for the deadlock to America, see Inverchapel to Bevin, 31 July 1946, PREM 8/627 Pt. 3: "If we leave the door ajar for the Americans to shut, as they undoubtedly will, part at any rate of the onus for the sequel will then rest on them."
63. Byrnes to Frank Aydelotte, member of the AAC, 3 Dec. 1945, Aydelotte Papers, Swarthmore College, Pennsylvania.
64. Bevin to Halifax, 12 Oct. 1945, FO 371/45381/E7757/G.
65. Ms. of Crossman diary, Jerusalem, 6 March 1946, SACMEC, Crossman Papers; David Horowitz, in charge of AAC affairs within the Jewish Agency, to Agency Executive, Jerusalem, 10 Feb. 1946, Central Zionist Archives (CZA)(Hebrew).
66. Statement to the press, 15 Oct. 1945, on the Mundt–Bolton visit to Palestine, Washington to Foreign Office, 10 Oct. 1945, CO 733/463 Pt. 1, No. 75872/134. The Congressmen were Carl Mundt (Republican/South Dakota) and Frances Bolton (Republican/Ohio).
67. Senator Bailey (Democrat) to Byrnes, 28 Oct. 1945, in Washington to Foreign Office, 30 Oct. 1945, FO 371/45401/E8410.
68. Moshe Sneh, Commander of the Jewish Resistance Movement at Inner Jewish Agency Executive meeting, 11 Dec. 1945, Jerusalem, CZA, No. S5/363 (Hebrew).
69. Report on meeting between Truman and Zionist groups, July 1946, Jewish Agency Executive Meeting, Paris, 5 Aug. 1946, CZA.
70. Memo by British Embassy, Washington, 9 Oct. 1945, FO 115/4218.
71. Memo by British Embassy in Washington on U.S. Jewish affairs, 29 Nov. 1946, p. 7, FO 371/52571/E11651.
72. Truman to his mother, Aug. 1946. Quoted in Margaret Truman, *Harry S. Truman*, New York, 1973, p. 299.
73. Truman to Eleanor Roosevelt, ibid., p. 385.
74. Truman to Bevin, 8 Dec. 1946, FO 371/61762/E221/G.
75. See note 71 above.

4

The AAC Takes Shape: Britain Proposes, America Disposes

The Anglo-American Committee of Inquiry into Problems of European Jewry and Palestine, announced simultaneously by Harry Truman in Washington and Ernest Bevin in London on 13 November 1945, was not quite the AAC that Bevin had envisaged. From the time in October that the Americans agreed to the idea in principle, up until the actual mutual acceptance of the terms of reference, scope and duration of the Inquiry, a lot of negotiations – even haggling – took place. In the end, it was apparent that America was determined to dictate the terms of the Inquiry. So much so that they warned that a premature British announcement of U.S. agreement to participate in such an inquiry prior to the mayoral elections in New York (in which a Jewish Republican was running against the Democratic candidate) might adversely affect the course of the negotiations for a loan to Britain being conducted at that time.[1] "This is the most cynical and dishonest performance I have ever seen," was the comment of one Foreign Office official.[2]

Bevin's initial guidelines for the Inquiry had been relatively comprehensive. The Committee, he suggested, were:

I. To examine what could be done immediately to ameliorate the position of the Jews now in Europe.
II. To consider how much immigration into Palestine could reasonably be allowed in the immediate future.
III. To examine the possibility of relieving the position in Europe by immigration into other countries, including the United States and the Dominions. In this connection, the possibility of using as temporary quarters the camps in North Africa under the control of UNRRA, should be considered.[3]

But following discussions by the Cabinet Committee on Palestine and various other concerned bodies of HMG, the role and scope of the Inquiry were redefined in more restricted terms. Palestine, in spite of Bevin's recommendation, was to be excluded from the terms of reference; so too was any mention of the possible absorption of non-repatriable Jews by Britain or the Dominions (since Britain was "under an obligation to find homes either here or elsewhere in the Empire for 100,000 Poles").[4] Instead, more prominence was to be given to America as a possible haven for displaced Jews. However, to prevent a situation which would "scare Americans off the Committee altogether," Ambassador Halifax was given permission to use his discretion when presenting the arguments which underlay the British desiderata.[5] But their substance was nevertheless clear. The Committee's role was redefined as follows:

I.   To examine the position of the Jews in Europe.
II.   To make an estimate of the number that could not be settled in the countries from which they originated.
III. To examine the possibility of relieving the position in Europe by immigration into other countries outside Europe, including the United States.
IV.   To consider other available means of meeting the needs of the immediate situation.[6]

By the time the British terms of reference reached Washington the U.S. administration had already received the Harrison Report on the DPs and was being subjected to a strong Jewish campaign, circumstances which militated against American acceptance of the British draft. The American counter-proposals articulated a completely different view of the role a joint inquiry was to play. The AAC was to concentrate on Palestine as a solution to the resettlement needs of the Jewish DPs. There was to be no question of America joining an inquiry for purely humanitarian reasons. The Committee was:

I.   To examine political, economic and social conditions in Palestine as they bear upon the problem of Jewish immigration and settlement therein and the well being of the people now living therein.
II.   To examine the position of the Jews in those countries in Europe where they have been the victims of Nazi and Fascist persecution, and the practical measures taken or contemplated to be taken in those countries to enable them to live free from discrimination and

oppression and to make estimates of those who wish or will be impelled by their conditions to migrate to Palestine or other countries outside Europe.

III. To hear the views of competent witnesses, including representative Arabs and Jews on the problems of Palestine, as such problems are affected by conditions subject to examinations under paragraphs 1 and 2 above, and to make recommendations to the Governments of the U.S. and Great Britain for an interim handling of these problems as well as for their permanent solution.

IV. To make such recommendations to the Governments of the U.S. and Great Britain to meet the immediate needs arising from conditions subject to examination under paragraph 2 above, by remedial action in the European countries in question or by the provision of facilities for immigration to and settlement in countries outside Europe.[7]

With minor changes these remained the final terms of reference. Palestine was now to be *the* focal point of the Inquiry and HMG could do little but haggle over semantics and even then their successes were limited. Bevin could not persuade the Americans to reverse the order of the first two terms (in the hope that the Arabs might be "persuaded to make a contribution if humanitarian grounds precede the racial").[8] Neither could he amend the section of Term II which enabled the DPs to decide for themselves whether or not to stay in Europe, preferring to leave the decision to joint arbitration. He also suggested changes in the wording of Term III. The term just "to hear," he wrote to Halifax, "creates the impression we just hear witnesses and dismiss them. I am anxious that the AAC should consult them ... this would have a profound effect and increase the chances of a permanent solution."[9] Ultimately, this was the only British modification accepted: "consultation" was substituted for "to hear."

The crucial American threat in the negotiations was that if Britain insisted on revisions or modifications, they would withdraw their initial approval of the wording of Term II. This spoke of the immigration of Jews to "countries outside Europe" in addition to Palestine. Since the last thing Bevin wanted was for Palestine to be left as the only possible haven, he was forced to agree to the U.S. draft as a whole.[10] This was a far cry from the original Foreign Office position that it was desirable "in any case ... not to mention Palestine by name in this connection."[11]

The British were also forced to give way on two other matters – the time limit of the Inquiry and its scope. "Americans like to think in terms of time-tables," wrote Halifax, who immediately sensed the existence of a stumbling block which was to cause Britain a good deal of subsequent frustration.[12] Bevin initially insisted on a flexible time-table, which would allow the Committee to present interim recommendations within as many as 120 days, and even then allow for an extension.[13] Byrnes, however, could see

no excuse for any Commission failing to report within sixty days ... In this country it has been the custom to fix a time and whenever it is not done, it is generally feared that the investigators will pass away before the investigation comes to an end.[14]

Moreover, the Senate Foreign Relations Committee was not to be swayed on this matter, since "all members of Congress have inconvenient commitments ... a time limit for them is the only straw at which they can clutch."[15] Bevin, therefore, reluctantly agreed to 120 days, with an ambiguous understanding with Byrnes that an extension might be considered. Byrnes's condition for this "flexibility" was: "If you are asked in Parliament, please do not refer to any understanding with the American government."[16] The imposition of a time limit was, in fact, to be regretted even on the American side of the AAC – as James McDonald, one of the American commissioners, wrote after the Committee had reported:

If we had not been constrained to finish our work within the 120-day period – a limitation which I felt ... was a mistaken concession to political expediency – we might have formulated a more constructive and definite political program.[17]

With regard to scope, the Americans were no less adamant. The problem of the displaced Jews embraced almost the entire continent of Europe, but the Anglo-American Commission could only seek a solution to the problems of those DPs who were then in the British and American Zones of Germany.[18] Byrnes came back from the White House with instructions (which he himself had probably drafted) to apply the Inquiry to the whole of Europe.[19] The pressure of the DPs on Palestine, instead of being confined to those wanting to leave the Allied Zones, thus grew enormously, especially when the Polish Jews were included.

Throughout, Britain was clearly in the weaker bargaining position, principally because HMG was the side most anxious to reach an agreement. At one point in the negotiations, Bevin was even ready to offer the Americans carte blanche, hoping that if he could get their agreement in principle, problems could be ironed out later.[20] But this did not come to pass. Bevin further made an attempt to agree to a delay in the announcement of the Committee's establishment until after the New York elections in return for an American agreement to switch Term I with Term II, giving humanitarian concerns precedence over political matters.[21] But the United States had no interest in horse trading. They were in too strong a position, intermittently producing the impression that they declined "to have any part in the suggested joint inquiry ... and that they were in fact changing their policy."[22] Finally, when irked by Bevin in the extreme, the Americans suggested that it would be better to leave final decisions to Attlee and Truman when the former visited America during the second week of November for talks on atomic research.[23] For Bevin, who seemed determined to let no one else attempt to solve the Palestine problem, this was a major provocation.[24] But his protests were ineffectual. Final agreement on all issues was eventually reached in Washington on 11 November 1945 between Attlee and Truman. No changes were made in the original American draft save the one already mentioned; and this in spite of Byrnes' assurance that after the New York elections the United States would be more conciliatory and "the Ambassador and I could settle the problem in half an hour."[25] It seems that rarely had post-war Britain found itself in such an inferior position as it did vis-à-vis America over Palestine.

The man who made the greatest impact on the negotiations was Lord Halifax, insofar as Britain was concerned. He provided Bevin with useful information and he was exceptionally sensitive to the vicissitudes of the American political temper. Thus, when he became aware that time was running against Britain's obtaining better terms, he suggested "immediately clinching, or a breakdown." [26] Withal, it took Halifax three long weeks into the negotiations to realize that "rats were at work. This the President himself and Byrnes."[27] While Byrnes acted with Halifax as if he were mediating between him and Truman, and had himself his own independent views – a rather strange role for a Secretary of State – he was, of course, merely interpreting the President's wishes. The rest was pose. At one point he even went so far as to represent himself as questioning the whole idea of the Inquiry: "Why should we examine the position of the Jews any more than the Frenchman,

Belgian, English, Irish, Scotsman," an idea which dovetailed with that of the British cabinet.[28] As if to add to Halifax's confusion, Loy Henderson, Assistant Secretary of State, also offered his services as *mediator* between his country and Britain![29] In all events, Halifax was certainly responsible for the fact that Britain didn't get an even worse deal.

The terms of reference of the AAC have sometimes been seen as a victory for Zionism, since they linked the problem of European Jewry to the future of Palestine.[30] Moreover, British officials of the period – who never saw a need for joint Anglo-American action on Palestine in the first place – were convinced, as has been previously noted, that Jewish and Zionist pressures had been instrumental in shaping the American draft. Neither claim can be substantiated. In fact, the terms of reference constituted a serious potential threat to the Zionists since they implied that the solution of the Jewish refugee problem was to be bought at the expense of a Zionist Palestine. In this context, it is significant that the terms of reference came as a complete surprise to the Jews and created an atmosphere of crisis at Jewish Agency meetings (see below).

THE TWELVE "APOSTLES"

Once the terms of reference had been settled, the next subject to engage the interests of both countries was the question of the membership of the Committee.

The impartiality of the candidates was thought to be the main criterion upon which appointment should be made. An extreme expression of this view came from St. John Philby who suggested a membership of Chinese, Hindus and Russian Communists who – not having had a Christian education – would be disinterested in the dispute between Islam, Jewry and Christianity over the Holy Land.[31] Yet there were some people in both countries who believed that the Inquiry should not be composed entirely of uncommitted members. The British Embassy in Cairo, for instance, proposed members of its own staff.[32] And someone in the State Department stressed that "men should be sent out who would like to carry out what is regarded as President Truman's policy ... if this is not done, the President may later find himself in an impossible position."[33] It seems that the more these sorts of pressure grew, the greater became the desire to "appoint persons of great weight and impartiality such as ex-judges and the like."[34] The outcome was a list of unknown names whom the frustrated adversaries regarded as "nonentities," the "Bander-log" or "Pygmies."[35] The British Foreign Office suspected a deliberate American intention not to appoint any "outstanding personalities on the American side of the Commission," so that "rejection of its recommendations will not be regarded as a national insult."[36]

The initial British proposals mentioned names of members of the Commons and Lords. Many of them refused, however, or were disqualified on the grounds that they had previously identified with one of the sides in the conflict.[37] Candidacies had included those of Sir Hector Hetherington, Vice Chancellor of the University of Glasgow, Sir J.F. Rees, Vice Chancellor of the University of Wales, and Sir Alexander Maxwell, Permanent Under Secretary at the Home Office, all of whom refused.[38] Membership of a Palestine commission was already viewed as a thankless duty, "a dirty assignment."[39] Furthermore, how could they possibly compare with the prestigious Peel Commission, and everyone knew how that had ended. Bevin's suggestion of appointing women was rejected because of the fear of Moslem agitation.[40] His idea – and it was strange coming from Bevin – that Field Marshal Smuts should preside over the Commission caused the Foreign Office to contend that the findings of such a Committee would never be regarded as unbiased.[41] Smuts was a known Zionist sympathizer and a friend of Chaim Weizmann. A suggestion that someone else from the Dominions be appointed was also turned down on the grounds that the United States would insist on members only from Britain proper.[42] The Foreign Office, on the other hand, suggested that Dr. Chaim Weizmann and Azzam Bey serve on the Inquiry, the latter to "satisfy himself and the Arabs that need exists for succour and that it is not Zionist propaganda."[43] Later Musa Alami was suggested in his stead, as being "more solid, less vociferous, and less filled with the sense of his own importance." Furthermore, since he was a Palestinian Arab and not an Arab-League appointee, Jewish opposition on this score would be neutralized.[44] The need for impartiality, however, ruled out the appointment of either Jews or Arabs. It was also doubtful whether any Arab or Jew could agree to join the AAC and politically survive.

The State Department's initial list contained only the names of judges, lawyers and people from the academic world, assumed never to have voiced an opinion on the subject of Palestine. The first ten recommended by the Department were: the President of the American Bar Association; the President of Princeton University; the President of Williams College; the former Dean of the Yale Law School; the Judge of the Fifth Circuit Court; the former President of the Institute for Advanced Studies in Princeton; the former Governor of North Carolina; a former Justice of the Supreme Court; the former Solicitor General of the United States; a professor of History at Duke University.[45] The avoidance of political circles contrasted with the situation in Britain where apparently it was still possible to find "unopinionated" Members of Parliament.

It soon became clear that the nominations would be made by the President according to his own particular criteria and, indeed, various lists were checked off by him with such comments as "don't know him," or "prejudiced!"[46] The President expressed the hope that a "judicially minded" commission would be able to prepare a "concrete recommendation" and accordingly appointed a judge to preside over it.[47] Yet he also took both State Department people and declared pro-Zionists, knowing that they would cancel each other.[48] The impartiality of the AAC may have thus been assured, but the contribution of the "mutually cancelling" members turned out to be negligible.[49] In the end, six Americans were chosen, who together with the six British members made up a committee of twelve, "like Moses' twelve spies and Jesus' twelve apostles, we twelve too are a mission to and for the Holy Land."[50]

The different backgrounds, beliefs and ideas of the twelve commissioners turned the AAC into a unique human, social and political association and made it an exception to all of the previous committees of inquiry on Palestine. Presiding over the British contingent was Sir John Edward Singleton who had been a Judge of the King's Bench Division of the High Court of Justice since 1934. Born in 1885 in Lancashire, he graduated from Pembroke College, Cambridge, where he read law, and was called to the Inner Temple in 1906, joining the Northern Circuit. During the First World War, he served in the Royal Field Artillery in France and Belgium and rose to the rank of Captain. In 1922–1923 he was the conservative Member of Parliament for Lancaster, but after losing his seat in 1923 to the Liberal candidate, he abandoned politics. Singleton was appointed a Judge of the King's Bench Division in 1934, and a Lord

Justice of Appeal in 1948, in which office he served until his death in 1957. During the Second World War he presided over several government inquiries into questions relating to submarine services, bomb sites, the comparative strength of the British and German air forces, etc.[51] Singleton was a man "of stout Lancastrian common-sense," a euphemism, apparently, for his unbending legalistic approach to matters.[52] His biographer writes of him that "he was not concerned ... to be remembered for the grace of his judge-ments but rather to perform that which he had to do."[53] While on the Inquiry, he was described as "dry and caustic, devoid of any sentiment that might have bearing on his case."[54] Fellow-commissioner Richard Crossman depicted him as:

almost a caricature of a Judge: the smooth aged skin with plump flesh underneath; the waistcoat beautifully cut over the slight paunch; the Pickwickian boyishness and simplicity combined with a judicial precision of wording and cautiousness. He is judicial in the strictly legal sense.[55]

Singleton vehemently defended Britain and the British when-ever allegations were made by Arabs or Jews against the Empire, and such allegations were not infrequent: "Each British member ... was made to feel that he was held personally responsible for the death of 6,000,000 Jews" and for bringing calamity on the Palestinian Arabs.[56] A man intolerant of wasted time, a man accustomed to being sole sovereign in his court, Singleton was forced to sit and listen to repetitive evidence and insults to his country, this latter a matter which he would usually have regarded as contempt of court. "I was anxious lest Sir John Singleton would explode," wrote Crossman.[57] As far as Palestine was concerned, the desire to protect British lives entirely dominated Singleton's thinking. To him a settlement of the conflict was of secondary importance to the security of British soldiers.[58] His rigid and sim-plistic belief in law and order was reinforced in Palestine by his natural aversion to terrorism – an aversion which had been sharpened by his experience during the Irish troubles.[59]

It was inevitable that such a man would clash with Judge Hutche-son, his counterpart as leader of the American contingent. Hutche-son was a man who believed in a free interpretation of the law, innovation and reliance on the "hunch."

Joseph C. Hutcheson was born in Houston, Texas, in 1879 of southern origin, "the son and nephew of Virginians who marched and fought and surrendered with Lee at Appomattox." He was educated at the Military Academy of Virginia and the State University of Texas Law School and after a brief period as City Solicitor, was elected – in 1917 – Mayor of Houston. A year later he was appointed district judge. On the Bench he was an "absolute monarch" and, as his biographer notes, "add to this the fact that the Judge's ancestry is Scottish-Irish and you get an idea of what to expect."[60] He considered himself a Jeffersonian democrat and strongly suported the view which sought to curb the jurisdiction of central government and devolve more powers on individuals and local bodies.[61] His inclination to the freest interpretation of the law was compounded by a hearty contempt for politicians and a minimal respect for officials. "Texas Joe" was known to burst into a rousing Texas "Yippee-ee," and was not above calling Roosevelt "a duplicitous son-of-a-bitch."[62] As a result, British first impressions of him were not of the highest order. It took the British almost two months to come to appreciate his powerful personality and to exchange the nickname "Texas Joe" for that of "the Judge."[63]

At best, aloof towards politics, and with no experience of international affairs, Judge Hutcheson presided over the American team, pursuing a judicial interpretation of the conflict and employing a great measure of intuition in his conclusions. "He is handicapped by what seems to me an unjustifiable feeling that our problem is analogous to a litigation whereas it is in fact one of political adjustment," complained James McDonald.[64] "I'm sick to death of being told how Texas judges prepare their judgements since we are not judges but a committee of inquiry," wrote Crossman later on the British–Hutcheson row which broke out in Lausanne over submitting ideas on paper rather than having a mere exchange of oral views – the latter being the Judge's "Texan way" of doing things.[65] Similarly, the Zionists decribed him as constitutional, judicial and non-political, who sought only for what was moral and just.[66] Relying more and more on his twenty-seven years' experience on the Bench, Hutcheson attributed only minor importance to the fact-finding and research sides of the Committee and following the lines of an article he wrote, "Judgement Intuitive: The Function of the 'Hunch' in Judicial Decisions," he relied on his insight to determine the rights and wrongs of a purely political issue.[67] As he wrote:

and when following it he meets the right solution face to face he can cease his labours and blithely say to his troubled mind – "Trip no further pretty sweeting, journeys end in lovers meeting, as every wise man's son doth know."[68]

Crossman noted that "Hutcheson said that you had to reach your conclusions first and then choose the facts which supported them; this was judicial procedure. Sir John argued that it was not."[69] It was, therefore, inevitable that the single-minded Singleton would eventually collide head-on with the "anarchist" from Texas – which is what happened later at Lausanne. The inability of the AAC to reach a purely just political solution for Palestine strengthened the Judge's non-political interpretation of the terms of reference, with the result that the AAC was, ultimately, unable to submit a settlement.[70] A furious Singleton refused to acquiesce and Hutcheson was left as the key figure in the recommendations. A year and a half later, however, the Judge had learned something when he wrote:

I certainly will not oppose it [partition] merely because it does not do exact justice, for I know that in international relations many solutions must be accepted which fall short of doing justice.[71]

But at the time his Scottish ancestry and Texan ways were the major criteria he used in judging the Palestine situation, and because he saw no reason for the establishment of a Scottish state in Texas, he likewise saw no reason why Jews should not assimilate in their countries of origin.[72]

Hutcheson's views on minorities confused his colleagues in the Committee. While he professed to have been instrumental in expelling more Mexicans than any other judge, he had defended blacks in a Ku-Klux-Klan-dominated Texas at a time when it was not popular to do so.[73] On the other hand, he strongly denounced the divided loyalties which he claimed that the Jews held, and regarded anti-Semitism as an outcome of Jewish success.[74] "Jews," he was reported as saying, "thrived on persecution – they numbered two millions in 1800 and were seventeen millions before the war."[75]

Among the course of action recommended by certain Zionists to win the support of the Judges was the suggestion that Singleton should be approached with data about Jewish shipping, since he was "terribly keen on the sea [and] maritime activity"; and Hutcheson should be accompanied by somebody who knew the story of the

Alamo, since he was "very aware of Texan history and the struggle for independence against the Spanish."[76] No one, however, could change Hutcheson's belief that the entire matter was a Jewish refugee problem and not one of political Zionism.

The rest of the commissioners were roughly divided into two national groups with the British active and anxious to solve their country's problems in Palestine, and the Americans taking the position of observers with no vested interests in the issue. Generally speaking, those who cornered and fought the witnesses were the British. They also made the biggest contribution to the Report, but, as it turned out, under the direction of the American Judge.

Two Americans, who were appointed to cancel each other out, did just that and their contributions were thus confined to secondary issues. James G. McDonald was in his early sixties when he came to the Inquiry with an impressive public career behind him, including participation in international affairs. As the League of Nations High Commissioner for Refugees from Germany (1933–1935) he sympathized with the plight of the German Jews, and advocated their cause as a staff member of the *New York Times* (1936–1938). During the war he served as chairman of the President's advisory committee on political refugees, thus acquiring first-hand experience of the international handling of the Jewish refugee problem. When he joined the AAC he considered his knowledge of the subject sufficient and the European stage of the Inquiry took place largely without him.[77] Gradually he found himself isolated from the rest of the Commissioners who appeared to avoid direct discussion in his presence.[78] McDonald was known for his pro-Jewish and pro-Zionist proclivities and they minimized his role even further. The two new suits of clothes in which he appeared at the Inquiry immediately raised suspicions of Jewish bribery.[79] During the entire course of the Committee's work he remained an outsider, a lone wolf, active only insofar as he neutralized his "opposite number," William Phillips.[80] "Mr. McDonald," Crossman wrote, "remained throughout the most enigmatic ... the British were relieved later on to find that it was not they alone who were baffled by him."[81]

William Phillips, a man in his late sixties, had had a distinguished diplomatic career as U.S. Ambassador to Italy; personal representative of President Roosevelt in New Delhi; member of the U.S. delegation at the London Naval Conference (1935); Director of the

London Office of Strategic Services (1942); political advisor to General Eisenhower and assistant to the Secretary of State (1945). Phillips was reported to be a strong opponent of British imperialism in India and while at the State Department had often referred to the "vestiges of colonial or mandate status in the form of special rights accorded to Britain or France" in the Middle East.[82] In a peculiar way, Phillips had to pursue pro-British State Department views regarding Palestine – while at the same time being described as a challenge to Britain:

He's an able fellow with a long experience and not much to do at the moment. Christ, there is no point in putting a good man out to pasture simply because he does not see eye to eye with the British in everything . . . is it not the best possible answer . . . [to the charge] that the U.S. members of the Committee are influenced by or merely puppets of their British colleagues?[83]

Phillips did not have to work hard to neutralize McDonald and preferred to see the Palestine conflict in its narrow rather than its broader Anglo-American context. Described as the "best-looking, the best-dressed and the best-mannered member of the Committee," he suffered much during the Inquiry from the bickering of his colleagues and was known as one of the "two weaker sisters" among the Americans, always in danger of "seducement" by the British.[84] "We would probably have behaved much worse had he not been there to remind us how gentlemen behave," wrote Crossman, thus dismissing Phillips' role in the Inquiry.[85] He might have served as a potential avenue of information for the State Department on closed AAC discussions, as he held many meetings during the Inquiry with various U.S. diplomats in Europe and in the Middle East.[86] But the State Department's surprise at the Report, and the lack of any evidence to the contrary, indicates that unlike the Zionists, the President, and Byrnes, they had no source inside the Committee and that Phillips did not even fulfil this function.[87]

The second "weaker sister" was Frank Aydelotte, sixty-six years old, one of the first Rhodes Scholars to come from the United States to Oxford (1904–1907) and since 1918 affiliated with the American Rhodes Trustees. He had been the President of Swarthmore College and Head of the Institute for Advanced Studies at Princeton. He regarded the Inquiry in the light of ideas which he had acquired at Oxford and defined as a "new conception of the kinship of the English speaking nations [and] how interwoven are our interests."[88] A practising Quaker, he further saw the Committee as Christian arbitration between the Moslem and Jew who were quarrelling in the Holy Land.[89] He never descended from these views into real-life Palestine, although he did reveal a deep interest in the history of the land.[90] Crossman likened him to "Happy of Snow White and the Seven Dwarfs, not only in his appearance but in his sunny temperament."[91] His interests plus the fact that for over a month he was sick, and remained at the Radcliffe Infirmary at Oxford for treatment while the Committee toured Europe, reduced his role in the AAC to something of a minor one.[92]

The fifth American was Frank W. Buxton, a man of sixty-nine. A Pulitzer Prize winner and the editor of the *Boston Herald* from 1929, he was recommended to the Committee by Byrnes upon the suggestion of Justice Felix Frankfurter. Buxton reciprocated by writing almost daily and supplying the latter with a wealth of detail on the conduct of the Inquiry. Byrnes, who met the Frankfurters socially, had as a result an excellent source of information.[93] Within the Committee a strong liaison developed between Hutcheson and Buxton which culminated at Lausanne in the latter supporting the Judge's views against those of McDonald and Crum, who advocated Jewish statehood.[94]

Bartley C. Crum, the sixth American, was a lawyer from Sacramento, California. The youngest member of the American team (born in 1900) this was the first time he had travelled outside the United States. Yet he had already had some experience of international affairs as counsel to the American delegation to the U.N. Conference in San Francisco. At the time of his appointment to the AAC he was preparing to leave for Spain to defend two members of the anti-Franco underground movement who were in danger of execution.[95] His campaign against the employment practices of southern railroads regarding Negroes and his chairing of a Spanish refugee rally at Madison Square Garden had won him a reputation of being a Russophile and a Communist. Referred to by some as "Comrade Crum," he was refused the necessary security clearance by Loy Henderson of the State Department.[96] Recommended to the Inquiry by his close friend David Niles, Truman's advisor on minorities, Crum had seen the Department's correspondence on his security clearance and from that moment onwards a minor vendetta erupted between him and the Department which lasted for many years.[97]

Because Crum owed his appointment to the Presidency, he reported regularly to Washington on the conduct of the Inquiry and received back instructions from the White House.[98] As a result, he soon found himself in McDonald's position, with the rest of the Committee refraining from open discussion in his presence.[99] His credibility was also called into question when he reported on apparently imaginary decisions of the AAC such as confiding to Alan Cunningham that the AAC had made up its mind that Britain should stay in Palestine for another seventy-five to a hundred years.[100] A Jewish Agency source commented that "for a long time already, I do not know how to refer to the news that I get from Crum."[101] Crum hoped to become a Congressman and later described his services to the AAC as crucial. His role as a commissioner was altogether marginal. Crossman summed him up as follows: "Reads nothing, drinks too much and changes his mind according to the last newspaper he received from the States."[102]

The British team included politicians, men of law, and civil servants. The only need for "balance" was the appointment of Conservative MP Manningham-Buller as a counter to left Labour MP Richard Crossman. With the participation of Wilfred Crick, an economist, it did look like a fairly efficient group. Under Judge Singleton, Major Reginald E. Manningham-Buller, a forty-year-old MP for Daventry, Northamptonshire, was the second judicial appointment. Educated at Eton and Oxford and married to Lady Mary Lindsay, daughter of the 27th Earl of Crawford, his traditional Tory background was complete when he was called to the Bar in 1927 and went to clerk in Justice Singleton's chambers. Though new as an MP, he had served during Churchill's caretaker Government as the Parliamentary Secretary to the Ministry of Works. (He continued to rise over the years, eventually reaching the House of Lords, where as Lord Dilhorne he earned a reputation for his work on the judicial functions of the Lords.)[103] Manningham-Buller had had some international experience before being appointed to the AAC, having taken part in a parliamentary delegation to Russia in 1945. Although it might have been natural for him to accept the authoritative opinions of Singleton, he gradually developed his own views and unlike Singleton was ultimately a party to the Report.[104] Coming to the Inquiry with some fixed ideas on foreigners and refugees, he was the one who later composed its report on the DPs, a report which indicated that his initial ideas had undergone a radical transformation.[105] Like Singleton, one of his main interests was in finding an immediate solution to the dangers threatening British troops.

Sir Frederick Leggett, who usually supported Manningham-Buller's initiatives, seemed to be the only British member with a wide experience of international organizations. He was recommended by Bevin, who hoped that his nomination would persuade the Americans to nominate Carter Goodrich (Leggett's American counterpart at the International Labour Organization), which "would give strong representation to the ILO point of view."[106] Leggett served as HMG's representative on its governing body from the early 1930s until 1944. Born in 1884, Leggett entered the civil service in 1904 and became Private Secretary to the Parliamentary Secretary to the Board of Trade (1915), and to the Minister of Labour (1917). In 1939, he became Under Secretary at the Ministry of Labour and was its Chief Advisor on Industrial Relations (1940–1942). Apart from his international experience at the ILO, Leggett served on the Government Mission of Inquiry into industrial conditions in Canada and the United States (1926). He had a reputation as a man who was "patient, careful, tolerant, broadminded, adept in the art of compromise."[107] The Seamen's Charter for All Nations was composed in the ILO Joint Maritime Commission under his chairmanship (June 1942), and during the 1940s he mediated the London dock disputes. Leggett and Bevin had been close friends since Leggett's service at the Labour Ministry and their friendship had developed during the period when they had both served on the Mission to Canada and the United States. Bevin had said of him that "he doesn't settle industrial disputes, he fondles them."[108] Perhaps he hoped that these talents would have some use in the later stages of the Inquiry, and indeed it was Leggett who proposed in Lausanne to leave the recommendations for the moment, turning first to the factual sections of the Report in order to demonstrate that there was a far broader basis of agreement among the twelve commissioners than they had expected.[109]

The only professed expert on the Committee, appointed to cover a specific area, was Wilfrid F. Crick, an economic adviser to the Midland Bank. Born in 1900 and a graduate of the London School of Economics (1923), Crick joined the Bank in 1928 where he became manager of the Intelligence Department. In 1936, he published *A Hundred Years of Joint Stock Banking*, which became a standard work on the subject.[110] From 1942, he advised the Ministry of Food on post-war economic problems. Crick was responsible for the Midland Bank's *Monthly Review*, had published various pamphlets, broadcast, and lectured at the London School of Economics on his special field. Bevin had known him for some time, and was reported to have a high regard for him as an economist.[111] With the general leaning of the Committee towards a non-political view of the Palestine situation, Crick found no difficulty in devoting his energies to the economic aspect of his mission. According to Crossman, he had a "logical mind [which] instinctively rejected ideologies and the mystique of political movements."[112]

The fifth Britisher was Lord Robert Craigmyle Morrison of Tottenham, a Labour MP for North Tottenham from 1922 almost uninterruptedly until October 1945 when he was created a Baron, thus strengthening the Labour Party in the House of Lords. Born in 1881, he became a teacher and later joined the British Army (1915) as a private and served for three and a half years in France. In 1929 he was appointed Parliamentary Secretary to Prime Minister Ramsay MacDonald, an office which he held until 1936.

To his colleagues on the Inquiry, Morrison appeared to be the "most British of the group; even more sensitive than Sir John about any possible questioning of the 'infallibility' of British officialdom."[113] Somewhat indifferent to the political aspect of the conflict, he was more concerned with and troubled by the awkward situation of the British soldier and the colonial officials who were in the midst of the Palestine muddle. And "wherever he travelled, Tottenham remained his yardstick," a characteristic which put him on similar ground to Hutcheson and Texas.[114] No special efforts had been made by either of the communities in Palestine to influence his mind. The Zionist view of him was that "he is not anti-Zionist and is too colourless to be 'anti' anything."[115]

The last Britisher was Richard Crossman, Labour MP for Coventry East from 1945, and assistant editor of the *New Statesman and Nation*. Born in 1907, the youngest commissioner was a Fellow and Tutor in Philosophy at New College, Oxford from 1930 until 1937. During the war he served in the Psychological Warfare

Department, using his intimate knowledge of Germany in Britain's riposte to Goebbels.[116] An author of standard books on political philosophy, Crossman had the reputation of being a brilliant intellectual who strove to apply logic and reason in everyday politics.[117] In *The Times* obituary of him in 1974, he was described as the "classic illustration of the strength and limitations of the intellectual in politics."[118] The Crossman controversy, which culminated in the 1970s following the publication of his *Diaries of a Cabinet Minister*, was a reflection of this paradox.[119] However, the implication which emerged from his *Palestine Mission*, that he had been the key figure in producing the Report, had nothing to do with the realities of the AAC, although long afterwards some authors, using his diary as the sole source, still came to the same conclusion.[120]

Possessing the sharpest and most sensitive eye within the Committee, Crossman saw the political impracticability of a unitary Palestine and consequently advocated partition. But since the leaders of the Committee were convinced that Jews and Moslems (to whom Crossman usually referred as Zionists and Arabs, thus emphasizing the national aspect of the problem) could live together in peace, perceiving at best the social and economic differences between them, Crossman didn't carry the day here. On the other hand, although he claimed to be unaware of the British intention to involve the United States in Palestine, he won the Committee over to a stand against an Anglo-American umbrella over Palestine.[121] He confided to McDonald that he was doing so because it would exclude Russia.[122] As he was the only British commissioner who still had to plan his political career and find an area in which to gain a reputation, there are certain similarities between his position and Crum's.[123] Perhaps it was mere coincidence, but in 1947 two books appeared on the Inquiry: that of Crossman and that of Crum. It may not have affected his sincere adherence to the Zionist cause, but it shows a more earthly side to his early Gentile Zionism. In the summer of 1947 one of his Committee colleagues wrote of him:

Dick is lousy with contradictoriness. It's merely a fortuity that he didn't argue for an Arab state in Palestine ... Palestine was to him merely a place for another enticing adventure ... he succumbs to rough talk from a Yankee ... all his associates distrusted him ... he had no influence over his fellows. Crum's remark that he wouldn't swap one Manningham-Buller for a dozen Crossmans wasn't bad. And yet Crossman had courage ... an appealing personality (he was the favourite of the secretarial staff).[124]

These then were the twelve commissioners. All of them "almost without exception" tended to be prima donnas in one way or another.[125] The main difference between them was that the Americans worked more together as a team. This, in fact, was disadvantageous to the British as it reduced their overall strength in relation to the united American contingent.[126] But there were other differences. The Americans were much more aloof from the political entanglements in Palestine. They could maintain the stance of objective observers, feeling sympathy for the enterprising spirit of the Jewish pioneers and contempt for the imperial power which was caught in the middle. They could bandy about moral principles with impunity.

The British, on the other hand, were more perceptive about the political constraints operating in the situation and were united in their desire to disentangle their country from them. It was the British contingent which fought and argued with witnesses.

Another difference between the two contingents was the amount of significance attached to the actual work of the Committee, and there can be little doubt that the British here were at a decided disadvantage, both before, during and even after the Report was submitted. Opposition to the very concept of the AAC at the various political, military and administrative levels of HMG were highly vocal and simply disabling. They simply did not want the Americans in and tried whenever possible to torpedo the AAC. Thus, for example, the beginning of the work of the Committee in January 1946 was dampened by the British Commander of the Arab Legion, John Glubb, who considered the AAC comparable to an American-Russian Committee sent to Kent to consider the settlement of 100,000 Jews there.[127] And more than once the Foreign Office emphasized the fact that the Committee was not in a position to dictate the policy making of HMG.[128] The British Administration in Jerusalem acted in a similar way. Their initial tendency was to minimize the importance of the Committee's visit in Palestine. The title, "Committee," and not "Commission," was interpreted as a deliberate choice of terms, intended to strip the Inquiry of any statutory powers. As a result, formal ceremonies such as had been accorded to the Peel Commission were ruled out and the visit was handled on a purely informal basis.[129]

One result was that while officialdom had no say in the politics of setting up the Committee, they dealt with the administrative side of things and the wealth of problems which the British team faced would seem to point to something more than bad luck. So much so that at one point Manningham-Buller complained to Bevin that the United States "will, I fear, feel that we on our side do not really attach much importance to the AAC."[130]

The British commissioners were allowed only two dollars a day for expenses and they often found themselves in most embarrassing circumstances vis-à-vis the Americans who were allowed twenty-five dollars.[131] "I really didn't expect to be rewarded for my work on this Committe, but didn't expect to have to pay for working on it," was another of Manningham-Buller's comments to Ernest Bevin.[132]

Technical assistance was another bone of contention between the British commissioners and their superiors, as the British Secreary to the AAC noted:

I don't know, but the Committee cannot be left unattended ... I write to you owing to my fear of being let down: early in December ... we were promised an officer to keep accounts, make travelling arrangements, etc. None was provided ... the Americans have an administrative officer and five shorthand typists. From Washington I wrote and cabled for clerical assistance ... None has been provided.[133]

Although the Foreign Office argued that there were few or no precedents for a committee of this kind and claimed when referring to financial aspects that neither the Treasury nor the Foreign Office were "disposed to have too much confidence in the discretion in these matters of one of the Secretaries," Bevin took the problem more seriously and submitted the matter to Attlee.[134] The damage, however, was done and confirmed the Americans in their view that Britain was ignoring the Committee.[135]

In all events, the AAC commissioners were bolstered by research and technical staff. The American secretary was Leslie L. Rood, a Lieutenant Colonel in the U.S. War Department Intelligence in Europe and the Pacific. Britain appointed Harold Beeley of the Eastern Department of the Foreign Office, who worked for Chatham House before the war, and composed the sections of the Annual Survey dealing with Palestine. These two were helped by Evan Wilson of the State Department and Graham Vincent, a British civil servant who during the war served in Washington on the British Joint Staff Mission. The U.S. side of the Committee's research group was reinforced during the second half of the Inquiry by Paul Hanna, author of a book on Palestine.[136] He was, so to speak, a counterpart to Beeley, following American concern that their ignorance on the subject would prove to be detrimental, especially in the Middle East, "where the British will have at their call all their official people."[137] Including secretarial and research assistants and court reporters, the personnel of the AAC totalled 38.[138] So it was with a reasonable entourage that the Twelve Spies or Twelve Apostles (as Hutcheson dubbed them) started upon their Mission to the Holy Land.

NOTES

1. Halifax to Foreign Office, 27 Oct. 1945, FO 371/45382/E8160.
2. Memo by Robert G. Howe, Under-Secretary, Foreign Office, 28 Oct. 1945, FO 371/45382/8230.
3. Bevin to Cabinet, 4 Oct. 1945, CAB 128/1, CM (45)38.
4. Cabinet Committee on Palestine, 10 Oct. 1945, CAB 95/14, P(M)(45)2.
5. Bevin to Halifax, 5 Nov. 1945, FO 371/45384/E8634.
6. Herbert Morrison, Lord President of the Council, Head of Cabinet Committee on Palestine, to Cabinet, 11 Oct. 1945, CAB 128/1, CM(45) 40.
7. Washington to Foreign Office, 24 Oct. 1945, FO 371/45382/E8060.
8. Bevin to Halifax, 25 Oct. 1945, FO 371/45382/E8060.
9. Ibid.
10. Bevin to Halifax, 27 Oct. 1945, FO 371/45382/E8245.
11. Undated comments by Foreign Office officials, FO 371/45380/E7479.
12. Halifax to Bevin, 13 Oct. 1945, FO 371/45381/E7757/G.
13. Bevin to Halifax, 20 Nov. 1945, FO 371/45385/E8935.
14. Washington to Foreign Office, 22 Nov. 1945, FO 371/45386/E9058.
15. Halifax to Bevin, 22 Nov. 1945, FO 371/45386/E9058.
16. Halifax to Bevin, 27 Nov. 1945, FO 371/45386/E9235.
17. James McDonald to Judge Proskauer, American Jewish Committee, 13 Nov. 1946, New York, AJC Archives, Proskauer Papers, Box 8.
18. See minutes of the Anglo-U.S. Study of the AAC Report, 13 July 1946, p. 1. "Outside the Allied occupied countries there was no direct action which could be taken by the U.K. or U.S. Govts," FO 371/52540/E6728.
19. Interview with Benjamin V. Cohen, Special Counsellor in the State Dept., Washington, May 1979.
20. See memo on conversation between Byrnes and Halifax, 29 Oct. 1945, FO 371/45382/E8177/G and Bevin to Halifax, 29 Oct. 1945, ibid.
21. Draft of a telegram from the Foreign Office to Washington, undated, FO 371/45382/E8161/G; Bevin to Halifax, 1 Nov. 1945, FO 371/45383/E8342.
22. Bevin analyzing U.S. moves, in Bevin to Halifax, 28 Oct. 1945, FO 371/45382/E8177/G. See also J. Balfour, First Secretary, British Embassy in Washington, to Foreign Office, 27 Oct. 1945, FO 371/45382/E8160.

23. Washington to Foreign Office, 27 Oct. 1945, FO 371/45382/E8160.
24. Michael Foot, *Aneurin Bevan – A Biography*, London, 1973, Vol. 2, p. 89; also Bevin to Halifax, 29 Oct. 1945, FO 371/45382/E8177/G.
25. Balfour to Foreign Office, 27 Oct. 1945, FO 371/45382/E8161/G.
26. Halifax to Bevin, 7 Nov. 1945, FO 371/45383/E8539.
27. Ibid.
28. Byrnes to Halifax, Washington, 22 Oct. 1945, FRUS 1945, vol. 8, p. 781; also minutes of the Cabinet, 11 Oct. 1945, CAB 128/1, CM(45)40.
29. Washington to Foreign Office, 31 Oct. 1945, FO 371/45382/E8304.
30. See Cohen, *Retreat from the Mandate*, p. 184; Bauer, *Flight and Rescue*, p.89.
31. Philby's memo to the AAC, Riyadh, undated, SACMEC, Philby Papers, Box 10, file 7; memo on the Palestine Report of the AAC, 6 May 1946, ibid.
32. Cairo to Foreign Office, 16 Nov. 1945, FO 371/45384/E8801.
33. Benjamin V. Cohen, Special Counsellor in the State Department, to Byrnes, 28 Nov. 1945, USNA, RG 59, Office of Near East Affairs, Palestine, Box 1.
34. Attlee to Cabinet Offices, 16 Nov. 1945, on his talks with Truman on membership of Commission, FO 371/45385/E8841.
35. Arthur Lourie, of American Zionist Emergency Council (AZEC), to F.B. Rundall, British Consulate, New York, in Rundall to A. Tandy, Washington Embassy, 8 Dec. 1945, CO 733/461 Pt. 4/75872/14B; N. Rose, *Baffy, The Diaries of Blanche Dugdale*, Vallentine, Mitchell, London, 1973, pp. 230-231.
36. C. Baxter, Eastern Dept., 26 April 1946, FO 371/52520/E4013.
37. Cunningham to Killearn, Cairo, 19 Nov. 1945, SACMEC, Ms. of Lord Killearn Diaries. On the candidacies of Lord Altrincham, formerly Sir Edward Grigg, the Minister Resident in Cairo, and of T. Reid, Labour M.P. for Swindon, who had served on the Commission that rejected Peel's partition proposal, see FO 371/45384/E8802, minutes of 9-23 Nov. 1945. On the candidacy of Gwilym Lloyd George, Liberal M.P. whose father was commonly quoted as supporting the "extreme Zionist interpretation of the Balfour Declaration," see note by John Martin, Colonial Office, 21 Nov. 1945, CO 733/463 Pt.2/75872/138/23.
38. FO 371/45384/E8802, various comments by Foreign Office officials.
39. Crossman, *Palestine Mission*, pp. 59, 199.
40. Bevin to Halifax, 14 Nov. 1945, FO 371/45384/E8778.
41. Bevin to Cabinet, 4 Oct. 1945, CAB 128/1, CM(45)38; comments by the Foreign Office, undated, FO 371/45380/E7450.
42. Comments by Howe, 14 Nov. 1945, FO 371/45384/E8802.
43. J. Henderson, Eastern Dept., 7 Oct. 1945, FO 371/45380/E7479.
44. T. Wikeley, Eastern Dept., 7 Oct. 1945, ibid.
45. David A. Simmons; Harold W. Dods; James P. Baxter; Judge Charles E. Clark; Judge Joseph C. Hutcheson; Frank Aydelotte; O. Max Gardner; Owen J. Roberts; Charles Evans Hughes; William Thomas Laprade, respectively, memo by Loy Henderson, 16 Nov. 1945, Washington, State Dept. Building, Lot 54 D403 Box 1815. On the 19 and 20 Nov., Henderson further recommended the President of M.I.T., Karl T. Compton; Mark Ethridge, the publisher of the *Louisville Courier* and Philip C. Jessup, professor of International Law at Columbia. Later five businessmen were also recommended, ibid.
46. See Byrnes's memo to the President, 21 Nov. 1945, Truman Library, President's Secretary's File, Box 184, Palestine; Samuel I. Rosenman memo, 19 Nov. 1945, Truman Library, Rosenman Papers, Box 3. Rosenman served as a special counsellor to the President. On the U.S. members of the AAC being solely under the jurisdiction of the Presidency with no avenues to the State Dept., see Halifax to Foreign Office, 19 Feb. 1946, FO 371/52510/E1518.
47. Memo by Frank Aydelotte on a telephone call from Truman, 5 Dec. 1945, Swarth-

more College, Aydelotte Papers, Box 3.
48. Washington to Foreign Office, 6 Dec. 1945, on the nomination of Ambassador Phillips and James McDonald, FO 371/45387/E9512. See also Halifax to Bevin on conversation with Byrnes, 9 Nov. 1945, FO 371/45384/E8604.
49. See Chapter 10.
50. Hutcheson to Committee, Lausanne, 1 April 1946, in Buxton to Frankfurter, 1 April 1946, Washington, Library of Congress, Frankfurter Papers, container 40.
51. In winter 1942, Singleton inquired into the delay caused to the 22nd Armoured Brigade's offensive operation in North Africa because of the need to strengthen the axles of its cruiser tanks. He strongly blamed the War Office for it. See WO 32/11028. On his wartime inquiries see CAB 120/54.
52. *Dictionary of National Biography, 1951–1960* (DNB), Oxford, 1971, p. 899.
53. Ibid.
54. Horowitz, *State in the Making*, p. 50.
55. R. Crossman, ms. of his Palestine Diary, entry for 30 Dec. 1945, SACMEC, Crossman Papers. None of this appeared in Crossman's *Palestine Mission*. See there pp. 23-24. On the "Pickwickian cherub," Ben-Gurion, see *Palestine Mission*, p. 132.
56. Crossman, *Palestine Mission*, p. 45. See below on the public hearings in Jerusalem.
57. *Palestine Mission*, p. 45.
58. Interview with Sir Harold Beeley, the British Secretary of the Committee, Oxford, Jan. 1980; report of the Jewish Agency Executive on the AAC hearings in Washington, 10 Feb. 1946, Jerusalem, CZA.
59. Crossman, *Palestine Mission*, p. 24.
60. *Chief Judge, U.S. Court of Appeals for the 5th Circuit, Joseph C. Hutcheson Jr.*, Washington, 1949, pp. 2,4,31.
61. Ibid., p. 23. His cardinal principle was the Jeffersonian precept that no man was ever "born with a saddle on his back, nor any born booted and spurred to ride him." Quoted in *Hutcheson*. On Crossman's reservations concerning this point in Hutcheson, see *Palestine Mission*, p. 29.
62. F. Flanshard, *Frank Aydelotte of Swarthmore*, Connecticut, 1970, p. 354; ms. of Crossman diary, undated, SACMEC, Crossman Papers.
63. *Hutcheson*, p. 30.
64. James McDonald diary, aboard "Queen Elizabeth," 18-23 Jan. 1946.
65. Ms. of Crossman diary, 4 April 1946, SACMEC, Crossman Papers; William Phillips diary, 2 April 1946.
66. Report on AAC Washington Hearings, Jerusalem, Jewish Agency Executive, 10 Feb. 1946, CZA. See also McDonald diary, Lausanne, 6 April 1946; aide memoire by Gideon Rufer on AAC hearings, Feb. 1946, Jerusalem, CZA, No. S25/6449.
67. McDonald diary, 18-23 Jan. 1946, aboard "Queen Elizabeth"; Joseph C. Hutcheson, Jr. "The Judgement Intuitive: The Function of the 'Hunch' in Judicial Decisions," *Cornell Law Quarterly*, vol. 14, no. 3, April 1929.
68. Ibid, p. 278, quote is from *The Tempest*.
69. Ms. of Crossman diary, Lausanne, 4 April 1946, SACMEC, Crossman Papers.
70. See also Phillips diary, 18-29 April 1946.
71. Hutcheson to McDonald, 11 Sept. 1947, Jerusalem, CZA, No. Z4/15440.
72. Arthur Lourie, Zionist Office, London, to Jerusalem, 25 Jan. 1946, Jerusalem, CZA, No. Z4/15440; Abraham Tulin to Abba Hillel Silver on AAC Washington Hearings, 17 Jan. 1946, ZANY, Tulin Papers, folder 35; W.J. Gold to Dr. Slawson, American Jewish Committee, 5 Feb. 1946, New York, AJC Archives; 1st British Infantry Division, Weekly Intelligence Review, no. 6, 14 May 1946, WO 169/22957.
73. On the Judge and the expelled Mexicans see Crossman, *Palestine Mission* (Hebrew

version only), p. 35. See also ibid (English), p. 29; Blanshard, *Aydelotte of Swarthmore*, p. 345.

74. Gershon Agronski, editor of the *Palestine Post*, to Dr. Weizmann, 26 March 1946, Jerusalem, CZA, No. S25/6447. Agronski quoted Hutcheson in a private talk with another Commissioner; report on Washington Hearings, Jewish Agency Executive, 10 Feb. 1946, Jerusalem, CZA.
75. Agronski to Weizmann, 26 March 1946, Jerusalem, CZA S25/6447.
76. Zionist Office, London, to Jerusalem (Shertok), 25 Feb. 1946, ibid.
77. Letter to Shertok from H. Hoffman, Frankfurt, 28 Feb. 1946, Jerusalem, CZA, No. S25/6449.
78. McDonald to representatives of Zionist Federation in Cairo, 3 March 1946. See report from Cairo to E. Sassoon, Head of Jewish Agency Arab Section, 5 March 1946, Jerusalem, CZA, S25/6420; see also Frederick Leggett to G. Cohen, interview, London, 5 Dec. 1960.
79. Leggett to G. Cohen, interview, London, 5 Dec. 1960.
80. Crossman, *Palestine Mission*, p. 31.
81. Ibid., pp. 30-31. See also SACMEC, ms. of Crossman's diary (Lausanne): "McDonald remains the great enigma, whisper that I have the supreme responsibility for achieving what Burke achieved in the reconciliation of the Americans. I can't quite remember what Burke achieved."
82. Phillips to the Regent of Iraq, Washington, 2 June 1946, see in Halifax to Foreign Office, 3 June 1945, FO 371/45239/E3744. Phillips' words had been explained in London as arising "in part from an erroneous suspicion that we are using our position in the Middle East to exclude the United States from that region." Comments of the Foreign Office, 4 June 1945, ibid.
83. Comments in U.S. Congress on appointment of AAC, in memo by Jewish Agency Office, Washington, 15 Dec. 1945, Jerusalem CZA, S25/6447.
84. Crossman, *Palestine Mission*, p. 30; A. Lourie to Goldmann on the Lausanne discussions of the AAC, 7 April 1946, Jerusalem CZA, Goldmann Files No. Z6/Bundle 18, No. 1.
85. *Palestine Mission*, p. 30.
86. On these meetings, see Phillips diary, passim.
87. Compare with Crum, Buxton and McDonald who gave information to the White House, the Zionists and Byrnes.
88. Frank Aydelotte, *The Vision of Cecil Rhodes*, Oxford, 1946, p. 85.
89. Blanshard, *Aydelotte of Swarthmore*, pp. 359, 361.
90. On Aydelotte and the Norman remnants of Athlit, see Crossman, *Palestine Mission*, p. 150.
91. Ibid, p. 30.
92. The rest of the Commissioners were afraid of catching Aydelotte's cold and let him have a room to himself aboard the "Queen Elizabeth." Blanshard, *Aydelotte of Swarthmore*, p. 352. While on the Committee, he spent his time on golf, and on the proofs of his Rhodes Scholar book. Aydelotte diary, 11 April 1946.
93. See the Frankfurter–Buxton correspondence in the Frankfurter Papers, container 40.
94. A strange situation developed within the U.S team when Hutcheson–Buxton opposed McDonald–Crum. Aydelotte and Phillips had to be the mediators. See Chapter 10 below.
95. Blanshard, *Aydelotte of Swarthmore*, p. 346. Crum used to say that the meetings with the Jewish DPs reminded him of the victims of the Spanish Civil War. See Eliahu Elath (Epstein), *The Struggle for Statehood* (Hebrew), Tel Aviv, 1979, vol. 1, p. 338.
96. Leggett to Hutcheson, 14 Dec. 1946, copy in Phillips Papers; oral history interview

with Loy W. Henderson, Washington, 14 June 1973, No. 156, pp. 108-110, Truman Library. Crum was accused of supporting the United Front, a group of liberal and leftist organizations in pre-war France, headed by Leon Blum.

97. Oral history interview with Loy W. Henderson, Washington, 14 June 1973, No. 156, p. 110, Truman Library. Veterans of the Near East Dept. still denounce Crum, the most recent, in Evan Wilson, *Decision on Palestine*, Stanford, 1979, p.202.
98. Mainly during the Lausanne period , see Chapter 10 below.
99. Leggett to G. Cohen, interview, London, 5 Dec. 1960.
100. See Cunningham to Hall, 5 April 1946, SACMEC, Cunningham Papers, Box 5, file 2.
101. Emanuel Neumann, Jewish Agency Executive, 19 March 1946, Jerusalem, CZA (Hebrew).
102. Crossman on Crum in Lausanne, SACMEC, ms. of Crossman diary, 3 April 1946.
103. L. Blom-Cooper and G. Drewry, *Final Appeal: A Study of the House of Lords in its Judicial Capacity*, Oxford, 1972, pp. 180-181.
104. Horowitz, *State in the Making*, p. 50; see also Chapter 10 below. On a favourable American assessment of him as the "ablest intellect in the British group," see McDonald's diary, 18-23 Jan. 1946.
105. Crossman, *Palestine Mission*, p. 24.
106. Bevin's proposal for British members of the AAC, 9 Nov. 1945, FO 371/45384/ E8802.
107. Zionist Office, London, on AAC members, 15 Dec. 1945, Jerusalem, CZA, S25/6447.
108. Bullock, *Ernest Bevin*, vol. 2, p. 120.
109. Crossman, *Palestine Mission*, p. 182, see Chapter 10 below.
110. Wilfrid F. Crick, *A Hundred Years of Joint Stock Banking*, London, 1936.
111. Zionist Office, London, on AAC members, 15 Dec. 1945, Jerusalem, CZA, No. S25/6447.
112. Crossman, *Palestine Mission*, p. 24.
113. McDonald diary, entry for 18-23 Jan. 1946, McDonald Papers, folder 14. Morrison was described as a very sentimental man who, often with tears in his eyes, defended Britain whenever witnesses seemed anti-British. See report on the Washington Hearings to Jewish Agency Executive, 10 Feb. 1946, Jerusalem, CZA.
114. Crossman, *Palestine Mission*, p. 24.
115. Zionist Office, London, on AAC members, 15 Dec. 1945, Jerusalem, CZA, No. S25/6447.
116. On Crossman and the Jews, see Bernard Wasserstein, "Richard Crossman and the New Jerusalem," *Midstream*, April 1975, p. 45.
117. *Plato Today*, 1937; *Socrates*, 1938; *Government and the Governed, A History of Political Ideas and Political Practice*, 1939; *How We are Governed*, 1939.
118. 6 April 1974.
119. See the introduction to the abridged version by Anthony Harvard, ed. *The Crossman Diaries: 1964-1970*, London, 1979, pp. 9-10.
120. See for instance, Ilan, *America, Britain*, p. 210; "The extent of influence that Crossman exercised while serving in the AAC ... is a case which leads one to reflect on the influence of individuals on the moulding of historical processes."
121. Crossman to Attlee, 7 May 1946, SACMEC, Crossman Papers.
122. McDonald diary, Lausanne, 6 April 1946.
123. Manningham-Buller was already on the road to success although only a young politician.
124. Buxton to Justice Frankfurter, 11 Aug. 1947, Frankfurter Papers, container 40.

Jewish Agency people had regarded Crossman in similar terms: "There are conflicting opinions about him: sometimes ... they say he is a real friend; sometimes they say: do not believe a single word he says. Sometimes you are in a position where you do not know whom to believe ... among them he is the most intellectual." Report to Agency Executive, 10 Feb. 1946 (Hebrew), Jerusalem, CZA.

125. Wilson, *Decision on Palestine*, p. 71.
126. Interview with Harold Beeley, Oxford, January 1980.
127. Memo by John Glubb, British Commander of Arab Legion, Jan. 1946, FO 371/52310/E3135; "Note on the Palestine Question," June 1946, pp. 7-8, FO 371/52542/E6869. Harold Laski replied through the Overseas News Agency, 12 July 1946, and rebuked "Brigadier Glubb ... and officers anxious to be regarded as the T. E. Lawrences of this generation," University College, Oxford, Attlee Papers, Box 6.
128. Comments by H.T. Morgan, Eastern Dept., 7 Feb. 1946, FO 371/52508/E1098.
129. Gibson, Palestine Solicitor General: Enactment of Legislation in Connection with the AAC, 10 Dec. 1945, Israel State Archives (ISA), Division 2, Chief Secretary's files, No. POL/33/45; Cunningham to Hall, 24 Jan. 1946, FO 371/52507/E855.
130. Manningham-Buller to Bevin, 22 Jan. 1946, FO 371/52507/E838.
131. Comments by the Foreign Office, Jan. 1946, FO 371/52512/E2377. See comment by the Treasury, 4 Feb. 1946, that because the AAC included two MPs "we had to be specially careful ... to avoid any suspicion of giving any concealed remuneration in view of the penalties under the *Places of Profit Act of Queen Anne*," T 220/20.
132. See note 131 above. On insurance problems of the British members, see also Singleton to Bevin, FO 371/52508/E1115.
133. H.G. Vincent, AAC British Secretary, to G. Lawford, Foreign Office, Jan. 1946, FO 371/52508/E955.
134. Comments by H. T. Morgan on administrative side of the Committee, Jan. 1946, FO 371/52512/E2377; I. Malletts of the Treasury, ibid.; see also comments of Foreign Office officials, FO 371/52507/E838. The matter reached Parliament where the Minister of War Transport had to explain the conditions aboard the "Queen Elizabeth," FO 371/52508/E1112. By winter 1948 some of the AAC's staff still had not been given their expenses, see FO 366/2702.
135. Crossman, *Palestine Mission*, p. 66. An exception to the above was John Martin, Colonial Office: "Government having cast a joint committee on the waters in the hope that a policy will return to them ... it behoves us, even if it cannot do much actual steering, to give the AAC as fair a wind as possible," letter to Shaw, 14 Nov. 145, CO 733/463 Pt. 3, No. 75872/138.
136. Paul H. Hanna, *British Policy in Palestine*, New York, 1942.
137. McDonald diary, 18-23 Jan. 1946. At the beginning, Hutcheson did not see any need for Hanna. He considered his own experience to be sufficient "and I do not want to add merely a book to our staff." Hutcheson to Byrnes, 29 Jan. 1946, NRC files of the U.S. Embassy, London, RG 84 59A 543, part 5, Box 1057.
138. Evan Wilson, *Jerusalem, Key to Peace*, Washington, 1970, p. 151.

5

The "Suffering Peoples" React

When Ernest Bevin introduced the AAC in the House of Commons in November of 1945, he expressed the hope that the recommendations of the Committee would facilitate the arrangements for placing Palestine under trusteeship, and serve as a basis for future discussions between HMG and the parties concerned. It was designed to find a permanent solution – "if possible an agreed one" – to be submitted to the United Nations. Pending receipt of the AAC's recommendation, HMG would consult the Arabs to ensure the continuation of monthly Jewish immigration into Palestine, thereby assuring that the Inquiry could be conducted in a relatively untroubled atmosphere. Bevin went on:

The House will realize that we have inherited in Palestine a most difficult legacy ... greatly complicated by undertakings given at various times to various parties [and] it will need a united effort by the Powers to relieve the miseries of these suffering peoples.[1]

The "suffering peoples" – the Palestinian Arabs and the Jews – could both point to breaches of these undertakings by the British. Neither saw in the AAC an instrument for ending their respective miseries.

The Palestinian Arabs regarded it as another futile stopgap, no better than the seventeen other committees which had already investigated the situation.[2] Omar Dejany, a young Palestinian Arab, added a further dimension:

Killing a man and walking in his funeral is a known proverb, but harming a man and inquiring from his people about the cause for their sorrow is a case which no vocabulary has yet known, but ... should be added to the English one ... There is nothing more strange on behalf of the English than appointing committees of inquiry as though they do not know the causes and remedies ... as though they are not ... responsible for our difficulties.[3]

The reopening of the question of Jewish immigration, without reference to the 1939 White Paper, which was believed to have settled the problem, was considered to be a major setback since the Arabs still clung desperately to the White Paper as their "Charter."[4] Similar protests were made with regard to the idea of trusteeship, since the promise of an independent Palestine had also been given to the Arabs in 1939.[5] They further claimed that "having U.S. citizens as members of the AAC is tantamount to handing over the representation to the Jews."[6] When the High Commissioner tried to convince Palestinian Arabs that this should be the last and final committee, Abdul Latif Saleh, a member of the Palestinian Arab Higher Committee, interposed that "they had heard that before."[7]

It was apparent to Britain as it was to the Arab League that in order to avoid a situation where "the findings of the committee which had been able to hear only the Jewish side would not only be of little value to HMG but might be extremely dangerous," it was necessary to revive the Palestinian Arab leadership.[8] Arab states by themselves were not enough. If there was one factor which helped to doom the Arab cause in Palestine to failure and defeat, it was (and perhaps still is) the relationship between the Palestinian Arabs and the Arab states. A process which began during the Arab rebellion of 1936–1939 and continued unabated culminated in the expropriation of the Palestinian Arab cause from its bearers. Palestine became a pawn in inter-Arab feuds, and the interests of the Palestinians were subjected to those of the various Arab states. In May 1948, the Arab states waged war in Palestine largely to prevent each other from gaining too large an advantage there.

Despite all the pre-war and war-time vows of Arab leaders to support the demand for an independent Palestine from 1945 on, the newly-created Arab League evinced a clear tendency towards the preservation of the status quo. Suggestions that Britain should continue to administer the country for another twenty to fifty years came from Azzam Pasha, the Secretary of the Arab League, and from the Iraqi Government.[9] The ninety million Moslems in the British Empire also failed to provide support since "Syd Mohamed Al Junah, the Moslem Indian leader, is interested in Moslem Pakistan more than in Palestine."[10] When action was finally taken in support of the Palestinian Arabs – such as the Arab League boycott of Jewish goods – it proved harmful to the economic interests of many Arabs in Palestine; they defiantly continued to trade in Jewish products since otherwise they would have had to go out of business.[11]

The process by which the Palestinian Arabs found themselves deprived of the initiative in their own cause began in October 1937, when, following the Arab rebellion, the Government of Palestine declared the Arab Higher Committee and the National Committee to be illegal associations. Accordingly, it dissolved them and deported their leaders. Haj Amin Al-Husseini, the Grand Mufti, had already fled, finding refuge in Germany and taking an active part in Nazi propaganda to the Moslem world. In the absence of their leaders, the tendency of the Palestinian Arabs was to group around political parties based on personal and family links. The differences which split the Arab parties in the summer of 1945 were not related to aims or ideologies ("the latter do not interest Arabs") but appeared to spring from a rivalry between the Arab National Bank and the Palestine Arab Bank, and the families who owned them and their respective newspapers (the *Falastin* and the *Ad-Difa'a*).[12] These parties sprang to life only when a crisis occurred in the Palestine conflict, and usually as a reaction to some Jewish move (which once raised the comment that "the Arabs are children even in blackmail").[13]

Moreover, such a situation could not fail to weaken the position of Musa Al-Alami, the all-party Palestinian representative to the Arab League. British observers noted that it made "the Arab League exasperated and forces on them a realization of the political bankruptcy of the Arab community in Palestine."[14] It was this realization which led to the expropriation of the Palestine case from the Palestinian Arabs.

The Arab League's handling of the Palestine question, however, was no better. The discussions on Palestine between Nuri Said, the Iraqi delegate and Azzam Pasha were coloured by their mutual rancour ("lunatic"; "dangerous influence, not from malice but because he is stupid, unbalanced and vain.")[15] Finally, the internal rivalries within the Arab world and the Arab League, notably that of the Hashemite-Saudi kingdoms, were the primary considerations of any Palestine policy (or lack of policy); each of the kings blocked any policy which promised too much gain to the other. In any case, the Arab states used the League to promote their own interests rather than those of the Palestinian Arabs.

The question of Palestine was among the first issues which Britain negotiated with the Arab League after its establishment, although it was not entirely happy at having to recognize the League as the sole Arab party to the conflict. Negotiations with League politicians caused some British officials to make remarks like "the egregious Azzam; vociferous and filled with the sense of his own importance," and "Sheik Yusuf Yasin whose irritant characteristics are notorious [an] obnoxious spokes[man]."[16] In the case of the League's declared economic boycott, the following view was not unusual:

All that seems to be required . . . is to show the Arabs a red light. Once they realize that their nasty (or hasty) [sic] action is likely to bring them into direct conflict with us, we may hope that they will walk more carefully.[17]

Yet HMG preferred the League to the Husseinis and Nashashibis of Palestine, and sought their approval for whatever policy it planned for Palestine, even in defiance of the latter's views:

it will be the Arab states which will have the prevailing voice. [Palestinian Arabs] would be most unlikely to stand out against any decision arrived at by the Arab states.[18]

Although it was clear to Bevin that British policy in the Middle East was based on "too narrow a footing, mainly . . . the personalities of kings, princes or Pashas;" he preferred those in the Arab capitals to those in Jerusalem.[19] Now, however, with the launching of the AAC, the Palestinians had somehow to be drawn back into the picture, despite their suspicions and scepticism and despite Britain's distaste.

For four months, from November 1945 to February 1946, weary negotiations went on between the Palestine Government, the Arab League and certain Palestinian Arabs, until a precarious tripartite agreement was reached. As a result, the Arab Higher Committee, which had been suppressed during the war was resuscitated. Jamal Husseini, the Mufti's cousin and one of the deported Arab Palestinians, was released from his exile in Rhodesia and the presentation of the Palestinian Arab case to the AAC thereby assured.[20]

THE ARABS ACCEPT

However, the main political interaction took place in Cairo, where HMG sought the Arab League's acceptance of Britain's new policy. The negotiations with the Palestinians were of a more perfunctory nature, designed to stave off any complaints from them of not being consulted. Britain expected very little in the way of a constructive contribution from the Palestinian leadership as it was now constituted. There was little hope for "a statesmanlike approach ... from our local brand of Arab political leader" who was described in the context as possessed by "an undercurrent of that intransigence, based on an inability to think otherwise than obstructively or selfishly about everything."[21] Accordingly, the acquiescence of the League was sought as a counter to Palestinian objections. In order to facilitate agreement on this matter, it was suggested that an Arab should be appointed to serve on the AAC or that a limited number of refugees should be admitted into Britain, thus enhancing the prospects of Arab agreement to Jewish immigration into Palestine.[22]

Most of the British officials in the Middle East who took part in the negotiations were, to say the least, unenthusiastic about the AAC. The main argument they used with the Arab leaders to explain its establishment was that it would provide an opportunity for presenting the Palestinian Arab case to the Americans. And the main hope of the Arabs in cooperating at all with the AAC was that it might prove another blow for Zionism, "since every investigating committee up to now has severed a limb from the Balfour Declaration," and all reports had up to now been rejected by the Jews.[23] Bevin made it clear to Lord Killearn, his ambassador to Cairo, who had reported that "they [the Arabs] obviously did not think it politic to display any enthusiasm about the proposals ... and in the usual oriental manner are afraid of yielding too promptly," that

if the result of consultation at the first stage even is seen to be an uncompromising and unhelpful rejection ... many people here would argue that further consultation with the Arabs would only be a waste of time ... it is to the interests of the Arab Governments to help me over this.[24]

And indeed, there were Arab voices that claimed it would be

better to leave the impression that it was the Jews who were uncooperative in order to demonstrate to the world "that the Jews are intriguers and a troublesome and turbulent people."[25]

The final Arab reply therefore accepted the British initiative – although in a manner and form which epitomized the entire Arab handling of the Palestine question. A session of the Council of the League was held – without Palestinian Arabs; its discussions were affected by the competitively patriotic attitudes of the various participants and coloured by the mutual hatred of Nuri Said and Azzam Pasha; what was drafted by the former was redrafted by the latter and vice versa. According to Killearn: "All this is typically Byzantine and stupid."[26] Furthermore,

Nuri said that of all the idiotic performances he had ever taken part in, this completely beat anything in his experience. It amounted in fact to this – that the Arab Conference was going to set out to teach us what certain words in English meant.[27]

The League's reply reflected this tangled web of ideas and relationships. Although worded in a way which "to the ordinary Western mind would appear to be a refusal," it was in fact ambiguous enough not to express an outright rejection, and indeed was interpreted in this way by Azzam Pasha.[28] According to Nuri Said, "when the reply said the door was closed to immigration, in fact it didn't mean that at all, but should be read as meaning that the door continued open."[29] It was left to HMG to find its way through this maze.

ZIONIST REACTION AND ACCEPTANCE

Zionist reaction to the AAC was, perhaps, even more scathing. The day after Bevin's announcement in the House of Commons, the Jewish Agency Executive met in Jerusalem in an atmosphere of crisis. Desperate and extreme expressions characterized the attitudes of both militants and moderates, who spoke of betrayal and deception:

The intention ... is no doubt the elimination of Zionism ... There is no mention of the Jewish people in this statement ... but only a Jewish community ... Our situation has become even worse because ... the Government of the United States has agreed to this ... Bevin tried to split Jewry into two, and the speeches of Silverman and Lord Samuel prove that this attempt has borne immediate fruit ... It is an attempt to liquidate the

Jewish race and it is far more than the liquidation of the Zionist enterprise. It reconfirms the theory of the assimilation of Jewry ... We lost a battle both in the British Government and in the American ... There is nothing more imprudent than to hold on to the illusion that we have more to say to the American Government ... It is a crisis of the whole of Zionist policy, the first in sixty years ... We will have to make sure that it doesn't turn into a war with the English and American peoples ... It is a disaster ... for the first time the majority of the British Parliament is against us ... Zionism needs to wage war for its own existence ... The Jew in the street will come to only one conclusion: there is no hope for Zionism, no hope for the Land of Israel ... Jews will start looking for another place to settle ... This is the greatest political failure that Zionism has had since ... the Balfour Declaration ... The Labour Party was let down. The Statement is so written ... to deceive all of them. The Chairman of the Party, Harold Laski, who is Jewish and very sharp witted ... he might have studied Talmud, thought it was all right ... Anyway, the trickery succeeded ... The whole document is destined to cheat the English ... In this business you also have America ... Truman has a thousand other problems, no doubt he had not even read it, only knew of the committee ... They [Britain] played a trick, created an international deception ... to create the impression that the whole thing is an Anglo-American agreement. After Truman knew the contents of the whole document, he announced that he still insisted on his immediate demand of 100,000 certificates. It means that he has disassociated himself from this joint business.[30]

Rarely had such acrimony been given vent. Their disappointment was the greater no doubt because of the high expectations which prevailed among world Jewry following the holocaust. The enlightened world, they had believed, was certain to make recompense.

The fact that the Jews had been massacred by the Germans as Jews, and not as citizens of their countries had had a profound and far-reaching effect on world Jewry. The idea of political Zionism as a solution to the Jewish problem began gaining considerable ground. Membership in the Zionist movement doubled during the war: there were more than two million Zionists in sixty-three countries.[31] What the Zionist movement had tried to achieve in the sixty years of existence up to then – a massive Jewish belief in its own national identity – Hitler had accomplished in less than ten years. As Crossman was to note a few months after he joined the AAC:

The Nazis and the anti-Semitic movements in the Satellite countries, by the ferocity of their persecution, transformed the surviving Polish, Hungarian and Rumanian Jews into a Jewish nation without a home.[32]

The war affected the Zionist movement in another way as well. By shifting the centre of the movement from Britain to the United States, it succeeded in mobilizing a vast and vocal public in support of its aims. Not only was America – because of its history – traditionally anti-British, but there were large Jewish centres of population in all the big cities, whose voice could be heard when necessary. Whereas support for Zionism in Britain had been confined to the upper classes, in the United States it had a broad power base and had to be taken into consideration by those in power. Many of the people who penned the daily 20,000 letters, telegrams and postcards, arriving at the British Embassy in Washington in protest against their Palestine policy, identified themselves as non-Jews.[33] And, indeed, Zionism had massive support among Christian organizations. Crossman attributed this sympathy to American identification with his ancestral pioneer,

who goes into the wilderness and turns it into a land of great agriculture and great industry ... America sympathizes with the National Home because it is something very American. Americans therefore are liable in their estimate of the Arabs' side to think of them as Red Indians ... Whereas to Englishmen there is something synthetic in the idea that somebody packs his bag and picks it up and travels somewhere and then becomes a citizen of that country and claims it as his native land.[34]

The shift to the United States brought about other political and individual changes which made Zionism more militant. The gradualist policy for achieving the National Home through an eventual majority was replaced by a demand for immediate independence, formulated in the Biltmore Programme of May 1942: Jewish statehood in all of Palestine after the war.

Activists like David Ben-Gurion and the Cleveland Rabbi Abba Hillel Silver replaced Weizmann, who still looked to Britain to become an "honest broker" and intermediary between Arabs and Jews.[35] The activists wanted an ally, not a middleman, and Britain could not fulfil the former function. Moreover, few Zionists shared Weizmann's wider view of the Palestine question as an inseparable part of the political reorganization of the whole Middle East. They considered the problems to be simpler, confined to Palestine alone.[36] Finally, Weizmann's special relations with Churchill, which had influenced much of Britain's war-time Palestine policy, were of little impact once Labour was in the saddle. Gradually the ageing Weizmann found himself excluded from Zionist policy making although he himself was not yet prepared to acknowledge this. He attributed his lack of information about the AAC's meetings in Lausanne to "postal, railways and other strikes," when in fact Zionist circles in Jerusalem received information daily.[37] His exclusion was also not apparent to the British, who tried to support him unsuccessfully against Ben-Gurion.[38]

And, of course, a major factor behind the demands for the establishment of the Jewish state was the existence of the Jewish refugees. A tendency to perpetuate and exacerbate the problem was discernible in post-war Zionist policy.[39] When Ben-Gurion was asked what his hypothetical choice would be between the admission of 100,000 DPs to Palestine, linked to the relinquishment of the state, or just the state, he decisively chose the state.[40]

The Jewish community in Palestine had also become more militant, ready to support Zionist aims through armed resistance:

The Jewish people in Palestine is capable of offering and is determined to offer physical resistance to a policy (be it within or without the White Paper) which does not square with Jewish aspirations ... Yishuv is being psychologically prepared for what will be in effect armed rebellion [and] material preparations do not seem to lag behind.[41]

It is on this background that Zionist reaction to Bevin's announcement of the AAC has to be understood. The Zionists and the Jews of Palestine were in a fighting mood, not ready to be placated by any commission. British explanations of the Statement were decried as an attempt to conceal "a most insidious emasculation of the whole problem."[42] Thus, the absence of any reference to the White Paper – apparently a pro-Jewish move – was sharply attacked as a sop used to placate Labour circles in Britain, while the White Paper was left intact.[43] But if the British and their White Paper had been the *bête noire* of Zionist aspirations, now that role was transferred, through the AAC, to the Americans. President Truman was accused of letting the Zionists down and of being party to "another Munich."[44] The formal reply of the Jewish Agency rejected Bevin's policy as providing for "the consultation of parties having no lawful competence in the matter." But it deliberately omitted the names of these parties, perhaps in order to include both the Arab states and the United States in the generalit .[45] American involvement in the conflict – beyond giving support to the admission of the 100,000 – was seen potentially as a camper on hopes for a Zionist Palestine. The apparently pro-Zionist linkage of the question of Palestine to the Jewish DPs was considered harmful to Zionism, a prelude to its consideration as a mere refugee issue rather than a national and territorial matter.[46] Yet the President was described at this stage as a simple man who had fallen into "a trap prepared by British diplomacy. The mistake ... will have to be exposed," and Washington was believed to have had no connection with the terms of reference of the AAC.[47] If lack of information and poor assessment had ever guided the Zionist movement, it was in connection with its views of the role of the President in this matter.[48]

Although it had not yet been decided to appear before the AAC, intensive Zionist preparations were undertaken in case a favourable decision was reached. Activity among the DPs was increased and American planes were used to deliver propaganda material from Palestine to Germany.[49] Plans were made for illegal immigrant ships to arrive in Palestine while the AAC was conducting its inquiry there.[50] There was a sudden decline in the number of Polish Jews applying in Warsaw for American visas, and an increase in the numbers attempting to reach Germany – "part of a manoeuvre to bring pressure on the AAC by producing a mass of Jews ... demanding entry into Palestine."[51] In Palestine and the United States, protests were launched against the intention to grant independence to Trans-Jordan. This was believed to be tantamount to "sabotaging the AAC by presenting it with the independence of Trans-Jordan as a fait accompli."[52] Britain was also accused of instigating the Arab boycott on Jewish trade in order to minimize the economic potential of the Yishuv in the eyes of the AAC.[53]

But the question of Zionist cooperation with the AAC had not yet been resolved. Numerous objections were voiced at the Jewish Agency Executive meetings.

Why should we go to our funeral? ... there is a silence which talks ... a powerful political act would be our non-appearance ... We are suspicious to begin with ... we are their opponents ... we are Zionists. They are prejudiced: a Jew may be "kosher," but a Zionist is a peculiar creature ... Why should we give our approval to this game? It could be very costly.[54]

Furthermore, it was apparent that with all the political infighting in the Zionist movement, and the impossibility of presenting one, united position, which the Arabs were sure to do, it would be simpler not to cooperate.[55] But it was the danger of alienating the powers, particularly America, that probably determined the final decision: since they had been presented with what appeared to be a fait accompli, where "the defendant must appear in court even though the sentence was passed on him at the outset," their only choice was to cooperate with the Committee. This was followed by an attempt to get from the Palestine Government a concession in the form of unrestricted immigration for the period of the Committee's deliberations.[56] The similarity with Arab tactics was apparent.

Both Arabs and Jews exhibited considerable opposition to the idea of an AAC, but they were both forced to recognize that the understanding between the two powers was stronger and had to be complied with. Their tactics from now on would be aimed at breaking this accord. As for the British and the Americans, they were confident in their policy and supported the view which (as later expressed) maintained that as long as there was a "wailing and gnashing of teeth by both sides of the controversy rather than by one side alone" an "excellent job has been done."[57]

NOTES

1. Text of Parliamentary Statement in Foreign Office to Cairo, 8 Nov. 1945, FO 371/45384/E8635.
2. Arab Higher Committee to Attlee, 15 Feb. 1946, CO 733/461 Pt. 4 No. 75872/18A.
3. Omar Dejany, "a young Arab Palestinian," to AAC, Jerusalem Hearings, 25 March 1946.
4. Summary of Arab reactions, comments by the Foreign Office, 10 Jan. 1946, FO 371/52504/E262.
5. Weekly political summary, Syria and Lebanon, 20 Nov. 1945, FO 371/45554/E9877. On Arab attitude towards trusteeship, see also comments by Foreign Office officials, 29 Sept. 1945, FO 371/45380/E7262/G.
6. Reports of District Commissioners, Palestine, 26 Nov. 1945, CO 733/456 Pt.2.
7. Meeting between Cunningham and Arab leaders, Jerusalem, 23 Nov. 1945, SACMEC, Cunningham Papers, Box 5, file 1.
8. Foreign Office to Washington, 5 Nov. 1945, FO 371/45384/E8634.
9. Baghdad to Foreign Office, 27 Aug. 1945, FO 371/45379/E6335; memo by Glubb Pasha, Dec. 1946, p. 6, CO 537/1783. See also minute by Baxter on interview with Saudi Arabian minister in London, 16 Aug. 1945, FO 371/45393/E6037.

10. Review of Weekly Intelligence, no. 7, 13-19 May 1946, 1st Infantry Division, WO 169/22957.
11. Review of Weekly Intelligence, no. 4, 5-12 Jan. 1946, 3rd Infantry Division, WO 169/22967.
12. Colonial Office memo on Palestine Arab Politics, 26 June 1945, FO 371/45471/ E5499; memo on Palestine Arab Politics, by GHQ Middle East Forces, Oct. 1945, WO 201/192.
13. Middle East Forces, Political Intelligence Centre, Fortnightly summaries, nos. 47 (10 Jan. 1946) and 56 (16 May 1946), WO 169/22936; Shaw to Hall, 24 Aug. 1945, p. 2, CO 733/456 Pt. 1, 75156/75/45; Fortnightly Intelligence Newsletter, no. 14 (29 April-12 May 1946), GHQ Palestine, WO 169/23022.
14. Memo on Palestine Arab Politics by GHQ Middle East Forces, Oct. 1945, WO 201/192.
15. Ms. of Lord Killearn diaries, Cairo, 4 Dec. 1945, SACMEC; Nuri Said to Brigadier Clayton, 29 May 1946, FO 371/52513/E5172.
16. Lord Killearn to General Spears, 14 March 1945, SACMEC, Spears Papers, Box 5, file 3; Comments by Wikeley, Eastern Department, Foreign Office, 7 Oct. 1945, FO 371/45380/E7479; Grafftey-Smith to Foreign Office, Jeddah, 26 Feb. 1946, FO 371/52511/E1817. Yusuf Yasin was the Saudi Delegate to the League.
17. Comments by Wikeley, 20 Jan. 1946, FO 371/52506/E624.
18. Recommendation of Cabinet Committee on Palestine, 8 Sept. 1945, CAB 129/2, No. CP (45)156. See also Cunningham: "Once the Arab states accept any solution ... the local Arabs would be of little account," comments on AAC Report, May 1946, SACMEC, Cunningham Papers, Box 5, file 2.
19. Bevin to Halifax, 12 Oct. 1945, FO 371/45381/E7757/G.
20. See comments by L. Henderson, Eastern Dept. Foreign Office, 17 Nov. 1945, FO 371/45395/E8813; AAC draft on Public Security in Palestine, p. 2, Lausanne, April 1946, SACMEC, Crossman Papers; Arab Higher Committee to High Commissioner, Jerusalem, 14 Feb. 1946, CO 537/1770. On the Arab Higher Committee's sub-committee which was set up to prepare the Arab case before the AAC, see report of Defence Security Office, Lt. Colonel Isham, Monthly Summary, no. 5, Feb. 1946, WO 169/23031. On attempts within the reinstated Arab Higher Committee to reverse the decision to testify before the AAC, see Weekly Military Intelligence Reviews, nos. 49 and 51, GHQ Middle East Forces, 1 and 15 March 1946, WO 169/22882.
21. Hall to Cunningham, 4 Jan. 1946, CO 733/463 Pt. 2 No. 75872/145; Cunningham to Hall, 22 Jan. 1946, FO 371/52507/E763. Shaw to Hall, 13 Nov. 1945, referring to Arab reaction to Bevin's statement, CO 733/463 Pt. 2, No. 75872/137.
22. Cabinet Committee on Palestine, memo to Cabinet, 8 Sept. 1945, CAB 129/2 No. C.P. (45) 156; Comments by Foreign Office officials, 7 Oct. 1945, FO 371/45384/ E7479; extract from Cabinet conclusions, C.M. (45)52, 13 Nov. 1945, FO 371/ 45384/E8797.
23. Weekly Political Summary, Syria and Lebanon, no. 189, 20 Nov. 1945, FO 371/ 45554/E9877; Weekly Political and Economic Report, 23 Nov. 1945, FO 371/45932/ J4120.
24. Killearn to Foreign Office, 14 Nov. 1945, FO 921/318; Bevin to Killearn, 1 Dec. 1945, FO 371/45396/E9306.
25. Amir Abdullah to Jordanian Prime Minister, 13 March 1946 in Amman (Alec Kirkbride) to Foreign Office, 14 March 1946, CO 537/1853; Syrian President to Geoffrey Furlonge, Minister in Damascus, in Damascus to Foreign Office, 16 Nov. 1945, FO 371/45395/E8813.
26. Cairo to Foreign Office, 5 Dec. 1945, CO 733/463 Pt. 2, No. 75872/137.
27. Conversation between Nuri Said and Lord Killearn, ms. of Lord Killearn diaries,

entry for 4 Dec. 1945, SACMEC.
28. Weekly Political Summary, Cairo to Foreign Office, 8 Dec. 1945, FO 371/45392/ J4160.
29. See note 27 above.
30. Minutes of Jewish Agency Executive Meeting, 14 and 21 Nov. 1945 (Hebrew) Jerusalem, CZA. Sidney Silverman, Member of Parliament, and Lord Herbert Samuel, first High Commissioner to Palestine, expressed their satisfaction with Bevin's statement when debated in the Commons and Lords.
31. J.C. Hurevitz, *The Struggle for Palestine*, New York, 1950, p. 267.
32. Crossman, *Palestine Mission*, pp. 212-213.
33. Washington to Foreign Office, 3 Oct. 1945, FO 371/45400/E7433.
34. Crossman to the R.I.I.A., London, 13 June 1946, p. 2, SACMEC, Crossman Papers.
35. Weizmann to Locker (Jewish Agency Office, London), 16 April 1946; Weizmann to Attlee, 16 April 1946, Weizmann Archives, Rehovot.
36. Meeting between Jewish Agency leaders and Weizmann, Rehovot, 4 March 1946, National Record Centre, War Dept. O.S.S. Report, No. A-67035 (NRC 253882), 7 March 1946.
37. Weizmann to Locker, 16 April 1946, Weizmann Archives, Rehovot.
38. See also E. Monroe, "Mr. Bevin's Arab Policy," p. 26 in Hourani, ed., *Middle Eastern Affairs*, No. 2, St. Antony's Papers, no. 11, London, 1961.
39. P.R. Stevens, *American Zionism and U.S. Foreign Policy, 1942–1947*, New York, 1962, p. 28. Bauer, *Flight and Rescue*, p. 79; Sykes, *Crossroads to Israel*, p. 354.
40. Ben-Gurion to Crossman, AAC Jerusalem Hearings, 11 March 1946.
41. John Shaw, Chief Secretary, Palestine Govt. to George Hall, the Colonial Secretary, 24 Aug. 1945, CO 733/456 Pt. 1, No. 75156/74/45.
42. Weizmann to Colonel Meinertzhagen, 15 Nov. 1945, Weizmann Archives, Rehovot. Meinertzhagen had served during the early 1920s as an intelligence officer in the British garrison in Palestine.
43. Ben-Gurion to Agency Executive, 21 Nov. 1945, Jerusalem, CZA.
44. Arthur Lourie, American Zionist Emergency Council (AZEC), to J. Rundall, British Consulate, New York, 8 Dec. 1945, CO 733/461 Pt.4, No. 75872/14B; Halifax to Foreign Office, 17 Nov. 1945, FO 371/45402/E8861.
45. Cunningham to Hall, 15 Dec. 1945, FO 371/52506/E643.
46. Leo Kohn, On the Appointment of the AAC, 10 April 1946, Israel State Archives, Kohn files, no. 57 6/P. Kohn served as political secretary of the Jewish Agency up to 1948.
47. Ben-Gurion to Agency Executive, 21 Nov. 1945, SACMEC,Cunningham Papers, Box 4, file 3.
48. On Truman's role in the wording of the AAC's terms of reference, see Chapter 4. Of importance was the unusual fact that the negotiations with the British were not leaked to Jewish circles in America. It supports the conclusion that the administration strove to challenge Zionism with an irreversible policy.
49. American memo, "The Mysterious Flights," USNA, RG 59, Office of Near Eastern Department, Palestine Affairs, Box 1.
50. C.in C. Middle East to War Office, 8 March 1946, FO 371/52512/E1971.
51. Warsaw to Foreign Office, 10 Jan. 1946, FO 371/57684/WR111.
52. Washington to Foreign Office, 13 April 1946, CO 537/1845. On the Colonial Office reaction that "The Agency are flogging a very dead horse," see Douglas Harris, 23 March 1946, CO 537/1848. Military Intelligence did not consider the offer of independence to be an anti-Zionist move: "The Jews ... will be possible through bribery and other means to infiltrate into [Trans-Jordan], action which wasn't possible under the watchful eye of the mandatory power," Gyles Isham, Defence

Security Officer, Monthly Summary no. 4, Jan. 1946, WO 169/23031.

53. Cunningham to Hall, 1 Jan. 1946, SACMEC, Cunningham Papers, Box 1, file. 1.
54. Minutes of Jewish Agency Executive meetings, 11 Dec. 1945, Jerusalem, CZA S5/363 and 7 March 1946, Jerusalem, CZA (Hebrew).
55. HQ Palestine War Diary, G. Granch, 26 Nov. 1945, WO 169/19745; Ben-Gurion to Jewish Agency Executive, 11 Dec. 1945, Jerusalem, CZA, No. S5/363.
56. 1st Infantry Division, Intelligence Summary, No. 2, 24 Dec. 1945, WO 169/19656; memo by Palestine HQ, 19 Dec. 1945, WO 169/19745; Defence Security Officer, Lt. Colonel Gyles Isham, 18 Dec. 1945, SACMEC, Cunningham Papers, Box 5 File 4. No change took place in immigration policy.
57. W. Rountree to James McDonald, 2 May 1946, New York, Columbia University, McDonald Papers, Folder 334. Rountree served as a secretary in the AAC. On this thinking, see also Richard Crossman, *A Nation Reborn*, London 1960, p. 61; "Arab Demands," evidence submitted to AAC by the Arab Office, Jerusalem, with Albert Hourani, Oxford.

6

The Evidence

Early in January 1946, the twelve commissioners gathered in Washington to begin their work. The members of the AAC assembled around tables arranged on three sides of a square. The two chairmen, who alternated in conducting the hearings, sat in the middle. To their right and left sat the rest of the commissioners in a fixed order that was preserved in every public hearing for the next three months. The witnesses sat facing the two judges, surrounded on three sides by the Committee, with the press and public behind them. Close beside the witnesses were the Committee's staff, who produced the verbatim reports of the proceedings which had to be in the members' hands by breakfast-time next day.[1]

It had been agreed that the commissioners would be

investigators, not adversaries, the appearers will in no sense be regarded as litigants, nor will the AAC regard itself as a mere trier of issues on a record adversarily made and therefore limited to what may be partisanly supplied. Quite the contrary ... the AAC intends to enter ... the field of available information. But we can't ... forget our function as deciders.[2]

To a large extent, the AAC managed to follow these guidelines, although the personal views of some of the commissioners and the complex nature of the problem they had to deal with did divert the investigation somewhat from its initial aims.

However, all twelve held some views in common which later strongly affected their recommendations. All of them regarded themselves as objective people inquiring into a conflict between two interested parties – a conflict in which their own countries possessed no aspirations of their own. They all abhorred the use of force as a means for bringing a settlement to Palestine. And they were all motivated by a Christian belief – the Americans more than the British – that resisted the exclusive demand of either Jew or Moslem to the Holy Land. The practising believers – Crum

the Catholic, Aydelotte the Quaker member of the Society of
Friends, and Judge Hutcheson the Presbyterian – all resented the
politicizing of the Holy Land, and regarded the possibility of a
"casino ... on Lake Galilee where they can gamble all night and do
other things accordingly," as a desecration of Christianity.[3] Consequently, when the AAC recommended that "Jew shall not dominate Arab and Arab shall not dominate Jews," it added that neither
should have the Land "where the great interest of the Christian
world in Palestine has been completely overlooked, glossed over or
brushed aside ... Palestine is a Holy Land ... and can never
become a land which any race or religion can justly claim as its very
own."[4]

But with the two judges presiding, the Committee was more a
court of inquiry than a latter-day Crusade.[5] And a severe court it
was. Judge Hutcheson disqualified evidence which was not submitted in the procedural way that had been decided upon; witnesses had to commit themselves to their testimony by attaching
their signatures to their typescript evidence; time and again various
subjects, mainly of a political character, were ruled out as not in
accord with the terms of reference; private conversations of commissioners with witnesses were considered as being of secondary
importance to the Inquiry.[6] The main instrument of the AAC was
to be its public hearings – with the two judges alternately presiding,
like a court-room in which justice was to be publicly sought and
publicly heard. It was found, however, that such a system was
not always compatible with the realities of the Palestine conflict,
since witnesses often spoke to the press and were forced to take
tougher stands than they might otherwise have done had this been a
different sort of inquiry.[7] With the terms of reference interpreted to
the effect that the Commission was expected to give a judicial
verdict rather than provide a political solution, the contribution of
the AAC to an essentially political problem could not be great.

One correspondent who accompanied the Committee described
the British judge as a "real hangman. Singleton looks like death
warmed over. When he points his pencil at the person giving
testimony he scares him half to death."[8] The judges cornered
and pressed witnesses with questions of "Yes or No," and often
challenged their signed statements, drawing protests from other
commissioners that they were acting like prosecutors.[9] Nevertheless, the court-room style cross-examination of the testimonies

turned out to be the most revealing part of the hearings. Consequently, some witnesses refused to be cross-examined, leaving only their public statements for the AAC's consideration.[10]

The one ex-diplomat in the Committee, Phillips, had serious reservations about the system:

A testimony in camera is so much more effective than at public hearings, in fact public hearings have become ... anything but constructive. Only the leaders of their respective organizations appear and they, speaking for their membership, have to present a rigid solution and position so any help towards compromise ... is ruled out at public hearings; hearings ... are a part of the theatrical performance which we are obliged to go through for the benefit of public opinion.[11]

It was not only the fact that the Middle Eastern rivals expressed extreme opinions during the public hearings. The AAC also got the impression that some Jewish DPs would have felt free to chose a haven other than Palestine had the Inquiry been a closed one. Some of the commissioners apparently exploited the hearings "in order to appear in the official proceedings rather than with the idea of obtaining information."[12] In addition, the determination of the commissioners to hear only public evidence led them to turn down the "secret trick" of the Zionists, namely to stick publicly to the demand for a Jewish Palestine, whilst privately pursuing the plan for partition.[13] This was not the committee with which to do such business, and Crossman's suggestion that Weizmann should be heard in camera, in order to discuss what the latter had confided to him about partition, did not materialize.[14] "If they have something to say, I shall listen to it on the Bench," was Hutcheson's unalterable position.[15]

Witnesses spoke mainly in English. Those who testified in French – in Syria for example – were heard by Frank Aydelotte and those who testified in German – mainly in Vienna – by Richard Crossman.[16] A barrier existed in the Middle East where the evidence of Arabic-speaking witnesses had to be translated by local or British or American translators. This contributed to the frustration the AAC felt in the Arab world. As Crossman put it:

Ignorant of their culture, their language and their life, we could not hope to establish any real contact with the Arab peoples ... everything must be accepted at second hand either from the official spokesmen or from the tiny group of westernized Arabs who could really express their thoughts and feelings in English.[17]

The secretarial section of the Committee was in charge of the voluminous quantities of written evidence submitted to the AAC, two hundred pounds' worth for each commissioner by the end of the Inquiry.[18] This, together with the verbatim typescripts of the daily testimonies, engaged the members of the AAC in intensive reading. It is against this background that one can better understand Crossman's comment that "Crum . . . reads nothing."[19] Witnesses were asked to submit a typed summary of their testimonies in advance and asked not to refer back to these summaries while testifying before the Committee. In most cases, this request was ignored and the AAC had to listen to repetitive speeches and statements.

The political research of the AAC was not held in the highest regard by the commissioners. The British members noted that their secretary, Harold Beeley, an expert in Middle Eastern studies, had never visited the area. "Our journey," Crossman commented, "was to be his first opportunity of seeing at first hand the countries on which he had lectured for so many years."[20] The U.S. European expert, Leslie Loud, was found to have little knowledge of his subject, owing his job to the fact that he was a friend of Evan Wilson, who, according to McDonald " 'had sold him' to the Judge. This is . . . personal nepotism."[21] But this pointed less to the incompetence of Loud than to Hutcheson's indifference to the need for a research staff: he considered his twenty-seven years on the Bench as the best instrument for conducting this Inquiry and maintained that he needed no staff to assist him.[22] The Americans' Middle East expert, Evan Wilson, was not valued by his compatriots either. "He's a nice enough boy, that's about all," wrote Buxton. He followed the example of Crum in approaching the "better staffed . . . extremely articulate" British secretarial unit for information.[23] Only with the appointment of Paul Hanna did American dissatisfaction die down.

Apart from both the oral and written evidence that was submitted, the commissioners initiated investigations into areas about which they felt somewhat ignorant. This was particularly true of Wilfrid Crick, the only man on the Inquiry in charge of a specific subject – the economic absorptive capacity of Palestine – and he repeatedly requested information on his subject.[24] In a similar way, the Committee as a whole asked UNRRA (United Nations Relief and Rehabilitation Administration) to submit evidence referring to such issues as the role of other voluntary bodies in the treatment of DPs, the extent of UNRRA control over the movement of Jews in Europe, the arrangements between UNRRA and the Allied Authorities, etc.[25] A detailed questionnaire was circulated through the Control Office among the DPs in Germany and Austria, requesting information on the choice of immigration havens and verification of the conditions which were claimed to be detrimental to Jewish reintegration in Europe.[26]

Neither the British nor the U.S. government went out of its way to supply the Committee with official proposals for the political future of Palestine. The American State Department was reluctant to offer the AAC any plans or directives lest "it might smack of an attempt to influence the Commission's findings."[27] As a matter of fact, when the U.S Senate passed the Wagner–Taft Resolution, calling for unrestricted Jewish immigration into Palestine and the establishment of a democratic commonwealth there, it was seen as an attempt to persuade the Committee to produce a pro-Jewish report. And in fact it was. As the "incorrigible" Senator Wagner stated:

We do not want the Committee to have the discretion to make its decisions on matters of fundamental policy. We should by this resolution let the Committee know what we want it to do, and we expect it to do just that without delay.[28]

This was not, however, a Committee which could be swayed in this manner, and according to Zionist circles, Hutcheson was furious. He said that he "had never gotten such an impudent letter. That a man would instruct him to judge not according to his conscience, but according to the conscience of somebody else."[29]

The British handling of the question was more complex. The risk that the Committee would settle on partition and the view that once it had reported it would be difficult for HMG to reject the recommendations made, or to substitute a scheme of its own, caused the British administration to consider a more active role than the one taken by the United States.[30] But the British Government's approach was less direct. When the Foreign Office wanted the AAC to inquire into a certain subject, such as the organization behind the Jewish migration from Eastern to Western Europe, for example, it decided that "it might be unwise to draw their attention to it explicitly . . . since [they] might feel that we were attempting to influence the course of the Committee's deliberations."[31] Instead, the British secretaries were informed and asked to draw the AAC's attention to the matter. The same approach was used when the Foreign Office was anxious that the practicability of Professor Lowdermilk's scheme for irrigation in Palestine be examined (see below).[32]

The laying down of any clear directive, however indirectly communicated, was hindered by the rift which emerged between the Colonial Office and the Foreign Office, the latter preferring the proposals contained in the White Paper and the former some sort of provincial autonomy. The plan to proceed along the lines laid down in the White Paper, whose "primary object was to force the two communities to cooperate" was considered to be quite futile by the Colonial Office, since the setting up of a successful bi-national government in Palestine seemed more remote than ever.[33] On the other hand, the Foreign Office rejected provincial autonomy on the grounds that it would be unwise to propose specific boundaries, however vague, since if they became known they would subject HMG to violent attack by both communities. The Colonial Office complained that Foreign Office officials "see the advantages of the scheme but shy off anything which even remotely savours of partition."[34] With no agreement between the two Offices, no proposal could be submitted. At the AAC's London hearings, however, the evidence of Amery, the former Colonial Secretary, considerably impressed the AAC in favour of partition, and persuaded the Colonial Office to unilaterally submit the plan for Provincial Autonomy. The plan was submitted anonymously, "thus largely defeating the object aimed at."[35]

Thus, while no directives for the political future of Palestine were supplied, the Colonial Office and the Government of Palestine did provide the AAC with a wealth of information about conditions in the country. In a note on the absorptive capacity of rural Palestine, for example, Douglas Harris refuted the Jewish claim for more land. He stated that a comparison of the congestion factors for the two communities indicated that on land of equal productive capacity, twice as many Arabs were subsisting as Jews. "It is no excuse for the Jews for not setting their own house in order before extending their holdings at the expense of the badly congested Arabs," he concluded.[36] It was perhaps of some importance that the two men in the Colonial Office who were considered sympathetic to the Zionist enterprise in Palestine and in charge of providing the AAC with information on the absorptive capacity of the country, namely Sir Douglas Harris and John Martin, later expressed the following views on the Jewish claim to the Negev, the desert-like part of Palestine. Harris said:

The statement so often made for propaganda purposes that nearly half of Palestine is still empty and available for settlement is, roughly speaking, true as regards its emptiness, but altogether false and misleading as regards its availability for settlement.[37]

And Martin noted:

No matter what may be said by HMG regarding the barren nature of the country at the time of its assignment to the Jews, the latter would be likely to turn around afterwards and say that they had been sold a "pup" and given large areas of useless land, for which they must be compensated by new areas elsewhere.[38]

The Palestinian Government also provided the AAC with a good deal of material relating to its own activities and conditions in the country during the last twenty-five years of British rule. Using the opportunity of the AAC's projected visit, Jerusalem asked London to approve development schemes in Arab education and health services, and the Jaffa–Rafa sand dune fixation project. "The AAC will wish to be appraised not only of the direction and extent of Government plans for development, but also of the likelihood of their being realized," wrote Cunningham.[39]

Colonial Office officials in London were less concerned about such impressions:

One might argue that to make a big splash now, somewhat late in the day, might be interpreted as a somewhat naive attempt by HMG to improve its development record in time to impress the AAC.[40]

It was also pointed out that "the Palestine Government had no reason to be ashamed of its record."[41]

The Executive Council in Jerusalem did feel, nonetheless, that it had to defend the Administration and its work over the last quarter of a century, and so a two-volume *Survey of Palestine* was prepared, under the auspices of the Chief Secretary's office. Facts and figures covering all areas of the Administration's activities from 1920 to 1946 were included, among them the chief problems that the Government had tackled and the Government's attempts to reconcile the two communities. Information provided by the two communities was also included, dealing with such subjects as education, health, housing, labour and wages, food and clothing, town and country planning, press, community and religious affairs, finance, irrigation and drainage projects, political parties, etc.[42]

This was, in essence, a descriptive survey which refrained from drawing any conclusions on the basis of the information collected. In the Introduction, Chief Secretary J.V.W. Shaw noted that "when an opinion has been expressed, it is generally because elucidation of the point covered has specifically been requested through you [the AAC]." A third volume of the *Survey* was prepared in March 1946, and covered subjects on which the AAC had specifically requested information, omitted from the first two volumes for political reasons. It was more detailed and included a résumé of the Government's views on major irrigation projects proposed for Palestine, on the absorptive capacity of the country, on possible demographic trends and on Palestine's currency in relation to sterling and the dollar.

It was no surprise when the Arab and Jewish communities challenged the validity of the *Survey*, but a fierce attack from the Anglican and Protestant clergymen in Jerusalem was clearly unexpected. They considered that the *Survey* devoted too much attention to the Catholic Church. The High Commissioner tried to cool them down and wrote to W.H. Stewart, the Anglican Bishop of Jeruslem:

If you want to make a public protest, that of course is your business. Personally, I would view with distaste in this country where the British community alone sets an example of tranquillity in an atmosphere of bickering, strife and violence, any action which would show that we cannot settle our own differences in the decency of privacy.[43]

In addition to the *Survey*, the Government prepared a confidential memorandum on the Palestine Administration, in which it described the political deadlock in the country, refuting or supporting the authenticity of claims made by the two communities. Among other things, for example, the memo refuted the Jewish claim that the Zionist enterprise in Palestine had brought benefits to the Arabs there:

Their plans for development and their elaborate social structure is intended primarily, almost exclusively, for Jews. There is nothing unnatural in this:

charity begins at home and if it ends there, so much the worse; if its beneficial influence can be extended without adversely affecting the main aim, so much the better.[44]

The Government defensively described its abortive attempts to create a community of interests in Palestine strong enough to prevail over the parochial aspirations of the contending sides. It admitted failure and, speculating on the effect military force would have had in this context, concluded that:

It may be that at any given time a few more battalions or aeroplanes or tanks would, as has sometimes been represented, have produced a different frame of mind in one or other of the local communities. It may be that it would not, but in any event, what frame of mind would it have produced in the other community?[45]

The Administration further quoted and strongly supported T. E. Lawrence's view of the Semites – in this context referring to both Jews and Arabs: their thoughts "were at ease only in extremes. They inhabited superlatives by choice. They pursued the logic of several incompatible opinions to absurd ends."[46]

The evidence of the High Commissioner, given in a meeting with the two chairmen of the Committee, added another depressing element to the picture. During a discussion on the Palestine Government and the London Colonial Office, Cunningham described a desperate Administration which received no instructions from London, and was in no position to offer a solution, although it had to bear the brunt of both Arab and Jewish criticism. Politically, the High Commissioner saw no solution which would not have to be forcibly imposed on one or both communities. Nor could he see a permanent solution which would not be essentially a political one: if this were the case, social or economic measures would have no chance of success. He tended towards partition, but stressed the vital importance of solving the humanitarian aspect of the conflict, since this would later ease the imposition of partition. In order to emphasize the depth of the conflict, he wrote that he had "recently been reading through [the] proceedings of [the] joint Conferences before [the] issue of [the] White Paper. How little [the] statement of [the] case has changed!"[47]

The bulk of the material given to the AAC was that submitted by the two main contenders, although some material was also submitted by politically disinterested bodies and individuals such as churches, pacifist organizations, and voluntary and welfare societies.[48] The official institutions of the Jewish and Arab communities in Palestine, together with their related world bodies, furnished the Committee with hundreds of memoranda and petitions, most of them repetitive and propagandist.

The two major bodies sponsoring the preparation and presentation of material to the Committee were the Jewish Agency for Palestine and the Arab Office, both in Jerusalem. The Arab Office was founded in March 1945 after the Alexandria Conference of what later became the Arab League. Under the direction of Musa al-Alami, it ran offices in the United States and Britain, providing information and propaganda about the Palestinian Arabs. The Arabs perceived the importance of a thorough presentation of their case to the AAC and through it to the Anglo-American public. It was clear to them that "the expenditure of millions of scarce dollars by the Arab Office would grow small potatoes in comparison with a fair statement and analysis of the Arab case by the Commission." Accordingly, they arranged for the Arab Higher Committee to testify before the AAC while the Arab Office prepared the written evidence.[49]

The material, in three volumes, was entitled *The Problem of Palestine*, and fell into two main sections. The first comprised a brief summary of the Arab attitude towards the conflict. The second contained various memoranda dealing with specific questions connected with the problem. A major line in this evidence depicted Zionism as a political movement aiming at the creation of a state: hence both immigration and land purchase were described as being part of a political strategy rather than humanitarian or economic concerns. The evidence contained an analysis of the various political solutions which were then being discussed, and rejected all of them except that which suggested an independent Arab state. The most vigorous attack was launched against the proposal for a bi-national state, since the Arabs believed this to be the compromise the Committee would be most likely to settle on. As for trusteeship, the Arabs were prepared to abide by it only if Arab states were represented on the controlling body. They refuted the assumption that the development of Palestine would reduce Arab hostility to Jewish settlement there, stating that this view was based either on a false psychology or upon the equally false assumption that Arab opposition to Zionism springs only from ignorance abetted by malice and will disappear with the spread of enlightenment and prosperity among the peasantry.[50]

In their survey and analysis of the Zionist case, the Arab Office rejected the argument that a Jewish state would provide a psychological haven for the displaced Jews, claiming that the present disturbances in Palestine argued quite the contrary. It further rejected the claim that a Jewish state would be a more stable ally for the West than an Arab Palestine. The Office also attacked all compromise solutions, noting that they "flatter the deep prejudice that truth always lies half-way between extremes and cannot in any way be pleasant." Compromise was a gesture of despair which would not lead to a permanent settlement.[51]

An attempt was made to depict the case of the Palestinian Arabs as a genuine struggle for independence, part of the general rise of nationalism in the Arab world. It was not a personal power struggle as was that of some non-representative leaders, but part of a plan, recently formulated by the Arab League, to replace the old Ottoman unity with a universal Arab society. In this context, strong emphasis was laid on the history of the Arabs and on the fact that they had inhabited the Middle East and Palestine for a millenium. The promises and undertakings of the Powers were presented in detail in order to show the legal international basis of the Arab cause. Efforts were made to illustrate the fact that Arab Palestine was striving to apply Western ideas: the feudal system was being dissolved and democracy expanded; social reforms were being instituted; progressive social theories were being examined; cultural and educational institutions were increasing; an Arab working class was crystallizing; there was a growing political awareness among Palestinian Arab women; and finally, the social base of national aspirations was broadening.[52]

But perhaps the main thrust of the Arab Office's evidence was to refute the idea of a higher civilization which assumed that if there was a less developed people the more advanced nation had the right, if not to dispossess them, at least to share the land with them:

Almost inevitably an Englishman or American ... recalls the history of his own people; he tends to understand the Jewish colonization in Palestine and Arab resistance to it in terms of white colonization of America and

Australia and the resistance of the Red Indians and Aborigines. The temptation to this is all the greater if ... his image of the Arabs is of a few backward nomads ... easily to be moved out or else concentrated in reserves where their peculiar dress and customs can be carefully preserved for the delight of the tourist ... he will tend to think that to champion the rights of the Arabs is no more than misplaced sentimentalism.[53]

That the idea was apparently attractive to Westerners can be found in the comment of Hugh Dalton, the British Secretary of the Treasury, who said that "he felt bad that Jewish resettlement should be held up merely by the intransigence of a backward local population."[54] And Buxton was not far behind:

Then came Buxton's turn, speaking in his flat Yankee frank manner ... he developed the idea of "eminent domain" citing as examples the United States' conquest of Mexico, the American conquest of the Indians and the inevitable giving way of a backward people before a more modern and pratical one. He thought that a strong people would naturally replace weaker ones.[55]

Crossman later put a more liberal face on this issue. Regardless of whether the Arabs could really be equated with the Red Indians,

Americans would find a certain embarrassment in too repeated a reminder that the rights of the indigenous population must at all costs be preserved against the needs of the colonists.[56]

But in the end the Committee was interested not in historical rights, nor in previous undertakings nor in the precepts of international law – all of which had been mobilized by the weaker side – but only in the present situation. This position was backed by the State Department's view that "we are not historians ... one can prove almost anything one wants to by historical argument."[57]

The evidence submitted by the "Jewish side" did not sidestep the "higher civilization" issue. It talked of progress and backwardness but never in terms of one civilization pushing out another. The Zionists did not see themselves as colonists in the colonial sense, merely as settlers in a underdeveloped land with which they had certain national–historical connections. Thus, the central line of the evidence – most of it submitted by the Jewish Agency for Palestine – emphasized the future development of the country. This was true of much of the other evidence submitted. The only pro-Zionist testimony which was entirely political was that of the South African Prime Minister, General Jan Smuts, who had been a member of the Imperial War Cabinet which issued the Balfour Declaration in 1917, and who attempted to show the AAC what the precise intentions of the Declaration were. He stated that the Declaration had been issued as a long-term policy and not as a tactical, short-term solution. Hence, Jewish immigration in the 1940s would still be in accord with it, whereas the White Paper of 1939 in fact contradicted it. But Smuts further stated categorically that the War Cabinet had deliberately been vague on the question of a Jewish state.[58] This part of his testimony was welcomed in London. "It will be of real value to the AAC seeing how strongly the contrary is being urged by representatives of Zionism."[59] Also, as noted above, of importance was Bevin's reaction to Smuts's defence of the Declaration: "The Balfour Declaration amounted to a unilateral declaration ... really a power politics declaration."[60]

Individual evidence was submitted as well by Lord Herbert Samuel, the first High Commissioner of Palestine, who proposed a plan to build a dam on the Litani river to increase Palestine's hydro-electric supply. The site of the dam was to be in what was Lebanese territory, which necessitated the annexation of fifty square miles to Palestine.[61] The Colonial Office was doubtful whether the Lebanese Government would agree to surrender part of its territory to enable more Jews to enter Palestine; the Foreign Office expressed the hope that Samuel "won't try to waste the AAC's limited time with his frontier rectification proposal." It also asked why the Lebanese Government should not request rectification of the frontier on its own account so that it could sell electricity to Palestine and thereby "hold a political weapon against it, i.e. would be able to cease the electricity supply?"[62]

A similar scheme presented to the AAC was the Jordan Valley Authority Plan, submitted by Dr. Walter C. Lowdermilk, assistant chief of the U.S. Soil Conservation Service. This plan, which bore some resemblance to that of the Tennessee Valley Authority, outlined the irrigation of some 706,000 acres of land and the development of agriculture and industry in Palestine for 4,000,000 more people. It sought the exploitation of the steep fall of the Jordan River into the Dead Sea to produce hydro-electric power, and the transfer of water from the Jordan to the Negev. Another feature of the Lowdermilk plan was the carrying of water from the Mediterranean to the Jordan Valley through twenty-eight miles of tunnels and open canals. This would enable the production of more hydro-electric power and the supply of Mediterranean water to the Dead Sea, leaving the Jordan waters for irrigation in the Negev.[63] This, like Samuel's Litani dam, did not appeal to some British officials who commented that

it is said that the age of miracles is not yet over and the people of Syria and Lebanon may be induced by their eagerness to assist the Jewish National Home to give up what is perhaps their most important river.[64]

A third paper submitted outside the official Jewish Agency evidence came from the Jewish Resistance Movement, a very short-lived umbrella organization of the three undergrounds. It discussed the future security of the country and adjacent states, and stressed that a Jewish state, equipped with appropriate weaponry, could militarily and politically "contribute our humble share" to the strategic interests of the Anglo-Americans in the Middle East and defend Christian and other minorities while policing the area. This could be done without the help of a "single American soldier" (see Chapter 2, p. 41). It gave Jewish acquiescence to an interim Anglo-American trusteeship in Palestine which would facilitate the eventual conversion of the country into a Jewish state. The paper rejected claims that a Jewish solution in Palestine would provoke the Arab countries to the point where they would dispatch forces to Palestine. Inter-Arab feuds and their internal problems would not allow them to make such a move. The paper concluded that Anglo-American regional interests would not be adversely affected by a Jewish solution. It also questioned the Arab threat to turn to Moscow and claimed that anti-British feelings existed in the Middle East regardless of the Palestine question, and would not disappear if a pro-Arab settlement was effected there.[65]

The Jewish Agency evidence was hamstrung by the political pluralism which characterized that body, representing as it did leftwing, rightwing and centrist Zionist parties. This was apparent in the evidence. Zionist officials were asked to give answers to questions which they had hitherto evaded, questions such as the Agency's attitude to partition, trusteeship, bi-nationalism, etc. As David Horowitz noted: "There was a general ignorance of what we were after" – the policy of the Zionist movement being "to say nothing in order to avoid controversies."[66] Unfortunately, this policy could no longer be pursued. But since there was no agreement even on the question of statehood, Ben-Gurion evaded that question, focussing instead on a demand for immigration of up to one million Jews and on the economic development of the country. Even here he evaded a detailed presentation of these general demands, not sure that unanimity could be maintained when it came to details.[67]

The Agency then could not agree on more than general principle, or go much beyond a concurrence on what *not* to present to the AAC. So, since the time had not yet come for a reconsideration of the Zionist political programme, the Agency had no choice but to resort to its Biltmore programme in public, while privately advocating partition.[68] Such tactics, as previously mentioned, did not work with the AAC.

Because the political stand of the Jewish Agency was not entirely clear (except for its demand for a Jewish Palestine as against an Arab Palestine), and because of the political history of the Mandate, and the British undertakings which followed it, which had not been unequivocally in favour of Zionism, it was decided to emphasize economic and social issues, to speak about the *future* of Palestine and to present numbers and figures rather than to use emotional arguments. Dwelling on the past was not proposed since the Jews could not claim an exclusive place in the history of the Holy Land. The understanding that the AAC was tired of speeches and general explanations, and expected only facts and figures in Palestine, guided the Agency's presentation.[69]

Another line in the Jewish evidence was to avoid criticism of the British Administration in Palestine. Shertok pointed out that "criticism of the Government meant a proposal for rectification based on the assumption that this Government would stay."[70] As to political polemics, the Agency sought to eradicate the distinction between Jews and Zionists, and further stressed the fact that the Jewish problem existed long before Hitler's time and was not only a question of post-war DPs.[71] Another line of evidence pursued – to satisfy the democratic beliefs of the American Judge – was the description of the establishment of the Jewish state as a democratic process which would be completed when further immigration turned the Jews into a majority.[72]

All the above points were highlighted in the thousand-page volume submitted by the Agency and later published.[73] There was hardly a subject relating to Palestine which was not discussed. Nor was it confined only to Palestine: the volume also outlined the past and future positive effects of the Zionist enterprise on the entire Middle East, all reinforced with charts, figures, and statistics. This was described against the background of Arab backwardness:

As far as the Middle East was concerned, the French Revolution might never have happened. For the doctrine of human rights and personal liberty had not penetrated the citadels of Islamic authoritarianism. Similarly, the Industrial Revolution might never have come to pass. The period of invention and discovery in the natural sciences, which had increased the productivity of all human effort and transformed the horizons of human welfare, had passed by the Arab East unknown and unheeded. The agricultural resources of these countries had dwindled through human neglect and persistent erosion. Whatever raw materials or sources of wealth lay beneath the soil were unexplored and unexploited. In fact, the squalor of the Middle East had become accepted as an integral part of its natural scenery. And together with poverty, both as cause and effect, there went ignorance and illiteracy.[74]

Detailed coverage was given to the economic absorptive capacity of the country, basically an imponderable, and to an attempt to prove that immigration would not impair the standard of living of those already in the country.

The hundreds of sophisticated graphs, tables and maps which illustrated the Jewish case, and the visits of the AAC to "settlements ... which are likely to remind the Americans of the western frontier days of the early American pioneering epoch," had their effect on the Committee. So much so that "Statler [= Crossman] compared Jewish evidence before the AAC to the easy manner in which a professional boxer would hold off a group of amateurs."[75]

The two sides did their utmost to influence the AAC, but neither history lessons nor arguments relating to the development potential of the country could divert the Commission from seeing an impasse in Palestine. In their view, all plans "however technically feasible they may be, will fail unless there is peace in Palestine."[76] The Jewish evidence had its effect on the Committee, but in an unexpected direction. Because it demonstrated the Arab weakness, the judicially-led Committee became the defender of the weaker side. Against this background, one can explain the Report's concentration on the development of the Arab sector of Palestine.

NOTES

1. Crossman, *Palestine Mission*, p. 31; Wilson, *Decision on Palestine*, pp. 69-71.
2. Hutcheson to AAC, Washington, Dec. 1945, McDonald Papers, folder 187.
3. Hutcheson at Jerusalem Public Hearing, 25 March 1946. On the Christian motivation of the Committee see also the report of the U.S. Legation, Damascus, on visit of the AAC to Syria, 20 March 1946, p. 2, NRC, Damascus Files, RG 84, 59A543; Blanshard, *Aydelotte of Swarthmore*, p. 359; Crossman, *Palestine Mission*, p. 138; Buxton to Frankfurter, 10 Sept. 1946, Frankfurter Papers, container 40. The Palestine Executive Council discussed the control of "Dancing and Swing Music at the Sea of Galilee" following a debate in Parliament. See 30th meeting 26 Sept. 1946, CO 814/41. See also appearance of Shaw, Chief Secretary Palestine Government, before AAC, Jerusalem, 22 March 1946, pp. 25-26, USNA, RG 43, AAC, Box 11.
4. AAC Report, p. 3 and Chap. VII of the Report on Christian Interests in Palestine, p. 33.
5. For the crusade expression see Lowell C. Pinkerton, U.S. Consul in Jerusalem, to Gordon Merriam, Chief of Near Eastern Division, State Department, 4 Feb. 1946, p. 2, Washington, State Department Building, Lot 54, D403 Box 9.
6. Phillips on hearings of Arab League representatives in Cairo, 2 Mar. 1946, Phillips diary.
7. Ibid.; also Crossman, *Palestine Mission*, p. 134.
8. Gerold Frank to W.J. Porter, U.S. Legation Damascus, in Damascus to State Department, 20 March 1946, NRC Damascus files, No. RG 59A 543.
9. Buxton to Frankfurter, 14 Feb. 1946, Frankfurter Papers, container 40. On Hutcheson the "prosecutor" see Washington cross-examination of H. Greenberg, 10 Jan. 1946, AAC public hearings. Hutcheson was reported to order witnesses to "answer the question, don't make a speech when you were asked to give an answer." Jewish Agency Executive, 10 Feb. 1946, report on the Washington Hearings, Jerusalem, CZA; McDonald diary, 26 March 1946.
10. See, for example, Arab League evidence, Cairo, 2 March 1946; Crossman, *Palestine Mission*, p. 110.
11. Phillips diary, 25 March 1946. See also Crum, *Behind the Silken Curtain*, pp. 185, 189; Crossman, *Palestine Mission*, pp. 133-134, 137.
12. Phillips diary, 8 March 1946.
13. On the "secret trick" see Joseph Heller, "From the Black Sabbath to Partition: Summer 1946 as a Turning Point in the History of Zionist Policy," *Zion*, vol. 43, no. 3-4, Jerusalem, 1978.
14. Crossman, *Palestine Mission*, p. 137.
15. Hutcheson in a conversation with Benjamin Cohen, Counsellor in the State Department, Dec. 1945, interview with Cohen, Washington, May 1979.
16. Aydelotte diary, 14 March and 6 April 1946. In Lausanne he got on very cosy terms with the golfers in the Committee: he paid the club fees because he spoke better French.
17. Crossman, *Palestine Mission*, p. 110.
18. Ibid., p. 32.
19. Ms. of Crossman diary, Lausanne, undated, SACMEC, Crossman Papers. See also Aydelotte diary, 21 April 1946.
20. *Palestine Mission*, p. 25; Leggett to G. Cohen, Interview, London 5 Dec. 1960.
21. McDonald diary, 2 Jan. 1946.
22. See p. 81 below on the appointment of Paul Hanna to the U.S. Research staff. Later Hutcheson completely changed his mind and praised Hanna's role in the drafting of

the Report. See memo by Hutcheson, May 1946, in USNA, State Dept., Palestine Material, 1946, Box 6755.

23. Buxton to Frankfurter, 17 Jan. 1946, Frankfurter Papers, container 40; excerpts from Crum, "Palestine Diary," in McDonald Papers, folder 93.

24. On Crick's detailed requests see Douglas Harris to John Martin, 21 Dec. 1946, CO 733/463 Pt.2 2/75872/138.

25. See AAC to UNRRA, London March 1946, FO 371/52512/E2191.

26. AAC (Mr. Vincent) to Control Office Germany, 15 Jan. 1946, FO 371/52507/E801.

27. Near Eastern Divison to Pinkerton, U.S. Consul in Jerusalem, 4 Jan. 1946. Washington State Depart. Building, Lot 54 D403, Box 1815; Wilson, *Decision on Palestine*, p. 70.

28. Washington to Foreign Office, on the Senate Resolution of 17 Dec. 1945, FO 371/45403/E9987; Cunningham to Hall, 1 Jan. 1946, on reactions in Palestine to the Senate Resolution, SACMEC, Cunningham Papers, Box 1, File 1. Wagner was a Democrat from New York.

29. Report to Jewish Agency Executive, 10 Feb. 1946 (Hebrew), Jerusalem, CZA. See also Hutcheson to U.S. Delegate to Damascus, W.J. Porter, in Damascus to State Dept., 20 March 1946, NRC Damascus Files, No. RG 84 59A543. A copy of the Senate resolution was sent to Judge Hutcheson.

30. See memo by Douglas Harris: "Constitutional Proposal for Palestine for the Use of the AAC," London, 14 Jan. 1946, CO 537/1754.

31. Comments of Foreign Office Eastern Dept. officials, Jan. and Feb. 1946, FO 371/52505/E537.

32. Trafford-Smith to Baxter, 16 Jan. 1946, FO 371/52506/E549.

33. Memo by D. Harris, 23 Jan. 1946, on meeting with Foreign Office officials to prepare evidence, to AAC, CO 537/1754.

34. Ibid. See also comments by Baxter and Howe, Foreign Office Eastern Department, 14 and 22 Jan. 1946, FO 371/52504/E389/G and FO 371/52507/E810 respectively.

35. Comment by Harris, 29 Jan. 1946, CO 537/1754.

36. Harris, Note on Absorptive Capacity of Rural Palestine, 14 Jan. 1946, CO 537/1754; comments by Harris, 18 Jan. 1946 and 21 March 1946, CO 537/1754.

37. Comment by Harris, 14 Jan. 1947, CO 537/2311.

38. Comment by Martin, 20 Jan. 1947, CO 537/2311. For a most favourable Zionist view of Harris and Martin, see Horowitz, *State in the Making*, p. 131.

39. Palestine High Commissioner to Colonial Secretary, 12 Jan. 1946, CO 733/465, No. 75873/16.

40. Trafford-Smith to Martin, 25 Jan. 1946, CO 733/465, No. 75873/16.

41. Colonial Secretary to High Commissioner, 30 Jan. 1946, CO 733/465, No. 75873/16.

42. Government of Palestine, Chief Secretary's Office, *A Survey of Palestine*, vols. 1 and 2, Jerusalem, Jan. 1946.

43. Cunningham to Bishop Steward, 31 March 1946, SACMEC, Jerusalem and East Mission Archives, Box 68, file 4. For correspondence with the High Commissioner, see ibid, Box 68, file 3.

44. Memorandum on the Administration of Palestine under the Mandate, Feb. 1946, p. 13, SACMEC, Cunningham Papers, Box 5, file 2.

45. Ibid., p. 16.

46. Ibid., p. 6.

47. Memo of High Commissioner to the AAC, Jerusalem, 22 March 1946, SACMEC, Cunningham Papers, Box 5, file 2. In an interview for Thames Television, 1977, the last GOC for Palestine, General Sir Gordon MacMillan, described the lack of support and loneliness which Cunningham had suffered in his relations with the senior echelons in Whitehall. See SACMEC, material collected for Thames Television programme on the Palestine Mandate.

48. See, for example, evidence by Cardinal Griffin, head of British Catholic Congregation, 14 Jan. 1946, FO 371/52505/E487; evidence of Dr. Emil Leimdoerfer on Lake Tana (Ethiopia) and on Angola as possible havens for Jews, SACMEC, Spears Papers, Box 4, file 7. Scores of memoranda had been submitted by various Arab bodies and by Jewish and Christian sects who based their writings on the Bible and on various messianic prophecies. See USNA RG 43, AAC, Boxes 1-14 passim.
49. Near East Division to U.S. Consul in Jerusalem, 4 Jan. 1946, Washington, State Dept. Building, Lot 54, D403, Box 1815. See also HQ, British troops in Palestine Fortnightly Intelligence Letter, No. 15, 13-26 May 1946, WO 169/23022; Ahmad Al-Shuqairi, *Forty Years in Arabic and International Life*, Beirut, 1969, p. 263.
50. Arab Office, Jerusalem, *The Problem of Palestine*, Vols. 1 and 2, March 1946; interview with Mr. Albert Hourani, Oxford, summer 1979.
51. Arab Office, *The Problem of Palestine*, vol. 1.
52. Ibid. In this context see Crossman, *Palestine Mission*, pp. 150, 167-168 regarding Palestine Arab Trade Unions. See also report by 1st British Infantry Division, 14 May 1946, on demonstrations of Arab women and schoolgirls in Jerusalem, Jenin and Haifa. Weekly Intelligence Review, No. 6, 6-12, May 1946, WO 169/22957.
53. See note 51 above.
54. Minutes of Cabinet Committee on Palestine, 6 Sept. 1945, CAB 95/14.
55. McDonald diary, 1 April 1946.
56. Lecture to the RIIA, London, 13 June 1946, p. 2, SACMEC, Crossman Papers.
57. Singleton to Dr. John Hazzam of the Institute of Arab American Affairs, Washington Hearings, 11 Jan. 1946; Gordon Merriam to Loy Henderson, 5 Dec. 1945, Washington, State Dept. Building, Lot 54, D403, Box 1815.
58. See copy of the evidence in FO 371/52509/E1413/G. Smuts was a member of the War Cabinet.
59. Comment by Douglas Harris, 2 Feb. 1946, CO 733/463 Pt. 2, No. 75872/138/7/1946, file on AAC: memoranda submitted by outside bodies.
60. See p. 47.
61. See correspondence on Hydro-electric Scheme for Palestine, Dec. 1945, CO 733/452, No. 75056 Pt. 1 & 2.
62. Comments by Harris, 17 Dec. 1945, CO 733/452, No. 75056, Pt. 2; Baxter, 12 Jan. 1946, FO 371/52580/E365 and J.T. Henderson, Eastern Dept., 17 Jan. 1946, FO 371/52580/E554. The Palestine Electric Corporation later submitted a paper to the Committee with comments on Samuel's plan, see FO 371/52580/E875.
63. Presented as the Lowdermilk, James Hayes and Abel Wolman plan for overall irrigation and hydro-electric development of Palestine. See Washington to Foreign Office, 14 Jan. 1946, FO 371/ 52505/E448. See also Walter Clay Lowdermilk, *Palestine, Land of Promise*, London, 1944. Lowdermilk developed his Jordan Valley Authority plan following a visit to Palestine (1939) to examine the conservation of soil against erosion. The Palestine Administration were not enthusiastic about his ideas, adding that "Dr. Lowdermilk is Ph.D ... .this presumably means that he is Doctor of Philosophy ... it would appear that he is not a hydraulic engineer," Water Commissioner, Palestine Government, 16 April 1944, Jerusalem, Israel State Archives, Chief Secretary, Section No. V/16/44.
64. Comment by Palestine Government Water Commissioner, 4 Aug. 1945, CO 537/1823.
65. See copy of paper, 25 March 1946, CO 733/463 Pt. 2, No. 75872/138/7/1946 and USNA,RG 43, AAC, Box 7.
66. Horowitz, *State in the Making*, pp. 34, 77. Horowitz was a member of the Agency's advisory committee which prepared the Jewish evidence.
67. Report to the Jewish Agency Executive, 10 Feb. 1946, about the AAC Washington hearings, Jerusalem, CZA, (Hebrew). Jewish Agency Executive, 24 Feb. 1946,

Jerusalem, CZA.
68. Heller, "Black Sabbath to Partition", pp. 325-326. The Biltmore Programme demanded the turning of Palestine into a Jewish commonwealth.
69. Horowitz, *State in the Making*, pp. 37, 41-42. Jewish Agency Executive, 3 March 1946, Jerusalem, CZA.
70. Jewish Agency Executive, 19 March, 1946 (Hebrew), Jerusalem, CZA.
71. Memo of Isham, Palestine Defence Security Officer, 22 Dec. 1945, SACMEC, Cunningham Papers, Box 5, file 2; PALCOR Press bulletin, 29 Nov. 1945 on Ben-Gurion's appearance before the Yishuv's National Assembly, CO 733/456 No. 75156 Pt. 2/151A.
72. Azriel Karlibach, *The AAC of Inquiry to Palestine* (Hebrew), Tel Aviv, 1946, p. 10.
73. Jewish Agency for Palestine, *The Jewish Case Before the AAC of Inquiry on Palestine as Presented by the Jewish Agency for Palestine*, Jerusalem, 1947.
74. Ibid., p. 346.
75. Horowitz, *State in the Making*, p. 42. The appeal to the past history of the powers was frequently used in the Jewish evidence; Report by Arthur Lourie to Nahum Goldmann, 30 March 1946, Jerusalem, CZA, Goldmann files, no. Z6, Bundle 18/1.
76. AAC Report, p. 9.

7

The Public Hearings, Washington and London: Texas Prevails

On 7 January 1946, the AAC's public hearings opened at the State Department building in Washington. Before meeting in America, the British and U.S. teams had assembled in their own countries and had been briefed by officials and army officers.[1] It was then that the decision was taken to open the Inquiry in America, since the Commission would thereby be "dealing with the future of the Jewish race where half the Jews in the world were."[2]

Those who composed the terms of reference certainly did not expect an investigation into the fate of the Jewish people. Yet much of the Inquiry was devoted to various aspects of anti-Semitism, to attempts to define the Jews in terms of a religion and nationality, and to the question of whether Zionism was compatible with western ideas of democracy and majority rule. With the Holocaust in the background, and the survivors constituting part of the terms of reference, the AAC tried, some seven months after the war, to find out why the Jews had suffered this fate. This was, however, too great an ambition. A leading Palestinian Jewish journalist and writer wrote at the time:

Among the commissions that inquired into conditions in Palestine, this is the eighth, but among the bodies that plunged into the full depth of the Jewish problem, this is the first ... it had never happened that the Powers ... dispatched their envoys to examine what distinguishes a Jew from his neighbour, what he feels at home and outside, what his past was and what his future will be. Never before did they sit for months and gather opinions – opinions not facts – from Jews about themselves.[3]

The Washington hearings, and, later, visits to Poland and to the DP centres in Germany convinced the Committee that anti-Semitism had survived the war and was even on the increase. There were many reasons for this, among them the post-war phenomenon of identifying the Jews with the Communist regimes. There was also tough economic competition in traditional Jewish occupations; Jews were being given preferential treatment by certain charitable organizations; there were arguments about the restoration of property; and "feelings that those Jews who fled to Russia avoided the horrors of war – much the same feeling as is sometimes evinced towards those English people who spent the war years in the USA."[4] But because anti-Semitism had been so strong before the war, some of the commissioners were interested in considering more profound explanations for it, such as the inherent malady of European democracy, or the non-assimilable character of the Jews.[5] This had been reinforced in the twentieth century by the so-called dual loyalty inherent in Zionism.[6] While the AAC could reach no conclusions about the causes of anti-Semitism, nor were they intended to, they were in total agreement about its prevalence at the time of the Inquiry. They differed strongly, however, over solutions to the problem, especially that of Jewish statehood.

The idea of removing all the Jews from the Continent was initially seen by the AAC as handing Hitler a posthumous victory, "a very dangerous precedent."[7] They considered assimilation in Europe to be the best solution, dismissing emigration to other countries as an unworkable proposition: "Do you believe," asked Hutcheson, "that this 'unhealthy rump' [using the words of a Red Cross representative to describe the surviving Jews] will be absorbed into the other nations of the world without bringing some of the ill-health with it?"[8]

The Committee strongly opposed the idea of the Jews being a people in need of a state (that is, the idea of political Zionism), and this view was expressed at the Washington and London hearings:

Is it a matter of pride that the Jews want to have a state, just to puff themselves up a little? .... Is not that a Germanic notion that to have freedom of the soul you have got to have and love a state? ... I cannot see why thay have to have it. While I am of Scottish descent, in America we do not want a Scottish state, the English do not want an English state. Why ... does the Jew want to have a Jewish state? ... why do the Jews have to do that in Arabia when I cannot do it in Texas? ... They want all the nations to withdraw and to run all their problems for themselves?[9]

Zionism actually strengthens the walls of the spiritual concentration camp. It is only the other side of the Nazi shield, the Jewish reaction to the

German disease. It is the anti-Semites and racists who want to clear the Jews out of Europe and place them together in Palestine.[10]

Throughout the Inquiry, only one commissioner, Richard Crossman, actually changed his mind about Jewish statehood, coming to the conclusion that Zionism and Judaism were irrevocably yoked together.[11] And, indeed, the AAC, in its final Report, did not recommend the establishment of a Jewish state in Palestine. In the autumn of 1947, the one man who had to be impressed by their arguments for a National Home still professed that it "has never appealed to me."[12] And what did not appeal to Judge Hutcheson did not appear in the Report.

The AAC was confronted with the fact that, first of all, not all Jews agreed to the idea of Zionism, and secondly, among those that did there were many whose reasoning was not entirely free of self-interest. A Zionist solution for the Jews of Europe would, Crossman noted, "safeguard American Jewry by preventing any immigration which might stir up anti-Semitism" in the United States. In England, contending Jewish viewpoints over the issue at the Hearings revived the storm which thirty years earlier had split British Jewry with the publication of the Balfour Declaration: how would it affect their status as equal citizens of Great Britain. During this debate, Crossman noted, "we felt acutely embarrassed."[13] And if, for one reason or the other, many Jews would remain scattered around the world, a state would not solve their problem. Thus, when, at the Washington hearings, Reinhold Niebuhr declared that world Jewry can survive "even if they do not have a Jewish state, but the price is terribly high," Judge Singleton countered with:

I do not see why that which you described as the price to the Jews would be any less by reason of the fact that a piece of land, not very big, was assigned to them and called the "Jewish State."[14]

There was a very crucial difference, as far as the AAC was concerned, between the Jewish Yishuv in Palestine and the Jews in Washington and London who advocated the idea of Jewish statehood as a solution to the problem, though all were represented as Zionists. The commissioners were prepared to seek a remedy for the persecuted, but they were less than sympathetic when confronted with the apparently divided loyalties of British and American Zionists. "We never expected the Arab to be other than an Arab, and we took for granted that his point of view would be quite

different from ours," wrote Crossman, but English and American
Jews who are Zionists are expected "to behave like us and to accept
our basic principles. When they failed to do so ... we felt annoyed
with them for being un-English and un-American."[15] In a statement
that permeated the entire Inquiry, Judge Hutcheson bluntly concluded that

I won't tolerate if in Texas things will be judged not from the American
point of view. I won't accept it, and if you want me to, you'll turn me into
Anti: Anti-Jewish, Anti-Italian. You say I'm an anti-Semite, perhaps you
are right ... a Jew can pray to his God, he can love Jewish songs as I love
Scottish songs.[16]

The AAC could not be moved from these views. They were not
ready to be lectured on and converted to Zionism by their Jewish
compatriots, since this would have constituted a judgement against
their own countries and sociopolitical systems. Zionism appeared
to them to contribute to the idea of divided loyalties and hence to
western anti-Semitism. This view was qualified only later, in Palestine: Zionism could be a solution for the persecuted Jews. There,
they were more attentive to Weizmann, who countered the charge
of disloyalty with the view that "it would not enter the head of an
American to suspect an Irishman." He also denied the connection
between anti-Semitism and Zionism. There was no Zionist movement in Yemen, yet a Yemenite Jew "cannot go on the pavement;
he cannot ride a horse; he has to stand up whenever a Moslem goes
by ... I do not know [whether] you could put that to the credit of
Zionism."[17] If Zionism had any influence on the AAC, it achieved
it in Jerusalem and not in Washington. In Palestine the Jews constituted a people, not merely a religious group.

Judge Hutcheson, who presided at the Washington hearings,
opened the first session by declaring:

While knowledge must precede understanding, and understanding must
precede judging, this is not always enough. Sometimes if we would judge
aright, we must let our minds be bold.

And so began the AAC hearings.

THE ZIONIST AND ARAB CASE PRESENTED

A variety of witnesses appeared on behalf of the Zionists, among
them noted public figures, economists who offered evidence to

demonstrate Palestine's ability to absorb large numbers of Jewish immigrants, Earl Harrison, Truman's envoy to the DP camps, who spoke of the grim condition of the displaced Jews, and, of course, members of the American Zionist Emergency Council. The testimony of AZEC members was first and foremost politcial: a demand for a Jewish Palestine. Dr. Emanuel Neumann, Vice-Chairman of the AZEC, further called for the transfer and exchange of populations along the lines of the Greek–Turkish exchange which took palce in Anatolia after the First World War.[18]

Another type of evidence, later referred to as the "Notestein Syndrome," was given by Frank W. Notestein, Director of the Office of Population Research in Princeton University. His testimony postulated that the Jews would never become a majority in Palestine, for even if Oriental Jewry with its higher birthrate was admitted to the country, the resultant increase would be cancelled out before 1960. "As an extreme measure, permit the whole of surviving European Jewry (assuming they were willing to go and could get there) to enter Palestine ... by 1980 at the latest, the Jews would again be a minority."[19]

The most "sensational" of the witnesses was Albert Einstein, who had been urged to testify by his Princeton colleague, Frank Aydelotte. People enthusiastically applauded when Einstein came before the Committee, "adoring women gazing at him like Gandhi."[20] In his heavy German accent, Einstein poured out his wrath on all involved in the Palestine conflict: on the British for fomenting trouble between Jews and Arabs; on America for taking part in a Committee which was no more than a "smoke-screen"; on the "anachronistic" Zionist demand for a Jewish state; and on the commissioners for participating in this "futile" inquiry. Naturally, he raised protests from every corner of the room.[21] According to Hutcheson, it was "no more illuminating than a lecture he himself once gave about relativity."[22]

The more interesting testimonies were those which touched on the question of Jewish statehood, and on this issue Hutcheson pitilessly cornered the witnesses who proposed it. To Chaim Greenberg of the American Labour Zionists, he even apologized beforehand: "Sir John and I know if we are going to hold a witness to an answer we are going to have to hold him tight. Otherwise he makes a beautiful speech." And then he asked his question:

Isn't the insistence at this time on naming this place a Jewish state or colony quite an anachronism, particularly in view of the general internationalism which the world is trying to take hold of?[23]

The good Judge found a rather tough opponent in another witness, the Reverend Reinhold Niebuhr. Niebuhr, of the American Christian Palestine Committee (ACPC), was one of the oustanding theologians and religious philosophers of his time.[24] His influence even in England was such that during the war Oxford students "rewrote" the Commandments to read:

Thou shalt love the Lord thy Dodd with all thy heart, and all thy soul ... and thy Niebuhr as thyself.[25]

Niebuhr, as a result, was not seen as a litigant, but as an objective representative of a known and respected group. The inspiring dialogue which developed between him and the Committee was often referred to in the AAC's later discussions.

Hutcheson: Do you think Palestine should be called a Jewish State?
Niebuhr: A people without a state will naturally use that expression to express what they lack ... when you say "Jewish state" you are saying you want some place where you don't have to bow to any majority ... the real difference between a Jew and a Finnish immigrant [in America] is that the Finnish immigrant doesn't have to worry ... as to whether there was a Finland ... even the Lithuanian will still have a geographical locus where Lithuanians are in the majority.
Hutcheson: The main difference between you and me is this: I really feel ... that there is no difference between an American Jew and myself. I have an ancestor that has been here 300 years. He came from Scotland. I don't think that I am a Scot or an Englishman; I am an American. It is the same way with a Jew.
Niebuhr: From the perspective of American democracy that is the case ... I happen to be an American of German ancestry, but I never face this problem that the Jew faces. If he goes into assimilation, then, if you universalize the assimilation business, then he is committing race suicide ... not only the individual had a right to live, but ... ethnic groups had a right to live.
Hutcheson: You think that if they have a state, it would not only help them there but would help the Jews all over the world?
Niebuhr: If the Jews have a homeland where there is a security for the perpetuation of their ethnic group, then the individual Jew

in the various nations will not have the collective survival impulse ... a Jew has an intolerable tension ... because he has to maintain a people scattered among the nations even while he relates himself to the culture of other nations ... that tension none of the rest of us have.

Crossman: Anti-Semitism is a certain state of mind in the Jew himself and in the Gentile acting on each other, which would be relieved by a Jewish home, in the sense that the Jew outside of Palestine would feel differently and also the Gentile would feel differently about it?

Niebuhr: Yes.

McDonald: What is your estimate of these fears ... that the establishment of the Jewish national homeland would jeopardize the status of Jews in America and elsewhere, would involve divided loyalty?

Niebuhr: I don't understand that ... I don't think the situation would be any different than with other groups that have a homeland. We expect that an Italian immigrant who becomes an American citizen will be a good American ... this doesn't change the fact that there are Italian American organizations [which] are more interested in regard to Italy, but we don't say that they are bad citizens ... there would be special interests in a Swedish group or a Finnish group.

Hutcheson: Everybody in this country deplores the German-American, the Polish-American, the Swedish-American political blocs ... when we find our people in those blocs, we find them voting not as Americans should, but as people of divided allegiance ... In my community we have very few Jews and very few Italians, but there is no animosity there at all, in Houston.

Niebuhr: We in America take a provisionally tolerant attitude toward all racial groups ... under the assumption of an ultimately complete assimilation. Now the Jew is in a different position, but if there were the answer for the Jew, if this were universalized, then there would be no Jews, because they would disappear ... We will be nice to them until they become completely American. If we mean by that that we don't want any racial, ethnic distinction, then I think that we are really asking the Jews to commit racial suicide.[26]

This dialogue was, in fact, the whole Washington enquiry in a microcosm: Jewish statehood, anti-Semitism, dual loyalty, the distinction between Jews and Gentiles, and even how things were "down there in Houston." It also accorded with Hutcheson's view that the Committee was only investigating "refugeeism and Zionism."[27]

GPDP-E*

Niebuhr's appearance raised the question of the attitude of non-Jews to the Palestine question. Anti-Zionist views had come largely from Protestant missionaries in the Middle East, while Presbyterian groups tended to support Zionist aspirations.[28] These attitudes should be compared to the evidence presented at the London hearings by leading Catholic figures. According to Joseph Cardinal Griffin, for example,

in the first place there do not seem to be any countries in Europe which it is necessary for them to abandon. The influence of Russia since 1917 has been consistently sympathetic to the Jewish communities, and it would seem that they can safely settle down throughout the countries of the Russian sphere of influence ... only the physically healthiest and mentally best balanced ... could become valuable citizens of ... Palestine.[29]

The AAC felt that the Washington hearings were "very useful as a means of blowing off the steam of the Zionist cause."[30] While they were proof of the power of Jewish and American feeling on the Palestine question, they did not yet tip the scales in the Zionists' favour.[31] It was the opinion of some that the Zionists were "prejudicing their case by the over-statement of their demands," particularly with regard to the demand for a state.[32] "Even Niebuhr had failed," commented a State Department source.[33] This apparent failure was perhaps the main reason for the campaign of the American Zionists to discredit the AAC in the press.[34] Another symptom of Zionist frustration was Ben-Gurion's comment on Emanuel Neumann's suggestion to the AAC to appoint an international committee on immigration to Palestine: "This is the worst proposal after the White Paper ... two Gentiles are worse than one Gentile; three are worse than two."[35]

Those who presented the Arab case in Washington hoped – futilely – to make their demands as important a part of the hearings as Refugeeism and Zionism. Their case had to wait until the Committee reached the Middle East.

The Institute of Arab American Affairs sent Dr. Philip Hitti, a distinguished professor of Semitic Literature at Princeton, and its Secretary, Dr. John Hazzam, to refute the Zionist claims and to moderate the impressions made by the Gentile supporters. They rejected the claim that Zionism had brought the benefits of progress to Palestine, further stating that they preferred gradual achievement and in their own way, without, as Hazzam put it, turning the country "into a cross between Pittsburgh and Coney Island." They found an attentive listener in Hutcheson who declared: "You are really talking about the avowed aim of the Jews of a political component fact in Palestine? . . . I can see that. I have enough Scotch-Irish in me to oppose it." But their emphasis on historical facts and on proving that Jews ruled Palestine for less than fifty years in King David's time did not impress the Committee. The only satisfaction the Arabs were offered was Hutcheson's comment that "if Great Britain has been perfidious to both of you, she has done pretty well." Their case suffered from not being viewed as an independent issue, like the DPs and Zionism; on the contrary, it was considered only as an obstacle to the solution of the Jewish problem. Hitti's argument that Palestine was only a myth, "the mischievous product of [Jewish] Sunday Schools," and that it merely constituted the southern part of Syria, was, in fact, a two-edged sword, since it undermined both Palestinian Arab and Zionist claims to self-determination.[36]

The reactions of the commissioners to the Washington hearings reflected their national and personal idiosyncracies. Crossman described the hearings as "Britain in the Dock," and wrote that "we Englishmen were driven not to obtain information but to counter a hostile argument . . . we were there to take punishment and we took it."[37] On the other hand, the American team exhibited a certain ignorance about the Palestine issue, revealing far less knowledge than the British. To emphasize this a Zionist source reported that "an American Senator, a supporter of Zionism, a friend of us, had asked why don't we grant the Arabs the status of minority; he naively thought that we are the majority in Palestine and the Arabs are the minority."[38]

The hearings saw Crossman looking for social revolutions and playing with socialist theories, as witnesses innocently furnished the AAC with data regarding development in Palestine.[39] James McDonald demonstrated his knowledge of history, and challenged witnesses who denied that the Jews constituted a nation with the work of two historians, Graetz and Dubnow, who had referred to the Jews as a people.[40] Hutcheson soon emerged as the most powerful figure in the American team, using his "real love of language . . . more explosively than any other member of the Committee" to apply his Texan experiences to the problem of Palestine.[41] He explained that he "had for a long time experience with immigration laws, holding court in border districts up and down the Mexican border, and I know something about immigration laws." He then proceeded to apply this experience to Palestine. He also managed to link his campaign against the Ku-Klux Klan with the AAC Inquiry, causing raised eyebrows among his colleagues.[42]

When the Washington hearings came to an end, and the AAC proceeded aboard the still blacked-out *Queen Elizabeth* to England, Crossman summed up his impressions up to that point as follows:

The Zionists are terrific ... they are passionately anti-British and have obviously organized nearly all the American Jews and all the Press. The case for the Arabs, and indeed the difficulty in putting a million Jews suddenly into Palestine, simply goes by default here ... By overstating their case and revealing their aims, the Zionists don't merely irritate the British. They have really worried our Texan Judge and fairminded men like Crum and Aydelotte and Phillips ... As democrats they are shocked. The American Arabs overstated their case just as badly.[43]

THE LONDON HEARINGS

Crossman was, as usual, highly perceptive in describing the change both of scenery and of priorities once the AAC moved from Washington to London:

To move from the American way of thinking of Palestine to the British is to move completely from one world to another. For when one comes back to London ... one comes to a Capital overtaxed with responsibility ... one is aware of intense concentration on the cutting down of military commitments and preserving our Middle Eastern position with the least force possible.[44]

The hallmark of the London hearings was its concentration on the Middle East, and the appearance of the son of King Ibn Saud "in his beautiful native costume" its most vivid manifestion.[45]

Austerity was still the rule in London. The hearing room was cold, and it took a four-day battle with the Foreign Office to get Judge Hutcheson his daily ration of fresh milk.[46] But the main difference from Washington was the absence of an influential Zionist lobby. The AAC were no longer dealing primarily with the pros and cons of a political *idea* which might or might not reach fruition; they were dealing with a conflict in which the Arab states had a say and where British interests were involved. But Jewish and Zionist issues were not entirely absent.

The London hearings started on 25 January 1946 in the hall of the Royal Empire Society. Hutcheson continued to challenge demands for a Jewish state, and Crossman continued to inquire into labour problems in Palestine. In one exchange, Hutcheson attacked the notion that the Jew has no control over his own destiny:

Has there ever been in the history of the world ... an instance where two great governments organized a committee for the purpose of trying to bring help to a people that you say are scattered and without influence ... there are many sick people in the world today, the Poles are sick ... this world sickness is not a phenomenon entirely applicable to the Jews ... you ought to live in New York City, you cannot get elected without the Jewish vote.[47]

It was perhaps easier for the Judge to speak about Jewish influence while in London, since in America he would have risked the reaction of the media and the Jewish community. In London the Press was less interested in the AAC altogether. In this context he referred to his own Texan experience, claiming that "I have a very fine neighbor, living about a block from me ... He's a Jew and he doesn't seem to be impressed with the fact that I live near him, nor am I that he lives near me."[48]

The Jewish testimonies were "to say the least ... pallid."[49] Reuters in London described the Jewish witnesses as "[unable] to give a simple answer to a simple question. They never say I don't know. They never say yes or no. They always make an evasive speech [with] too much slickness."[50] The strongest pro-Zionist testimony came from Dr. James Parkes, a Protestant historian and theologian, who after describing the Jewish case for a state, concluded that assimilation would never work in an environment where the Jewish culture was on a higher level than that of their neighbours. Jewish–Slav friction in Eastern Europe would, therefore, be perpetual.[51] The Committee, however, was not impressed by Parkes's testimony.

The British Jewish Board of Deputies advocated the idea of a British Dominion in Palestine, which seemed a rather moderate position after what Hutcheson called the "rising crescendo" of the denunciation of Britain's position in Washington.[52] But on that same day, McDonald, who was used to American Jews, noted in his diary that

Brodetsky's seeming evasiveness was the inevitable result of his being unable to be frank because he dare not, in public, say some of the things which he and his colleagues would probably say to us in private.

In this context, a Foreign Office official later commented: "It is a pity that this body has gone Zionist."[53]

The Jewish Fellowship – an anti-Zionist body – also put on an impressive show at the London hearings. Its spokesmen were Sir Brunel Cohen, who had lost both his legs in the First World War, Colonel Louis Gluckstein and Colonel Tom Sebag-Montefiore. According to McDonald, "unlike Lessing Rosenwald ... [they] were distinguished looking and ... had impressive records of public service."[54] Still he challenged them as well with Graetz's and Dubnow's histories of the Jewish people. Crossman characterized Gluckstein as

the pukka sahib anti-Zionist British Jew. He stated that he thought it very poor form to pack your baggage and leave your country when things got difficult. I asked him whether he would think the same were he a Polish Jew.[55]

In all, the Jewish Agency was of the opinion that

our case was not greatly advanced in London. Those ... who were friendly in New York remained friendly here. On the other hand, the American Chairman (who, I gather, is very homesick) ... is becoming more confirmed in his opposition to a Jewish state.[56]

One marked difference between the London and Washington hearings was the fact that the Arab case was no longer championed by volunteers and academics. The Arabs were represented by Arab leaders, some of the highest rank.[57] It was also assisted by political figures such as the former M.P. General Sir Edward Sears, and the Labour M.P. Thomas Reid, a member of the 1938 Woodhead Commission. It was Spears who arranged for the Arab delegation to the London United Nations Conference to appear before the Committee ("it would be a thousand pities to lose a unique opportunity").[58] The Arab "No" to immigration and a Jewish state had far more force behind it than the one heard in Washington.[59]

Another difference in the London hearings was the appearance of former British Middle-Eastern experts and officials who could report on their first hand experience.[60] General Spears, who had been the British Minister to the Levant states, 1942–1944, and Sir Ronald Storrs, totally rejected Jewish demands in Palestine.

Spears even expressed the view that Zionism was rooted in Nazi philosophy, and reflected in the Jewish idea of expansion (*Lebensraum*), and in the Nazi-style training of youth.[61]

One of the most impressive contributions was made by Leo Amery, who outlined a plan for the partition of Palestine, in which the Jordan River and the Jordan Valley Authority would be assigned to the Arab state as compensation for the loss of the rich coastal plain to the Jews. The AAC was so impressed by his argument that discussions were held in Whitehall to the effect that the Committee should be furnished with the Provincial Autonomy Plan for Palestine to counteract Amery's partition proposals.[62] (This was the baptism of fire for the Provincial Autonomy Plan, and although not successful, it gradually gained the support of various bodies in Whitehall and was advocated more enthusiastically in July of that year. Then too it was seen as the last barrier against partition.)

The London hearings were presided over by Judge Singleton, and according to Phillips, "having formed the habit of twenty years of judgeship," he behaved as if he were going to prosecute the witnesses.[63] Lord Morrison, who was tired of Hutcheson's lengthy discussions on political philosophy, commented to Dr. Parkes – who was merely answering the Judge's question – that "this Committee has not been appointed to deliver lectures, nor to write books, nor even to read books,"[64] a comment aimed at Hutcheson. In addition, as a minor reflection, perhaps, of the differing British and American opinions of the Soviets, the Americans showed some enthusiasm over the testimony of the British Communists and described them in the warmest terms.[65]

UNANIMITY – IF NOT UNITY

Personal differences between the British and American teams became more pronounced as the work of the Committee progressed, and frictions among the members of the British contingent were common knowledge. According to Buxton, "Manningham-Buller complains to me about Crick and Crick confides in me his dislike of M.-B." and "if Sir John Singleton knew what Manningham-Buller ... says about him, a beautiful friendship would be disrupted." Leggett made a hobby of causing arguments between Manningham-Buller and Crossman, and Crossman was, altogether, the *prima inter prima donnas*. In comparison to the British, who were in general considered the brainier, more plausible, more resourceful and more articulate, the Americans at least were a unified group. This was not because they refrained from intermural gossip and grumbling, but because "their judge" was authoritative enough to overcome it.[66]

In all events, what went on among the plebs was topped by the running war between the two judges. They were constitutionally unable to get along with each other and spent much time forming "camps" to reinforce their respective positions. This "mini-war" engaged the rest of the Committee in attempts to keep the peace. According to Aydelotte:

Our two chairmen ... talk too much ... a Judge is completely master of the situation in his own courtroom. But a committee like this refuses to be dominated by any chairmen, and when you have two nations concerned the situation gets still more difficult ... Our two chairmen were ready to fight and they were backed up – Hutcheson by Buxton and Singleton ... by Manningham-Buller, though Manningham-Buller showed more real independence than Buxton who was almost a complete yes-man to the Judge.

And according to Crossman:

Two judges aren't chairmen at all but representatives of American and British isolationism at their worst. Anything which Texas Joe suggests is automatically opposed by Sir John ... and anything Sir John suggests is automatically opposed by all six Americans.

In these arguments, which usually occurred over minor issues, the American Judge regarded the attitudes of his compatriots as a matter of personal loyalty. But often a mission of mediation, usually composed of Leggett, Phillips and Aydelotte, managed to pacify the judges until the next fight broke out.[67]

Originally the Committee had intended to conduct the entire Inquiry as a team. Moreover, they planned to meet daily for organizational purposes. These daily meetings were kept up – even on board ship – until the Committee left London. But there was too much which militated against continued close teamwork: the length of the Inquiry, the repetitiveness of the sessions, the homesickness, the personal clashes, etc. When the Committee left London, they did not sit again together without witnesses until they met in

Lausanne. It was the end of any team spirit, if there had even been any to begin with.[68]

Politically, however, London was probably the most important station on their trek. For it was there that the Committee, en masse, attended a formal luncheon with Ernest Bevin and, at his behest, undertook to produce a unanimous report. On this occasion Bevin solemnly promised that if the Committee submitted a unanimous report, he would try his best to implement it.

According to Crossman's testimony, Bevin's appeal and promise made an enormous impression on the Committee, "on all of us, especially my American colleagues."[69] One can, therefore, trace the Committee's subsequent insistence upon a search for unanimity to this meeting. The outcome was, of course, crucial to the fate of the Inquiry: the AAC was forced to settle on the lowest common denominator.

What was Bevin's reason for asking for unanimity? Was it the Foreign Office who urged him to impose such a constraint in order to foil the attempt to bring the Americans into Palestine? Was it, perhaps, a sincere pledge given by Bevin in order to allay American suspicions that the Inquiry was a stalling device, "a refuge, as governments often do, in another commission," as Amery said at the hearings? Or, perhaps, Bevin made his pledge secure in the knowledge that the realities of the situation in Palestine would convince the Americans of the wisdom of British policy?[70]

Whatever the motivation, it is of little importance compared to the effect that it had on the Committee itself. And now, with unanimity, if not unity, their byword, the commissioners set out for the next lap of their mission: Europe.

NOTES

1. See Aydelotte diary, 14 Dec. 1945, and Crossman, *Palestine Mission*, p. 22.
2. Washington to Foreign Office, 15 and 18 Dec. 1945, FO 371/45389/E9828 and FO 371/45389/E9914.
3. Karlibach, *The AAC of Inquiry*, p. 8.
4. Manningham-Buller, 13 Feb. 1946, p. 2, USNA, RG 43, AAC, Box 12.
5. Crossman, in Jerusalem Hearings, 8 March 1946.
6. See report to Jewish Agency Executive on Washington Hearings, Jerusalem, 10 Feb. 1946, Jerusalem, CZA.
7. Crossman to Weizmann, Jerusalem Hearings, 8 March 1946; Crossman, *Palestine Mission*, p. 27.

8. Hutcheson to L. Marton, Rumanian delegate to the International Red Cross, Vienna, 22 Feb. 1946, USNA, RG 43, AAC, Box 1.
9. Hutcheson to Reinhold Niebuhr of the Christian Council for Palestine, Washington Hearings, 14 Jan. 1946; Hutcheson at London Hearings, 28 and 30 Jan. 1946.
10. Crossman, *Palestine Mission*, p. 27.
11. Ibid, p. 74.
12. Hutcheson to McDonald, 11 Sept. 1947, McDonald Papers, folder 187.
13. Crossman, *Palestine Mission*, pp. 40, 74, 76.
14. Washington Hearings, 14 Jan. 1946.
15. Crossman, *Palestine Mission*, pp. 73-74.
16. Hutcheson to Reinhold Niebuhr, Washington, 13 Jan. 1946. In report to Jewish Agency Executive on the Washington Hearings, 10 Feb. 1946 (Hebrew), Jerusalem, CZA.
17. Jerusalem Hearings, 8 March 1946.
18. Washington Hearings, 8 March 1946.
19. Washington Hearings, 12 Jan. 1946; report to Jewish Agency Executive, 10 Feb. 1946, Jerusalem, CZA; analysis of Notestein evidence in British Embassy Washington, to Foreign Office on Jewish Affairs in the United States, 12 March 1946, FO 371/52568/E2198.
20. Crossman, *Palestine Mission*, p. 47; McDonald diary, 11 Feb. 1946. See also Blanshard, *Aydelotte of Swarthmore*, pp. 350-351.
21. Washington Hearings, 11 Jan. 1946. See also McDonald diary, 11 Feb. 1946.
22. Halifax to Foreign Office, 13 Jan. 1946, in Washington's Weekly Political Summary, India Office, L/P & S/12/1111.
23. Washington Hearings, 10 Jan. 1946.
24. On the ACPC, see Carl Hermann Voss, "The American-Christian palestine Committee: The Mid-1940s in Retrospect, *Midstream*, June–July 1979.
25. June Bingham, *Courage to Change: The Biography of Reinhold Niebuhr*, New York, 1972, p. 284. Dodd was a revered English theologian.
26. Washington Hearings, 14 Jan. 1946.
27. Hutcheson to Philip Hitti, Washington Hearings, 11 Jan. 1946.
28. See Frank Manuel, *Realities*, p. 3.
29. Memo by Cardinal Griffin, Head of British Catholic Congregation, London, 14 Jan. 1946, pp. 3-4, FO 371/52505/E487.
30. Phillips diary, 25 Jan. 1946.
31. Phillips to Abraham Tulin of AZEC, in Tulin to Rabbi Abba H. Silver on "Our accomplishment in Washington," 17 Jan. 1946, ZANY, Tulin Papers, folder 35.
32. Washington to Foreign Office, 13 Jan. 1946, CO 537/1736.
33. Benjamin Cohen, Counsellor in the State Department, interview, Washington, May 1979.
34. Goldmann to Shertok, 20 Feb. 1946, Jerusalem, CZA, Goldmann Papers, No. Z6 Bundle 18, file 15.
35. Ben-Gurion to Zionist Executive, 24 March 1946 (Hebrew), Jerusalem, CZA. On Neumann's testimony, see Washington Hearings, 8 Jan. 1946.
36. Washington Hearings, 11 Jan. 1946; Blanchard, *Aydelotte of Swarthmore*, p. 349.
37. Crossman, *Palestine Mission*, pp. 43,45.
38. D. Horowitz to Jewish Agency Executive, 10 Feb. 1946 (Hebrew), Jerusalem, CZA.
39. Crossman to Robert Nathan, 7 Jan. 1946, Washington Hearings.
40. McDonald to Lessing Rosenwald, President of the anti-Zionist American Council for Judaism, Washington Hearings, 10 Jan. 1946.
41. Crossman, *Palestine Mission*, p. 30.
42. Hutcheson to Judge Proskauer of the American Jewish Committee, Washington

Hearings, 9 Jan. 1946; Hutcheson to Niebuhr, Washington Hearings, 14 Jan. 1946; see also Hutcheson to Dr. M. Roydon, London Hearings, 29 Jan. 1946.

43. *Palestine Mission*, p. 47.
44. Crossman to R.I.I.A., London, 13 June 1946, SACMEC, Crossman Papers.
45. William Phillips, *Ventures in Diplomacy*, p. 278.
46. Crossman, *Palestine Mission*, p. 60.
47. Hutcheson to Dr. James Parkes, London Hearings, 30 Jan. 1946.
48. Hutcheson to Professor Selig Brodetsky of the British Jewish Board of Deputies, London Hearings, 25 Jan. 1946.
49. Horowitz, *State in the Making*, p. 62.
50. Reuters London to Reuters Jerusalem, 2 Feb. 1946. Copy in Jerusalem, CZA, No. S25/6450.
51. London Hearings, 30 Jan. 1946. Parkes undertook research for Chatham House on the Palestine question.
52. Hutcheson to Selig Brodetsky, London, 25 Jan. 1946; Crossman, *Palestine Mission*, p. 68.
53. Comment by Baxter, 16 May 1946, on the Board's attitude towards the AAC Report, FO 371/52521/E4197.
54. McDonald diary, 30 Jan. 1946.
55. Excerpt from Crossman diary, quoted in Bernard Wasserstein "Richard Crossman and the New Jerusalem," *Midstream*, April 1975, p. 47.
56. Zionist Office, London, 3 Feb. 1946, report of Abraham Linton, Jerusalem, CZA, no. Z4/15440.
57. Prince Faisal Ibn Abdul Aziz of Saudi Arabia; Farris Bey al-Khurry, President of the Syrian Chamber of Deputies; Hamid Bey Frangieyeh, Foreign Minister of Lebanon, McDonald diary, 1 Feb. 1946.
58. Spears to Colonel Wadi of the London Iraqi Legation, 14 Jan. 1946, SACMEC, Spears Papers, Box 4, file 3.
59. See McDonald diary, 1 February 1946.
60. Lord Samuel, the first High Commissioner for Palestine; Ronald Storrs, the first Governor of Jerusalem; Sir Hubert Young, the head of the Colonial Office's Eastern Dept.; Leo Amery, the Colonial Secretary, 1924–1929.
61. London Hearings, 20 Jan. 1946.
62. See discussions in Colonial Office, Jan. 1946, CO 537/1754.
63. Phillips diary, 7 Feb. 1946.
64. London Hearings, 30 Jan. 1946.
65. Ibid, 1 Feb. 1946. See also Phillips, *Ventures in Diplomacy*, p. 278.
66. Buxton to Frankfurter, 15 Feb. and 25 June 1946, Frankfurter Papers, container 40; Leggett to G. Cohen, interview, London, 5 Dec. 1960.
67. Crossman diary, Lausanne, undated, SACMEC, Crossman Papers; Aydelotte diary, 12 and 20 April 1946. See also Buxton to Frankfurter, 4 April 1946, Frankfurter Papers, container 40; Blanshard, *Aydelotte of Swarthmore*, p. 362.
68. Aydelotte diary, 4 March 1946; McDonald diary for the period of 18-23 Jan. 1946 and previous entries for the pre-Washington Hearings period; Phillips diary, Vienna, 23 Feb. and 1 April 1946. See also Crossman, *Palestine Mission*, p. 83.
69. Crossman, *Palestine Mission*, p. 66.
70. Sykes, *Crossroads to Israel*, p. 343.

8

Europe: A Bird's Eye View of Misery

The arrival of the members of the Committee in Europe after a month of theoretical discussions, and their confrontation with Jewish suffering in the flesh, proved a most shocking experience, one which haunted them long afterwards. Although they visited different areas, divided as they were into sub-committees, their overall impressions were of a similar nature.

Not all of the commissioners and their staff actually kept to the schedule. Aydelotte, Crossman and Beeley, the British secretary, all came down with colds and stayed behind in London for some time. Wilson, the American secretary, was dispatched to Cairo to prepared for the AAC's visit there toward the end of February. In Europe, Phillips fell ill in Frankfurt, and McDonald apparently took time off to pursue some personal pleasures (he was said to have been last seen in a row boat on Lake Constance) and was even attacked by Crum "for gallivanting round Europe on his own and for his own amusement."[1] But singly or in groups they did visit the major DP centres in France and in the American, British and French Zones of Germany and Austria. They also went to Poland and Czechoslovakia and there met with the representatives of other Eastern European communities. Finally, the full Committee was reassembled in Vienna to prepare the European chapter of the AAC Report. And a sub-committee stopped off in Italy afterwards.

IS RE-INTEGRATION POSSIBLE?

Before arriving on the Continent, the Committee had circulated a questionnaire among the DPs which was designed to give some indication of their present and future hopes and requirements.[2] The questionnaire asked for statistical data concerning the total numbers of Jews in the camps, their nationality, their origin and their ultimate destination. It also asked about conditions affecting Jewish re-integration in Europe and about the DPs preferred place of residence. In relation to this last point, interviewers were advised that "Questions should not be so phrased as to suggest any particular answer, nor should opportunity be given for an answer which reflects ... a haven which on any one day might be rumored in the community to be the best."[3] The questionnaire also dealt with housing, diet, bedding, clothing, medical services, facilities for locating relatives, employment opportunities, etc. The aim was "to get some idea about what the people themselves want, and not argue about their disposal as if they were cattle."[4] The census was carried out by the Control Commissions in the British and U.S. Zones, with the aid of the military units stationed there and the UNRRA authorities. The information submitted to the AAC was then classified according to its degree of reliability, and analysed to provide precise statistics. It was found, for example, that 90 per cent of those questioned wanted to emigrate to Palestine, whereas only 6 per cent preferred America. The main factors working against Jewish re-integration in Europe were listed as unhappy memories, the anti-Semitic attitude of the public and a fear of personal violence. The abnormality of camp life and a critical shortage of shoes led the list of Major Complaints.[5] With regard to nationality, none of the Jews questioned were native-born Germans or Austrians: the overwhelming majority were Polish.[6]

Later in Lausanne the AAC was briefed by military representatives and given up-to-date information on the DP problem. Thus, the personal meetings with camp inmates, the information available through the survey, and the later meeting with the Military, all furnished the Committee with fairly comprehensive information about the DPs.[7]

The various sub-committees in Germany visited DP centres around Hanover, Hamburg and Munich, as well as Jewish orphanages and homes for the aged. At a farm previously owned by Julius Streicher, the publisher of the vicious anti-Semitic Nazi weekly *Der Stuermer*, the AAC met a group of young Jews preparing to emigrate to Palestine and settle as a kibbutz.[8] McDonald made a similar visit to a kibbutz-style group in Biberach camp, near Ulm and Stuttgart, and the two judges visited the Army Headquarters in Berlin.[9] Gradually the picture of the displaced Jews lost its polemical and abstract aspect and became a reality, perhaps even too much so, with reactions to the "penetrating smell" and comparisons with the Germans: "How much cleaner they are than the Jewish people."[10]

The initial attitudes of the Committee members towards the displaced Jew, and his demand to leave the Continent to settle in Palestine, were equivocal and not entirely sympathetic. The judges felt that

if this general cry of Zionism ... could be piped down some ... these German Jews would like to rebuild again. The main trouble in Europe is coming from the Jewish people, particularly the Zionists; if some way could be found to get these fanatics into Palestine, it would be temporarily for the good of the world, though what would happen afterwards I don't know.[11]

From Germany the sub-committees moved to Austria where, in addition to excursions, they met with the Chancellor and with the Ministers for the Interior and Education. A rather depressing meeting was held with the Kultusgemeinde, the central body of Austrian Jewry. According to Crossman, "a prosperous looking lawyer, a crippled old soldier and a thin and threadbare minor official," were brought in, "the wreckage of a proud and prosperous community."[12] The question of property restitution dominated the meeting in which Judge Hutcheson lectured them on how "we in America would go about restoring titles to property illegally taken away from somebody."[13]

After visiting the Jewish home for the aged and the Rothschild Hospital, the AAC interviewed the Catholic Bishop of Austria, who claimed that "we do not fight against the Jews, only against the Jewish spirit," and accused the Kultusgemeinde of collaboration with the Gestapo. Here Hutcheson ruled out counter-questions which he believed to be "irrelevant, immaterial and inconsequential." He also warned the interpreter not to disclose what he was going to say and stated that the Jews should have their synagogues, but in segregating and creating social or cultural organizations, they only caused anti-Semitism and made life unbearable for themselves. (The interpreter reported this to the Jewish Agency the next day.)[14]

The Austrian sub-committee also heard evidence from representatives of Jewish communities in Eastern Europe about conditions then prevailing in the Communist-controlled countries. The participation of Jews in the new regimes, including the Party and the police, had introduced a new kind of anti-Semitism. "He [Hitler] lost the war and now the Jews are ruling us," was the way one witness summed up common sentiment in Hungary and Rumania.[15]

In their reports, each member of the sub-committee on Austria took one aspect and analysed it: Buxton dealt with housing and overcrowded living conditions; Crick described hospital and health facilities, noting that on the whole they were satisfactory "although some people have to be literally taught to use ordinary mechanical arrangements in the lavatories."[16] The overall Austrian report was then prepared by Manningham-Buller, and the emphases here were different:

The Jews were not armed . . . the bad hats had been weeded out. The flats . . . were good with two or three rooms, bathroom, kitchen, etc. The only genuine anti-Semitism in Austria before the war was due to Jewish monopoly of certain businesses such as banking and of certain professions . . . especially to the difficulty for a non-Jew in getting admitted as a doctor, owing to Jews securing their admission to the limited number of places by bribery. The occupants used different names and papers . . . a pretty common practice among the Jews . . . the people would disappear from the camp and their points cards would be handed over to new arrivals. The Jews have money. Some go to the theatre and pay for their tickets, and some engage in black-market activities. The fact that their basic ration is larger than that of the local population enables them to exchange some part of their ration . . . for money. Anti-Semitism was primarily due to the fact that the DPs enjoyed the best hotels and a bigger ration than the rest of the community.[17]

The German and Austrian experience did not, therefore, yield the unanimously positive attitude which the AAC Report finally took towards the displaced Jew. It was the inquiry in Poland which overshadowed all the above impressions.

But in the centres in Germany and Austria, other aspects of the Jewish DP problem came to light. The preferential treatment given to Jews, for example, had made their camps attractive to non-Jewish refugees, and the Army was forced to screen newcomers, giving them a Yiddish test. Also, according to a military source, "the people in the centres will do a good job themselves. If a Gentile came in saying he was a Jew, he would have a hard time."[18]

The American military were, on the whole, rather apologetic in the explanations of their relations with the Jewish DPs. They attributed Jewish migration from the Communist countries into the western zones to the "lack of opportunity for the Jews in their old sphere." The American authorities insisted that the massive movement into their zones should not be ascribed to connivance on their part, but to the fact that "it happens it is on the route to Palestine."[19] This apologetic mode was repeated throughout the entire investigation and was due to the fear of the military that they might be severely criticized again; Buxton reported that there was

an echo of Earl Harrison in all Army quarters, plus the resulting uneasiness that perhaps this Committee will also make an adverse report . . . Two American generals whose areas we examined were so jittery that I rather pitied them.[20]

The AAC pointed to the bribery and corruption among the UNRRA and military officials who dealt with the DPs.[21] Together with the Committee's claim that clothing stored in Army warehouses never reached the DPs because of administrative problems, this resulted in an increase in the Army's uneasiness.[22] The unsettled atmosphere was highlighted in a conversation with a British colonel "who explained that the Jews are the great danger to our civilization and that we should deal with them as the Americans dealt with the Negroes."[23]

Manningham-Buller's main criticism, however, was directed at the lack of coordination between Britain and the United States in handling the question:

The American authorities in Austria are definitely facilitating the flow of migrants from Vienna onwards . . . It radically conflicts with British policy, which is to discourage the flow of these migrants, and it is highly regrettable that the two English-speaking communities should follow such divergent practices and, it should seem, without both of them kept fully aware of what the other was doing . . . It was apparent to me that many of the American officers . . . were also keen Zionists . . . My inability to secure any accurate information as to the movement of Jews . . . leads me to the conclusion that they have a shrewd suspicion of what occurs, but that it might be embarrassing to them to possess accurate knowledge.[24]

The Anglo-American rift over the DP problem was also mirrored in Truman's complaint that "the British are suppressing information with respect to our contributions: the average man in the countries being benefitted by our shipments of food supplies is totally ignorant of such supplies."[25] Moreover, Britain refused to permit the United States to establish consulates in the British Zones.[26]

The Committee was also puzzled by the difference in the British and U.S. governments' reports on the situation of Jews in Eastern Europe. British reports pointed to a lack of discrimination in Hungary, to a waning of the Palestinian incentive concomitant with economic and social re-integration in Rumania, and a belief that "Poland offers no cause for panic or mass exodus."[27] The State Department, on the other hand, reported that "unlike Polish Jewry, anti-Semitism did not perish in Poland." It further drew attention to a sharp increase of anti-Semitism and an increase in the numbers wanting to go to Palestine from Hungary, as well as the fact that Jews were in a worse position than any other citizens in Bulgaria.[28]

Another aspect of the European stage of the AAC was the role the Zionists played on it. In every country visited, a Zionist–Jewish body was set up to present the Jewish Agency case. Representatives of the Joint, the UNRRA and the I.G.C.R. (Inter-Governmental Committee on Refugees) were sounded out before being brought to the AAC. People who were suspected of holding non-Zionist views were "spirited away" from the camps before the arrival of the Committee.[29] Other witnesses were manipulated:

Morrison asked ... to see two left-wing Jews, anti-Zionists. He had a bad conscience since he had seen only Zionist Jews all over Europe. We heard it just in time and we took care that two "appropriate" Communists would appear before him and would be able to assure him that they, too, were for free immigration and a Jewish commonwealth in Palestine.[30]

In Vienna and Lodz the Zionists organized demonstrations near the Committee's lodgings, and attempts by British, American and Russian military police to break them up only ended in "dramatic incidents" during the resulting confusion.[31] In Italy, Jewish demonstrators carried banners derogatory to the AAC; Phillips confided to his diary: "It was shocking to see small children, not much above the baby age, marching two and two carrying their banner." In Bari car tyres belonging to Committee members' cars were punctured.[32]

As time drew on, Judge Hutcheson grew more and more impatient with details, and the shift from abstract discussions to a confrontation with reality caused him even greater consternation. Phillips noted that he continued to be very homesick and his ambition was to shorten our program so that we may be ready to work on the final Report before the end of March. He believed that little can be accomplished by our sub-Committees in Germany and rather that much time will be lost in the effort.[33]

According to Crossman, the Judge considered that the whole matter of Jewish migration from East to West could be settled on the "Texan model," by closing the frontier and deporting any Jew who crossed it.[34]

As for the Committee as a whole, according to Crossman, "whenever [it] dispersed, its corporate spirit rapidly disappeared."[35] Relations between the British and the Americans had not improved and Hutcheson was the only American who met the British socially.[36]

The European experience, however, did affect the thinking of the Committee members. Gradually the British were said to have become "reconciled to a bold stroke," and, after the depressing encounter with the DPs, ready to recommend large scale immigration to Palestine.[37] "Texas Joe," who was reported to "be bristling with anti-Zionist fervour," had been mollified when confronted with the human side of the problem.[38] Crossman described the final effect of Germany and Austria as follows:

The first and most important lesson [was] the impossibility of maintaining any contact between the displaced Jew and the British and American peoples ... Policies which seemed sane enough in the White House or in Downing Street struck these wretched people as sadistic brutality. Measures which made sense to them appeared to busy British and American politicians downright unreasonable ... We had not really touched the reality of camp life, but had seen a bird's eye view of it, circling above its misery and claustrophobia. But even this ... had made us wish that the policy makers ... before they came to any more decisions, could at least do what we had done.[39]

There was another aspect of the problem which gradually possessed the AAC. The commissioners were witness to a process whereby DPs – with whom they could not communicate, and whose thoughts they could not completely decipher – were wandering across the Continent, disappearing from one area and reappearing in another, in a movement beyond the Army's control. It was like a nightmare, and nobody knew how many people were involved. One U.S. general considered this movement of undocumented masses as the seeds of World War III.[40] Leggett observed that they "were likely to break camp, wander about and become a problem for the military forces."[41] And Crossman became metaphorical: "This mysterious migration behaved just like water on a hillside after a heavy storm … nothing can stop it permanently unless the water is dammed at the top or the rain stops."[42] It seemed that many feared that the entire DP population would combine to raid the West in the style of the Huns, with the Jews serving as the spearhead for the penetration of Bolshevik ideas.[43] The first aim, therefore, was to put some kind of halt to this wandering, which would freeze the situation and create a legally manageable "melting pot" subject to a *sub-judice* situation, thus enabling the AAC to find a solution.[44] It was believed that if the Jewish DP camps could be closed on the basis of the poor "absorption capacity of Bavaria," i.e., its inability to house all the Jewish migrants, then perhaps the wandering would stop.[45]

POLAND: A HAUNTED GRAVEYARD

As noted before, the AAC's visit to Poland obscured all other impressions and attitudes, both those gained in Europe and those soon to be gained in the Middle East. The problem of Palestine was to take second place. After seeing human ashes and bones in Warsaw, and even finding urns containing ashes in their hotel rooms, the Committee could write that "we can well understand and sympathise with the intense desire of the surviving Jews to depart from localities so full of such poignant memories."[46] This recommendation was made by the same people who had persistently opposed Jewish demands to leave Europe.

The sub-committee that visited Poland included Crick, Buxton and Manningham-Buller. According to Crick, meetings with Polish officials and Jewish witnesses were held in "an atmosphere of conspiracy, lawlessness, violence, robbery, forces of foreign power, espionage and Government disliked by most and loathed by many."[47] Conversations with the Polish Prime Minister, his Foreign Minister, the Polish Plenipotentiary for Repatriation, and the governor of the Bank of Poland all gave the impression of an attentive and considerate regime which was nevertheless helpless in the face of Polish hatred of the Jews.[48] The British and U.S. embassies in Poland, which provided the sub-committee with preparatory evidence, considered the prediction of a quarter of a million Jews in Poland within five years as "nonsense." They also refuted the claim that without Zionist instigation Jews would not have left Poland: "The Jews are resolved to clear out of here and they will do so," stated the Ambassador.[49]

In a two hour interview, the sub-committee listened to the views of Rabbi Kahane, the acting Chief Rabbi of Poland and the Chief Rabbi of the Polish Army. The witness, described by the First Secretary of the British Embassy as "the best they had yet come across," was one of the last ten rabbis in Poland. The forty-five year old Kahane, who was not a Zionist, and was not considered as one by the Embassy, painted a shocking picture of Polish Jewry:

> The vested interest of the Christian Polish trading classes predisposed them violently against the resurgence of the Jew in Polish national life … The atmosphere of terror was too strong; particularly in the outlying villages and in the small towns, where the Jewish community might number at most twenty people, the danger was too great. Pogroms were an everyday occurrence … Synagogues were destroyed, Jewish families burned in their homes, Jews removed from passenger vehicles … and murdered by the roadside. They had even resuscitated the age old libel of ritual-murder; a child had disappeared in a small town near Lublin, someone had talked of ritual murder; two days later the entire Jewish community, consisting of nine persons, had been burned in their house.[50]

For the sub-committee, the importance of this statement lay in the fact that it was entirely confirmed by the Embassy, which even considered the witness to be too optimistic: "His opinion is of greater value than mine, but I should be surprised if there are as many as 50,000 Jews in this country in January 1948."[51]

From Warsaw the sub-committee moved to Lodz, where it heard witnesses and watched German films which had been shown to the Poles during the Nazi occupation in order to promote anti-Semitism – "able pieces of work," according to Manningham-Buller.[52] Later, in front of the Grand Hotel where the sub-committee stayed, 2,000 people demonstrated with banners and flags, demanding free emigration and admission to Palestine.[53]

Towards the end of the visit to Poland, the three commissioners put their separate impressions down on paper, thus creating the "Polish folder," which was later copied and distributed among the rest of the AAC. The conclusions of the sub-committee were unequivocal: any recommendations to remedy basic conditions in

Poland would be futile since anti-Semitism and widespread lawlessness were the rule.[54]

The sub-committee concluded that a considerable amount of education would be needed to elevate the Jewish survivors to a level where they could play a useful part in a civilized community. They did not rule out Palestine as a place where this training could be given. And in the context of emigration to Palestine Manningham-Buller – already convinced that the Jews must leave Poland – wrote: "While I doubt whether an organization had been created from outside to assist these people to get out of the country, I think it likely that a grapevine had come into existence."[55] This was a different Manningham-Buller from the one who had written the Austrian report. Still, his suspicions of the Russians were never quieted:

We visited one reception centre in Lodz ... the manager spoke only Russian. He was assisted by a corporal who spoke only Russian, and accompanying us on our tour of the premises was another person who spoke only Russian. It would have been a brave man or woman who said anything to us which conflicted with Russian desires ... The Russians may want this migration from Poland because it will create difficulties for the British and Americans in Europe and accentuate the situation with regard to Palestine, and because they fear the influence and propaganda in Poland of a large number of Jews who have seen the inside of the USSR.[56]

This British obsession with Russia was made light of by the American Buxton, who reported in a letter to Frankfurter that he had warned Manningham-Buller to "look under the bed ... to make sure he wasn't sleeping over a Russian bear," adding: "I've become a vulgar American, Felix, and love the role."[57]

Another sub-committee visited Prague, although the Czechoslovak authorities had been initially reluctant to receive the Committee. Fearing a loss of "face" and "prestige" if two outside powers came to investigate their internal affairs, the Czech Foreign Secretary finally accepted the British Ambassador's assertion that "now that U.N.O. had arrived, countries must really be prepared to accept some degree of limitation in their sovereignty."[58]

Crum and Leggett, who formed the Czechoslovak sub-committee, conducted a series of meetings with representatives of the Jews in Slovakia and Bohemia–Moravia. The country had become a transit camp for refugees fleeing from Poland, and the Czechs were eager to hear the Committee's views on this problem.

Crum and Leggett suggested moving people from the camps in Germany to Palestine, since

> once such a movement began the Jews in other parts of Europe would realize that the hope of eventual immigration to Palestine was not a mere chimera, and would be content to wait more patiently where they are instead of flocking desperately ... into the British and American Zones.[59]

This was a different Leggett from the one who had previously considered the DPs' Zionist attitudes as living proof of General Spears's allegations about the Nazi character of Zionism.[60]

At the Prague meetings, Crum was reported to have asked Communist Czech officials their opinion about Russia's attitude to Jewish migration, and to have asked others whether they regarded the Czechoslovak Government as a benevolent administration. "Not unnaturally he received no reply ... Sir Frederick Leggett and I found [it] embarrassing, though the former tells me that he is used to this sort of talk by his colleague."[61]

The Committee's journey back to Austria was interrupted when the commissioners were arrested by the Czech authorities. This followed an American military raid into the heart of Czechoslovakia to look for the documents of the gangster Karl Hermann Frank, the German Sudeten Nazi leader. After a short while the group was released. Leggett fell asleep during the detention, causing one committee member to comment: "What does a Britisher do in time of crisis? Falls asleep!"[62]

Towards the second half of February the entire Committee assembled in Vienna to discuss the European inquiry. The sick had recovered and even McDonald was located. The question of an interim report was at stake and the impressions left by the camps and Poland were still strong. Nevertheless, the call of those who had toured Czechoslovakia to clear the camps and send the inmates to Palestine did not win the support of the full Committee. As a matter of fact, it almost split them in half, when Singleton insisted on an interim report recommending only the closure of the camps. "A gentle hint from above" reminded Hutcheson that Truman wanted a report recommending immigration to Palestine.[63] If such a report could not be submitted, he preferred to have no report at all. "I'm for emptying the camps," he said, "and for people going to Palestine. I don't give a damn about what the Arabs think. But *now* it is impossible to recommend it."[64] The AAC decided, therefore, not to issue a report, and harmony was preserved.

The commisioners proceeded to the Middle East still moved by what they had seen in Europe. They could not yet alleviate the conditions of the DPs, but it had become only a question of time.

THE SOVIET ENIGMA

The inquiry into the situation of the Jews in Europe omitted the largest concentration of Jews, the more than 2.5 million in the Soviet Union and its satellite states in Eastern Europe. It was clear that the U.S.S.R. was described as holding "many of the important cards in the Palestine situation [since] they control most of the exportable Jews of Europe."[65] The inability of Britain to reach a firm conclusion regarding Russia's Palestine policy was characteristic of their post-war crisis, and resulted in their surprise at Russia's support for the U.N. partition resolution of 1947.[66]

In one of Britain's first assessments of post-war Russia's attitude towards Palestine, they anticipated that the Soviets would reject the AAC's request to inquire in their areas, and in this context there was little doubt that they were anti-Zionist:

They were opposed, on principle, to any movement, secular or religious, which may confront any section of the population, however small, with problems of conflicting loyalties. In addition, the Soviet Union now regards itself as a Great Moslem power.[67]

This became the cornerstone of post-war British attempts to analyse Moscow's policy. The Soviets' so-called anti-Zionism was interpreted as the other side of a pro-Arab policy, and the initial approach to them suggested that the AAC was not established in order to assist Jewish migration into Palestine. On the contrary – as they informed Moscow:

Insofar as they can enable the Committee to realize that the Jews in their territories (or in territories controlled by them) do not, repeat not, either need or desire to go to Palestine, they will to that extent be assisting the Arabs.[68]

The Soviets rejected this overture, stressing in their reply the absence of any "manifestations of racial discrimination," and their anger at the fact that they had been excluded from and not informed about "the creation, purpose and function" of the AAC.[69]

Moscow's plea of "official ignorance," the way in which the Soviet press avoided the subject of Zionism, and Soviet refusal to grant access to the AAC were all interpreted by the British Chargé d'Affaires in Moscow as bearing out the argument "that the Soviet Government are as firmly opposed as ever to Zionism."[70] But when a similar analysis was applied to a lecture given by Lutski, the Soviet expert on Palestine, on Zionist ambitions for a Jewish "bourgeois state" in Palestine, the ambiguousness of Russia's actions became evident. The fact that he was allowed to say what he did suggested to some observers that the Soviets were preparing to come out in support of the Arabs against the Zionists. But, on the other hand, the fact that the Soviet press, in its coverage, was reluctant to side with the Arabs and suppressed all reference to the lecturer's condemnation of Zionism, indicated a much less clear-cut conclusion, suggesting at best that the Soviets were sitting on the fence.[71] This feeling increased when repeated reports pointed to active Soviet involvement in illegal immigration and were expressed in comments like:

The Russians are out to win the Arabs' good opinion, and if it becomes known that they are not even enforcing their own regulations to prevent illegal immigration, their stock will go down accordingly.[72]

Russia was in some ways the key to Britain's post-war foreign policy, although the subject is beyond the scope of this book, and the Russian aspect of Britain's Middle Eastern policy will not be discussed in the context of the AAC. There is no evidence that Moscow had any influence on the Committee, save the feeling that the Russians were standing in the background, ready to exploit a western mistake. Some parallel did exist, however, between the equivocation which stemmed from the support given to illegal immigration and the uncertainty about Russia's policy in the Middle East as a whole. Russian criticism of Britain's Palestine policy, however strong, was considered to be based on a recognition of Britain's position there (unlike their attitude in other world theatres). It was designed only "to cause as much discomfort for the British ... so as to keep them occupied and give them less time to contemplate or devise anything against Russia."[73] It was a fact that Stalin had shortly before expressed his reluctance to Bevin to see a British retreat from Egypt since "it would be a disadvantage to everyone."[74]

British attempts to evaluate contradictory Russian moves were further hindered by the fact that the Soviets concentrated on campaigning against "British Imperialism" in the Middle East, while taking a milder attitude towards U.S. interests there. It took the British nearly a year to convince the Americans that Russia's basic Middle Eastern policy aimed at weakening both their influences in the area.[75] This understanding was not felt in the traffic of Jewish DPs into Palestine. America supported this traffic, and it looked to Britain as if the United States were "unwittingly cooperating with the U.S.S.R. to embarrass HMG in their exercise of the Palestine Mandate ... which is critical for the whole Middle East."[76]

NOTES

1. Crossman to Mrs. Zita Crossman, 28 Feb. 1946, SACMEC, Crossman Papers; also *Palestine Mission*, p. 83; McDonald diary (folder 14) Feb. 1946. He visited tourist sites, attended ballet and opera performances and some sessions of the Nuremburg Trials.
2. See Chapter 6.
3. Memo outlining the matters to be examined by the AAC in Europe, 15 Jan. 1946, FO 371/52507/E801.
4. G. Henderson, Foreign Office, 7 Oct. 1945, FO 473/45380/E7479.
5. Findings for the AAC in British and U.S. Zones, FO 945/383, 14 Feb. 1946, and FO 945/655, undated.
6. See answers of Allied Commission for Austria (British Element), New York, UN Archives UNRRA files, Box 52071, file no B/JR/2/Austria.
7. See USNA, RG 43, AAC, Box 12; USNA, State Dept. Palestine material, 1946, Box 6754, No. 867N. 01/3.
8. Jewish Telegraphic Agency, 15 Feb. 1946.
9. McDonald diary, 11 Feb. 1946.
10. Report on visit of AAC to Seegasse camp near Vienna, p. 3, Jerusalem, CZA, No S25/6453.
11. Hutcheson on visits to DP camps in Germany, 13 Feb. 1946, and on visit to Berlin, 14 Feb. 1946, McDonald Papers, Box 15 (Europe).
12. *Palestine Mission*, pp. 100-101.
13. Report by the Committee interpreter in Vienna, 22 Feb. 1946, Jerusalem, CZA S25/6453.
14. Ibid., p. 3; also report by Crossman on visit to Vienna, p. 2, undated, USNA, RG 43, AAC, Box 12.
15. Testimony of Dr. Ernst Marton, Rumanian Delegation to the Red Cross, Vienna, 22 Feb. 1946, USNA, RG 43, AAC, Box 1.
16. Visit of sub-committee to U.S. zone, Austria, 19-21 Feb. 1946, pp. 9,10, USNA, RG 43, AAC, Box 12.
17. Report on visit in Austria, 25 Feb. 1946, p. 2, ibid.
18. U.S. Military to AAC, Lausanne, 9 April 1946, p. 6, Hutcheson Papers.
19. Ibid., pp. 18, 46.
20. Buxton to Frankfurter, Vienna, 24 Feb. 1946, Frankfurter Papers, container 40.

21. McDonald diary, 5 Feb. 1946.
22. AAC meeting with the Military, Lausanne, 9 April 1946, p. 2, Hutcheson Papers.
23. Crossman to Mrs. Zita Crossman, 28 Feb. 1946, SACMEC, Crossman Papers.
24. Manningham-Buller, Austria report, 25 Feb. 1946, p. 4, USNA, RG 43, AAC, Box 12.
25. Truman to U.S. Cabinet, 3 May 1946, Truman Library, papers of Matthew J. Connelly, Secretary to the President, Set 1, Box 1 – Notes on Cabinet meetings.
26. AAC meeting with Chief of Visa Dept., U.S. Dept. of State, 19 Feb. 1946, USNA, RG 43, AAC, Box 1.
27. Foreign Office: Position of Jewish Communities in East Europe, 24 Jan. 1946, material submitted to the AAC, USNA, RG 43, AAC, Box 4.
28. Ibid., Dept. of State, Intelligence Research Report, 15 May 1946; American Legation, Budapest, to AAC, 25 March 1946; American Legation, Sofia to AAC, 3 April 1946. For a comprehensive report prepared by the Dept. of State for the use of the AAC on Jewish survivors in post-war Europe, 3 Dec. 1945, see USNA, RG 43, AAC, Box 5.
29. Bauer, *Flight and Rescue*, p. 202.
30. Gideon Roufer to Jewish Agency, Vienna, 25 Feb. 1946 (Hebrew), Jerusalem, CZA, No. S25/6453.
31. U.S. Political Adviser, Vienna, to Dept. of State, 28 Feb. 1946, USNA State Dept. Palestine correspondence, 1946, Box 6753, no. 867 N 01/2-2846; also Bauer, *Flight and Rescue*, p. 202.
32. Phillips diary, Bari, Italy, 26 Feb. 1946.
33. Phillips diary, 3 Feb. 1946.
34. To Mrs. Zita Crossman, 28 Feb. 1946, SACMEC, Crossman Papers.
35. *Palestine Mission*, p. 83.
36. Report to the Jewish Agency, Vienna, 22 Feb. 1946, Jerusalem, CZA, No. S25/6453.
37. Singleton to Buxton, in Buxton to Frankfurter, Berlin, 15 Feb. 1946, Frankfurter Papers, container 40.
38. Crossman to Mrs. Zita Crossman, 28 Feb. 1946, SACMEC, Crossman Papers.
39. *Palestine Mission*, p. 85.
40. Washington to Foreign Office, 2 Jan. 1946, on General Morgan's allegations about organization standing behind this movement, FO 945/655.
41. To U.S. Commanders, Lausanne, 9 April 1946, p. 11, Hutcheson Papers.
42. *Palestine Mission*, p. 93.
43. G. Roufer to Jewish Agency on AAC Hearings, Vienna, 21 Feb. 1946, p. 3, Jerusalem, CZA, S25/6453.
44. AAC Report, p. 14; comment of Foreign Office Refugee Dept., 23 Oct. 1945, FO 371/51125/WR3209; Refugee Dept., MacKillop, 25 Feb. 1946, FO 371/57759/WR 552.
45. Dr. Goldmann to Jewish Agency Executive, 19 March 1946, Jerusalem, CZA.
46. Jewish Telegraphic Agency, 19 Feb. 1946; AAC Report, p. 13; G. Roufer to the Jewish Agency, 21 Feb. 1946, p. 2, Jerusalem, CZA, No. S25/6453; AAC Report, p. 13.
47. Berlin, 14 Feb. 1946, USNA, RG 43, AAC, Box 12.
48. Details on meetings in the "Polish file", USNA RG 43, AAC, Box 1; report by British Ambassador, Cavendish-Bentinck, to Foreign Office, 20 Feb. 1946, Annex I & II, FO 371/57688/WR736.
49. Cavendish-Bentinck to Foreign Office, 20 Feb. 1946, FO 371/57688/WR736.
50. Report of J.W. Russell, First Secretary, Warsaw Embassy, to Ambassador Cavendish-Bentinck, in Warsaw to Foreign Office, 20 Feb. 1946, Annex I, FO 371/57688/WR736. Russell commented on Rabbi Kahane's age: "This in itself is a

good illustration of what has happened to Polish Jewry ... the average age of any rabbinical college ... before 1939 was somewhere in the neighbourhood of 65." Ibid.

51. Ibid.
52. Report on visit to Poland, 13 Feb. 1946, USNA RG 43, AAC, Box 12.
53. Karlibach, *The AAC of Inquiry*, p. 279; Bauer, *Flight and Rescue*, p. 202.
54. Buxton report on Poland, 16 Feb. 1946, USNA, RG 43, AAC, Box 12.
55. Report by Manningham-Buller, 13 Feb. 1946, p. 4, ibid.
56. Ibid., p. 3.
57. Buxton to Felix Frankfurter, 15 Feb. 1946, Frankfurter Papers, container 40.
58. Prague to Foreign Office, 28 Jan. 1946 and 5 Feb. 1946, FO 371/52508/E1098 and FO 371/52509/E1201.
59. In Prague, Ambassador Shuckburgh, to Bevin, 18 Feb. 1946, FO 371/52511/E1760.
60. Crum, *Behind the Silken Curtain*, p. 87.
61. Prague to Foreign Office, 18 Feb. 1946, FO 371/52511/E1760.
62. Leggett to G. Cohen, interview, London, 5 Dec. 1960. On the arrest, see Shuckburgh to Foreign Office, 16 Feb. 1946, FO 371/56035/N2278.
63. G. Roufer to Jewish Agency, 21 Feb. 1946, Jerusalem, CZA, S25/6449; Aydelotte diary, 19 April 1946, p. 16.
64. Conversation between Crum and Hutcheson, in Roufer to Jewish Agency, 25 Feb. 1946 (Hebrew), Jerusalem, CZA, S25/6453, emphasis mine.
65. Memo by J. Bennet, Foreign Office, International Relations Dept., 26 Jan. 1946, CO 537/1459.
66. See also Evan Wilson, "Where We Went Wrong," in *Decision on Palestine*, p. 157.
67. Frank Roberts, Chargé D'Affaires in Moscow, to Foreign Office, 14 Jan. 1946, FO 371/52506/E620. See also Moscow Embassy files, FO 181/1010, Palestine, Part I, unsigned and undated minutes regarding the request for access for the AAC.
68. Draft of telegram no. 228 to Moscow, 24 Jan. 1946, FO 371/52506/E560. The final copy had a different wording.
69. In Moscow to Foreign Office, 16 Feb. 1946, FO 371/52507/E761.
70. Moscow to Northern Dept., Foreign Office, on Soviet Attitude Towards Jews, 25 Feb. 1946, FO 371/56851/N2954/1481/38; Frank Roberts to Foreign Office, 14 Jan. 1946, FO 371/52506/E620.
71. Moscow, Sir M. Peterson, to Foreign Office, 22 July 1946, FO 371/52543/E6962.
72. Comment by Morgan, Eastern Dept., Foreign Office, 5 April 1946, following the sailing from Constanza of the steamer *Smyrna* with 1,500 immigrants, FO 371/52514/E3089/G. See also suggestion by Campbell, Cairo, 2 Aug. 1946, to publicise this and the Office reply that past experience with publicity of such in the Arab press was not encouraging, FO 371/52548/E7479.
73. Political Intelligence Centre, Middle East Forces, General H.Q., 10 July 1945, no. 75, item 19, WO 169/19593.
74. Moscow Conference of Foreign Ministers, 17 Dec. 1945, CAB 133/82.
75. Moscow to Foreign Office, 8 Aug. 1946, FO 371/52551/E7720.
76. Foreign Office to Washington, 25 Sept. 1946, FO 371/57773/WR3052.

9

The Middle East and Palestine: Zeroing In

In a letter to Judge Proskauer, President of the American Jewish Committee, James McDonald gives a fairly representative summary of the Committee's reaction to the Arab Middle East:

In the Arab states we were introduced, most of us for the first time, to a new world. We had excellent chances to see and to hear and thus to take in, as we would not have done otherwise, the meaning and significance of Arab nationalism.[1]

In Cairo and, to a lesser extent, in the other Arab capitals, the AAC heard the case for Pan-Arab unity and the newly-born Arab League did its best to appear as the embodiment of this trend. Since this attempt to demonstrate the solidarity of the Arab world and the triumph of unity over parochialism took place on Arab soil, and was made by representatives of independent states, the stateless Zionists were placed in a position of inferiority. Nevertheless, this new situation did nothing to advance the Palestinian Arabs' claim for self-determination. While very much impressed by the objections of the Arab states to a Zionist Palestine, the commissioners were similarly impressed by the lack of Arab support for an independent Arab Palestine.

According to the original schedule, the AAC was to conduct its hearings in Egypt at the Mena House Hotel, opposite the Giza Pyramids, towards the end of February. Cairo was at that time subject to student riots against the presence of British troops in Egypt, and strict security arrangements surrounded the city and the Committee.[2] As a result, the hearings were postponed and in their free time the commissioners found that golf, sight-seeing, formal dinners, dancing, good food, good wine, good shops and swimming all made Cairo the most pleasant chapter of the Inquiry. There was, however, a price to be paid for all this gaiety: "Aydelotte defeated Texas Joe at golf in Cairo and it caused a serious break between them."[3]

ARAB CASE PRESENTED

At last, on 2 March 1946, the Secretary General of the Arab League opened the hearings with a brilliant speech explaining the League's attitude towards the Palestine question. Azzam refuted the Zionist claim to Palestine and rejected the assertion that the Arabs would benefit from Jewish know-how. "The difference," he said, "between ignorance and knowledge is an education of ten years at school." He reiterated Arab objections to further immigration and to any modification in the land-purchase regulations and concluded:

Our brother has gone to Europe and to the West [and] come back a Russified Jew, a Polish Jew, a German Jew, an English Jew. He has come back with a totally different conception of things, Western and not Eastern ... But the Jew old cousin, coming back with imperialistic ideas, with materialistic ideas, with reactionary or revolutionary ideas ... he is not the old cousin and we do not extend to him a very good welcome.[4]

Azzam's testimony was delivered in English and most of the other League representatives were forced to follow the simultaneous translation. From time to time someone would protest in Arabic against something Azzam had said or make a comment, thus bogging down the proceedings. Apart from the usual objections to Zionism, already rehearsed in Washington and London, a recurring Arab argument was the claim that Zionism had introduced ill feeling between Jews and Moslems in the Arab states. Fadel Jamali, the Director General of the Iraqi Foreign Ministry, claimed that his government had tried to curb such ill feelings, "but we cannot convince ignorant people that not all Jews are Zionists, that Zionism is one thing and Judaism is another." As a result, every Arab country with a Jewish minority was directly concerned with finding a settlement for Palestine. In his view, Palestine should remain in Arab hands with the Jews being accorded the same status as the Kurds in Iraq: "They [the Kurds] are our brethren, they are our Scotland," stated Jamali. Habib Bourgiba, then leader of the anti-French nationalist party in Tunisia, expressed similar views. He reiterated the commitment of Tunisian Arabs to the Palestinian cause, but devoted most of his presentation to publicizing the case for independence of the four Maghreb states.[5]

In Cairo, the AAC also heard two of Egypt's religious leaders, Sheikh el-Bakri, the Grand Chief of the Sufi Orders, and Sheikh Hassan El-Banna, the President of the Moslem Brothers Association. They added Islam's fierce religious objection to Zionism, exhibiting an irreconcilable attitude, much harsher than that of the politicians. When Sheikh El-Banna noticed that smoking had been prohibited in the chamber lest it be offensive to some, he suggested that "similarly ... you do not offend others by inducing certain elements to enter Palestine which do not only smoke but fire too."[6]

None of these arguments were new to the Committee, but the setting, the atmosphere and the language were different, and all of these factors reinforced the impression of Arab resistance to Zionism until "there were phrases used recurrently which referred to a state of war."[7] While the testimony – as noted – tended to concentrate on the Arabs' vehement objection to a Jewish Palestine, rather than on the Palestinian Arab claim for independence, Palestinian representatives had spent some time lobbying the various Arab Governments prior to the Cairo hearings, but to no avail.[8] The concept of Arab nationalism was acceptable; a separate Palestinian nationalism was not.

The AAC spent some of its time in Cairo meeting with British and American officials, both civil and military, and learning something of the type of expert who dealt with the Arab Middle East.[9] Apart from social meetings, the AAC met in camera with the British Commanders in Chief in the Mediterranean and Middle East. Colouring their account of the Palestine crisis with numerous details of Jewish underground warfare, the C. in C. also pointed out the potential threat from Palestinian Arabs. If Arab states were drawn into the conflict then this threat could express itself in anti-Jewish and anti-Christian xenophobia. Major General Oliver, Chief of the General Staff, Middle East Force, warned the AAC that there would be troubles throughout the Middle East if a solution favourable to the Jews were decided upon. The conclusion, therefore, was that militarily a solution favourable to the Arabs would present fewer problems. Hutcheson immediately replied:

The precise amount of military force one solution or another will require is a matter for the military to determine based upon what we should decide to do, rather than for us to determine based on what the military tell us they think will happen ... In the terms of reference no suggestion was made in regard to military questions and our two Governments, innocent and naive as they seem to be, propose that this matter be settled as on the football or cricket field among gentlemen, and whatever is finally decided they will all fix it among themselves and go home.[10]

The C. in C. gave a detailed account of the Jewish arms build-up but were unable to answer questions regarding its aims; their answers, therefore, did not suggest an official attempt to assess the long-term intentions of the Jews. An interesting dialogue, later repeated in Jerusalem, exposed this gap in British military thinking on Palestine. Again it was Hutcheson who elevated the hearing to this level:[11]

Hutcheson:	Do any of you have the opinion that the preparations which you describe as a sort of guerilla army ... are with the idea of maintaining the struggle there without regard to what solution is recommended, the struggle to include a war against Arab and Mandatory Power?
Gen. Oliver:	I see what the Judge is getting at.
Hutcheson:	How far this matter has got out of bounds and become an effort at conquest ... is it only a meagre preparation or a fairly sound, a vigorous preparation for the exercise of force which will enable these people to have a temporary if not a large permanent success so as to create a belligerent status?
Air Marshal Medhurst:	May I give you my opinion and then perhaps my two colleagues will give you theirs. I think that their army is there ... gradually to extend their territory by displacing the Arab and to make it as difficult as possible for the Mandatory Power ... to carry out its obligations ... That is my personal opinion.
Hutcheson:	It does not serve any useful purpose in protecting the Jew from the Arab, does it?
Gen. Oliver:	No.
Hutcheson:	The only purpose that it could serve would be to assist in the illegal running-in of immigrants; it is mainly a basis for bringing in other people. How does that army really work to help them outside immigration? ... It may be I did not express myself very well. I did not mean to say, what is the purpose of it, but what was the actual focus of it. Is the interference all directed to the question of immigration, or is it interference with other things, that is what I want to get at. Is it a military purpose rather than a political purpose? What is the purpose of it?

Air Marshal Medhurst:	Anything that will be a nuisance. For instance, they blew up a large number of viaducts on the railway.
Hutcheson:	That had nothing to do with immigration at all?
Air Marshall Medurst:	Nothing to do with immigration at all.
Hutcheson:	Then it is not all to do with immigration?
Air Marshall Medhurst:	No.
Hutcheson:	These things are not directed to immigration, they are directed to being as much of a nuisance in every possible way, with the idea, I suppose, of carrying on some sort of guerilla war against the Mandatory Power to make the Mandatory Power sick of it, so that they will quit? It is more directed to the Mandatory Power than to the Arabs?
Admiral Tenant:	Yes, I think the Arabs and Jews at the moment are quite friendly.[12]

It was abundantly clear, therefore, that instead of giving an official appreciation, the C. in C. were expressing their own opinions about an issue which should have been well understood by those who were dealing with the Jewish revolt. The protracted cross-examination by Hutcheson was probably the first time that the Military had attempted to define the strategic aims of Jewish resistance. Two weeks later in Jerusalem, the G.O.C. Palestine was questioned with similar results, and it seems that this ignorance was a major factor in Britain's inability to confront the Jewish resistance successfully.

SIDE STOPS: THE MAJOR ARAB CAPITALS

The meeting with the Military brought the official Cairo hearings to an end and the AAC proceeded to Palestine. Both before Cairo and after Jerusalem other Arab capitals were visited by sub-committees. Originally, the Committee was only to visit Cairo and Jerusalem, but the following excerpts from dispatches to the Foreign Office explain why the commissioners had to make tours of the Levant, Trans-Jordan and Saudia Arabia as well, despite the fact that the AAC and Foreign Office officials were aware that very little would come out of them:[13]

The AAC should go to Lebanon where they would see how Moslems and Christians lived harmoniously. [They] would also see that the standards of living there were higher than in Jerusalem and thus realize the weakness of the Jewish argument that Zionism had raised the standard of living in Palestine beyond that of all other Arab countries.

Tensions between the Hashemites and the rest are now so acute that all or none ... must be visited or there will be trouble. It is tiresome but necessary to work on this level of nursery squabbles.

He [King Ibn Saud] may develop some sense of grievance if ACC is, e.g., received by enemies in Egypt or hears Amir Abdullah in person, and he himself is not given the opportunity to expound his views.

Most important for psychological reasons that the Committee should visit Baghdad.

If they visit Egypt and fail to come here, Iraq will certainly feel slighted and will be prejudiced against the acceptance of the AAC's findings.[14]

Singleton, Manningham-Buller and Buxton visited Baghdad on 16–18 February 1946, and conducted a series of personal interviews with Iraqi politicians, Moslem clergy and Christian and Jewish leaders. They were also received by the Prime Minister and the Regent.[15]

Morrison, Leggett and Phillips visited Amman and were received by the Emir Talal, whose father, the Emir Abdullah, was then attending the London ceremonies in honour of his country's recent independence. The usual sort of hearings were held in Amman, where politicians and notables expressed their objections to Zionism.[16]

Hutcheson, Morrison and McDonald visited Damascus on 16–18 March 1946. Here too representatives of various political, trade, commercial and religious groups gave evidence on Palestine. The commissioners were received by the Syrian President and were impressed by the apricot plantations on his estate which "proved something of an eye-opener for the sub-committee, whose members had perhaps underestimated the ability of the Arabs as farmers."[17] During the hearings Moslem clergy questioned the need for the Inquiry altogether, saying:

This reminds us what happened in Europe some six hundred years ago when an investigation was launched to determine whether or not women were human beings. Proofs that they were were no less obvious than those that Arabs have rights in Palestine![18]

Something new did however emerge in Damascus: the meetings with Syrian officials were not concerned as much with Palestine

as with Syrian grievances against France. "Their feeling of bitterness I have not heard expressed towards the French in many,
many years," wrote McDonald, who did not miss one Damascus
museum.[19] Hutcheson spoke about how "in the Arab-Jewish
clamour, the interests of Christianity were being lost sight of ...
Palestine [does not] belong by right to either Arab or Jew and ...
they would both have to get used to the idea." The Judge then
recited extracts from Grey's "Elegy" in one breath and let out
sulphurous expressions of astonishment with the next.[20]

The visit to Lebanon on 17–20 March did reveal the development of Zionist–Maronite relations under French auspices. The
Lebanese Christian President, unlike his Moslem Head of Cabinet
and Minister, was quite ambiguous about a settlement in Palestine
and finally supported the continuation of the British Mandate.
A surprising statement came, however, from the prelates of the
Maronites in Lebanon, Archbishop Moubarak and the Patriarch
Monsignor Arida. They supported the Zionist aims in Palestine
and claimed that the Lebanese President did not speak for the
Maronites because he "is a nice man but weak and fearful ... a
poltroon."[21] Fears of Moslem domination and the effects an Arab
Palestine would have on the Christian population were repeated in
these interviews, a résumé of which was given to the press by the
prelate. Similar evidence was presented by the Assyro-Chaldean
Christians.[22]

The reference to the President brought on an argument with the
prelates who refused to issue a démenti.[23] "How the Archbishop
could make such a statement about the President and expect to get
away with it in Lebanon," as Hutcheson pointed out, was beyond
the Committee's understanding and Hutcheson then asked for "the
low-down on that flare up." Here a most interesting relationship
came to light between the French, the Maronites, and the Zionists
who viewed the Moslems and the British as the common enemies
of the French Levant, Jewish statehood and Maronite existence.
Although according to George Wadsworth of the U.S. Legation in
Beirut, "nothing came out of this contact except the encouragement of the Zionists to plough in Lebanon the soil already well-
spaded by the French," the AAC did get to hear a different opinion
of the Arab Middle East.[24]

On 19 March the same sub-committee (Singleton, Manningham-
Buller and Buxton) which had visited Baghdad was received by

King Abdul Aziz Ibn Saud of Saudi Arabia at his palace in Riyadh. Here the King made the following statement:

The Jews are our enemies everywhere. Wherever they are found they intrigue and work against us ... As an example let us imagine two persons, one with tied hands and no arms and the other with free hands and armed, with some wild birds hovering over their heads. Can you say that these two persons are equals and are on the same footing? This is exactly the case of the Arabs and the Jews in Palestine ... With the power of the sword we drove the Romans out of Palestine. We fought hard for it. Paid heavily for it and sacrificed a lot. How, after all this sacrifice, would a merchant come and take Palestine out of our hands for money?[25]

Singleton, getting into the picturesque style of Riyadh, then asked a question which amounted to begging His Majesty "to be patient with him in asking a *ridiculous* question [and] referred to the decision ... which suggested the partition of Palestine."[26]

The commissioners each received a golden dagger and an Arabian robe and headdress from the King, whom Buxton described as "the most engaging old boy I've met ... He even showed us his harem, to the scandal of his attendant, and offered to find a wife for Singleton." In return the sub-committee gave the King perfume, in accordance with palace etiquette.[27]

Ibn Saud described himself as "Britain's spy in the Arab world."[28] He enjoyed a special status in Britain's Arab policy, certain British moves being for his ears alone.[29] As far as Palestine was concerned, he was reported to have spoken "humanely of the Jews as being men like others."[30] This didn't prevent him from ordering the execution of any Jew who might seek to enter his dominions, according to one testimony.[31] He was also reported to have said that

if he had a beloved friend and later he discovered this friend hated the Jews, he became even more endeared to him than before ... "Praise to God for 1,400 years there have been no Jews in my territory." H.M. further stated he had never in all his life set eyes on a Jew to his knowledge – though he nearly did once. This was when he had newly taken Hassa and was visiting the Bazaar and smelt a strange smell that was unknown to him. On enquiring, he was informed it was the place intoxicating liquor was made. He asked for the Jew in question to be brought to him at once, but unfortunately (fortunately for the Jew) the Jew in question had escaped with the retiring Turkish garrison.[32]

Regarding the situation of the Jews in the Arab states where they lived (no Jews lived in Trans-Jordan or Saudi Arabia), these visits provided the AAC with certain information. The Committee was told that the arrival of 100,000 Jews in Palestine would endanger their Oriental brethren in the Arab countries.[33] Meanwhile, however, the Jewish witnesses living in Arab countries stated that their living conditions were satisfactory, or at least no worse than that of any other minority.[34] The witnesses themselves, however, were very circumspect, causing Singleton to comment that "certainly you know a lot of things, but the special conditions and the law of the country force you to be cautious."[35] Similarly, Zionist reports from Lausanne reported the Judge's concern following the testimony of the Syrian Jews.[36] Their evidence, which appears in its entirety in the following passage, probably goes a long way to explain that concern:

> In the name of the Jewish congregations of Syria and the Lebanon we declare that we are loyal citizens of our countries and enjoy all the rights and have nothing to complain of. Therefore, we totally object to Zionist aspirations

Hutcheson: Do you have something more to add?
Dr. David Pinto: No.[37]

The evidence accumulated in the Arab capitals convinced the AAC that if Palestine were handed over to the Zionists the entire Middle East would rise in revolt. The Committee – especially the British team – was, therefore, concerned about such a danger to Anglo-Arab relations. And yet, once in Palestine, a complete conversion occurred. "I agree with Lord Morrison," wrote Crossman, "who is possessed by the one idea that there's going to be a war here unless we can prevent it [but not] a war as I imagined between Jews and Arabs ... No, a war between the British Army and the Jews."[38] The AAC was so impressed by Zionist strength in Palestine that they left the country thinking almost entirely in terms of Anglo-Zionist rather than Anglo-Arab relations. This caused the British Government to criticize their commissioners for letting HMG down and producing "a Report ... grossly unfair to Great Britain."[39]

LAST STOP – PALESTINE

What most struck the Committee once their train had crossed the Sinai–Palestine border on 6 March 1946 and entered Gaza were the security arrangements and the demonstration of power. This impression was fortified during the entire stay in Palestine. The atmosphere was compared to that of occupied Europe during Nazi days.[40] Telephones were tapped and letters and messages intercepted; bomb scares were a frequent occurrence, and the police were heavy handed in dealing with crowds along the commissioners' route.[41] The tense atmosphere was accentuated by the interception of two ships carrying illegal immigrants, and the discovery of arms caches in Birya, in Northern Galilee. Thus, despite the attempts by Jewish Hospitality Committees to be more friendly towards British troops ("attempts to counterfeit a hospitable front in order to impress the AAC ... it has not impressed or deceived the British soldier") the commissioners could not fail to recognize the turbulent conditions then prevailing in the country.[42] Yet the landscape, the sun and the air reminded the Committee's own "displaced person" of his Texas home. According to Crossman, Hutcheson could "feel at home whereas we feel ourselves utterly remote from England."[43] Hutcheson was to continue to judge Palestine against his experience of Houston.

The Jerusalem hearings were due to start on 8 March. Extensive reports had been prepared by the two sides and by the Administration, and the commissioners had to read through these on the night before since they were a necessary supplement to the oral evidence.

THE ZIONIST CASE REITERATED

The preparation of the Zionist case had been undertaken by a committee of the Jewish Agency which studied the Washington and London hearings for useful pointers: since Morrison, for instance, was interested in the allegation that Britain kept silent about the extermination of the Jews, the Agency decided to re-emphasize it; similarly they decided to cater to Crossman's vision of social revolution in Palestine by the exposition of the social changes which Zionism had brought to Arab society.[44]

One crucial issue for the Zionists was the controversial appearance of the bodies which advocated political plans differing from those of the Agency. Ben-Gurion threatened to expel from the Zionist movement anyone who made a separate appearance before the AAC or supported a programme which was less than Biltmore.[45] The leftist Hashomer Hatzair, which advocated bi-nationalism, had, therefore, to remain silent, along with those who favoured partition. Weizmann, however, resented "these totalitarian methods" and warned that "the AAC is bound to get to know about it, and will wonder whether all our professions of tolerance and so on are really to be taken as seriously as we would like them to be taken."[46] It was the British view that "there is little likelihood . . . of any Jew opposed to Zionist principles having the temerity to express his views before the AAC, thus exposing himself to the wrath of the Yishuv and the bullets of the Stern Gang."[47]

The Zionist testimony began with Dr. Weizmann's presentation. He was now in his early seventies, sick, weary and bitter, and he began with a survey of world Jewry since the 1880s. Talking very slowly he appeared as the prophet of the Movement, deducing the future from the past, and speaking in general rather than specific terms. "We warned you," he said, "we told you when Hitler burned the synagogues in Berlin . . . I said those fires will spread to Westminster Abbey." He claimed that once the Jews achieved statehood, Gentiles would cease to see them as a peculiar people, and he totally rejected the claim that the creation of a Jewish state would give rise to divided loyalties. He called on the Committee to decide on the most just solution:

[Arabs have] so many kingdoms, two kingdoms, four republics; six seats in U.N.O.; one seat in the Security Council . . . there may be some slight injustice politically if Palestine is made a Jewish state but . . . Arab national sentiments can find full expression in Damascus and in Cairo and in Baghdad.

He then referred to the Yishuv in Palestine, comparing it to two other twentieth century attempts to settle Jews on the land – in the Argentine and in Russia (Birobjan). Both projects had been complete failures, and Weizmann suggested that the whittling down of Zionist rights in Palestine would cause the latest settlement scheme to go the same way. "The British," he said "are empiricists and they like to see how a thing works out," but the land restrictions turned the Yishuv into a ghetto. Weizmann then described the qualities which made him a contender for the leadership of the Agency, then under Ben-Gurion: he still felt that "the Rock of Gibraltar on which I build my Zionist policy is absolute co-operation with Great Britain." He added:

For four years I found myself in disagreement on the tempo and on the desire of my friends ... to fix the end of our Zionist policy ... I maintained the thesis that as long as we can colonise – sometimes slowly, sometimes more quickly, as long as we can bring Jews into Palestine, then the National Home will automatically develop eventually into a Jewish State. It is no use pressing this subject beyond certain limits.

Weizmann's answer to a question from Buxton, that the absorption of the 100,000 in Palestine might take more than a year, further demonstrated the gap between him and the Agency. Throughout the hearings Weizmann never tied himself down to details, and had subsequently to write to the AAC to rectify this answer. Even this did not change the commissioners' attitude towards him, an attitude which is apparent from the following exchange:

Dr. Weizmann: I am trying to curtail what I have to say.
Justice I am sure, Dr. Weizmann, we would not like you to curtail
Singleton: it at all on our part.
Mr. Crick: Dr. Weizmann, I will not keep you a minute or two, you have had a very long day.

Weizmann was the only witness who commanded such respect from the AAC.[48]

It was now time for the more pragmatic testimony of Ben-Gurion, the Chairman of the Jewish Agency. His style was different from Weizmann's: he told the commissioners that anti-Semitism was "your baby, a Christian baby." His familiarity with what had been said in previous hearings was apparent from his reference to Dr. Hitti's testimony in Washington, where the latter had claimed that there was no such thing as Palestine in history. "Arab history," said Ben-Gurion, "was made in Arabia, Syria, Persia and in Spain and North Africa. You will not find Palestine in that history." Regarding the political aims of the Agency, he answered Crossman's question about choosing between the 100,000 or giving up the Jewish state in the following way:

Suppose Hitler had in his hand 100,000 Englishmen and he told Mr. Churchill – either you give me the British Navy or I will slaughter all these 100,000 Englishmen. I know what those 100,000 Englishmen would answer – would not they die gladly rather than renounce the British Navy?

The difference between this view and Weizmann's gradualism was obvious, and caused Crossman to comment that "I noticed the difference in substance and not in style."[49] There was also a later exchange with Singleton:

Singleton: Is the Hagana under some sort of control by the Jewish
                Agency?
Ben-Gurion: There is no organization of such a kind under the control of
                the Jewish Agency as far as I know.
Singleton: Have you answered my question?
Ben-Gurion: Yes.
Singleton: The Jewish Agency has nothing to do with the Hagana?
Ben-Gurion: No Sir ... The word Hagana has a double meaning. The
                word "Hagana" means defence, but when you use
                "Hagana" it is a proper name of a secret organization. With
                defence we have to do; with an organization which is called
                "Hagana," no.
Singleton: I should just like to know where are the Headquarters of
                that organization (laughter).[50]

The statement of the Agency's political case was concluded by
Moshe Shertok, head of the Political Department of the Jewish
Agency. He referred to allegations that the Zionist enterprise
had obstructed Arab development in Palestine: "A huge Jewish
omelette was made and not one Arab egg was broken. Moreover,
using largely the same frying pan, the Arabs managed to make
quite a decent omelette for themselves."[51]

It was now the turn of the Agency's economists to present their
plan for the future of the country, and to reply to the arguments
which related to Palestine's absorptive capacity. These men were
the subject of merciless criticism. Crick, for example, challenged
them to "cite any example of a ... country undertaking such a
drastic contraction of the price and cost structure as you are
contemplating without entailing widespread unemployment and
bankruptcy." And Crossman asked: "Do you now foresee an acute
economic crisis in which immigration is blamed [for], a situation
like civil-war?"[52] Yet, this, in some ways, turned out to be the
strongest part of the Jewish case. Variables like land, water,
industry, infrastructure, birth rate, employment, life-expectancy,
infant mortality, etc., were all discussed with regard to the past
and future of the two communities in Palestine, compared with
conditions in Arab states and several European countries, and
supported with maps, charts, diagrams, etc.[53] This caused a British
observer to comment that

well supplied with statistical charts, economic data and other impedi-
menta, the Jews seem to have given much thought to the preparation of

1. The Anglo-American Committee, Lausanne, April 1946. Left to right: row 1 – Reginald Manningham-Buller, Judge Singleton, Judge Hutcheson, Frank Buxton, Lord Morrison; row 2 – Frank Aydelotte, William Phillips, James McDonald; row 3 – Bartley Crum, Wilfrid Crick, Richard Crossman, Frederick Leggett.

2. The Committee on arrival in Jerusalem, March 1946.

3. From left to right: Wilfrid Crick, Richard Crossman, Frederick Leggett and Bartley Crum on their way to the public hearings, Jerusalem, the Y.M.C.A. building, March 1946.

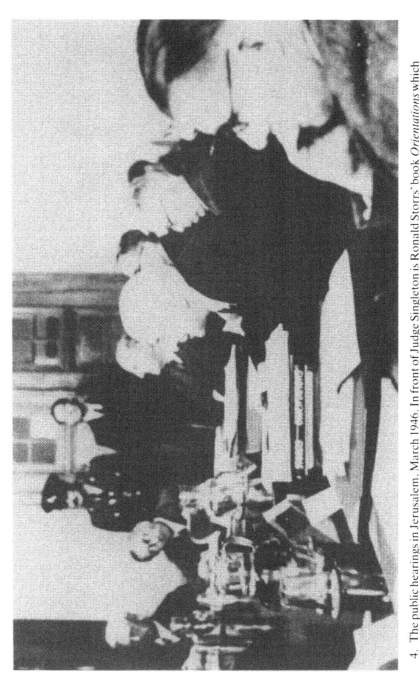

4. The public hearings in Jerusalem, March 1946. In front of Judge Singleton is Ronald Storrs' book *Orientations* which describes his period of service as Military Governor of Jerusalem (1917–1926)

5. Jerusalem public hearings. March 1946. Consultation among members of the Committee. Standing is James McDonald.

6. Top row: Richard Crossman, William Phillips, Frank Aydelotte and the American secretary Evan Wilson with Druze religious leaders. The Galilee. March 1946.

7. Evan Wilson and Richard Crossman at the Kibbutz Tirat Zvi nursery. The Beisan valley. March 1946.

8. Richard Crossman meeting local Arabs. The Beisan valley, March 1946.

their case, whilst on the other hand, the Arabs seem to be relying mainly on the power of the spoken word.[54]

The AAC also heard Jewish witnesses in camera, and held private meetings with Weizmann and other Agency leaders. So while concern for the internal unity of the Zionist movement produced public adherence to Biltmore, partition was being advocated in private meetings with Weizmann and Shertok in Rehovot.[55] But this was not the Committee with which to do such business. The Report's conclusion that "the Biltmore programme had the support of the overwhelming majority of Zionists" did not reflect the real situation so much as it reflected the reluctance of the American Judge to attribute importance to private evidence given outside the hearings.[56]

BETWEEN ZIONISM AND PAN-ARABISM: PALESTINE INDEPENDENCE

An American memo described the Arab preparation for and interest in the AAC in the following way:

Arabs of Palestine ... their idea of impressing the AAC with their case seemed to lie more in the direction of a sumptuous luncheon at Katy Antonious's or a ceremonial visit to a large estate rather than any systematic marshalling of facts and figures to make a convincing presentation ... For the most part Arab leaders did not appear to take much interest in the Committee's proceedings – which one might have thought would be a matter of life and death to the Arabs of Palestine – and in fact the members of the Arab Higher Committee often did not bother to fill the seats which had been reserved for them at the hearings – and this when hundreds were being turned away daily for lack of space.[57]

Added to these impressions were the reluctance to show the commissioners picturesque Arab villages lest it produce "folkloristic attitudes" and the absence of Moslem Arabs (unlike Christians) from the hearings.[58]

The main theme of the Arab evidence given in Jerusalem was the elevation of their case to a clear demand for independence, and it was the Palestinians who concentrated on this demand.

It was not easy to introduce this line to the commissioners. Hutcheson, for example, did not really understand their argument for separate statehood and later asked whether it was not enough that Syria was separated from the Palestinian Arabs and made independent.[59] Weizmann's assertion that Damascus, Cairo, and Baghdad could replace Jerusalem as a national centre for the Palestinians had had its effect as did the Arab League's insistence on Pan-Arabism. Against this background, one can understand just how difficult it was for the commissioners to accept the arguments for a separate Palestinian Arab nation. The following excerpts from the Jerusalem hearings illustrate this point:

Would you say that Arab nationalism, I mean talking about Palestinian Arabs, was Palestinian in its feeling or more general? Is it a nationalism which is Palestinian or Trans-Jordanian or Syrian or do the Arabs feel a single nationalism? The difference of state is relatively unimportant?[60]

The Arab world, as you choose to call it ... formerly there were people around in a sea of Arab civilization ... now they are trying to cut them out into little sections, demand certain national attributes and feelings?[61]

The statement of the Arab case began on 12 March 1946 with the testimony of Jamal Husseini, who spoke on behalf of the newly re-established Arab Higher Committee. Husseini had recently been released from exile in Rhodesia for this purpose (see Chapter 5).[62] Husseini dealt with immigration, the sale of land, the progress of industry, and the historical background, aiming his evidence at statements made by Weizmann and Ben-Gurion. He refuted the Jewish claims to Palestine and presented the Arab demand for statehood with great eloquence and confidence, calling for the early withdrawal of the British. He assured the committee that bloodshed would not follow:

If these pampered children, if these spoilt children of the British Government, the Zionists, know for once that they are no more to be pampered and spoilt, then the whole condition will be turned to what it has been before the First World War. We will become friends probably.

And if it did not work out like this, why then,

The people in this world have always cut their difficulties and knots by coming to grips with one another. Let us do it. Why not do it? You have done it in every war of your history ... why should not we have this war? Why should you laugh at it? It is quite natural. This is God's way. That is God's creation.[63]

Jamal had some difficulties in reconciling some of his own statements with the accepted principles of democracy, particularly those relating to the representative character of the Arab Higher Committee and his absentee leader, the Mufti.[64] He was questioned by Crossman and Crum about Haj Amin Husseini's wartime activity. More than indicating the latter's allegiance to the Nazis, these questions exposed the two commissioners to the criticism of their colleagues.[65] No one expected anything but the defence of his cousin from Jamal, and the lengthy dialogue which ensued confirmed an earlier assessment of members of the AAC who "put their questions in order to appear in the official proceedings."[66]

Husseini's testimony left a deep impression on the AAC.[67] Even his criticism of the wording of the Balfour Declaration, which referred to the Arabs only as the non-Jewish citizens of the country, was relevant to his testimony, most of which related to Zionist deeds and Arab reactions to them. Still, even he was unable to endow the claim for Palestinian self-determination with the aura of an independent issue, detached from Pan-Arabism and Zionism.

It was now the turn of the Arab Office, which was described as being "free from the obsolete catchwords and myopia of the old gang [and] who could speak the language of today."[68] Ahmad Shukeiri was the first to speak, stating that "if it is a question of degree of violence, the Arabs are prepared to break the record."[69] His speech seemed "bellicose both in matter and delivery."[70] Next came Albert Hourani, who employed a different style and emphasis altogether.

Hourani discussed the pros and cons of three compromise solutions for Palestine – partition, bi-nationalism and a continuation of the status quo – and a fourth – an Arab Palestine. His emphasis was *not* on Zionist actions and Arab reactions, but on the interest of the country's Arab inhabitants, and the need for a lasting solution. He did not rule out the use of force in effecting a settlement, or the inevitable involvement of Britain and the United States in the conflict. On this issue his words were highly perceptive:

There is a certain inclination in Great Britain and America to state the problem in terms of a conflict of two races and two nationalisms, and to picture the British and American governments as impartial peacemakers and judges in no way involved in the conflict ... This is not the correct view. You will never understand the problem aright unless you realise that Great Britain and America are essentially involved in it. They are not only judges, they are also actors in the tragedy.[71]

His demand for independence, according to one British observer, "did something to prove the existence of Palestinian Arabs" to a sceptical Committee:[72]

We all recognize that there are dangerously unstable elements in nationalism. Nationalism goes wrong when the nation worships itself; it falls into sin; but to say that is one thing and to condemn nationalism is another. I believe there can be a healthy nationalism.[73]

He explored the practicality of every compromise plan, and was especially critical of bi-nationalism, which, according to a British source, is "from the Arab point of view ... much more of a danger than Ben-Gurion's because it is more reasonable."[74]

Hourani concluded the Arab case with a plea for Palestinian independence: in his view the Palestinian Arabs deserved that independence not because they were part of the awakening Arab world or because the Zionists wanted their land, but because Western thinking recognized the right of all peoples to self-determination. According to British sources, with this argumentation "he won the hearts of the Committee even if he may not have won their minds."[75] He did not repeat the argument of earlier witnesses who had looked back nostalgically to the days of the Ottoman Empire and complained that now they were "being governed in the same way as certain backward peoples inhabiting other territories."[76] This sort of talk had merely caused Singleton to say that "if on both sides there was more realization of what both sides owe to Great Britain's help ... Palestine might be a more peaceful place."[77]

The only Zionist witness to defy the Jewish Agency ban on "dissident" testimonies was Dr. Judah Magnes, the President of the Hebrew University, who appeared on behalf of the Ichud (Union), a group of intellectuals who supported the idea of bi-nationalism.[78] Magnes, a San Francisco-born liberal rabbi, stated that the natural rights of the Arabs and historical rights of the Jews should be regarded as being of equal validity. This could help in the institution of a bi-national state in which the Arabs would be given ample opportunity for self-government and the Jews would be granted ample immigration rights. Such an arrangement would result in the Arabs agreeing to Jewish immigration and the Jews relinquishing all demands for independence. In the short run, the demands of life would be strong enough to bring about a measure of cooperation.[79] It would be "the one country in the world where the Jews would be a constituent nation, that is, an equal nationality within the body politic and not just a minority as everywhere else." In order to satisfy the various international and religious groups who were involved in the conflict, an absorptive capacity board was to be set up under the direction of the Jewish Agency, the Arab League and the Mandatory Power. To support his argument, Magnes took the example of Switzerland where differences in language, religion and culture had not been obstacles to political unity. Consequently he rejected the idea of partition.

It was a courageous act to defy the Agency and it had, in fact, been necessary to place Magnes under police protection.[80] He held his audience almost spellbound for more than two hours, and as he concluded his evidence there were tears in the eyes of many, and he was warmly congratulated by Hutcheson who said to him: "In the words of my Leader – 'Behold an Israelite indeed in whom there is no guile.'" Although, according to McDonald, Magnes "reached the hearts of more than perhaps any other speaker," the Committee attributed very little weight to his testimony. His parity principle ("a newer form of democracy") did not accord with the democratic beliefs of the commissioners, especially not with those of Hutcheson. Above all, Magnes was unable to prove the existence of a Palestinian identity strong enough to unite the Zionists and the Arabs. "Too much has happened in the last years for a solution," noted McDonald.[81]

CIVIL AND MILITARY BRITISH ASSESSMENTS

The evidence of the Palestine Administration and the Military was – for obvious reasons of security – presented in camera.

The first meeting was with Lieutenant General J. C. D'Arcy, the G.O.C. in Palestine.[82] His evidence related mainly to the Jewish military build-up in Palestine. He said that there was now a fairly well-equipped Jewish army under the direction of a General H.Q., and that any attempts to disarm it would be very difficult, if not impossible. In the event of a future Arab–Jewish confrontation, asked Leggett, "would that mean a considerable slaughter of the Arabs?" D'Arcy's answer was clear: "Yes, indeed." The impression gained from D'Arcy's testimony was that from the military angle the easiest solution to the Palestine problem would be a *Jewish* one:

He could enforce a pro-Jewish solution [on the Arabs] without much difficulty; in enforcing the Hagana would be very helpful; a pro-Arab solution would ... require three divisions [to enforce on the Jews]; in such a solution Arab support would be of no value.[83]

A Jewish solution would also be the most acceptable in the context of Anglo-Jewish cooperation in, and beyond, Palestine:

Crossman: Imagine they were given their independence and were
              allowed to have an army and we were there in Haifa
              and Lydda, having our treaty relations, are they the sort
              of people able to produce a serious standing army with
              supplies from outside?
D'Arcy: Yes, I think so.

D'Arcy's views were – implicitly – entirely different from those of the C.in C. in Cairo. His evidence implied that there would be disastrous consequences if an Anglo-Jewish war broke out, since "Jews ... are prepared to fight and die." This thought was later to haunt the commissioners, especially the British, and concern about Arab reaction was now replaced by concern about Zionist reaction.

D'Arcy stressed the fact that the military strength of the Yishuv was impressive and thorough training was given to members of the Hagana. He illustrated his evidence with documents which had been seized in Birya. The material included photographs of a police station in Zikhron Yaacov on the Mediterranean coast. The following dialogue ensued:

Crum: I do not understand what these postcards are?
D'Arcy: They are pictures of Zikhron Yaacov police station; in fact
              it has a camp there now.
Crum: Those are postcards that are on sale publicly, are they not?
D'Arcy: I cannot tell you; I cannot answer that ... May I now read
              you some of the standing orders which were found in this
              place at Birya:

Standing Orders for Palmach [Special units of the Hagana] *Detachment*

1. It is the duty of the enlisted group ... to carry out any instructions given
   by the Yishuv's supreme bodies.
2. In order that the group's duties shall be carried out in a proper manner,
   permanent training will be conducted.
3. The group will be self-supporting by doing its own work.
4. The presence of good relations between the members and the recognition of the basic Zionist principles ... are important factors.
5. The group ... has been created outside the framework of the local

authorities and is continually harassed by them.

6. All activities within the framework of the group are carried out in absolute secrecy. (Copies passed).

McDonald:	The words "Top Secret" on here, is that added by you or was that on the document?
D'Arcy:	That was added at my headquarters.
Crossman:	What sort of classification do you think the Hagana would give this document on their side?
D'Arcy:	I think the document itself will explain; it is obviously top secret.
Crossman:	Is it a document of which each member is given a copy?
D'Arcy:	I should not think so ... from the nature of the document it insists on secrecy so much I imagine it is not a thing that would be issued to every man.
Aydelotte:	It would probably be read to them.
D'Arcy:	I imagine so. You will see they are the sort of orders a small military unit or sub-unit would issue in those circumstances ... May I pass on?
Singleton:	Please do.

This dialogue could suggest either a lack of information among the British fighting the Jewish undergrounds or, alternatively, their low regard for the AAC. It could also stem from a reluctance to be specific with the Committee, in accordance with instructions given to the C.in C. by the C.O.S.[84] In any case, it did not convince the Committee of the Military's ability to cope with the question of security in Palestine, nor did the following dialogue between Hutcheson and D'Arcy:

Hutcheson:	I have been listening to all these minor tacticians but my field is higher military strategy ... The question I want to ask you is from the standpoint of higher strategy as to the purpose for which these things have been formed ... Is it designed primarily against the Palestine Government, or primarily against the Arabs, or is it a stand-by force which is to be in case things take a turn for the worse for the Jews [or] to take hold of the country against both British and Arabs ... Is [it] an Irish movement to throw the British out or a movement to knock the Arabs out if the British get out of the way? ... What is its real purpose?
D'Arcy:	The Hebrew press I think will give you the answer ... I will read to you an extract from one of the papers ... It is talking about the attack on the police posts at Sarona and others, about which I have spoken, and the attacks on the aircraft

	on the various airfields [reads the description of the attack on the airfields].
Hutcheson:	You see, that illustrates the battle ... I thought you were going to read ... a statement of the purpose of these armies ... This is a tactical statement. It does not give any idea of the general purpose, whether this is a way of independence against the Palestine Government or against the Arabs, and I suppose you have no answer as to what it is.
D'Arcy:	May I supply you with cuttings from the Hebrew press and a transcript of speeches by leaders?

Obviously the G.O.C. did not understand the question: Hebrew press cuttings were no substitutes for an official British strategic assessment. D'Arcy's difficulties in answering Hutcheson probably did not stem from a reluctance to express an opinion on a basically political issue, since two months later he had no inhibitions about dismissing his Government's American initiative in Palestine.[85] The fact that the C.in C. in Cairo, who had been asked the same question a fortnight earlier, did not bother to warn D'Arcy, supports the conclusion that simple ignorance was an important factor in Britain's inability to cope with Jewish resistance, and not London's inhibitions.

The in camera evidence of the Chief Secretary of the Government, John Shaw, revolved primarily around the relationship between the Jewish Agency and the British Administration and differences between the latter and the Colonial Office in London. (Singleton insisted there could be no differences whereas Crossman insisted there were.)

The Committee, now in its third week in Palestine, had begun to acquire some knowledge of the country's affairs under the Mandate and wanted to know from Shaw, among other things, whether certain phenomena, such as the land purchase restrictions, were unique to Palestine or were to be found in other colonies, and which of the various forms of administration – Crown Colony, Dominion or Mandate – was the most appropriate for Palestine.

The Chief Secretary likened the position of the Jewish Agency in Palestine to that of a state within a state, and pointed out that it created a solution which could only be rectified by the withdrawal of either the Administration or the Agency. This assessment added another gloomy dimension to the Committee's concern about a possible Anglo-Jewish war.

Shaw's message was clear: partition was almost impossible because of the presence of a large Arab minority in the would-be Jewish state:

Already the town of Jaffa, with its 60,000 more or less fanatical Moslem Arabs, has become almost as much to the Arabs . . . as Tel-Aviv does to the Jews . . . and it is extremely difficult to find any scheme of partition which does not put Jaffa in the Jewish state.[86]

It was his opinion that 100,000 immigrants could be admitted only after the disbandment of the Agency and the disarmament of the under grounds. As for the Arabs, he said: "I feel from [their] psych logy, however paradoxical it may sound, they would accept 100.00) better than a lesser number [which] would meet greater suspic on as being likely to prove but the thin edge of the wedge." When a month later the Committee did recommend the admission of 10(000, they may have been considering this "psychology."

The re was yet another in camera meeting held by the AAC, this one with Jerome Farrell, the British Director of Education in Palestine. Of all the meetings, this one had the most immediate repercussions. The "traditional" relationship between the Colonial administrators and the upper-class natives, such as prevailed in most of the Arab countries or in India, had never been a notable part of Jewish–British relations in Palestine. Rather, the contrary was true. During the war, for example, the Arabs were described as "superficially attractive and . . . have achieved comparative popularity with British officers . . . by their fondness for sport and their being less grasping than the Jews."[87] The Palestinian Jew, the informant continued, was said to have combined "many of the worst traits of the Russian, the Pole and the Jew. It is an unfortunate combination." Glubb Pasha, in his reaction to the AAC Report, tried to "explain" the problem:

The life of the Jewish people is an unending tragedy. Driven ceaselessly from one country to another they are first welcomed and then driven out or massacred. Nobody can endure them long because they don't assimilate. Pharoah welcomed and then expelled them. Nebuchadnezar, Tigleth-Pileser and other monarchs found the Jewish question insoluble. The Romans drove them from Palestine. All the countries of Europe have received and expelled them . . . the list is unending. It is difficult to apportion praise or blame. Persecution has bred hatred and bitterness in the Jews and people who hate and sneer are unpopular with their neighbours.[88]

In all events, Farrell's testimony was "traditional" in this sense:

Farrell: Jewish family ... had ideas of amusement which were not
                mine. They do not live in the house so much; they live out-
                door more in cafés, cinema and places like that. Because of
                this the Jews often maintain they have a higher standard of
                living than the Arabs.
Crossman: Most Englishmen go to the cinemas and pubs too. This does
                not seem to be a special defect of the Jews.
Farrell: It's a special defect of Central Europeans.

To this he added a comparison of the Jewish Youth Movement and
the Hitler-Jugend, as well as other insults.[89] The reaction was swift:
"Both American and British members," the High Commissioner
noted, "made a special point of coming to tell me that his showing
before them was one of fanatic anti-Semitism ... I sent for Farrell
and told him that he should go as soon as he could."[90] Farrell left,
but not before leaving the following legacy:

Any statement unflattering to the Jews will excite a strong immediate
reaction against it. But after a decent interval ... the Jews stealing Jove's
thunder will pretend that this is their own ... there is little evidence that
Jews will assimilate advice sugared by flattery. The sugar is relished and
the good counsel expelled ... As it now seems to me, there is no common
moral and theological ground upon which politically organized Jewry and
a Christian civilization can stand together in harmony. The inhuman mass
selfishness of concentrated Jewry ... is a phenomenon so far ... without
parallel in history ... To counter so fatal a virus as that with which the
Jewish youth is being injected ... the Balm of Gilead neither prevents nor
cures [such] rabies. "Unassimilated" Judaism, after rejecting successively
both Hellenism and Christ, is now reducing its own traditional faith ...
from monotheism to the older henotheism which leads to that racial self-
worship which Albert Rosenberg borrowed from the Jews for Nordic ends
... For many years, and despite many indications I myself failed fully to
understand why in the National Home, Palestine, it should be necessary to
reinforce the natural separation ... by exaggerated attention to Hebrew
language and other, more unprofitable, Hebrew studies. Ultimately,
however, though late, the reason became clear, that the aim was not a
passive, cultural and religious Judaism, but the nurture of an active,
selfish, aggressively secular and imperialistic spirit liable to direct itself to
domination over neighbouring people.[91]

An informal conversation which the judges held with the High
Commissioner concluded official hearings in Palestine. But before,
during and after the session the commissioners had also toured

the country, visiting almost every type of settlement in Palestine: Moslem villages and cities, Christian, Druze, Nomad and Samaritan settlements, kibbutzim and Jewish towns. The commissioners also saw various Arab, Jewish and Government agricultural and industrial enterprises: the Negev and the Jordan Valley were surveyed from the air.

During a visit to the potash plants on the Dead Sea, the American judge quoted from the Old and New Testaments.[92] At the Holy Places in Jerusalem and on the Sea of Galilee, Frank Aydelotte rediscovered the Bible, finding in it a welcome relief since "it was getting on my nerves to hear people talking Arabic and Hebrew."[93] Crossman, as was his wont at all times, constantly looked for signs of trade unionism, social revolution or labour problems wherever he went, modestly noting that his colleagues were "not very good at seeing things so they do not much want to look at Palestine."[94] Leggett tried to apply some of his skills of mediation in industrial disputes. He described how "employers and work people … though they are not equal, will probably find a way in which they can live together." Why, he asked, were the Arabs and the Jews unable to settle their political differences in the same way?[95] McDonald was reported to have spent his time helping Ben-Gurion prepare his evidence. Phillips humbly observed, in his "Observer in Palestine," a visit to the Samaritans in Nablus where

four tall distinguished priests, with long grey beards and fine classic features, conducted us to their chapel … These white robed high priests with spotlessly clean hands, respectfully unroll the ancient scroll, while pointing out in subdued voices the beauty of its script.[96]

Apart from his excitement at all that was picturesque in Palestine, he rarely interfered in the hearings.[97]

MIXED EFFECTS

The visit to Palestine gradually began to wear on the commissioners, who became less patient with each other and with those trying to influence them. The cloak-and-dagger atmosphere in the King David Hotel got on Crum's nerves. He would obligingly drop documents on the floor of the hotel to test the efficiency of the agents there.[98] The two judges could hardly bear each other. "It is quite ridiculous leaving before we have really realized what were the matters there," Crossman wrote, "but I think this Committee would disintegrate if it were to go on much longer. I hesitate to think what might happen when we get to Lausanne ... with two such chairmen in charge."[99]

The visit to Palestine ended but its complex effects lingered on. The hostility which the Arabs felt towards the Zionist enterprise was apparent throughout the Arab Middle East, but even more so in Palestine. Nor was it something which had been whipped up by the effendi; it was a deep feeling which would obstruct any attempt at cooperation.[100] Hutcheson gave credence to the Arab claim that they would "drive everyone into the sea" and considered Jewish persistence in the face of such opposition "the greatest mystery ... in this Holy Land." This led him to regret all the lost opportunities of the past, such as the 1922 lopping off of Trans-Jordan, and, in fact, produced a kind of paralysis in his thinking with regard to the possibilities of the present.[101]

On the other hand, the demands of American and British Jewry for statehood sounded a good deal less impracticable after the Committee had seen the Yishuv in Palestine. Here was something real and there was no way to ignore it. In Palestine theoretical debates on the nature of the Jew were rare and the AAC found no "divided loyalties" among the Palestine Zionists. Things no longer looked artificial. On the contrary, according to Aydelotte:

I left Washington pretty strongly anti-Zionist and very much of Lessing Rosenwald's opinion. But when you see at first hand what these Jews have done in Palestine ... the greatest creative effort in the modern world. The Arabs are not equal to anything like it and would destroy all that the Jews have done ... This we must not let them do.[102]

Once again sympathy for the pioneering spirit had been aroused. As Buxton put it:

How my Vermont father, who used to glory in the land cleared by him and his brozhers [sic] would have been amazed at the greater deeds of the Palestinian Jews! ... Vermont is almost stoneless by comparison. I came away from those farms less cocky and more humble and not quite so certain that American pioneers left no successors.[103]

To a large extent, the AAC's encounter with the Yishuv added to the deadlock in Palestine. There was little room to manoeuvre between Arab hostility and Zionist achievement. Furthermore, the real threat of an Anglo-Jewish war had been made evident.

Crossman, according to Beeley, "became convinced that ... the Jews represent a greater military danger than the Arabs," a view not shared by HMG's military advisers.[104]

The net result was that the Twelve Commissioners embarked on a line of thought clearly opposed to the concepts of HMG and its Foreign Secretary, Ernest Bevin.

NOTES

1. Lausanne, 9 April 1946, New York, AJC Archives, Proskauer Papers, Box 8, Palestine. See also Crossman, *Palestine Mission*, p. 117.
2. McDonald diary, 28 Feb. 1946.
3. Crossman diary, Lausanne period (undated), SACMEC, Crossman Papers. See also *Palestine Mission*, pp. 116-117.
4. Cairo Hearings, Mena House Hotel, 2 March 1946, USNA, RG 43, AAC, Box 10.
5. Cairo Hearings, 5 March 1946, USNA, RG 43, AAC, Box 10. See also assessment of Bourgiba's evidence in U.S. Legation, Cairo, to State Dept., 21 March 1946, USNA, State Dept., Palestine Papers 1946, Box 6754, No. 867N 01/3-2146.
6. Cairo Hearings, 5 March 1946, USNA, RG 43, AAC, Box 10.
7. McDonald diary, 2 March 1946.
8. On this lobbying, see USNA, Strategic Service Unit, report no. 66922, 11 March 1945.
9. See "Proconsuls and Pro-Arabs" in Crossman, *Palestine Mission*, pp. 109-113. On meetings with people of the American University of Beirut, see Phillips, *Ventures in Diplomacy*, p. 291; *ESCO Foundation for Palestine*, vol. 2, Yale University, 1946, p. 1119.
10. Cairo Hearings, 5 March 1946, USNA, RG 43, AAC Box 10, pp. 6-7, 23-24.
11. Evidence of General Oliver and Air Marshal Sir Charles E. Medhurst, Air C.in C., Mediterranean and Middle East, Cairo, 5 March 1946, USNA, RG 43, AAC, Box 10, pp. 24-27.
12. Vice-Admiral Sir William Tennant, Flag Officer, Levant and Eastern Mediterranean, was representing C. in C. Mediterranean, whose H.Q. were at Malta.
13. Buxton to Frankfurter, Berlin, 15 Feb. 1946, Frankfurter Papers; comments of Foreign Office officials on Beirut to Foreign Office, 6 Feb. 1946, FO 371/52509/E1185.
14. Cairo to Foreign Office, 17 Feb. 1946, in conversation with counsellor of Lebanese Legation, FO 371/51510/E1453; Jeddah to Foreign Office, 2 Feb. 1945 and 17 Feb. 1946, FO 371/52508/E1013 and FO 371/52510/E1463; conversation with the Iraqi Chargé d'Affaires, 4 Feb. 1946, FO 371/52509/E1197; Baghdad to Foreign Office, 31 Jan. 1946, FO 371/52508/E976.
15. See in Baghdad to Bevin, 19 March 1946, FO 371/51513/E2860.
16. Glubb, Note on the Report of the AAC, May 1946, p. 2, FO 371/52542/E6871; Phillips, *Ventures in Diplomacy*, pp. 291–292.
17. William J. Porter, U.S. Damascus Legation, to State Dept., 20 March 1946, p. 4, NRC, Damascus files no. RG 84 59 A543. Arab agricultural development became a subject for refuting Zionist progress. See Crossman, *Palestine Mission*, p. 127. See also King Ibn Saud to AAC, FO 371/52517/E3765, p. 2, and Damascus Hearings,

spokesman of the Syrian Chamber of Commerce, Jewish Telegraphic Agency, 19 March 1946.

18. Karlibach, *The AAC of Inquiry*, p. 412.
19. McDonald diary, 16 and 17 March 1946.
20. U.S. Damascus Legation to State Dept., 20 Mar. 1946, NRC, Damascus files no. RG 84 59A543, pp. 2, 4.
21. McDonald diary, 18 and 21 March 1946.
22. See details in Jewish Telegraphic Agency, 24 March 1946; Karlibach, *The AAC of Inquiry*, p. 416. On support for Zionism among Aleppo Christians, see British Consul, Aleppo, to Beirut Legation, 4 May 1946, FO 371/52523/E4360. The Jerusalem Representative of the Palestine Maronites did not appear before the AAC "for reasons of ill-health," Jewish Telegraphic Agency, 25 March 1946.
23. Weekly Political Summary, Syria and Lebanon, no. 207, 26 March 1946–10 April 1946, FO 371/52857/E3229.
24. Hutcheson to George Wadsworth, U.S. Legation Beirut, 23 March 1946, NRC, Beirut files, no. RG 84, Box 230; Wadsworth to Hutcheson, Beirut, 3 April 1946, ibid. Wadsworth attributed the prelates' attitudes to Maronite–Lebanese internal politics, ibid.; British Weekly Political Summary Syria and Lebanon, no. 207, 26 March 1946–10 April 1946, FO 371/52857/E3229. See also on Jewish sympathy with French interests in the Levant, in Palestine to Colonial Secretary, 27 June 1945, CO 733/456, No. 75155/143.
25. Minutes of the AAC interview with King Ibn Saud, 19 March 1946, pp. 2, 4, 6, 7, FO 371/52516/E3754.
26. Ibid., p. 8, my emphasis.
27. Buxton to Frankfurter, 4 April 1946. Frankfurter Papers, container 40. For more on AAC and palace etiquette, see Jeddah to Jerusalem, 10 March 1946, FO 371/52512/E2169.
28. Grafftey-Smith to Bevin, Jeddah, 11 Feb. 1946, FO 371/52510/E1512.
29. Memo by Colonial Secretary, 28 Sept. 1945, No. CP(45)196, FO 371/45380/E7262/G.
30. Unsigned draft minute to Bevin on immigration, Jan. 1946, FO 371/52503/E200.
31. James M. Landis, U.S. Director of Economic Operations in the Middle East, to President Roosevelt, 17 Jan. 1945, FRUS, 1945, vol. 8, p. 681.
32. Manuscript of Lord Killearn diaries, minutes of conversation with the King, Cairo, 14 Jan. 1946, SACMEC.
33. See Nuri Said in conversation with Brigadier Clayton of the British Middle East Office, Cairo, 28 May 1946, FO 371/52528/E5305.
34. Jewish Agency, Arab Section, report on AAC visit to Iraq, undated, Jerusalem, CZA S25/6412.
35. To Rabbi Sasoon Khedouri, Chief Rabbinate of Iraq, Baghdad, 17 March 1946, in Karlibach, *The AAC of Inquiry*, p. 415.
36. Arthur Lourie to Nachum Goldmann, Geneva, 7 April 1946, Jerusalem, CZA, Goldmann files, No. Z6, Bundle 18, No. 1.
37. Damascus Hearings, 17 March 1946, in Karlibach, *The AAC of Inquiry*, p. 414.
38. Crossman, *Palestine Mission*, pp. 141-142; meeting between Attlee and the British commissioners, London, 14 May 1946, FO 371/52524/E4514.
39. Crossman quoting Attlee, 7 May 1946, SACMEC, Crossman Papers.
40. Evan Wilson to Thames Television, Washington, 13 June 1977, SACMEC, Thames Television programme "Palestine Mandate."
41. Aydelotte diary, 10 and 24 March 1946; Phillips, *Ventures in Diplomacy*, p. 285; Crossman, *Palestine Mission*, pp. 126-127, 131; McDonald diary, 9 March 1946.
42. 3rd Infantry Division, Weekly Intelligence Review, 2-9 March 1946, WO 169/22967; Fortnightly Intelligence Newsletter, H.Q. Palestine, 3-17 March 1946, No.

11, WO 169/23021.
43. Crossman, *Palestine Mission*, p. 126.
44. Undated memo of Jewish Agency Arab Section, Jerusalem, CZA, No. S25/6478.
45. Ben-Gurion to the Jewish Agency Executive, 27 Feb. 1946, CZA. See also discussion of the Executive, 27 Jan. 1946, ibid.
46. Weizmann to Shertok, 11 March 1946, Jerusalem, CZA, S25/10171. Shertok answered, 17 March 1946: "The fact that there is complete freedom of expression in the House of Commons ... does not mean that when HMG goes to an international conference it takes the opposition along with it to present a second case." CZA S25/6367.
47. 3rd Infantry Division, Weekly Intelligence Review, No. 10, 22 Feb. 1946–1 March 1946, WO 169/22967.
48. Jerusalem Hearings, 8 March 1946. Crick protested the comparison with the Warsaw Ghetto: "It is shocking to us ... seeing the remains of a Ghetto in Warsaw." As to restrictions on immigration, Weizmann said of the Colonial Secretary Lord Passfield's 1929 comment that there is no room to swing a cat in Palestine: "I wish you could count up not only the ... cats which have been swung since that time, but the number of immigrants coming." Compare this final exchange with Hutcheson to Ben-Gurion: "Thank you for your speech and for your finish," Jerusalem Hearings, 11 March 1946.
49. Jerusalem Hearings, 11 March 1946.
50. Jerusalem Hearings, 26 March 1946. See also Kirk, *The Middle East, 1945–1950*, pp. 211-212.
51. Jerusalem Hearings, 26 March 1946.
52. Questions to S. Hoffien of the Jewish Agency Economic Branch, 11 March 1946.
53. See testimonies of David Horowitz and Eliezer Kaplan, Jerusalem Hearings, 11 and 26 March 1946.
54. 3rd Infantry Division, Weekly Intelligence Review, No. 12, 10-17 March 1946, WO 169/22967.
55. Crossman, *Palestine Mission*, pp. 134-137, on his and Crum's visit to Rehovot; Aydelotte diary, 25 March 1946, and his and Phillips' visit.
56. AAC Report, p. 26.
57. William Yale, counsellor at the State Dept., Impressions on Palestine, 1 April 1946, Yale Papers, Harvard University, Houghton Library.
58. Albert Hourani, in charge of the presentation of the Arab Office before the AAC, interview, Oxford, Nov. 1979.
59. Hutcheson to Dr. Bernard Joseph of Agency Executive, CZA, Jewish Agency Executive, 31 March 1946.
60. Crossman to Henry Cattan of the Arab Higher Committee, 23 March 1946.
61. Hutcheson to Hourani, 25 March 1946.
62. See note to Colonial Secretary on meetings between Cunningham and Musa Alami, 8 Jan. 1946: "Without him [Jamal] each would be more extreme than the other ... what Musa says in regard to letting the Arabs loose on the Committee without control is right," SACMEC, Cunningham Papers, Box 5, file 1.
63. Jerusalem Hearings, 12 March 1946. Some Arabs attributed this fatalism to the Rhodesian exile, where Jamal engaged in Yoga. Interview with Mr. Hourani, Oxford, Nov. 1979.
64. See Palestine H.Q. Fortnightly Intelligence Report, No. 10, 3-16 March 1946, WO 169/23021; also Crossman to Hector McNeil, Minister of State at the Foreign Office, hoping for a representative Arab leadership "to replace the present set of charming degenerates," Lausanne, 22 April 1946, FO 371 52524/E4469. For a different view, see AAC Report, p. 17: "No evidence that the Arab notables who appeared before the Committee ... did not reflect accurately the views of their

followers."

65. McDonald complained about this "destructive questioning." McDonald diary, 12 March 1946. The Government assessment was that Jamal paid lip service to his own family and party leaders when he mentioned the Mufti. See Cunningham to Colonial Secretary, 2 April 1946, CO 537/1708.
66. Phillips diary, 8 April 1946.
67. Especially on McDonald: "sensational ... brilliant and fluent ... one could not but admire his courage," McDonald diary, 12 March 1946.
68. Cunningham to Hall, 2 April 1946, SACMEC, Cunningham Papers, Box 1, file 1. The "old gang" was a term used in relation to the Arab Higher Committee during the riots of the 1930s.
69. Jerusalem Hearings, 25 March 1946.
70. H.Q. British Troops, Fortnightly Intelligence Newsletter, No. 11, 17-30 March 1946, WO 169/23021.
71. Jerusalem Hearings, 25 March 1946.
72. Cunningham to Hall, 2 April 1946, SACMEC, Cunningham Papers, Box 1, file 1.
73. Jerusalem Hearings, 25 March 1946.
74. In camera hearing of Edwin Samuel, Jerusalem, 25 March 1946, Hutcheson Papers. Samuel was the director of the broadcasting services in Palestine.
75. H.Q. British Troops, Fortnightly Intelligence Newsletter, No. 11, 17-30 March 1946, WO 169/23021.
76. Hearing of Henry Cattan, 23 March 1946 and Auni-Bey Abdul Hadi, 12 March 1946.
77. To Cattan, Jerusalem Hearings, 23 March 1946.
78. Jerusalem Hearings, 14 March 1946.
79. To Magnes' suggestion that Arabs and Jews be appointed to responsible posts in the Palestinian Administration, the Chief Secretary, Shaw, answered that it "puts the cart before the horse, and willingness to cooperate must precede appointments." Paper by Shaw to AAC on Palestinian Citizenship, 25 March 1946, USNA, RG 43, AAC Box 11.
80. Cunningham to Hall, 5 April 1946, SACMEC, Cunningham Papers, Box 5, file 2.
81. McDonald diary, 14 March 1946.
82. D'Arcy testimony, Jerusalem, 14 March 1946, USNA, RG 43, AAC Box 11.
83. Arthur Lourie to Goldmann, 30 March 1946, Jerusalem, CZA, Goldmann files, Z6 Bundle 18, No. 1.
84. Repeated in Colonial Secretary to High Commissioner, 11 April 1946, SACMEC, Cunningham Papers, Box 1, file 1.
85. See Chapter 3, p. 52.
86. Shaw testimony, Jerusalem, 22 March 1946, USNA, RG 43, AAC, Box 11.
87. Note for the War Secretary, 20 Nov. 1943, unsigned, WO 32/10260.
88. June 1946, p. 16, CO 537/1856.
89. Farrell testimony, 22 March 1946, Hutcheson Papers.
90. Cunningham to George Gater, Colonial Office, 24 May 1946, CO 733/460, No. 75771/2/46. See also Phillips: "The Secretary of Education is a hopelessly stupid man ... a good example of the highly unfortunate Govt. which the British are maintaining in Palestine." Phillips diary, 27 March 1946.
91. Jerome Farrell: Notes on Jewish Education and the McNair Report, 30 Nov. 1946, CO 733/476/75089/2. The McNair Committee inquired into the question of Jewish education in Palestine, 1945-1946.
92. D. Horowitz, *State in the Making*, p. 75.
93. Aydelotte diary, 29 March 1946; Blanshard, *Frank Aydelotte of Swarthmore*, pp. 357, 361.
94. Crossman, *Palestine Mission*, pp. 150, 167-168; Crossman to Mrs. Zita Crossman,

23 March 1946, SACMEC, Crossman Papers.

95. Leggett to Magnes, Jerusalem Hearings, 14 March 1946.
96. Phillips, *Ventures in Diplomacy*, p. 289. His chapter on the AAC is called "An Observer in Palestine."
97. Phillips diary, Jerusalem, 8 March 1946.
98. Cunningham to Hall, 5 April 1946, SACMEC, Cunningham Papers, Box 5, file 2.
99. Crossman to Mrs. Zita Crossman, 23 March 1946, SACMEC, Crossman Papers.
100. Crossman, *Palestine Mission*, p. 144. Evan Wilson wrote that the only place where the AAC found Jews and Arabs together was at the asylum for the insane in Acre. "In Palestine you don't have to be crazy to mix with the other community – but it helps." *Decision on Palestine*, p. 75.
101. Hutcheson to M. Jaffee, AAC in camera hearings, 21 March 1946. Hutcheson Papers; Lourie to Goldmann, 7 April 1946, Jerusalem, CZA, Goldmann files, Z6, Bundle 18, No. 1.
102. Aydelotte diary, 11 April 1946.
103. Buxton to Frankfurter, 4 April 1946, Frankfurter Papers, container 40.
104. Comment by Beeley, 26 May 1946, FO 371/52524/E4469.

10

Lausanne: Unanimity First

"This is one of the loveliest spots on earth," wrote Aydelotte, a few days after the Committee reached Lausanne. "It is a kind of return from the frontier to civilization again."[1] Crossman happily added that there was "not a soldier, not a policeman, not a detective to be seen ... we were no longer V.I.P.s; we were not even worth a single journalist's presence."[2] While this was obviously an enormous change from Palestine, the most difficult stage of the Inquiry still lay before the commissioners and Judge Hutcheson expressed his concern in his opening words:

I pray that my tongue may cleave to the roof of my mouth and my right hand forget its cunning if I forget that we are a joint committee and, forgetting, permit myself to be moved by a sense of narrow nationalism or of division as between British and American. If I differ then with my colleagues, I shall differ on the merits of the proposals and not on the basis of nationality.[3]

As it turned out, the commissioners and their respective governments had to make supreme efforts to bring the Inquiry to an agreed end. At certain crucial moments, it appeared that unilateral national reports were a distinct possibility.

On long term immigration policy, the initial proposals in Lausanne ranged from free immigration or limited immigration to immigration according to the White Paper (i.e., an end to it). With regard to a political settlement, proposals ranged from a Jewish state through partition, bi-nationalism and to an Arab state (as proposed in the White Paper). In the interim, however, immigration of the 100,000 and the extension of the Mandate (this time termed "trusteeship") seemed the only options which the AAC could unanimously agree upon. Otherwise two, or even three, reports might emerge.[4] As to the long term prospects, Aydelotte wrote:

We had a good meeting this morning and reached agreement on ... no Jewish state, no Arab state, but some kind of bi-national or tri-national state or union, under Mandate or Trusteeship ... The negative statement we agreed on, but we are not yet agreed on the positive form.

He would continue to lament this fact: the inability of the AAC to agree to anything but what not to do in Palestine.[5]

On some issues the majority of the Committee were in agreement. They believed, for example, that had they recommended the withdrawal of British troops, the result would have been immediate and prolonged bloodshed.[6] On the other hand, they did not expect a major outburst of violence following the publication of their report, as Buxton later wrote: "We felt that they would be non-satisfied, but not dissatisfied. We foresaw some blood-letting by uncontrollable Arab and Jewish marauders," but, he added, even their objections would shortly subside.[7]

As to long term policies, the British chairman explained that "time had been too short, they [the AAC] were not an appropriate drafting body and they had felt that it was better to leave this aspect ... to be decided in the light of future events."[8] Since the whole issue was expected to be tabled before the UN, the Committee decided that it was pointless to work out the minutiae of a final settlement. They produced, therefore, only short term recommendations which "could ward off the danger of war and give to the British Government at least six months' breathing space," enough to keep things under control until the transfer of Palestine to a UN trusteeship.[9] In view of the fact that the Government had originally "cast a Joint Committee on the waters in the hope that a policy will return to them after many days," a policy designed, inter alia, to assuage Bevin's fears that a UN solution would automatically involve the Russians, it is easy to understand Attlee's opinion that the Committee had let him down badly.[10]

AMERICAN INVOLVEMENT: PRO AND CON

A serious question which engaged the Committee was that of letting America take some responsibility for Palestine. The British were of the opinion that the admission of immigrants would expose the Palestine Administration to the wrath of the Arabs. They rejected the idea of seeking assistance from the Hagana and sought help rather from America. The Americans, on the other hand,

would have been only too happy to use the Hagana for this purpose, rather than their own forces, were the AAC to recommend
such action. McDonald wrote that in a dialogue between the two
judges, Singleton asked whether

policemen who had defended us would welcome the cooperation of the
Hagana and what wives and mothers of such policemen would think. We
don't see why we should continue to bear these heavy burdens made
heavier by American demands ... J.H. [=Hutcheson] then spoke, again
stressing that we were not in a position to commit the United States to
cooperation.[11]

Crossman makes two separate references to this:

From the first, our American colleagues had been convinced that Mr.
Bevin had outwitted Mr. Truman in getting the Committee at all and
had been on the lookout for any British attempt to involve the Americans further. This stress, therefore, on the need for American military
assistance, aroused their keenest suspicions that the whole Committee had
been framed for this express point of view.[12]

No indication was given to us what-so-ever that you desired to push
responsibility on to America ... At a lunch given to the Committee
in London, the Foreign Secretary stated unequivocally that, if the Committee reached unanimity, he himself would carry the Report into effect.
He made no reference what-so-ever to American assistance being a sine
qua non. Moreover ... at Lausanne, the Foreign Office official [Beeley]
... always stressed that it was not in British interests to work for a joint
Anglo-American control of Palestine.[13]

This matter, however, was not considered substantive enough to
justify the presentation of separate reports. Nor was the question of
the change in the status of the Jewish Agency and the disbandment
of the underground movements. Wilfrid Crick proposed conditions
attached to the admission of the 100,000:

It should be expressly understood that the Jewish Agency would withdraw
its support of ... further illegal immigration ... That the Agency would ...
render all possible assistance to the Mandatory Power in maintaining law
and order ... In particular, it would exercise its influence upon the Jewish
population to avoid provocative actions, such as illegal military training
and accumulation of arms ... and that it would facilitate entry ... of the
authorities ... for the purpose of search and arrest (the above are without
prejudice to further proposals regarding the Jewish Agency).[14]

In the atmosphere which prevailed in Lausanne this drew an
immediate response from McDonald, who announced that he

would not sign a Report which did not strengthen the Agency and broaden its powers. "I want to emphasize," he said, "that I am not asking merely that 'bouquets' be showered upon the Agency."[15] This stunned even the Americans, who saw it as a "wild idea, like asking for the strengthening of Tammany Hall."[16] Judge Hutcheson declared that if McDonald defended the Agency, "he would join in a smashing attack on it."[17] On the other hand, under pressure from McDonald, Crum and Buxton, the British too had to shelve their restrictive recommendations since

they ... heard that if the Jewish Agency were attacked, the Mandatory Power and the dear old Palestinian officials would also be surveyed, and that the Agency could defend itself better than London and Palestine could justify all that has happened.[18]

Thus, subject after subject was omitted from the Report in the interests of unanimity.

American attitudes on disarming the underground movements also challenged Britain's current thinking on Palestine, which saw the negation of the demands of one side as a substitute for the fulfilment of the wishes of the other side. As Manningham-Buller argued:

It is not enough for us to say that there shall be no Jewish state to make Palestine safe for Jewish immigrants ... it is important to allay Arab fears that every immigrant is a recruit for the force that will one day seek to seize the country.[19]

Here, however, after much haggling, American tradition proved the weightier:

Judge Hutcheson had quoted from the United States Constitution on the right of the people to bear arms and from Thomas Jefferson on revolutionary bands; ... He [Buxton] explained that the Hagana was not an army in any formal sense ... but like the American revolutionary army was "a rabble in arms in the fine sense."[20]

To this was added certain anxieties which had plagued the members since their visit to Palestine:

Nothing could be more terrible than a recurrence in Palestine of the Irish Black and Tans ... The disarming of the Hagana ... I cannot help feeling that if our Report were to do this, we should have on our consciences the responsibility for the death of many more British soldiers.[21]

The main concern was to lessen the tension which prevailed in

the country. This could be achieved by consenting to immigration
and abolishing the White Paper, the two issues which had caused
the Yishuv to resort to armed resistance. There could be no compromise, however, between this attitude, which sought to deal with
the causes of resistance, and that of Attlee, which advocated disarmament as the remedy to the problem of security in Palestine. As
Crossman pointed out to Attlee: "Our policy reduced the military
risks whereas yours enormously increased them."[22]

The immigration of the 100,000 was not a source of contention
within the Committee, nor was the question of long-term immigration after the admission of the 100,000. "I think," concluded
Manningham-Buller, "all disagree with the 1939 White Paper in
that respect." He ruled, however, that future immigration into
Palestine should be based on purely humanitarian grounds, adding,
"Is anything to be gained by repeating . . . the Balfour Declaration?
. . . I cannot think of any useful purpose that it would achieve other
than that of possibly placating American opinion."[23] The Americans – who disagreed – answered him in the following way:

> British policy in the Middle East is . . . Arab-oriented. There will therefore
> be strong pressures . . . to halt or drastically curtail Jewish immigration on
> political grounds. If the Committee did not specifically repeat the terms of
> the Balfour Declaration . . . it could be argued . . . that the National Home
> . . . could be "maintained and developed" without much further immigra-
> tion.[24]

Here as well the Report acceded to the American view, specifically linking the development of the National Home to further
immigration. Thus, in addition to the controversial subjects left out
of the Report, unanimity was preserved by British capitulation to
U.S. demands.

It was the opinion of some that if immigration of the 100,000
were permitted, the Yishuv would have to concentrate on solving
the enormous economic problems consequent upon it. This would
alienate the "extremists" who would continue to pursue their
"totalitarian political ambition." It was also expected to provide
the Jewish Agency with a serious problem: "By giving them a good
deal of what they ask, we have put the Agency 'on the spot.' "[25]
Crossman predicted even more serious difficulties for the Zionists
if the country were partitioned and the Jews given independence:
"Ben-Gurion himself would have to tell the Jews . . . the limitations

of the Judean state for Jewish immigration."[26] This idea appealed to people in both London and Washington, although it was soon shown to be illusory.[27]

The constitutional settlement discussed by the AAC in Lausanne was, in fact, confined to a choice between partition or a single country. All the other proposals offered by witnesses during the hearings relating to the political future of the country had been rejected before the Committee arrived in Lausanne. As a matter of fact, there is no evidence to suggest that the commissioners even considered the question of the political future of Palestine outside the public hearings. All the work done on this issue was done by the two research assistants of the American team, Paul L. Hanna and Leslie L. Rood. They analysed and, without exception, rejected all of the plans, initialling P.L.H. or L.L.R. on every draft. The only reason partition remained to be considered in Lausanne was because Crossman remained adamant in his adherence to it.

When originally considering the political status of Palestine, the AAC had looked for a guiding analogy, either in Western history and political institutions or even within the loose, decentralized Ottoman Empire.[28] The unique nature of the conflict was brought home to them when they came to study the official documentation which accompanied the Mandate – the Balfour Declaration, the various promises to the Arabs, the White Paper of 1939 and so on. Studying these added to the confusion of the Committee members, and it did not take long for them to conclude that the past was dead:

You demand justice now. In 1917 you were granted the Balfour Declaration and later the Mandate, but we stand now after the destruction of the whole world. Is it the only thing that you can't get rid of? It was possible to change borders; the League of Nations was destroyed; a new one had risen; and only the Balfour Declaration is not changeable? We have to work from today's point of view ... from today's justice.[29]

From then on, each plan for Palestine was considered in terms of its practicability; it was ruled out if force was required to give it effect and made without reference to past commitments. An all-Jewish or an all-Arab state was ruled out from the beginning. The remaining propositions were then discussed in the light of the possible reactions of the two communities in Palestine, the Arabs in the Middle East and the Jews in America, and the repercussions that each plan was likely to have on their country's external and internal politics. The finality of every settlement was the ultimate test, and all proposals failed to pass it. The plan for partition was dismissed on the grounds that, as Shaw had noted, there "would be a tendency for the dam to burst its banks."[30] Likewise, bi-nationalism was ruled out because it was clear that each community would continue to strive for its own ends: "the Jews regard themselves primarily as Jews, the Arabs as Arabs."[31] In this context, it is difficult to support Evan Wilson's view that the AAC implied a bi-national state when it recommended the continuation of the Mandate: the Committee had been told that in a bi-national state, Jews and Arabs would have parity of representation in the central governing institutions of the country irrespective of the size of each community.[32] Any other form of bi-nationalism which recognized the existence of an Arab majority would be an Arab Palestine. On the other hand, to balance an Arab majority of 1.2 million with 600,000 Jews was a non-democratic act which the Americans, especially Hutcheson, vehemently resisted.

A proposal to proceed with partition, and to attach the resulting Arab state to Trans-Jordan, was similarly rejected. The Committee accepted the arguments of the Chief Secretary of the Government in Palestine that "Palestine is maritime, a part of the Mediterranean region, having ties with the West and with Egypt. Trans-Jordan is Arabian, with a traditional orientation towards Damascus and a dynastic bias eastward to Iraq." Furthermore, he added, King Abdullah of Trans-Jordan was unpopular among Palestinian Arabs.[33] With the realization that an independent Arab state within a partitioned country would not be economically viable, and with the rejection of the merger of such a state with Trans-Jordan, the last chance of the AAC settling on partition disappeared.

Early in the Inquiry, the AAC had been warned not to submit a compromise solution since if such a solution "failed to satisfy either Jews or Arabs [it] might well result in a heavier and more protracted military commitment than any other solution."[34] The Committee, however, could not comply with this request, stating that the amount of force required to effect a solution would not be a component in their thinking.[35] They would continue to look for some kind of compromise which would require enforcement (partition) or a compromise which would require no action, namely the extension of the Mandate. In the end, they chose the latter course, and recommended that the country remain politically intact. This was in complete contradiction to their earlier "strong feeling that merely to recommend continuing immigration under a regime similar to the existing one will offer no solution."[36]

Perhaps one of the reasons for the failure of the AAC to find a suitable political plan for Palestine was the strong emphasis the commissioners placed on the principles of democracy and self-determination. The transfer of Palestinian Arabs to neighbouring Arab states was ruled out as being contrary to such principles, because, as Hutcheson told representatives of the Yishuv's National Council, "I as a citizen of Texas, would not like to be told I could go to Virginia." The principles of strict majority rule could not be applied since the

great imponderable ... which prevents the ordinary doctrine of fair elections and fair plebiscites in fixing majorities [is] that it is not a mere question of a majority or a minority but that the Jew's situation is that he has got to have a majority somewhere in order to live and this is the place where he should have it.[37]

But the idea of the AAC recommending a Jewish state solely to achieve a Jewish majority could not satisfy the American chairman. Hutcheson always challenged the Zionist representatives to submit an alternative set of principles based, as the American constitution was, on the principle of human rights. "How would I draw my constitution for the Jewish state merely that there should always be a majority of Jews? ... you have to have a principle for a state ... answer me 'Yes' or 'No.' "[38] Similarly the Wilsonian principle of self-determination would not allow him to settle on partition, since it would have run contrary to the professed desire of the existing majority in Palestine. Nor could he support a recommendation to

import people into a country for the deliberate purpose of creating there a majority in order to dominate the country and take control away from its inhabitants ... we could not have made ourselves parties to such a scheme of creeping conquest by colonization.[39]

Although this was, in some ways, Hutcheson's own personal democratic campaign, he did manage to impose his views on his colleagues, resorting from time to time to his authority, declaring that "as chairman of this Commission I rule that ... ," or demanding as chairman the right of veto.[40] Karlibach, a noted Jewish-

Palestinian correspondent, defined this aspect of the Inquiry as follows:

We, the victims of the failure of democracy, try to prove that our return to Palestine would be a democratic process. The eternal minority supports majority rule, and nevertheless demands to turn a majority in Palestine into a minority, and asks it from the majority champions according to the majority law book.[41]

As far as Hutcheson was concerned, there was still another reason for his objection to partition: "As a Christian I object on behalf of the Christian people of the world to have the Holy Land, like Christ's vestments, divided between Jew and Arab."[42]

So in the end, the solution was to make only implicit references to the subject and to recommend the extension of the Mandate in the new guise of trusteeship. There was no doubt that such a recommendation would induce a sense of grievous frustration in both parties involved in the Palestine conflict, but it was hoped that they would feel only unsatisfied, not dissatisfied.

Less than a month before, Edwin Samuel, head of the Palestine Broadcasting Service (later Viscount Samuel), had testified in camera in Jerusalem:

One of the problems in this country is its unpredictability . . . the future of India, the position of Russia and the Middle East strategy, have all a considerable influence on the future of Palestine . . . it would be a good thing if the Committee were to recommend a policy for the next five years only. The White Paper's great demerit was that it tried to crystallize the policy for all time. Five years ago nobody could have foreseen the D.P. problem and the massacre of the Jews in Europe. We require a continuation of trusteeship, and should rule out an Arab state . . . and a Jewish state . . . you will have equal disappointments. The Jews will start a clamour; and then the Arabs will cheer up when they see how disappointed the Jews are. And when both realize that neither has won, the majority will settle down.[43]

The Report followed this statement so closely one might have thought that Samuel actually directed the meetings at Lausanne.

Surprisingly, the AAC regarded world politics as being irrelevant to the Inquiry, and on the few occasions when the relevance of Russian policy to the Palestine situation was discussed, it was mainly at the instigation of Crossman, and, to a lesser extent, Crum. Crossman considered that the Russians were a peaceful people and there was, therefore, no need to discuss Palestine in global terms. He repeatedly introduced the question of Soviet involvement in the Middle East and since the Military's answer to it was of minor importance, he refused to see Russia as an enemy, and consequently objected to an Anglo-U.S. trusteeship in Palestine which would eventually result in the exclusion of Russia.[44] Similarly, his British colleagues saw no reason to involve America in Palestine, thus implicitly denying the need for an Anglo-American alliance in the area against a Russian threat. According to the British, "American financial assistance ... would merely divert Palestinian trade to the United States; joint trusteeship with America would be fraught with tremendous difficulties; it would be a major disaster."[45] It seems that the longer people were away from London, the more they saw the United States as a threat rather than the Soviets, and the British members of the AAC were no exception to this.

LAST MINUTE PRESSURES

The discussions in Lausanne did not pass without crises and ultimatums, which at one stage in the proceedings necessitated Government intervention. In a meeting between Philip Noel-Baker (Minister of State at the Foreign Office, who happened to be in Lausanne for the dissolution of the League of Nations) and Singleton, which had been arranged by Crossman, Singleton heard about the importance of a unanimous Report in accordance with Bevin's unanimity pledge.[46] Later Bevin's pledge was attributed by the Foreign Office to "some semi-jocular reference of his."[47] It had no effect on the British chairman, who continued to make immigration conditional upon the disbandment of the underground movements. Later, when he realized that he was the only British member sticking to this point, he bowed out for tactical reasons. Crossman, who happens to be the only source for this meeting, ascribed the presentation of a unanimous report to it, and thus, indirectly, to himself. However, Frederick Leggett who played the mediator in Lausanne, heard about this meeting for the first time only in 1960.[48] In 1946 Crossman himself gave a different version of how Singleton interpreted Noel-Baker's unanimity mission. It bore no resemblance to the Report:

Sir John understood that Noel-Baker meant a unanimous Report against immigration and the Jews generally, and not favourable to them.[49]

This is perhaps a good example of how misleading it is to rely on Crossman as the sole source for any statement.

Of greater importance were the communications which the U.S. team received from the White House. The American judge's tendency to leave or to ignore controversial subjects worried the Zionists lest some of the restrictions contained in the White Paper should, after all, survive the Committee. One anxious Agency man wrote that, for "our *Shofet* [= Judge] ... it is extremely essential that the Boss in Washington would cable him."[50] The Jewish Agency's approach finally resulted in a Presidential message being sent to Hutcheson. The wording was general, expressing confidence in the Judge's methods and reaffirming the need for justice for the DPs.[51] But it immediately brought about a change in Hutcheson, who behaved as if "God had given him a revelation."[52] He informed the British that "he does not give a damn what they want, but he would like to know immediately so that the Americans can get down to the drafting of *their* recommendations."[53] After a few more warnings about a separate Report, a joint draft appeared.[54]

This gave rise to some changes among the British team. Led by Manningham-Buller, five members agreed to withdraw their conditions for the immigration of the 100,000 (in particular the disbandment of the underground movements and the reorganization of the Agency). According to Arthur Lourie of the Jewish Agency:

Singleton was eventually virtually repudiated by his whole group. From that moment on, his hold on his own people was broken and Bell [= Manningham-Buller] established himself as the dominant influence among the Britishers.[55]

More than once, the conference in Lausanne was on the verge of exploding, and not always because of matters of substance. After three months of collecting material, Singleton demanded a week to sift the facts before getting down to recommendations. Hutcheson viewed this as a British attempt to stall and saw no reason why the Committee should not report within three or four days.[56] Phillips was of a different opinion: "I know the British method of work, which is slower and more painstaking than ours."[57] It did not take long before the two judges were (again!) not speaking to each other.[58] In addition to this, the American judge, unlike his British colleagues, required no written analyses or papers, and called merely for an exchange of oral views. Homesick, he sought to speed up procedures. This was also the reason why he objected to the institution of sub-committees to prepare the chapters on Palestine and the DPs, regarding it as an unnecessary waste of time.[59] He considered the three months in the field plus his Bench experience to be sufficient.

Gradually the atmosphere became heated. "We have got to a point where petty nationalistic emotions and even personal prestige are threatening the success of our work," noted Aydelotte, and a few days later: "All are suffering from confinement and lack of exercise."[60] It resembled a "conclave" where even the secretaries and the stenographers were excluded. The atmosphere was heavy with suspicion, intensified by the active presence of the press.[61] Unflattering and blunt comments appeared in the commissioners' private diaries; there were rumours of an affair between a married member of the Committee and a girl on the staff; there were hints of homosexual relations among three other members.[62] McDonald expressed himself as follows: "Perhaps I am thinking with my intestines as is the custom of one of our colleagues, but in any case the language ... of your report brings me to the verge of vomiting."[63] Of the judges' incompatibility, Aydelotte wrote: "We are getting tired of the pomposity of [them] and ... considering a revolt." In the American camp Hutcheson saw every divergent opinion as a show of disloyalty to him and to the American cause, and Crossman's support of partition earned him a similar label among the British team. Of the two groups, more individuality was discernible among the British, which meant that the American judge could depend upon more votes to support his case. Attempts by Aydelotte and Phillips to dissociate themselves from national ties and play the role of harmonizers, and attempts by Crum and McDonald to advocate partition, were suppressed by Hutcheson who was assisted by "old Bux."[64]

Of greater importance were the national divisions within the AAC. The American group met separately, both for social purposes and to consider matters of substance before coming to the plenary.[65] McDonald confided to his diary that "in J.H.'s room he showed us a highly confidential and explosive analysis on the position of the British. It was so loaded that we agreed to turn all the documents back before we left the room." Crossman's dissent from the views of his British colleagues in supporting partition did not change the national distribution. Crossman was originally "all over the place and landed nowhere" and even appeared at the beginning to support an Arab Palestine.[66] His later shift towards partition smelled more of expediency – dissent was news – than of the Committee's "surprising non-national divisions."[67]

As it turned out things were finally settled by Hutcheson and Manningham-Buller.[68] However, when the draft was concluded and the parties ready to attach their signatures to it, they discovered that Singleton had slipped into it the requirement that, prior to the admission of the 100,000 and any further immigration, consultations be held with the Arab states. When submitting this draft, Singleton stated that it was identical with the one the two sides had agreed upon.[69] The uproar was terrible, as were the mutual recriminations. The Americans later scanned the drafts "to make sure nobody was trying another Sir John on us ... Hanna ... sat up all night to safeguard us."[70]

Lausanne was coloured by another phenomenon – the presence of a Zionist delegation, which closely followed the discussions through their contacts with McDonald and Crum.[71] Their preference was for a mild unanimous Report rather than a minority Report supporting the Jewish cause. Again, the achievement of unanimity should be seen as a result of developments inside the AAC (in this last context as a result of Hutcheson's warning that he would "smash" the Agency if McDonald did not drop his demand to strengthen it), and not as a result of Zionist influence.[72]

FINALLY, AGREEMENT

An agreed draft was finally composed and unanimity preserved, but the price was high as the common denominator was low, and no details were included. Did the commissioners thereby play into the hands of those in the Foreign Office who conceived the condition of unanimity as an insurmountable obstacle, or at least a guarantee of a non-effective Report, one which would check Anglo-American cooperation in Palestine? Or was this the natural result of the desire of any committee of inquiry to draw up a unanimous report? Bevin genuinely wanted unanimity, although his officials tried to brush it aside as a mere "semi-jocular" expression. In any case, "the

American chairman ... treated this remark in all seriousness."[73] The outcome was that the

practicability of any plan for Palestine cannot be determined unless that plan is worked out in detail. This was not done in the Peel Report or in the Report of the AAC, with the result that the Palestine problem has never been solved.[74]

And thus, on 20 April 1946, the Report was signed and "tout est fini, accompli, reasadjutica [sic] (God damn this machine)."[75] The Americans were left with a feeling of triumph, the British with the feeling that they had given way to American pressure. On the night of 29 April, the American judge invited his eleven colleagues to a dinner. The menu was as follows:

Grapefruit au Choix
(Juif ou Arabe)
Potage Balfour
Tournedos Truman aux Champignons Bevin
Pommes à la mode de Texas
Salade de Recommendations
Sabayon à la Gruber
Café Hagana
Châteauneuf du Mufti.[76]

THE FINAL PRODUCT

The final AAC Report dealt with five subjects: immigration, land, the form of government, development and security.[77] The order of presentation in which immigration was pushed out of first place and into second, the absence of certain subjects, and matters which appeared in the comments following the recommendations (but not in the recommendations) – all indicated the compromises and the give and take which characterized the meetings in Lausanne.

The Committee called first for a governmental and UN solution to the general problem of the DPs, either by emigration or by rehabilitation in Europe. They then recommended that 100,000 Jewish DPs be authorized to enter Palestine as rapidly as possible. They commented that "we know of no country to which the great majority [of the Jewish DPs] can go in the immediate future other than Palestine," and added: "Those who have opposed the admission ... if they cannot see their way to help, at least they will not make the position of these sufferers more difficult." As to immigration in the long term, the Report recommended that it should continue, in accordance with the obligation of the Mandate to facilitate Jewish immigration for the development of the National Home. It also added:

> We reject the view that there shall be no further Jewish immigration ... without Arab acquiescence, a view which would result in the Arab dominating the Jew. We also reject the insistent Jewish demand that forced Jewish immigration must proceed apace in order to produce as quickly as possible a Jewish majority.[78]

Thus the Committee dealt with the problem of the displaced Jews (in Recommendations 1, 2 and 6) establishing a direct link between the DPs and the question of immigration into Palestine.

Recommendation 7, which related to land policy in Palestine, considered the Land Transfer Regulations of 1940 to be discriminatory and recommended that they be rescinded. While they were considered to discriminate against the Jews, the AAC also thought them unfair to the Arabs. An Arab landowner who lived in a zone where sales to Jews were restricted did not have the same rights as his brethren living in the free zone. They could sell their land for "a fantastic price" and thus add to the congestion of the other zones by moving there.[79] In addition to this, the Committee considered the confinement of land sales to zones to be consistent only with partition, since it would encourage the two communities to take root in their respective provinces, and this ran contrary to the AAC's belief that the country should remain undivided.[80]

As to the future form of government in Palestine, dealt with in Recommendations 3 and 4, the AAC concluded "once for all" that the country should be neither Arab nor Jewish. And since in the Arab–Zionist struggle over Palestine the Christian interest "has been completely overlooked, glossed over or brushed aside ... we ... emphatically declare that Palestine is a Holy Land ... and can never become a land which any race or religion can claim as its very own."[81] In addition, although the reason given for the indefinite extension of trusteeship in Palestine was the prevailing hostility between the two communities, the desire to secure the continued presence of a Christian Power in the country figured very prominently.[82]

Social and economic development were dealt with in Recommendations 5, 8 and 9. "One of the chief causes of friction," it was stated, "is the great disparity between the Jewish and Arab standards of living." The Report, therefore, advocated equality of standards in economic, educational and social affairs. It also called for large scale agricultural and industrial developments, some of which should be undertaken through cooperation with adjacent Arab countries. As to education, the AAC called for the introduction of compulsory education and for greater Government control over Arab and Jewish schooling in order to avoid propaganda-based instruction.[83]

Security was dealt with in Recommendation 10, the last subject to be dealt with and the shortest. The section was entitled "The Need for Peace in Palestine." The tenor of this chapter was relatively mild in comparison to the emotion which the issue had brought out in the Committee's discussions. Security and the disarmament of the Yishuv were no longer pre-requisites; on the contrary: "We recommend that if this report is adopted ... any [armed] attempt ... to prevent its execution will be resolutely suppressed." The only connection made between security and immigration was a call to the Jewish Agency to assist in the maintenance of law and order "for the good of all, including the new immigrants."[84]

The prevalence of "too many uncertain factors" prevented the Committee from proposing a more ambitious and detailed plan, although they were appointed for this very reason.[85] It seemed, however, that the conflicting national and personal backgrounds, the different methods of working, the Crusader mentality, the inclination to perceive things non-politically, the perplexity of the issues, and the legacies of the White Paper and Peel Report could not lead to anything but a cautious Report.

The question is whether in 1946 a random group of British and Americans could meet the Jewish displaced persons, Arabs and Zionists and produce more than a description of the prevailing difficulties in Palestine with a recommendation for the extension of the Mandate. Perhaps the AAC demonstrated that it was impossible to go beyond these limits. Since the implementation of a more active plan was to be a British, and to a certain extent, an American responsibility, one can understand the reluctance of the AAC to recommend a more active course. This also explains the fact that the UNSCOP (United Nations Special Committee on

Palestine), which was composed of representatives of eleven outside member countries with no responsibility for the implementation of its recommendations, was able to settle on partition just a
year later.

The ten recommendations were followed by nine chapters
summarizing the AAC's findings on the position of the Jews in
Europe, the political situation in Palestine, its geography and
economics, Jewish and Arab attitudes, Christian interests, Jews,
Arabs, and Government, public security and general matters.
There were also seven appendices giving facts and figures concerning the position of the Jews in various European countries; the
estimated Jewish population of Europe; the Mandate document,
the AAC itinerary and a list of the staff. Maps on rainfall, population and land, prepared by the geographers on the staff, were also
included.

With reference to the language of the Report, Hutcheson, who
used English freely, differed from the pedantic Singleton. But he
argued that "its rhetorical finish or lack of finish will neither heal
nor hurt." Aydelotte, on the other hand, wrote in his journal that
"most of our members really cannot tell the difference between
good English and bad."[86]

The publication of the Report put an end to the lull which had
enveloped Palestine policy-making for more than four months.
Within a few days, little attention would be paid to the commissioners, and by July their Report would become history. Intensive correspondence continued among them for years afterwards,
and this points to some of the friendships that were built between
January and April 1946.[87] There, and in their memoirs, they
lamented the shelving of their Report.

Four months of intensive labour went for nothing. The enormous expenses
of transportation and accommodation for the Committee members and
large staff of experts, assistants and clerks were wasted.[88]

And although this was written after 1948, it was perhaps typical of
the writer, William Phillips, that he lamented the waste of money
rather than the AAC's failure to prevent the war that followed.

NOTES

1. Aydelotte diary, 2 April 1946.
2. Crossman, *Palestine Mission*, p. 174.
3. Hutcheson to Committee, Lausanne, 1 April 1946, Frankfurter Papers, container 40.
4. Crossman to Hector McNeil, Minister of State in the Foreign Office, Lausanne, 22 April 1946, FO 371/52524/E4469. See draft of it in SACMEC, Crossman Papers.
5. Aydelotte diary, Lausanne, 3 and 9 April 1946. In this context came the agreement to discontinue the White Paper. Aydelotte's Lausanne chapter is very detailed and more inspiring than the diaries of his colleagues.
6. Singleton on Public Security, Lausanne, 9 April 1946, SACMEC, Crossman Papers.
7. Buxton, "A Report in Retrospect," *The New Palestine*, vol. 37, no. 20, 20 June 1947, p. 136. On Hutcheson's copy of the article, there is a comment by the Judge: "This is an excellent discussion. Buxton was one of my best men," Hutcheson Papers.
8. Singleton to Attlee, London, 14 May 1946, FO 371/52524/E4514.
9. Crossman, *Palestine Mission*, p. 184; Crossman to McNeil, London, May 1946, FO 371/52524/E4469.
10. Martin to Shaw, 14 Nov. 1945, CO 733/463, Pt. 2, No. 75872/138; Crossman on Attlee's reaction, in Crossman to Attlee, 7 May 1946, SACMEC, Crossman Papers.
11. McDonald diary, Lausanne, 6 April 1946.
12. Crossman to McNeil, Lausanne, 22 April 1946, p. 2, FO 371/52524/E4469.
13. Crossman to Attlee, 7 May 1946, SACMEC, Crossman Papers.
14. Crick's Memo on Immediate Immigration, 5 April 1946, McDonald Papers, folder 16. He also asked whether this immigration should not be conditional on America sending "forthwith to Palestine ... a token military force and a cadre for embodiment in the civil administration." As to other restrictions on the Agency, see Crick to Bevin, 26 April 1946. The restrictions were omitted from the Report "for the sake of unanimity, as well as to avoid inflaming an already delicate situation." They included a constitution acceptable to the Trustee; opening of the Agency's accounts to independent scrutiny; no more allocation of certificates by the Agency; no more activities in countries neighbouring Palestine. SACMEC, Cunningham Papers, Box 5, file 2. On reactions to Crick's proposals, see memo by John Martin, 30 April 1946, FO 371/52519/E3961, and memo by Cunningham, 8 June 1946, FO 371/52535/E6182.
15. Memo by McDonald, 16 April 1946, p. 2, McDonald Papers, folder 16.
16. Aydelotte diary, Lausanne, 16 and 20 April 1946. Tammany Hall was equal to corruption and nepotism within the elected bodies in New York as from 1910.
17. McDonald diary, 16 April 1946.
18. Buxton to Frankfurter, Lausanne, 4 April 1946, Frankfurter Papers.
19. Memo on immigration, 15 April 1946, p. 3, McDonald Papers, folder 16.
20. Halifax to Foreign Office, 3 May 1946, on Buxton's reaction to Attlee's demand to disarm the illegal armies, FO 371/52520/E4055.
21. Crossman, Note on the Jewish Illegal Army, Lausanne, 3 April 1946, McDonald Papers, folder 16. See also Crossman to Attlee, 7 May 1946, p. 5, SACMEC, Crossman Papers.
22. 7 May 1946, SACMEC, Crossman Papers.
23. Memo on immigration, April 1946, McDonald Papers, folder 16.
24. P. L. Hanna, U.S. staff, Lausanne, 10 April 1946, McDonald Papers, folder 16.
25. Crossman to McNeil, 22 April 1946, FO 371/52524/E4469.

26. Crossman on partition, Lausanne, 7 April 1946, p.3, ZANY, McDonald file. See Cunningham to AAC, Jerusalem 22 March 1946: "As long as the Jews were not responsible for the control of the country, complete irresponsibility would be shown as to numbers which would be admitted," SACMEC, Cunningham Papers, Box 5, file 2. See also Harris, Colonial Office, who expected the Jewish trade unions to object to further immigration on the grounds of unemployment and a lowering of standards of living. Enclosure to Provincial Autonomy, 29 June 1945, CO 733/463, Pt. 1, No. 75872/132. See also Cunningham to Hall on Clayton's partition, 20 Sept. 1946, CAB 127/280; Anglo-U.S. study of the AAC Report, scheme of Provincial Autonomy (No. P 30), 13 July 1946, p.5, FO 371/52541/E6794/G.
27. On the U.S. view see Wilson, *Decision on Palestine*, p.156.
28. McDonald to Lord Samuel, London Hearings, 29 Jan. 1946.
29. Report to Jewish Agency Executive, 10 Feb. 1946 (Hebrew), Jerusalem, CZA.
30. Evidence of John Shaw, Chief Secretary Palestine Government, Jerusalem Hearings, 22 March 1946, USNA, RG 43, AAC, Box 11, p.21.
31. Unsigned memo, McDonald file, ZANY.
32. Wilson, *Jerusalem, Key to Peace*, p.64; Wilson, *Decision on Palestine*, p.88; unsigned memo, Bi-Nationalism or Partition, McDonald file, ZANY.
33. Shaw on "Practicability of attaching the Arab state, assuming Partition, to Trans-Jordan," 25 March 1946, USNA, RG 43, AAC, Box 11.
34. Memo by C. in C., Middle East to AAC on Maintenance of Law and Order in Palestine, p.4, Cairo, 1 Feb. 1946, USNA, RG 43, AAC, Box 10.
35. Hutcheson to C. in C. Cairo, 5 March 1946, USNA, RG 43, AAC, Box 10, p.23.
36. Crum, code name "Francis" to representative of Zionist Office, London, 3 Feb. 1946, Jerusalem, CZA, No. Z4/15440.
37. Jerusalem Hearings, 13 March 1946.
38. To Dr. H. Greenberg of the Zionist Labour Party, Poalei Zion, Washington Hearings, 10 Jan. 1946.
39. Lecture to Bar Association of Houston, Texas, 31 May 1946, Truman Library, Truman Papers, 204, Misc. Box 772.
40. Jerusalem Hearings, 11 March 1946; Ms. of Crossman diary, Vienna, SACMEC, Crossman Papers.
41. *The AAC of Inquiry*, p.10.
42. Lausanne, 1 April 1946, Frankfurter Papers.
43. Jerusalem Hearings (in camera), 25 March 1946, pp.1-2, Hutcheson Papers.
44. Report to Jewish Agency Executive, 10 Feb. 1946, on meetings with Crossman during the Washington Hearings, Jerusalem, CZA. See also meetings with British C. in C., Cairo, 5 March 1946, pp.11-12, and meeting with G.O.C. Palestine, Jerusalem, 14 March 1946, pp.20-21, USNA, RG 43, AAC, Boxes 10 and 11 respectively.
45. Meeting of British members of AAC with Attlee, 14 May 1946, FO 371/52524/E4514.
46. Presumably he acted independently in seeing Singleton. Bevin later commented on the Report: "Show this to Noel-Baker. Rumour persists that he advised this. He had better see the P.M. and make clear what actually happened." Comments on Baghdad to Foreign Office, 26 April 1946, FO 371/52519/E3869/G. See also Ilan, *America, Britain and Palestine*, p.211.
47. Foreign Office to Paris (U.K. delegation to conference of Foreign Ministers), 11 May 1946, FO 371/52522/E4268.
48. Leggett to G. Cohen, interview, London, 5 Dec. 1960.
49. In Buxton to Frankfurter, 18 Nov. 1946, Frankfurter Papers, container 40.
50. Meyer Weisgal, Jewish Agency, New York, to Goldmann, 5 April 1946, CZA, Goldmann files, Z6, Bundle 18/1. See also McDonald diary, 17 April 1946: "Crum

told me a new communication from Harry to J.H." On telephone calls between Crum and Niles, see Niles to Matthew Connelly, Secretary to the President, 16 April 1946, Truman Libary, President Official file No. 204, Misc.Box 771.

51. Elath, *The Struggle for Statehood*, vol. 1, p. 342.
52. Goldmann to Agency Executive Conference, Paris, 2 Aug. 1946, CZA.
53. Buxton to Frankfurter, Lausanne, 4 April 1946, Frankfurter Papers, container 40. My emphasis.
54. On Hutcheson's ultimatum (16 April) to the British, see Lourie to Goldmann, 21 April 1946, CZA, Goldmann files, No. Z6, Bundle 18/1; McDonald to Hutcheson, 2 July 1946, McDonald Papers, folder 187.
55. Lourie to Goldmann, 21 April 1946, CZA, Goldmann files, no. Z6, Bundle 18/1.
56. Ibid., 3 April 1946.
57. Phillips diary, Lausanne, 12 April 1946.
58. Lourie to Goldmann, 3 Apr. 1946, CZA, Goldmann files, No. Z6, Bundle 18/1.
59. Phillips diary, 31 March and 1 April 1946. Hutcheson hoped that this would also prevent a split in the Committee. "Attempt to stall" was the Judge's reaction to Leggett's move to table the agreed facts first, McDonald diary, 1 April 1946.
60. Aydelotte diary, 2 and 6 April 1946.
61. Blanshard, *Aydelotte of Swarthmore*, p. 375. On C.I.D. agents, tapped telephones, opened mail, etc., see Wilson, *Decision on Palestine*, p. 203; correspondence between the Foreign Office and Washington Embassy, Aug.–Sep. 1946, FO 371/52554/E8337 and FO 371/52558/E9307.
62. Letter to Buxton from a member of the AAC staff, undated, Frankfurter Papers, container 40; ms. of Crossman diary, Lausanne, SACMEC, Crossman Papers.
63. McDonald to AAC, 12 April 1946, McDonald diary.
64. Aydelotte diary, 4 and 30 March, 1, 7, 9, 13 and 15 April 1946; Buxton to Frankfurter, 4 April 1946, Frankfurter Papers; McDonald diary, 20 April 1946. See Aydelotte on Hutcheson: "He would like to be surrounded by five 'yes men'; luckily there are only one or two," diary, 1 April 1946.
65. Phillips diary, 5–8 April 1946; Aydelotte diary, 9 April 1946. On the attempt of Buxton, "the most maladroit of all our members" and Hutcheson to organize a separate picnic for the Americans, see Aydelotte diary, 2 April 1946.
66. McDonald diary, Lausanne, 1, 5 and 6 April 1946.
67. Ilan, *America, Britain and Palestine*, p. 208.
68. "The best, ablest, most substantial of the Englishmen ... the same big and dark and stubborn M.B.," Buxton to Frankfurter, 19 April 1946, Frankfurter Papers.
69. Aydelotte diary, 19 April 1946; McDonald diary, 19 April 1946.
70. Buxton to Frankfurter, 19 April 1946, Frankfurter Papers.
71. McDonald diary, 6 April 1946; Jewish Agency Executive meeting of 2 June 1946, CZA. A Treasury official who resented the stay in luxurious Lausanne, had added: "The AAC ... will retire to Lausanne where, so they say, they will not be subject to pressure ... or other lobbying. If you choose to believe this story, I can't prevent you," H. G. Brooks, 14 Feb. 1946, T 220/20.
72. See more on this in Agency Executive meetings, Jerusalem, 12 May 1946, and Paris, 4 Aug. 1946, CZA.
73. Foreign Office to Paris (U.K. Delegation to Foreign Ministers Conference), 11 May 1946, FO 371/52522/E4268.
74. Cunningham to Creech-Jones, Colonial Secretary, 11 April 1947, FO 371/61773/E3235.
75. Buxton to Frankfurter, 20 April 1946, Frankfurter Papers.
76. Aydelotte Papers, Box 2, correspondence with Judge Hutcheson. All the commissioners added their signatures to the menu. Hutcheson added: Houston, Texas. Ruth Gruber was an American reporter who accompanied the AAC.

77. Published later in London as Cmd. 6808.
78. AAC Report, pp. 2, 3, 6, 7.
79. AAC Report, p. 7.
80. Ibid., p. 8.
81. Ibid., p. 3.
82. Ibid., pp. 4, 5.
83. Ibid., pp. 5, 10, 22.
84. Ibid., p. 10.
85. Ibid., p. 6. Here it was in relation to the need to fix a number for annual immigration.
86. Hutcheson to Committee, Lausanne, 1 April 1946, in Frankfurter Papers; Blanshard, *Aydelotte of Swarthmore*, p. 374.
87. See the private papers of Crossman, Aydelotte, McDonald, Buxton, Hutcheson and Phillips. These also include letters from Leggett and Crum.
88. Phillips, *Ventures in Diplomacy*, p. 297.

11

Hanging Fire

The fears and hopes of both Jews and Arabs, held in check during the AAC deliberations, were now given freer rein with the publication of the Report. There was, as had been assumed there would be, "a gnashing of teeth" on both sides. Expressions of "unsatisfaction" as compared with "dissatisfaction" were largely, though not entirely, semantic. Both sides literally hung fire.

ARAB REACTIONS

Arab reaction to the Report had been anticipated and was expressed rather figuratively by the Amir Abdullah of Trans-Jordan:

I have no better comparison to this Committee's decision than the case of a man who, on seeing a piece of cake in the hand of a poor little orphan, inherited from his forefathers, slapped him on the face and tried to take the piece of cake in order to give it to another boy who has numerous wealthy and influential relatives and cousins all over the world.[1]

In Saudia Arabia, it was less poetic and more pointed:

The hostility felt by Arabs for this hateful Zionism is no whit less than any hatred felt by the Nazis towards those Jews in Europe; on the contrary – the hatred nurtured in Arab breasts for this malignant tyranny is stronger than any hatred of Nazis for Jews.[2]

But reactions were not only verbal. In Beirut, the U.S. Information Centre was set on fire. In Baghdad violent demonstrations were held in front of the British Embassy, where there was an exchange of fire with the police which resulted in several casualties, some fatal.[3] The Syrian President cancelled a visit to Britain and the United States, officially for medical reasons.[4] The Egyptian reaction, however, was a mixture of apathy and interest. This was attributed to their preoccupation with the revision of their own

Treaty since a solution in Palestine would jeopardize their chances by excluding Palestine as a possible place of retreat for the British forces then in Egypt. But, as an official in Cairo complained, the Egyptians are "a volatile people" and not easily capable of revealing interest in anything.[5] It was of some importance that Sidki Pasha's reaction to the Report, which amounted to strong support for partition and some positive views on the Yishuv's achievements, was ascribed in Cairo to the fact that the Egyptian Prime Minister "much associated with Jewish interests in business."[6]

Typically, the reactions were from the Arab states and not from the Palestinians. No one had expected independence: what had been expected was "sympathy for the Jews, justice for the Arabs, and Palestine for the British."[7] And so the frustration flared up when the Report was published, the Saudi Foreign Secretary claiming: "You have not done this even to Germany and Japan!"[8]

The cancellation of the White Paper and with it the land transfer regulations and the indefinite extension of the Mandate all resulted in Palestine itself in "a ferment of racial polemics, which, on the Arab side, reached a degree of bitterness unequalled since 1939."[9] Strikes, demonstrations, threats and calls for an uprising overwhelmed the country, although Arab villagers revealed a somewhat perfunctory attitude, frequenting Jewish cafés and using Jewish buses during the strike.[10] Arab members of the British Council and Anglo-Arab clubs resigned in protest.[11] At public appearances of Jamal Husseini and other leaders, money was raised to buy arms.[12] Both in Jerusalem and Cairo there were calls for the evacuation of Arab women and children to Egypt in preparation for a declaration of Jihad in Palestine.[13] There was a sharp exchange between Cunningham and Husseini when the High Commissioner rejected his claim that these were merely defensive measures, telling him that " 'defence' reminds him of Hitler, who also used this term."[14]

In the precarious system of Arab politics in Palestine, the Report weakened the position of the moderates, Jamal Husseini and Musa Alami. Their apparent failure to prevent an anti-Arab report precipitated a campaign against the newly established leadership of the Arab Higher Committee. But following Attlee's speech in the Commons, which appeared to reject the Report, the Palestinian Arabs returned to their internal squabbles, and their reliance on the diplomacy of the neighbouring countries.[15] Thus, the revival of

Arab politics in Palestine, generated by the AAC, soon subsided.[16] An extract from the private diary of Ben-Gurion (privately owned and published here for the first time) shows the Zionist leader weighing the Report from an Arab point of view:

The "good things" given to the Arabs are basically negative: not a Jewish state; protection of peasants and small land owners; ability of the neighbouring countries to block development. The Arabs will have a genuine basis for decrying the fact that they have been deceived and deprived of the rights which were promised to them by the White Paper.[17]

All in all, there was hardly an article of the Report which was not rejected by the Arabs. Even the recommendations which specified the need to develop the Arab sector were seen as a mere bribe aimed at facilitating the acceptance of future immigration. According to Azzam Pasha, "If ten extreme Zionists had got together in a New York room, they could not have devised anything more to the sole advantage of Zionists." He blamed America for putting pressure on Britain to produce an anti-Arab Report. "The Americans," said Azzam, "could get votes while the British would get the bullets."[18] Two of the recommendations in particular were considered objectionable, the first that territorially Palestine should belong to the three great religions.[19] On this subject the Arab League issued a sharp statement:

A land does not belong to religious communities living outside it ... but to its people. The suggestion that because Christendom in general is spiritually attached to Palestine and because the majority of Arabs are Moslems, their title to it as their country must not be accepted is ... an alarming throwback to the spirit of the Crusades.[20]

The second recommendation to which even stronger Arab pressure was directed was the one anchored in the view that the conflict was, to a large extent, the result of the gap between Arab and Jewish standards of living, and that the remedy lay in closing this social and economic gap. To the Arabs, this clearly implied the inferiority and backwardness of their culture vis-à-vis the Jews:

The Arabs of Palestine enjoy a standard of living and culture, economy, industry and agriculture which is not below that of the Arabs in Egypt, Syria, the Lebanon and Iraq. In all these countries there are Jewish communities having a high standard of living and, in spite of this, there is no friction between these communities and the other inhabitants on account of difference in standard of living.[21]

It was also now time for some action to be taken by the one-year-old Arab League. Under the auspices of King Farouk of Egypt and Azzam Pasha, a conference of Arab kings and heads of state assembled in Inchass on 28 and 29 May 1946 to discuss the Report. There was at first rather extreme talk of taking up arms against Britain (if the Report were implemented), encouraged by a letter from the Mufti which was read to the Conference. But this soon gave way to more practical suggestions such as the institution of a fund to buy land which was on the verge of being sold to Jews.[22] In addition, it was decided to convene an emergency meeting of the League's Council to discuss the actual measures to be taken against the Report. It was to take place in Bloudan, Syria, on 8–10 June 1946.

It was at the Grand Hotel in Bloudan in 1937 that the Arab states had presented a common front against the Peel Commission's recommendation of partition, and so might augur well for the future. But the June conference got off to a less auspicious start with the decision of the Council to dissolve and reorganize the dispute-ridden Arab Higher Committee, and loud protests from the opposition in the Committee. They complained that they were being treated by an "outside body as though they were immature children."[23] The reorganization was carried out by the League's Internal Committee appointed to deal with Palestinian Arab politics. The key figure in this body was Jamil Bey Mardam of Syria, who in December 1945, following the announcement of the AAC, had succeeded in re-establishing the Higher Committee. The Arab Higher Committee, it will be remembered, had been suppressed during the War.[24]

The Political Committee (unlike the Internal Committee) did not include a Palestinian delegate. In the discussions, the Iraqi Foreign Minister, Fadel Jamali, alleged that the League had let the Palestinians down, and demanded strong measures against Britain and America.[25] He was outnumbered, however, by the moderates. The latter were backed by a telegram from Ibn Saud, begging the conference to take moderate decisions rather than promise the Palestinians "heart-winning pledges which could be disastrous for them when we wash our hands of these pledges."[26] The delegates felt less confident, however, when they faced Jamal Husseini, who demanded more action from his brethren. He called for the immediate establishment of a Palestinian Arab Government-in-exile, which could, within six to seven months, set up an army of 100,000 soldiers to resist the implementation of the Report. Arms and ammunition were available from French, American and British army surpluses in the Middle East. According to Jewish Agency intelligence reports, Jamal claimed that militarily, his plan had received the support of Arab strategists, who had pointed out that an army of 100,000 combatants, plus 60,000-70,000 auxiliaries, would also solve the unemployment problem of the Arab countries. The plan left a deep impression on its hearers at Bloudan but could not survive the conference's tendency to handle the problem politically rather than militarily. Azzam agreed only to the institution of a liaison committee between the League and the reorganized Higher Committee to examine Jamal's demands and to deal with their financial aspects.[27] In addition, a Land Rescue Fund of one million pounds and a Propaganda Fund to win support for the Arab boycott were established. These decisions were followed by a note to HMG, protesting U.S. intervention and naming Britain as the only authority in Palestine with whom the Arabs would negotiate. A note was also dispatched to Washington, denouncing America's pro-Zionist attitude.[28]

There was a secret appendix attached to the public pronouncements and even today some Arab writers still feel the need to apologize (literally) when they disclose its contents.[29] However, already in June 1946 the Syrian President referred to the appendix as a "propaganda bluff" and by October 1947 at the Arab League meeting at Aley, Lebanon, the "Bloudan secret decisions had been honourably buried."[30] The secret appendix which amounted to a declaration of "active hostility by all means short of war" listed economic, political and cultural measures to be taken against Britain and the United States if the Report was implemented. The effectiveness of these steps can be deduced from the following passage: "The King [Abdullah] is so indignant with the Prime Minister and Minister for Foreign Affairs ... for having subscribed to this paper ... that we may well see a change in the Council of Ministers as a result."[31]

There were other hush-hush aspects to the Bloudan meeting.[32] At Azzam's request, Britain sent Brigadier Clayton and the head of the Arab section of the Palestine C.I.D., John Briance, to Bloudan to exert a "moderating British influence." The United States sent Dr. Philip Hitti for the same purpose.[33] The conference was also marked by stringent security precautions, which made it difficult for Zionists, Americans and British to obtain accurate information.[34]

The main spirit of Bloudan was clear: the Arab states settled on the diplomatic option (to the frustration of the Palestinians) and were ready to negotiate the future of the conflict only with Britain. This was another blow to the few people in London who expected the AAC to make Palestine an Anglo-American responsibility.

JEWISH REACTIONS

In the Jewish camp, both the supporters of the Report and those who rejected it viewed the recommendations as a turning point for Zionist policy. The dilemma of choosing between no immigration and the rejection of the Report, or no statehood and its acceptance, almost precipitated a split in the Zionist movement.[35] The question was further complicated by the fact that rejection of the Report would mean opposition to a joint Anglo-American policy.[36] As Weizmann put it: "We cannot fight the British Empire, so how can we fight both Britain and America?"[37] What saved the Agency from a painful decision and the Yishuv from certain vendetta, was Attlee's demand to disarm the underground movements.[38] British hopes that the Report would cause a split in the Zionist camp were dashed by the British themselves.

The Yishuv's moderates supported the Report, some with the feeling that the results of the Inquiry could have been even worse. Weizmann declared that the Zionist movement had

reached a most important stage after the Balfour Declaration. We finished a war with a great achievement ... States do not fall from heaven, they have to grow organically. Do not press ... we pushed and pressed and they pushed us back ... But we shall start immigration, land purchase, industry ... and thank God we survived the crisis and must take care that the Report will be approved.[39]

The main controversy in the Yishuv revolved around the question of immigration versus statehood. Weizmann considered that relinquishing the idea of the Jewish state was a reasonable price to pay for the immigration of the 100,000: "We cannot have both things [and] it would be better to discuss [immigration] than the imaginary Jewish state."[40] There were others who claimed that "Zionist political aims have been sacrificed to philanthropy," and that the Report's insistence that self-government would be granted only when hostilities ceased and the two communities began to cooperate was an indefinite postponement of statehood.[41] Magnes, in a letter to the *New York Times* (3 June 1946) saw the conditions of the Report as an example of "putting the cart before the horse." In his view the growth of goodwill between Jews and Arabs was contingent upon the two communities working together. Further criticism was levelled against the Report's implicit recommendation that Jews should be taxed to improve Arab education and social standards. But perhaps the harshest criticism is to be found in Ben-Gurion's Paris diary:

Well, the conclusions are worse than I feared ... This is a double elimination both of the White Paper and Zionism ... The worst thing is American approval for the abrogation of the Jewish people's right over its country ... It seems that the hands of N.G. [= Nahum Goldmann] and M.S. [= Moshe Sharett] are in this treachery. The 100,000 totally confused them ... We are facing a terrible crisis ... What the Report lacks is more worrisome than what it contains – no reference to the lack of a homeland for the Jewish people, no historical link between the Jewish people and its land. Instead there is a new principle: Palestine belongs equally to the Moslems, Jews and Christians. Actually an eternal British colony ... "National Home" for the British Army. It is difficult to understand how the American members signed such a shameful document ... The Americans were caught in the trap which the British Foreign Office had prepared and you have American approval for the elimination of Zionism. Crum and McDonald think they have achieved a brilliant triumph and done an historical service to the Jewish people! Now Crum demands the price – expression of thanks to Truman. "If there's no enthusiasm," he says, "that is ingratitude," and "Do not be Talmudic," says McDonald![42]

The question of the absorption of the 100,000 raised the thorny problem of accommodation, and corroborated the High Commissioner's report that the Agency was reluctant to give publicity to the housing shortage. The shortage was already being felt with the demobilization of 900 Jewish soldiers from the British Army (the first of 11,000 expected to return to Palestine during the summer of 1946).[43] Jewish sources in Palestine and in America denied that U.S. troops would be required to help in the absorption of the 100,000. They gave repeated assurances of the Zionists' ability to handle Arab opposition to mass immigration and to assist the British in policing the country.[44] One reason for this may have been the fear among the Jews in America that "if American troops are killed in Palestine, Jewish blood will flow in New York."[45]

There was also strong Zionist opposition to the "theocratic state" which they thought the Report wanted to establish in Palestine.[46] The Agency complained that Britain has "a pure Christian conception: they want to turn Palestine into a holy vessel, forbidden to be touched; a museum of antiquities and the repository of holy relics."[47] Others protested against halting developments around the Lake of Galilee and along the Jordan River in consideration of Christian sensitivity.

These protests, however, did not change the basic facts which, to a great extent, limited the scope of the Agency's reaction to the Report. The Zionists realized that if America accepted the Report it would mean a radical change of policy, and one which would be detrimental to their political aims. On the other hand, they were too weak to prevent the Anglo-American understanding which they thought the full Report had produced.[48] They therefore would have to settle for the impossible, i.e., for immigration alone. In this way, they hoped to avert the change of policy which the full Report implied, and to return to the status quo ante. This thinking resembled that of the Americans who had the same reasons for supporting the admission of the 100,000 (see chapter 12 below). It also resembled the thinking of officials in London who wanted the status quo ante in which America had had no say in Palestine. But one could find some rethinking among the Zionists regarding the wisdom of the shift from London to Washington. It looked to Ben-Gurion as if America were making an attempt upon the political life of the Jewish people.[49]

NOTES

1. In Cunningham to Hall, 8 May 1946, CO 733/463, Pt. 2, No. 75872/138/13.
2. In Jeddah to Foreign Office, 30 June 1946, FO 371/52536/E6311.
3. U.S. Legation, Beirut, to State Dept., 9 May 1946, NRC, Beirut files, RG 84, Box 230; British Embassy, Baghdad, to Foreign Office, 28 June 1946, FO 371/52533/E6012.
4. Beirut to Foreign Office, 6 May 1946, FO 371/52891/E4119.
5. Ronald Campbell to Foreign Office, 22 June 1946, FO 371/53332/J2813. See also Cairo to Foreign Office, 5 May 1946, FO 371/53331/J1992; Cairo to Foreign Office, 31 Aug. 1946, FO 371/52556/E8732/G. Elias Sassoon, Jewish Agency, Arab

Division, to E. Elath, 23 May 1946, CZA, Elath files, No. S25/451.

6. Cairo to Foreign Office, 26 April 1946, FO 371/52521/E4084.
7. G.O.C. Palestine, to C. in C. conference Cairo, 17 April 1946, WO 201/2079.
8. Yusuf Yassin, Saudi Foreign Secretary, in U.S. Legation, Jeddah. to Washington, 2 May 1946, USNA, State Dept. Palestine papers 1946, Box 6755, No. 867 N.01/5-246.
9. Cunningham to Hall, 4 June 1946, SACMEC, Cunningham Papers, Box 1, file 1.
10. The weekly, *Al Wahada*, Jerusalem, 20 May 1946. Quoted in PALCOR News Agency, 23 May 1946. The weekly suggested national strikes on Saturdays when Jewish services were closed.
11. British Council, Jerusalem, 6 May 1946, FO 924/516, No. LC 2751/914/452.
12. The Jewish Agency blamed the Administration for organizing these appearances in order to show the unworkable character of the Report, CZA, Sassoon to Elath, 6 June 1946, Elath files, No. S25/451; reports by District Commissioners, Nazareth and Jerusalem, 20 and 21 May 1946, respectively, CO 537/1707.
13. Ahmad Shukairi, *Forty Years in Arabic and International Life*, Beirut, 1969, p. 268 (Arabic); Cairo to Jerusalem, 24 May 1946, FO 371/52526/E4832; Cunningham to Hall, 10 May 1946, FO 371/52524/E4438.
14. Note on interview with Jamal Husseini, 3 May 1946, Cunningham to Martin, 11 May 1946, SACMEC, Cunningham Papers, Box 5, file 2.
15. Cunningham to Martin, 4 June 1946, Cunningham Papers, Box 1, file 1.
16. See also Sykes, *Cross-Roads to Israel*, p. 356.
17. Ben-Gurion diary, p. 6, Paris, 22 April 1946 (Hebrew). By then, Ben-Gurion had, surprisingly enough, already seen a copy of the Report.
18. See in Cairo to Foreign Office, 3 May 1946, FO 371/52520/E4026.
19. Arab Office, London, 9 May 1946, FO 371/52523/E4436.
20. In U.S. Embassy, London, 2 May 1946, USNA State Dept. Papers, 1946, Box 6755, No. 867, N.01/5-246. See also Arab News Bulletin, published by Arab Office London, 14 June 1946, CO 537/1740.
21. Iraqi Ministry for Foreign Affairs on AAC Report, Baghdad, 19 June 1946, in Baghdad to Foreign Office, 21 June 1946, FO 371/52532/E5929. See also Beirut to Foreign Office, 15 June 1946, FO 371/52529/E5512.
22. Record of meeting with King Abdullah, 1 June 1946, FO 371/52553/E8148.
23. U.S. War Dept., Strategic Services Unit Report, 25 June 1946, No. A-70663, NRC No. 301462.
24. Political Summary, Syria and Lebanon, 11 June 1946, FO 371/52858/E6193.
25. On the protests against this "insult [and] invidious declaration," see Ibn Saud to Grafftey-Smith, in Jeddah to Foreign Office, 16 June 1946, FO 371/52314/E5615/G.
26. "Memoirs of an Arab Senior Official" (anonymous), *Al-Ahram*, 23 June 1977 (Arabic). On Ibn Saud's call for moderation, see Grafftey-Smith, Jeddah to Foreign Office, 16 June 1946, FO 371/52314/E5615/G. On a similar Syrian call, see Beirut to Foreign Office, 11 June 1946, FO 371/52528/E5353.
27. Intelligence report, Jewish Agency Arab Section, Jerusalem, 18 June 1946, CZA S25/9023.
28. H.Q. Palestine, Fortnightly Intelligence Newsletter, No. 17 for the period 10-23 June 1946, WO 169/23022. See also Beirut to Foreign Office, 16 June 1946, FO 371/52529/ E5480.
29. See "Memoirs of an Arab Senior Official," *Al-Ahram*, 16 June 1977; Shukairi, *Forty Years*, p. 271.
30. U.S. War Dept., Strategic Unit Report, No. A-68990, 17 June 1946, NRC, No. 275591; Beirut to Amman, 12 Oct. 1947, FO 816/89.
31. Foreign Office comment, 14 Aug. 1946, on Amman, Sir A. Kirkbride, to T. Wikeley, Eastern Dept., Foreign Office, 23 July 1946, FO 371/52551/E7830.

32. Shukairi, *Forty Years*, p. 270.
33. See Cairo to Foreign Office, 14 May 1946, FO 371/52523/E4408. Interview with Mr. Briance, London, Jan. 1979. On Clayton's appearance, see the U.S. Legation, Damascus, 12 June 1946: "[it] caused the uproar of those present as to the motives of the coming of the well-known intelligence general," NRC, Damascus files, RG 84, 59A, 543. On Hitti's, ibid., 11 June 1946.
34. Interview with Mr. Briance, London, Jan. 1979; Jewish Agency Arab Section, 13 June 1946, CZA S 25/9023. A physician checked the food in Bloudan against deliberate poisoning.
35. Shertok at Jewish Agency Executive meeting, 20 June 1946, CZA.
36. D. Horowitz at Jewish Agency Executive meeting, 2 June 1946, CZA.
37. U.S. Office of Strategic Services (OSS) report on Jewish Agency Executive meeting, 2 May 1946, No A-68795, USNA, RG 43, AAC, Box 2.
38. J. Heller, "The AAC of Inquiry on Palestine, 1945-1946," p. 23 (in typescript); Horowitz, *State in the Making*, p. 94.
39. Jewish Agency Executive meeting, 1 May 1946, CZA. An OSS paper, 2 May 1946, reported a different Weizmann at the same Agency Meeting: "[I] repeatedly asked ... not to demand a Jewish state ... now the whole Zionist political situation had been placed in the same position as before the Balfour Declaration," OSS No A-68795, USNA, RG 43, AAC, Box 2.
40. OSS Report, No A-68794, on Agency Executive Meeting, 2 May 1946, USNA, RG 43, AAC, Box 2.
41. U.S. Consulate, Jerusalem, to Washington, 2 May 1946, FRUS 1946, vol. 7., p. 591; Goldmann on Report, 10 July 1946, USNA, State Dept. Palestine Papers, 1946, Box 6756, no. 867, N.01/7-1046.
42. Paris, 22 and 23 April 1946 (Hebrew).
43. Cunningham to Hall, 4 June 1946, CO 537/1708; Annex 4 of the results of the Brook–Harriman discussions on the immigration of the 100,000, London, 17-27 June 1946, PREM 8/627 Pt. 2.
44. AZEC report July 1946, appended to U.S. Dept. of War memo on possible opposition to Report, USNA, RG 43, AAC, Box 13; analysis of Jewish press 29 April–5 May 1946, H.Q. 1st Infantry Division Intelligence Review, No. 5, 7 May 1946, WO 169/22957.
45. Inverchapel to Foreign Office, 29 June 1946, FO 371/52535/E6215.
46. Chaim Greenberg, "Ten Recommendations: a Critique," *Jewish Frontier*, May 1946.
47. Inner Executive, Jewish Agency, 21 May 1946, CZA S5/340; AZEC analysis of the Report, New York, 1 May 1946, ZANY, AAC confidential file.
48. Ben-Gurion Paris diary, 22 April 1946.
49. Ibid.

12

The Report at Stake, London and Washington

With the signing of the AAC Report, Palestine policy-making in both London and Washington took on new life. The fears and hopes of all those involved, which had incubated during the period of governmental inactivity, now erupted.

In Whitehall, there were changes in style and jargon in inter-office correspondence and every subject was reopened for discussion. The status of the Jewish Agency, which had achieved recognition and respectability in the 1930s, was now challenged, and large scale military raids on the Yishuv, hitherto avoided, now seemed appropriate. Approaches to the UN were suddenly given attention, and officials soon found themselves involved in endless correspondence about Palestine. Some even resorted to crude arguments, as did Glubb Pasha, who stated that "the sufferings ... of a few hundred thousand Jews, cannot be weighed in the balance with the future of the British Commonwealth, which numbers hundreds of millions." At the centre of all this activity stood the British handling of the AAC Report.[1]

The discussions within the Cabinet Defence Committee, which took place two days after the Report was signed, raised a number of questions which were later to affect the Government's attitude to the Report. Bevin was clearly in favour of accepting it in its broad outlines, hoping that the unanimity achieved by the AAC "was an augury of cooperation by the U.S. Government in solving the problems of Palestine." He believed that HMG's aims in Palestine – such as the cessation of Jewish armed resistance – could be fulfilled through the supply of American troops, and he urged the Cabinet to come to a quick decision about the Report. The Prime Minister, on the other hand, said that he took a less rosy view of the Report than the Foreign Secretary. No other country except Palestine was to make any contribution of substance to the problem of absorbing the [DPs]. He found little grounds in the Report for the view that we could obtain American cooperation . . . On the contrary, [it] proposed a policy which would set both the Arabs and the Jews against us and that we should implement alone. The administration of the country was to be such that neither side dominated the other. We were to hold the balance between them.

The Colonial Secretary was also far from convinced of the Report's usefulness and "observed that there was no positive recommendation . . . for the disarmament of the illegal organizations." The feeling was that the policy to which the Government hoped to return after "having cast a Joint Committee on the waters" promised to yield nothing but frustration, and some simply asked why "could we not relieve ourselves of these responsibilities?"[2] The initial enthusiasm, therefore, subsided, and the Cabinet Committee passed the Report on to a group of officials – the same officials who had consistently opposed the Foreign Secretary's initiative to have the Americans in Palestine. Bevin's desire to use the Report as a quick means of developing Anglo-American understanding over Palestine was not, therefore, supported by his colleagues.

The handling of the Report at the administrative level had, in fact, begun at Lausanne. There the two secretaries of the Committee, the American Evan Wilson and the British Harold Beeley, prepared a seven stage procedure for its implementation, which began with the handing over of the Report to Bevin and Truman and ended with UN approval of a British Trusteeship over Palestine.[3] They were working on the assumption that both governments would approve the recommendations. Earlier, Beeley, who had expected a tough line to be taken against Jewish resistance, had suggested that the British and American C.O.S. cooperate in combatting the underground movements.[4] In London, the Colonial Office prepared itself for the Report by assuming that after their visit to Palestine, the AAC would be unlikely to make "such ridiculous and sweeping a proposal as that put forward last autumn by the President" with regard to the 100,000.[5] All this advance planning, however, became totally irrelevant once the Report had actually appeared. Reality proved stronger.

The committee of officials who examined the Report was chaired by Norman Brook of the Cabinet Secretariat and submitted its conclusions within forty-eight hours: they totally rejected the Report, stating that as far as the DPs and the situation in Palestine were concerned "it cannot be said that the discussion of these aspects has been in any way advanced by the Committee's recommendations." In their view the decision to continue the Mandate seemed to be in direct contradiction to the UN Charter (Article 76) which advocated the independence of dependent areas, and the AAC's recommendations for Arab educational, economic and social betterment were seen as bribes unlikely "to weaken their antagonism to the Report." The officials also believed that the Arabs would see the proposed development projects as designed to facilitate the admission of more immigrants. In addition the cost of implementing the recommendations would be astronomical since the Mandatory Power would have to provide for the education of an additional 200,000 children. The officials argued that because of Arab opposition to the Report – which could affect the security of the whole of the Middle East – and because of the financial burden involved, HMG should not attempt to implement the recommendations alone, but should seek the assistance of either the United States or the UN, preferably the latter.[6]

Despite the adverse reactions of the Cabinet Defence Committee and officialdom, Bevin was determined to continue his attempts to secure American financial and military aid, but from now on he was working in an atmosphere hostile to any kind of Anglo-U.S. cooperation in Palestine based on the Report. It was different from the "augury of cooperation" Bevin had attempted to describe at the Cabinet Committee.

The Report was now discussed mainly between London and Washington, although the Colonial Office and the Palestine Administration were still examining the technical problems involved in the implementation of its recommendations and reaching negative conclusions.[7]

The British members of the AAC contributed – perhaps unwittingly – to this hostile atmosphere. Things which had deliberately been left vague in the Report were interpreted by the commissioners in their meeting with Attlee in a way which even further deterred people from supporting their recommendations. Treasury officials who were concerned that the AAC had not considered American financial aid for Palestine were not reassured by Crick's excuse that U.S. money "would merely divert Palestinian trade to the United States and impose on the Administration the burden of an unnecessary dollar loan." As for the disarmament of the Hagana, Leggett confirmed that he was in agreement with the Report, which did not make disarmament a precondition of immigration.[8] Crossman, who painted a rosy picture of Palestine's economy for Attlee, told Hector McNeil that "if you read between the lines of our somewhat discreet economic section ... you will realize that Palestine is heading for an acute economic crisis."[9] In general, people in Britain had a low opinion of the Report and Attlee, in a meeting with Crossman, commented that it was "unfair" and had "let them down."[10] Nothing Crossman said to him produced any better results:

Crossman expatiated on the Haifa Refinery, the pipeline, the Holy Places, and the Stern Gang and so forth, and paused ... Silence. Crossman then moved over to the Jordan Valley, the potash and the Gulf of Aqaba, and ... paused again. Silence. Somewhat nettled, Crossman passed on via the Suez Canal and the tanker fleets back to the Haifa Refinery and after twenty-nine and a half minutes obstinately fell silent. After nearly half a minute's pause, Attlee commented "I saw your mother last week."[11]

The Military were particularly opposed to the Report:

The reaction throughout the Middle East..would be disastrous to British interest ... there will be a long period of unrest ... the military implications of which are formidable ... In Palestine itself we clearly foresee ... a general Arab rising ... more serious and more widespread than in 1936 and 1938/39 ... The reinforcements we shall require ... would be needed for a prolonged and indefinite period. We [will have] to resort to calling back men already released; [we will have] difficulty in sustaining the morale of British troops called upon to take action against Arabs in support of Jews whose terrorist activities have already inflicted upon them irritations, insults, hardships and casualties ... There is no way of meeting the requirement from British resources. We cannot walk back on our commitments in Germany, India and elsewhere. Nor ... from Italy and Greece [and] the chances of obtaining American army reinforcements are slight; Middle East oil resources ... make the retention of Arab friendship essential [since] we should seek to develop areas more remote from Russian attack.[12]

These statements, joined to the fact that Arab opposition had been growing more vocal over the last two months, removed any hesitations on the part of the Military.

AND IN THE ARAB CAPITALS

British representatives in the Middle East reacted in a similar way: the British Ambassador in Baghdad, for example, told Iraqi protesters that "nothing they could say on the subject ... could be any stronger than some of the telegrams he had dispatched to London." The ambassadors to the Arab countries were, in fact, predicting a total collapse of Britain's interests in the Middle East: a breakdown of the negotiations on the revision of the Anglo-Egyptian and Anglo-Iraqi treaties, acute problems for commercial and trading ventures – already being felt by the Goodwill Trade Mission to the Levant – and the total breakdown of Bevin's Partnership Policy with the Arab world. "Must we lose the good name," they asked, "which we gained from a just and courageous policy in Syria by following ... a policy of enforced colonization unparalleled in history?"[13] The ambassadors particularly objected to the Report's emphasis on the economic and social inferiority of the Arabs, and to its recommendations for the development of the Arab sector of Palestine. This was seen as a revival of the "old fallacy of a hope of settlement of communal strife by way of economic interest:"

Even if Tel Aviv were the dream city of Arab desire ... the Arabs consider the indefinite continuation of Jewish immigration too high a price to pay for an increasing standard of living ... We ourselves did not share the German views about the blessings of alien "kultur" and some of us prefer our own to the American "gadget" civilization. Neither the Germans nor the Americans understand this ... These denials of their national claims mean more to them than recommendations about standards of living, university education, etc., which will help to sell the Report to the British and U.S. public.[14]

Anxious warnings came from India about attempts by the press to stir up Moslem feeling by

urging that the Holy Land of the Prophet is being cut up for "infidels" ... this should be a successful move since the illiterate Moslem masses who have very little knowledge of geography (a statement that I can confidently endorse) would not be able to distinguish Palestine from Arabia.[15]

These were the views contained in the ambassadors' formal communcations with London; in their internal correspondence, they described the Report as superficial, dishonest, amateurish and insincere, arguing that "100,000 immigrants simply go to swell the unproductive Jewish elements already congregated in the towns." In addition they believed that the implementation of the Report would hinder the British withdrawal from Egypt:

with all the consequences of loss of goodwill ... without ... any troops in Egypt, our position in Palestine would be very isolated and any combined Egypto-Arab action against us ... would probably be too much for us ...[16]

It was clear that Britain could not pursue a policy of force in Palestine and evacuation in Egypt at one and the same time.

THE BRITISH PRESS SPEAKS OUT

An interesting factor which perhaps played a significant part in paving the way for the rejection of the Report (and the ultimate adoption of the Provincial Autonomy Plan [see below]), was the reaction of the British press. In early May, the Report was receiving a mixed press, sometimes in the same editorial or article. The unanimity of the Report was praised, but the *Spectator* (3 May 1946) felt that the Committee had been more successful "in diagnosing problems than in solving them ... [and] after [the] Report, as before it, a solution for Palestine has still to be discussed." *The Economist* (4 May 1946) called for the adoption of the Report not so much because of its merits but because "on balance, there seems no alternative ... and the plan contains nothing which is an absolute violation of inalienable rights on either side." Another opinion, however, was voiced in *The Sunday Times* (5 May 1946) by Sir Reginald Coupland, who had been a member of the Peel Commission. It asked why Palestine could not follow the Indian example of having autonomous areas which looked after their own affairs except in certain matters of common interest, entrusted to a central administrative body. This article signalled a new mood in the press, which now ceased to discuss the implementation of the Report and began to consider alternative solutions. The AAC was now attacked for its fourth recommendation which advocated the continuation of the Mandate and the dependent status of the country. In a later editorial (25 May 1946), *The Economist* suggested that the AAC's priorities and the Report's fourth recommendation should be reversed: self-government and independence should precede cooperation. Only then, with practical responsibility and with Palestinians serving in the Government, would extremism be curbed. In general, *The Economist* found that the AAC's recommendations

smell of defeatism [and] appease the world's conscience at the expense of the Mandatory ... Without Palestinian responsibility, the Committee's recommendations are mere palliatives, when not actual irritants.

The Observer (2 June 1946) expressed the opinion that the AAC had followed the "well beaten track of all Palestine commissions – reversal of whatever policy may be uppermost at the moment, with a douceur to each of the principal parties concerned," including the assurance for HMG of their continued strategic presence in the country. And "if security demands that we have a place for our troops there, this does not mean that they should be keeping order with machine guns in town and countryside."[17] In July 1946, these themes found general expression in the Provincial Autonomy Plan.

After the first reaction, discussions about the Report centred around key issues like the disarmament of the underground groups, the admission of the 100,000, financial aspects, cooperation with America, and reference to the UN.

THE MILITARY TAKE ACTION: "AGATHA"

The committee of officials made it clear that the AAC had not made the admission of the 100,000 DPs conditional upon the disbandment of the Jewish armies, but in their opinion, if the Report were adopted, it should be.[18] The Military, however, were of the opinion that it would be impossible to achieve even this, since "the whole Arab world [would] regard us as accepting a bribe on a big scale if we allowed immigration on condition that arms were given up."[19]

The situation was further complicated by Attlee's refusal to implement the Report until the Jewish armies had been disarmed, and his insistence that this be undertaken with the assistance of American troops. This aroused the deep objections of the Middle Eastern officers who were totally against accepting any American military assistance. The G.O.C. Palestine argued that this was a good propaganda move providing that the Americans would not comply. He stated that he had enough troops in the country to carry out a general forcible disarmament of the Jews, and their leaders; if the latter were not apprehended this "would be similar to disarming the Wehrmacht and leaving intact the German General Staff."[20] D'Arcy discussed the matter with Attlee on 16 May 1946 and may have convinced him that "Operation Agatha" – a wide scale military operation against the Yishuv – could be successfully carried out without the Americans. It was of some importance that Bevin's request to get, at the least, American agreement to the disarmament of the Yishuv, was turned down by the Cabinet "despite the importance of securing the continued cooperation of the United States in Palestine and the Middle East."[21]

"Agatha" was put into operation and according to General Dempsey, the C. in C. in the Middle East, it was a great success. "Palestine is a wasps' nest. We dug it up ... and captured a good many wasps. The remainder are now buzzing about angry and bewildered."[22] It now seemed pointless to request the assistance of U.S. troops, and Bevin accordingly dropped the idea.[23] This was a victory for those who objected to American troops in Palestine on the grounds that "the position of the C. in C. would be extremely complicated."[24] The AAC had evaded the question of Jewish disarmament in the hope of preserving a general British–U.S. agreement over Palestine, but by carrying out "Agatha" alone, Britain had taken a course which would make sharing the Mandate with Washington more difficult.

The question of the 100,000 promised to be less controversial. In November 1945, Bevin had objected to what he saw as a Jewish attempt to push their DPs "to the head of the queue," but in April 1946 he personally ordered the Foreign Office to assess the extent to which Jewish refugees should have priority over others.[25] Later, when the admission of the 100,000 became conditional upon U.S. military assistance and Jewish disarmament, his attitude changed again:

In Palestine there are illegal armed forces. If we put 100,000 Jews [there] I would have to put another division of British troops there. I am not prepared to do it. [Hear, hear].[26]

However, it was clear that the problem of the 100,000 would not hinder the attempt to come to an agreement with Truman on Palestine, especially after "Operation Agatha" on 29 June 1946. Then it seemed that there were no longer any illegal armed forces in Palestine which could be reinforced by the immigrants, nor Jewish undergrounds which British forces could not confront without U.S. troops.

FINANCIAL DIFFICULTIES

One subject which aroused loud protest was the financial burden involved in implementing the Report. It was estimated in Jerusalem that as much as £200,000,000 in capital investment would be needed for the establishment of compulsory education, health services, welfare centres for the Arabs and the absorption of the 100,000.[27] In late April the Treasury stated that the cost of housing and resettling the 100,000 (estimated at £100,000,000) was almost as great as the ten-year development budget for the entire Colonial Empire (£120,000,000), and concluded: "We cannot afford it, and in any event, the UN will not allow us to remain indefinitely." The Treasury had previously noted that

The utmost consolation that the AAC hold out for the Administering Power is that its difficulties ought to be appreciated by the other members of the UN.[28]

Further investigation, however, produced lower estimates. The commissioners believed that HMG "would not spend one penny [but] would actually gain £1 capitation fee per head of immigrant."[29] There were also reports that the Jewish Agency was ready to carry much of the financial burden and was already negotiating in France about surplus U.S. Army huts. This all led to the conclusion that the case against the plan on financial grounds alone was less strong than it was originally felt to be.[30] Commenting on the Jerusalem figures (£234,000,000), the Treasury remarked that "nothing would have been more fatal than to overstate the difficulties and we suggest that it would be inadvisable to quote these figures to the Americans."[31] Comparison of this with another view that "in utterances ... in America we should not admit weakness (except financial weakness which is now understood)" reveals the type of thinking which prevailed in the summer of 1946 with regard to some aspects of Anglo-American relations.[32]

THE AMERICANS: DO WE NEED THEM?

The question of cooperation with the United States was obviously the most important one. It was also the first time, in fact, that London had actually discussed the details of Bevin's aim of involving America in Palestine.

The committee of officials emphasized the disadvantages of inviting America to share in the implementation of the Report. Their view was that despite the advantages of military assistance and some help in discouraging Soviet intervention, U.S. presence in Palestine could have disastrous consequences for Britain's interests in the Arab Middle East. Such a step would confirm American public opinion in the view that the AAC was merely an attempt to entangle the United States in Palestine. Furthermore, it was most unlikely that the United States would send soldiers to coerce Jews or Arabs during an election year.[33] In addition, the C.O.S. argued that since Palestine was the fulcrum of British strategy in the Middle East, Britain must remain in sole charge of the country.[34]

An April meeting between Bevin and Byrnes in Paris had not produced any agreement on Britain's needs in Palestine. Bevin insisted that immigration be conditional upon Jewish disarmament and American military assistance.[35] He further blamed the United States for permitting its Jews to support the Yishuv with weapons. According to the report by a U.S. State Department source

the point has about been reached where he [Bevin] must consider the possibility of a complete British withdrawal from Palestine. At present he is forced to retain four divisions there and this cannot go on indefinitely. He realizes that after British withdrawal, there might be Russian penetration in the area and that it would weaken the whole situation in the Middle East, but he sees little hope of any improvement unless we accept a share of the responsibility.[36]

This does not appear in Bevin's version of the conversation, probably because Bevin had little support in London for his idea of linking the continuation of a British presence in Palestine to an agreement with America.[37] In all events, this was the first time that the United States had been threatened in this way, and it probably had the effect of elevating the subject in Washington to a global level, perhaps even precipitating the search for a successor to Britain in Palestine. It may also have encouraged a U.S. reappraisal of Zionism as a political asset in the Middle East.

Whatever the case, Attlee told Parliament on 1 May 1946 that the 100,000 would only be admitted into Palestine after the U.S.

forces had assisted Britain in disarming the Jews.[38] These were, however, the very points which stood in the way of Anglo-U.S. cooperation, both politically and personally, since they threatened to jeopardize Truman's own 100,000 achievement.

The question of involving America in the implementation of the Report was also marked by Middle Eastern and general Anglo-U.S. considerations. The original intention was to get to grips with the Americans on the AAC Report as soon as possible.[39] At that time, however, the U.S. Congress was debating the loan to Britain and this forced a delay on the Palestine issue until the conclusion of the debate.[40] A similar thing happened with regard to the question of a British withdrawal from Egypt. Bevin attributed America's readiness to discuss the details of the Report to Britain's willingness to negotiate such a withdrawal, adding that it had "had a salutary effect on the attitude of the U.S. Government towards cooperation in the Middle East."[41] He said, however, that he would prefer to solve the problem of Egypt first, expressing the hope that the Egyptians would then be helpful over Palestine.[42] The questions of the loan and withdrawal from Egypt had, therefore, been given priority over the question of Palestine, and this suggested that there was some discrepancy between the alarm Britain had raised over her position in Palestine and her actual priorities in practice.

The initial opinions on a joint implementation of the Report also revealed something about London's interpretation of American interests in the Middle East. It was thought, for example, that if America sent forces to Palestine, its aim would be the solution of *local* problems rather than the pursuit of regional strategic aims. These limited interests were not, therefore, "an insuperable difficulty," and it was anticipated that an agreement could be reached, providing "we had control of the organization of the defence of the area."[43] By attributing philanthropic motives to America and power politics to Britain, the Foreign Office was misreading the reality of the situation in the Middle East in 1946. Similarly, their assessments of U.S. Palestine policy made in April and May did not all prove to be correct. One such error was the "axiomatic" view that American intervention and cooperation outside the Western hemisphere "can be best sought under the umbrella of UNO."[44] When London finally referred the problem to the United Nations, America failed to satisfy British interests there. In addition, the conclusion of Lord Inverchapel, Halifax's successor in Washington, that Truman's Palestine moves lacked "his predecessor's skill in these tight corners" and "the old master's touch at press and similar conferences," was far from accurate.[45] To describe the President in 1946 as a weak person, open to Zionist manipulation, did not accord with Truman's tough decisions over such matters as the atomic bombing of Japan.

It was almost inevitable that the attempt to achieve an Anglo-U.S. understanding in Palestine, based on the Report, would break down: it could not resist the combined opposition of almost everybody in London. Bevin reluctantly accepted the situation, although he still genuinely believed that the Report could provide the cornerstone of an understanding. In July 1946, the Cabinet Secretary, Norman Brook, gave two reasons for his suggestion that "it would be wiser if HMG conducted the negotiation alone": the Arab claim that the United States had no *locus standi* in the matter and the fact that American participation would cause other countries to intervene.[46] A couple of months earlier, these very reasons had induced Bevin to attempt to *introduce* America into Palestine, believing that its participation would dissuade other countries from intervening.

An analysis of Bevin's behaviour in this context would show that he was now actually following a line against his own better judgement. Everybody in Britain wanted an end to Jewish military resistance, but Bevin was not prepared to pay for this with the abandonment of Anglo-U.S. understanding. He simply attached more importance to Anglo-American understanding than to Anglo-Arab relations: "We should not be unduly alarmed by some initial clamour from the Arab states." It is quite possible, therefore, that Bevin saw the Report as elevating Palestine to a new status where, on British authority, some sort of American responsibility had been created. He stressed the fact that "the enquiry had been made by an Anglo-American committee, and the Report should be considered by the two governments jointly."[47] He would have preferred to be able to say that following the Report Britain was no longer free to act exclusively in Palestine, and was not even free to decide whether or not to adopt it. But others in Britain did not believe that a new situation had been created. For them, the adoption of the Report was an independent British decision and America could help Britain only in its implementation. In the light of this view, one can understand that the committee of officials arrived at the conclusion that Britain had to adopt the Report *before* approaching America.[48] Information reached the Jewish Agency in May 1946 that "Bevin is not ready to accept Attlee's line ... he negotiates with America, emphasizing the positive sides more than the negative."[49] Crossman also tended to blame Attlee more than Bevin for the rejection of the AAC's recommendations.[50] His views were probably correct.

HMG IN A BIND

In the weeks following the signing of the Report in Lausanne and the recommendations of the committee of officials appointed by the Cabinet to examine it, HMG found itself in a double bind. The committee of officials, it will be recalled, suggested seeking either American or UN cooperation in implementing the terms of the Report, and considered the UN option as the lesser of two evils. Seeking U.S. cooperation would, according to the committee, first require HMG to take a decision adopting the Report, a step which would have disastrous consequences in the Arab world. In such a case, the Arab states and/or Russia were sure to table the subject before the Security Council. Appealing to the United Nations directly would not prove much more beneficial since, as a Foreign Office source was to articulate it, "it is almost inconceivable that a two-thirds majority ... would be in favour of helping the United Kingdom to develop a strategic base in Palestine."[51] In short, Britain would be damned if she did and damned if she didn't. The only apparent advantage of seeking UN assistance directly would be to forestall the Arab "clamour" attendant upon British adoption of the Report. In all events, a committee composed of representatives of all the British government departments concerned preferred the UN option to cooperation with the United States. This preference was so strong it survived even the Foreign Secretary's flat rejection of it. "Ministers felt that ... if we continued to keep the matter solely between ourselves and the U.S. Government, the suspicions of the Soviet Government might be aroused." The Soviet threat which weighed so heavily on Bevin and in face of which he sought Anglo-American cooperation in the first place, was not shared by all his colleagues.[52]

In the end, the Cabinet found a middle way out of their predicament: they decided to negotiate with the United States over the

Report without first making any decision about it themselves. Apparently Bevin's insistence that HMG was no longer free to make decisions on Palestine alone had won the day. But the Cabinet probably settled for this option not so much because of Bevin's view but because it was simply the easiest road to take: it meant no immediate change in Palestine. No change in Palestine was also the view of the United States, which did not consider the Report as altering in any way Britain's exclusive position in Palestine, and was ready to discuss only the implementation of the Report, leaving the decision about its adoption to Britain.

THE AMERICAN APPROACH

America's handling of the Report exhibited a clear tendency to see the Palestine issue as a non-political, refugee problem. This was first evident in early May when the President emphasized only the recommendation for admitting the 100,000 and again later in July when it was stated that "the United States is in general agreement with the Report ... and early action should be taken on the immigration of the 100,000 ... and on other recommendations."[53]

From May 1946, Britain attributed Truman's emphasis on immigration to personal weakness and to Zionist manipulation, as if "the 100,000 are the crux of the problem and there are really no sound reasons for delaying their transfer to Palestine."[54] Truman however was fully aware of the broader picture, commenting as he did that "I doubt if the 100,000 necessarily means a change of policy, but the whole Report does."[55] Like Bevin he realized that the Report had effected a change in Palestine. But unlike Bevin, he attempted, by advocating only immigration, to continue the pre-AAC situation, repeating that the country was a British responsibility. As to the Arabs, he was supported by Niles's view that "if the transference of the 100,000 Jews [is] responsible for a future war, the world is certainly in bad shape."[56] Later, the proviso that no U.S. forces would be employed in Palestine, nor would the United States act as co-trustee there, cleared the way for a Presidential agreement (in July) to accept the whole Report.[57] But the main reason for this was still the 100,000, since Britain had made it clear that it would not negotiate their immigration unless America was ready to discuss the entire Report.

Concentrating on the refugee aspect was also in America's own interests. In one very explicit example of U.S. intention to pressure Britain on Palestine, General Hilldring, in charge of the Division for Occupied Areas in the State Department, wrote:

In order to further our interests in Germany and Austria ... I think that all the Jewish pressure should be directed against the British ... This result, I believe, can be achieved only if this government pursues an aggressive public policy of needling the British to implement the Committee's recommendation for entry of 100,000 immediately and without reference to future action on any other aspects of the Report ... A public offer by the U.S. Government to assume primary responsibility for the movement of all the 100,000 from Europe to Palestine ... the net cost of [it] to the U.S. Government would not be more, and perhaps even less, than the expense of maintaining Jewish DPs in camps ... for another year.[58]

Britain was, therefore, wrong to ascribe America's concern for the 100,000 to a Zionist conspiracy.

As in Britain, so in the United States, the Military and representatives in the field warned Washington about the probable effects of the Report's implementation. They anticipated violent Arab reactions which could inflame the Middle East, inciting riots against Christians and other minorities, and resulting in serious damage to Anglo-American interests. According to their estimate, it would take seven to eight armoured and infantry divisions plus three to four hundred planes about two years to restore peace in the area.[59] Reports from the Arab countries emphasized the "fear of Zionist imperialism [which] is felt to be more dangerous than that of the British or French since it works silently and under cover."[60] And as early as April, U.S. legations in the Near East were on the alert for disturbances, and legation staff were being advised to make themselves as "inconspicuous as possible."[61] Such opinions, no doubt, lay behind the Joint U.S. C.O.S. paper:

We urge that no U.S. armed forces be involved in carrying out the Committee's recommendations. We recommend that in implementing the Report, the guiding principle be that no action should be taken which will cause repercussions in Palestine which are beyond the capabilities of British troops to control ... in implementing the Report ... no action be taken which would ... orient the peoples of the Middle East away from the Western powers.[62]

This duality – American refusal to send troops to Palestine, but at the same time concern about Britain's ability to police the country – was characteristic of U.S. Near Eastern policy.

There were, as well, discussions in the State Department during May and June on whether the Committee had, in fact, disregarded the Arab case, and a paper on the subject was prepared by the American Secretary of the AAC, Evan Wilson. He pointed out the opportunities which the AAC had had of looking into the Arab case, and concluded that "The Report, when considered as a whole, will be found to contain many advantages from the Arab point of view ... It is significant that the Report has also been criticized by the Zionists."[63] The State Department also refuted the allegation that the Report conflicted with the UN Charter (which called for independence to be granted to Mandated territories) by denying the Palestinian Arabs' right to self-determination: "Since the AAC was not acting under the Charter, any possible denial by it of the right of Palestine to independence cannot be a violation of article 80(1)."[64]

It was probably U.S. public opinion that helped clear the way for the view that the Report implied much more than an investigation of the refugee aspect of the Palestine problem. Some were quick to see the British request for U.S. troops as an attempt to secure support for the "tottering British position in the Middle East."[65] But others, notably *The New York Times*, in an editorial (3 May 1946) emphasized that

we cannot ask Great Britain to abrogate the White Paper ... without assuming some responsibility for imposing a substitute policy involving grave risks of violence and disorder ... We cannot very well wash our hands of the consequences of our advice and our actions.

It seems that in Britain the press was instrumental in bringing about the rejection of the AAC Report; in America the opposite was true.

As to the reactions of the American commissioners, the most vocal was Crum, who did not cease to vilify Britain and the State Department. He thought it a good idea to "refresh" Bevin's memory about his unanimity pledge.[66] He dismissed the Department's fear that the Arabs would apply to Russia as preposterous: "One might as well envisage an appeal by Rockefeller or Lamont to Moscow to help them obtain a reduction in income tax."[67] Some people even labelled it the "Barkley Krum [sic] report".[68]

In Britain, therefore, the Report was to be rejected; in America – accepted. Both Bevin and Truman realized that, following the signing of the Report, America was already involved in Palestine. Truman wanted to put an end to this involvement by concentrating on immigration alone. Bevin wanted to preserve it by emphasizing the whole of the Report. Those in Britain who objected to U.S. involvement in Palestine would therefore push for its total rejection. The Americans, who saw no other chance of the 100,000 being admitted to Palestine, would call for its total implementation. Under such circumstances, the AAC Report could not possibly survive.

NOTES

1. See May 1946 correspondence and comments in FO 371/52519/E3951 and FO 371/52521/ E4089; C.O.S. assessment of the publication of the Report and the disarming of the Jewish undergrounds, 14 and 16 April 1946, No JP (46)76 and JP(46)83, respectively, CO 537/1755; Glubb Pasha to Montgomery, 13 July 1946, Pt 6, WO 216/207, and the almost identical view expressed by the Assistant Chief, Air Staff, in Prime Minister Meetings (P.M.M.) 30 April 1946, No. P.M.M. (46) 18, p. 3 AIR 20/4963.
2. Minutes of Cabinet Defence Committee, 24 April 1946, No DO (46)61, FO 371/ 52517/ E3839/G; see also Wikeley, Foreign Office Eastern Dept., to Bevin, Notes for discussion with Defence Committee, 23 April 1946. There the need for acceptance of the Report and for an American armed division were also stressed, FO 371/ 52517/ E3840/G.
3. Lausanne, 15 April 1946, Washington, State Dept. Building, Lot 54, D 403, Box 9, No 543080/3.
4. Beeley to Baxter, Jerusalem, 25 March 1946, FO 371/52514/E3057/G. See also draft of unsent telegram from Foreign Office to Washington, April 1946, ibid.
5. Douglas Harris, Procedure in Connection with Palestine Policy, 21 March 1946, CO 537/1755.
6. Report of committee of officials, 27 April 1946, CAB 129/9, No. CP (46)173. See also draft report, 26 April 1946, FO 371/52517/E3943/G.
7. See correspondence, late April–May 1946, between Jerusalem and the Colonial Office, CO 537/1748.
8. Meeting of British commissioners with Attlee, 14 May 1946, FO 371/52524/E4514.
9. Crossman to McNeil, 22 April 1946, FO 371/52524/E4469.
10. Attlee on Report, quoted in Crossman to Attlee, 7 May 1946, SACMEC, Crossman Papers.
11. Douglas Jay, *Change and Fortune*, London, 1980, p. 133. Jay was a personal assistant to Attlee.
12. C.O.S. Committee, Report to the Cabinet, Military Implications of the AAC Report, 10 July 1946, No COS(46)188(0), PREM 8/627, Pt.3; Army Council Secretariat, Brief for War Secretary on C.O.S. Attitudes to AAC report, 11 July 1946, No. ACS/B/2071, WO 32/10260. See also Glubb, June 1946, on 12-15 divisions which would be required to deal with security in the Middle East following the adoption of the Report, FO 371/52530/E5668.
13. In U.S. Legation, Baghdad (James S. Moose) to State Dept., 21 May 1946, USNA RG 43, AAC, Box 12; Cairo to Foreign Office, 25 April 1946, FO 141/1090; report

by Lord Davidson, who led the Goodwill Trade Mission, 30 May 1946, BT 60/93/1 Pt. 1; Baghdad to Foreign Office, 10 May 1946, FO 371/52523/E4358.

14. Grafftey-Smith, Jeddah, to Foreign Office, 23 April 1946, FO 371/52516/E3663/G. See also Baghdad to Foreign Office, 25 April 1946, FO 371/52516/E3756/G.

15. Sir Frederick Burrows, Governor of Bengal, to Attlee, 6 May 1946, in Mansergh and Moon, eds., *India: The Transfer of Power, 1942–1947*, vol. 7, London, 1977, p. 446.

16. Walter Smart, the Oriental Counsellor, on Report, Cairo, 2 May 1946, FO 141/1090, No. 101/156/46; memo by Ronald Campbell, 1 May 1946, FO 141/1090 No. 101/148/46; memo by Walter Smart, 29 April 1946, ibid.

17. The same author was believed by the U.S. London Embassy to have written the editorials in *The Economist* and *The Observer*. He was Christopher Holme, former Political Relations Officer in Palestine and, in May 1946, the sub-editor of *The Observer*. See survey of British Press, 3 June 1946, USNA, State Department, Palestine material, 1946, Box 6755, No. 867 01/6-346.

18. Cabinet Paper No. CP (46)173, 27 April 1946, p. 15, CAB 129/9.

19. C.O.S meeting, 26 April 1946, No. JP(46)86, AIR 20/4963.

20. C.O.S. meeting with Lt. General D'Arcy, G.O.C. Palestine, London, 15 May 1946, FO 371/52525/E4774/G.

21. Cabinet Meeting, 20 June 1946, CAB 128/5, No. CM(46)60. Bevin was at that time in Paris.

22. Dempsey to Montgomery, 4 July 1946, WO 216/194. See H.Q. Palestine, Fortnightly Intelligence Newsletter, 24 June–7 July 1946, No. 18: "The Jews are quite unbalanced, dangerously emotional and psychologically insecure [but] this may be the result of centuries of persecution," WO 275/63.

23. Bevin to Beeley and Brook, Paris, 10 July 1946, PREM 8/627, pt. 3.

24. D'Arcy to C.O.S., 15 May 1946, FO 371/52525/E4774/G.

25. Memo by Mackillop, Foreign Office Refugee Dept., 30 April 1946, FO 371/57691/WR1275. "Priority over all others except Spanish Republican refugees," answered the Refugee Dept. Ibid.

26. Bevin to Labour Party Conference, Bournemouth, 12 June 1946, FO 371/52529/E5546.

27. Ibid., the Palestine Govt. reached the sum of £234,000,000. See note by the Treasury on the Report's financial consequences, May 1946, CO 537/1748, No. 75872/138D. See also Cunningham to Hall, 2 May 1946 (two telegrams), FO 371/52520/E4040.

28. A.S.D. Winnifrith, 26 April 1946, T 220/20; 24 April 1946, T 161/1251, No. S-54034.

29. Crossman to McNeil, 8 May 1946, FO 371/52524/E4469. See also meeting of British commissioners with Attlee, 14 May 1946, FO 371/52524/E4514.

30. Treasury memo, 28 May 1946, T 161/1251, No. S-54034.

31. Note by Treasury on Report's financial consequences, May 1946, CO 537/1748, No. 75872/1380.

32. Charles W. Baxter, Eastern Dept., Foreign Office, 9 Aug. 1946, FO 371/52551/E7832.

33. Report of committee of officials, 27 April 1946, p. 6., CAB 129/9, No. CP(46)173. 1946 was a congressional election year.

34. Waterfield to Gater, 24 May 1946, FO 371/52350/E4855/G.

35. Paris to Foreign Office, 27 April 1946, FO 371/52517/E3786/G.

36. Memo by Matthews, Director of Office of European Affairs, U.S. State Dept., to Washington, Paris, 27 April 1946, FRUS, 1946, vol. 7, p. 588.

37. See Paris to Foreign Office, 27 April 1946, FO 371/52517/E3786/G.

38. See copy of announcement in Hall to Cunningham, 1 May 1946, SACMEC, Cunningham Papers, Box 1, file 1.

39. Attlee to Bevin, 7 May 1946, FO 371/52522/E4223/G.
40. Cabinet Meeting, 11 July 1946, CAB 128/6 No. CM(46)67.
41. Cabinet Meeting, 20 May 1946, CAB 128/5 No. CM(46)50.
42. Report by Beeley and Brook on meeting with Bevin, Paris, 10 July 1946, PREM 8/627, Pt. 3.
43. R. Howe, Under Secretary of State, Foreign Office, 25 May 1946, FO 371/52527/ E5065/G.
44. Memo by Baxter on consequences in America of British rejection of the Report, 26 April 1946, FO 371/52520/E4013.
45. Inverchapel to Bevin, 11 June 1946, CO 537/1736; 7 June 1946, CO 539/1759.
46. Brook to Howe, 23 July 1946, FO 371/52543/E7067/G.
47. Cabinet Meeting, 29 April 1946, CAB 128/5 No. CM (46)38.
48. Report of committee of officials, 27 April 1946, p. 6, CAB 129/9, No. CP (46)173.
49. Eliezer Kaplan, Jewish Agency Executive, 19 May 1946 (Hebrew), CZA.
50. Crossman to Monroe, interview, 19 Oct. 1958, SACMEC, Monroe Papers.
51. J.G. Ward, Foreign Office, International Relations Dept., 5 June 1946, FO 371/ 52521/ E4089. See also J. Bennet, International Implications of AAC Report, 24 April 1946, CO 537/1459.
52. See, e.g., correspondence among Foreign Office staff in late May 1946, FO 371/ 52521/ E4089. On Bevin's objection to reference to UN, see Cabinet Meeting, 29 April 1946, CAB 128/5 No. CM(46)38; Foreign Office correspondence, 8 May 1946, FO 371/52521/E4098; Foreign Office to Washington, 18 June 1946, CO 537/1736; Cabinet Meeting, 25 July 1946, CAB 128/6, No. CM(46)73.
53. Memo by Board of Alternates to U.S. Cabinet Committee on Palestine, undated, USNA, RG 43, AAC, Box 13. Truman also gave his agreement on 9 July 1946 to a questionnaire of the Alternates which specifically mentioned support for "NO Jewish NO Arab state in Palestine." See FRUS 1946, vol. 7, p. 644.
54. Inverchapel to Foreign Office, 7 June 1946, CO 537/1759.
55. Truman to Niles, 7 May 1946, Truman Library, President's Secretary's File.
56. Niles to Truman, 27 May 1946, Truman Library, President's Official File No. 204, Misc. Box 171.
57. Questions submitted to the U.S. Cabinet Committee on Palestine by their Board of Alternates, undated, USNA, RG 43, AAC, Box 13.
58. Hilldring to Dean Acheson, the Under S.O.S., 3 May 1946, FRUS 1946, vol. 7, p. 592.
59. Memo to Mr. Dorr, U.S. Cabinet Committee on Palestine, 3 July 1946, p. 3, USNA, RG 43, AAC, Box 13.
60. Phillip Ireland, First Secretary, U.S. Cairo Legation, report on visit to Arab countries, 15–30 May 1946, in Cairo to Byrnes, 1 July 1946, NRC, Cairo Files, RG 84, Box 104.
61. Baghdad to Washington, 26 April 1946, USNA State Dept. Palestine Papers, 1946, Box 6754, No. 867/N.01/4-2646. On similar British precautions, see in U.S. Legation, Baghdad, to State Dept., 9 May 1946, ibid., Box 6755, No. 867, N.01/5-946.
62. Joint C.O.S. memo, Washington, 21 June 1946, FRUS 1946, vol. 7, pp. 632, 633.
63. Evan Wilson, Palestine Report from Arab Standpoint, 8 June 1946, NRC, Beirut files, RG 84 Box 230.
64. Legal effect of UN Charter with respect to the Palestine situation, undated, USNA, RG 43, AAC, Box 2.
65. Washington to Foreign Office, 10 May 1946, India Office, L/P&S/12/1112.
66. Washington to Foreign Office, 10 May 1946, FO 371/52523/E4353.
67. Speech in San Francisco, 15 May 1946, CO 537/1759.
68. W. Millis, ed., *The Forrestal Diaries*, New York, 1951, p. 189.

13

The End of the Report:
Anglo-American Discussions,
June–July 1946

The demise of the AAC report was not immediate, nor was it dramatic. It was drawn out over a period of more than three months during which time a series of discussions between the United States and Britain were held in London. They began with the Brook–Harriman talks in June (led by Norman Brook, Secretary of the Cabinet, for Britain, and Averell Harriman, American Ambassador to the Court of St. James, for the United States) and continued with the Brook–Grady talks in July. Harry F. Grady was an American career diplomat and a member of the Cabinet Committee set up in Washington early in June to deal with the aftermath of the AAC Report (see below). The Anglo-American discussions – the first such joint talks on a Middle-Eastern subject since winter 1944, when Wallace Murray of the State Department Near Eastern Division negotiated in London regarding the relations between the two powers in the area – ended with the presentation in Parliament of the Morrison–Grady Plan for Provincial Autonomy in Palestine, on 31 July 1945, and the temporary withdrawal of the United States from involvement in the Palestine question. There remained for the AAC and its Report only the eulogy, and this was handsomely supplied by "Texas Joe" Hutcheson, two days later. The Grady team, he reported to his fellow commissioner, James McDonald,

left my room in Washington assuring me that they would take the Report as their Bible and insist on its being carried out as a whole ... If what I have read of what they have done is correct, it appears like another case of Satan quoting Scripture to his purposes.[1]

During the second half of 1946, Anglo-American negotiations on the Report were begun in earnest. According to Bevin, the United

States "now seemed to be willing to remove this question from the realm of propaganda and to study its practical implications on a business-like footing."[2] Towards the end of the month, a list of questions dealing with various aspects of the Report was forwarded to Washington. Among the subjects raised were the probable reactions of the two communities in Palestine, repercussions in the Middle East, military and financial commitments, the effect on British and American interests in the Middle East, the role of the UN in a settlement and the discussion of trusteeship.[3] This then was the basis for the discussion which followed.

THE TALKS BEGIN: BROOK–HARRIMAN

The planning of U.S. Palestine policy was given into the hands of a Cabinet Committee under the chairmanship of Secretary of State Byrnes, with the Secretaries of War (Robert Patterson) and the Treasury (John Synder) as members. The Secretaries appointed three alternates, and the Board of Alternates was chaired by Grady, a lawyer who had served as a special envoy of President Roosevelt in various parts of the world.[4] The Cabinet Committee was set up at the initiative of the State Department, and more particularly of Loy Henderson, the chief of the Near Eastern and African division.[5] This partly explains American readiness to discuss the whole Report as against the President's initial tendency to negotiate only over the 100,000.[6]

After three weeks of preparation in Washington the Board of Alternates drafted a plan for bi-national government in Palestine under UN trusteeship, a plan which seemed in accordance with the recommendations of the AAC.[7] In the meantime, however, talks were begun in London between Harriman and Brook on the admission of the 100,000. What Washington failed to take into account were certain indications that HMG might soon adopt a new approach to the Palestine question. The British press, as noted before, was calling increasingly for an alternative to the AAC Report, and the idea was supported by a conversation between John Martin (of the Colonial Office) and Evan Wilson. Martin, according to Wilson, suggested that "the 100,000 be admitted only to a portion of Palestine, thus reassuring the Arabs. Implicitly Martin meant partition by this."[8] Nevertheless, Grady's instructions were to give full support to the Report, while avoiding the issue of U.S. involvement in Palestine. And in order to forestall any rumours of American troops being sent to Palestine, the soldier in his team was to be no more than a Lt. Colonel.[9]

The first of the joint discussions began in London on 17 June 1946. Three days earlier, Bevin had written to Attlee that

there is evidently some danger that the US government will attempt to commit HMG to acceptance of the 100,000 before decisions have been taken on the AAC's Report as a whole. It therefore seems advisable to sound another note of warning on this point.[10]

The success of this second warning can be deduced from Harriman's speech at the opening of the Conference with Brook, in which he said that he was "concerned only with the physical implications ... for the settlement of 100,000 Jews in Palestine."[11]

And indeed, for eleven days the only subject discussed was the immigration of the 100,000, i.e., the Report's second recommendation. Averell Harriman and Norman Brook presided over their delegations which included "a combined galaxy of Palestinian talent that we shall have to go a long way to equal."[12] And the wealth of detail that was considered included methods of selection, priority groups (children, skilled workmen, people over sixty, etc.), transportation, embarkation ports, rates of movement, reception in Palestine, assignment given to the Jewish Agency, the cost involved, and so forth and so on.[13]

The question of the 100,000 was not a bone of contention between the two sides, and the discussions were mainly technical. It is true, however, that by this time the figure of 100,000 had lost all meaning: at the time of the 1945 Harrison Report, this was the approximate number of Jewish DPs, but by later summer of 1946, there were probably over 250,000.[14] The necessity of Jewish emigration from Europe was universally accepted, except, perhaps, by the Control Authorities who considered "that the Jews who had been living in freedom [sic] in Germany and Austria throughout the war, should not now be encouraged to emigrate to Palestine."[15]

An interesting aspect of the June Conference (and the later Brook–Grady study) was the fruitless attempt to get other non-European countries – besides Palestine – to agree to take in Jewish emigrants. Reference was made to the period 1933–1946, during which time a quarter of a million Poles, in addition to 200,000 other refugees, among them 70,000 Jews, were resettled in Britain, and 430,000 Europeans emigrated to America.[16] There was, however no positive response to inquiries made in Eritrea, Tripolitana,

Cyrenaica or the Dominican Republic.[17] Disappointing answers were also given by the British Dominions which stressed that "it would be exceedingly difficult to single out persons of Jewish race from among the various groups of refugees with whom we have to deal." The South Americans were also unhelpful since they were giving immigration priority first to Italians and then to Catholics.[18]

BRITISH HOLDING OPERATION

But as far as the British were concerned, the Brook–Harriman talks were little more than a holding operation. Following the publication of the AAC Report at the end of April, and up to, during and after Grady arrived in London, Whitehall was airing the possibility of offering another scheme in its stead: the Provincial Autonomy Plan. This plan had first seen the light of day in August 1945. Drawn up and presented by the Colonial Office, it was one of the eight plans for Palestine proposed to the Labour Cabinet – and rejected. At the time the Foreign Office had objected strongly, seeing it as the "thin end of the wedge of partition."[19] And in January 1946 it had been presented (anonymously) to the AAC, precisely because the Colonial Office believed that "if we do not do this, the AAC may come down on the side of partition without being fully aware of the implications."[20] By 11 July 1945, the Cabinet referred to the plan as the alternative to partition "with the advantage that it separated sovereignty from cultural autonomy."[21]

It was the considered opinion of most people involved in the Palestine issue in Britain that Jew and Arab would never be able to live peacefully in one unitary country; and this lay at the basis of the feeling of disappointment with the AAC Report. For while the Report described the divisions between the two peoples accurately, it still supported the continuation and development of a unitary bi-national country. Provincial Autonomy, on the other hand, would prevent partition from going too far while at the same time promoting it in certain aspects, thus satisfying those who insisted that some form of partition be instituted.

During the better part of July 1946, while the British were working out the details of this old-new constitutional scheme in preparation for the *joint* Anglo-American conference, they were also doing their best to keep the plan from the Americans. Their reason was simple: they were determined that any substitute plan would have to be a totally British plan, implemented by Britain alone. American cooperation, military or political, was not wanted:

The Committee [of the C.O.S.] took the view that it would be dangerous to hand over copies of the scheme to the Americans ... They would much prefer that he [Norman Brook] should refrain from discussing the scheme at all with the Americans, but agreed that if this were impossible, he should confine discussion of it to general terms and avoid giving details.[22]

The C.O.S. had no doubts about the advantages of the plan. On the contrary:

From a preliminary examination of the plan ... the General Staff consider that it offers the best solution which will bridge the period of the next three to five years, during which it should be possible to obtain the military facilities we require.[23]

As far as the C.O.S. was concerned, there was really only one criterion for judging whether Provincial Autonomy was better or worse than the Report: the possible Arab and Jewish resistance to it, and the number of troops required to quell it.[24] Attlee was infuriated by the C.O.S.'s fear of any scheme "which would in *any* [sic] way offend the Arab" and of their political "devotion to the impossible."[25] Brook's draft, in comparison, sought to judge the plan according to "whether it is one which affords to the Trustee a practical means of discharging the undertaking given to the two communities."[26]

If there was objection to Provincial Autonomy, it came from the British authorities in Palestine and the Middle East. According to Cunningham, it contained most of the disadvantages of partition without its main advantages:

It would be better to accept partition ... A provincial autonomy scheme would be acceptable to neither the Jews nor the Arabs, whereas partition would anyway be acceptable to the Jews ... My main objection to the P.A. [sic] scheme is that it does not remove the difficulties arising from ... Jewish immigration. I agree that the control of immigration must remain the concern of the central Government [but] however generous [it] may be ... it will never satisfy the voracious fervour for the admission of Jews to Palestine of the present fanatical leaders of the Yishuv and [we] would continue to be faced with the same problems ... I agree that there would be great advantages in leaving us in general control in Palestine, but I do not believe that this requirement is so great as to justify adopting the scheme as a whole.[27]

Further objections came from the Attorney-General in Palestine, who complained that because the assent of the High Commissioner would be required for all bills passed by local legislatures, he would attract "all the opprobrium connected with legislation." In addition, he predicted provincial nationalistic legislation which would provoke retaliatory legislation.[28] Others in Palestine objected to the plan because it would restrict the integration of the Jewish National Home into the Middle East by separating the Jews from the surrounding Arabs.[29]

Provincial Autonomy would nevertheless solve one of the most difficult problems raised by partition – that of establishing frontiers. The boundaries of the provinces would be merely administrative.[30] If there were fears that the scheme would result in partition after all, the Foreign Secretary's views (which were a complete reversal of his past and future objections to partition) helped to overcome them. He told Norman Brook that he was actually considering a proposal

under which the major part of the Arab province would be attached to Trans-Jordan and the Arab portion of Galilee to Lebanon. This would make possible the establishment of an *independent Jewish state, perhaps with a rather larger territory than that allocated to the Jewish province in the Colonial Secretary's plan.*[31]

The savour of partition inherent in the Provincial Autonomy Plan was not, therefore, so much of a deterrent as before. Since the preparation of a new policy was expected to take some six months, one can understand the readiness to settle on a plan which already existed and had apparently been successfully applied in India.[32] The Cabinet, therefore, concluded that subject to possible C.O.S. reservations, Provincial Autonomy was "a constructive and imaginative plan."[33]

The real enthusiasts behind the Provincial Autonomy Plan were, naturally, the Colonial Office, who were determined to push forward with their plan regardless of any opposition from the Middle East. Apart from Colonial Secretary George Hall's belief in the merits of the plan, his enthusiasm can also be attributed to the traditional and ongoing rivalry between the Colonial Office and the Foreign Office. At the decisive Cabinet meeting on 11 July, a number of factors joined together to tilt the balance in favour of the Colonial Office. First of all, Bevin was in Paris at the time.

Secondly, all those who were unalterably opposed to American involvement in the Middle East threw their support behind Provincial Autonomy. For them the major defect of the AAC Report was exactly the same as Bevin's reason for initiating the Inquiry and supporting its results: he saw it as a stepping stone to Anglo-American cooperation in the area. Against this background, one can easily understand Bevin's reluctance to return to London on 31 July to announce the Autonomy Plan in Parliament, in spite of Attlee's request.[34] Herbert Morrison, Lord President of the Council, announced it in his stead, and thus had his name attached to the plan.

DISPOSING OF THE AAC

In all events, before getting on with Provincial Autonomy, the AAC Report had to be disposed of. And, indeed, in accordance with previous Cabinet instructions, the British delegation to the Brook–Harriman and Brook–Grady discussion had prepared a set of papers stressing the fact that the Report was unworkable. They pointed out the various problems which the AAC had not covered, such as the lines on which immigration should take place after the admission of the 100,000. Should it, asked the Colonial Office, be

on lines which would lead to placing the Jews in a position ... of dominance with the demotion of the Arabs to a position of hewers of wood and drawers of water? Equally[should] it preclude the possibility of any further settlement of Jews in the National Home, and were the Palestine Jews obliged to adapt themselves to an Arabized culture? [Therefore] with the admission of the 100,000 ... there should be no further immigration ... until the impact of this move has been studied.[35]

Doubts were also expressed about the prospects for developing self-governing institutions in light of the AAC's implicit hope that under the Mandate, the mere passage of time would make it easier for the two sides to cooperate. The AAC's recommendations for the development of Arab communal organizations similar to those established by the Jews were seen as a move which would accentuate the gap between the communities and thus perpetuate two different social systems. There was also a paper devoted to finance which specified the wealth of problems inherent in the AAC's general recommendation to bridge the gap between the Jewish and Arab standards of living.[36]

Thus, when the Colonial Secretary, at the 11 July meeting of the Cabinet, tabled a paper outlining the political, military and financial difficulties involved in putting the Report into effect,

there was general agreement that the recommendations in the Report of the AAC offered no practical prospect of progress towards a solution of the constitutional problem in Palestine and discussion turned on the alternative policy.[37]

These four lines constituted the Cabinet's only reference to the AAC Report.

Having thus, in Bevin's absence, so readily disposed of the AAC Report, the Cabinet agreed not only to table the Provincial Autonomy Plan but to enumerate the tactics which Brook should employ with the Americans in their forthcoming discussions: his team should not indulge in destructive criticism of the AAC Report, but "seek the appropriate moment for bringing forward this alternative plan ... after they had exposed the weaknesses in the recommendations (No. 3 & 6) regarding the future constitution of Palestine and further immigration policy." These weaknesses were thought to be the Report's failure to suggest practical measures to ensure that one race would be unable to dominate the other, and its failure to emphasize the rest of the world's obligation to share in the solution of the Jewish DP problem.[38]

The Colonial Secretary then turned his efforts to Cunningham, noting that, in his view,

progress in the solution of the problems with which Palestine is confronted ... is likely to be negligible for so long as Palestine continues as a unitary bi-national state ... I find it difficult to escape the conclusion that a bi-national state ... other than one administered bureaucratically and by force of arms, is an impracticable conception.[39]

It was a matter, Hall continued, of allowing "each race to manage its own affairs," and he concluded with the point that "the Cabinet was inclined to agree in this conclusion!"

This then was the situation when the Americans, led by Grady, and committed to accepting the AAC Report, arrived in London to commence discussions with Brook, who was to offer Provincial Autonomy at "the appropriate moment."

THE TALKS CONTINUE: BROOK–GRADY

The U.S. delegation came to London with the scheme for constitutional development in Palestine worked out by Grady's Board of Alternates in Washington.[40] It was based on the assumption that neither community would dominate the other or attempt to turn Palestine into a totally Arab or a totally Jewish state. Either a mandatory power or the UN would continue to administer the country. An international advisory board would be appointed by the UN to direct the development of the country. Two legislative houses would be established: the lower house would be elected without regard to nationality, but half of the upper house would be elected by the Jewish community and the other half by the Arab community. Deadlock in the upper house would be averted through the powers of the chief administrator, i.e., the mandatory power. At five year intervals, the UN would consider the termination of the country's dependency. Immigration would continue to be regulated by the Government of Palestine. This plan, as noted, was entirely consistent with the recommendations of the AAC, and consequently, at odds with the aims of the British team.

Against this background, Brook introduced the Provincial Autonomy plan, but not before the difficulties of implementing the AAC Report had been pointed out. At the same time, two other moves were made by Brook to facilitate American approval for the British Autonomy plan. First, in the conference's three subcommittees – one for economics and finance, one for political questions and one for the DP problem – Britain agreed to the completion of the movement of the 100,000 within one year (an earlier British estimate had suggested two years against a U.S. estimate of five months).[41] Secondly, the question of American military assistance was completly avoided, notwithstanding Howe's reservation that

if we were to find . . . that we could not carry the proposed policy into effect and then made a request for American troops, our failure to discuss this possibility during the present conversations would give rise to the suspicion that we had never had any serious intention of actually implementing this policy, but had simply been playing for time.[42]

It seems that the Under-Secretary of State at the Foreign Office was not familiar with the aim of some of the British negotiators to keep the United States out of Palestine. The British found Grady an easy negotiator; he "fully appreciated the difficulties" of the 100,000 immigration "and agreed that twelve months was meant to be a target rather than a firm undertaking."[43] According to one British source, he "certainly did brush aside many objections raised by his colleagues to British proposals."[44] His team was even said to be in "an indecent hurry to agree, mostly because of Grady who pretends to have such instructions."[45] Concerning the emigration of Jews from Europe, he called first for emphasis to be put upon their remaining in Europe, or for the exploration of the possibility of immigration to Latin America.[46] When the Provincial Autonomy plan was submitted, he first pressed for full control over immigration into the Jewish province to be given to the Jews, but later withdrew this proposal.[47] His behaviour may explain the British Treasury's comment that we have "successfully sold ... the Americans the Provincial Plan."[48]

Strangely enough, discussion of the Plan revolved not around its deviation from the AAC Report and from Grady's programme for a unitary country, but around such matters as frontiers and finance. While the British sought to enlarge the Arab province in order that the scheme be palatable to the Arabs (in response to C.O.S. wishes), the Americans sought to expand the Jewish province. But, wrote Brook to Attlee, "we have now succeeded in persuading the Americans to withdraw their proposals ... and the differences between us have been narrowed down to the delineation of the southern boundary of the Jewish province below Jaffa."[49] He further noted that

while the balance of political advantage in the ... Provincial Autonomy is about equal for both Arabs and Jews, its economic advantages are somewhat heavily weighted in favour of the Jews. We can therefore argue that the balance should be adjusted in favour of the Arabs.

The frontiers were to be purely administrative, thus obviating the need to administer island areas, a problem that would have arisen had the country been partitioned.[50] Yet some still thought that

from the psychological aspect, the location of the boundaries would inevitably be regarded as one of the most important factors ... It would inevitably be a point on which critics would fasten.[51]

For similar reasons, the Negev and Galilee were excluded from the

Jewish province.[52] The Negev, or South Gaza area, was regarded as the only area which was capable of absorbing the natural increase in the Arab population. Since irrigation could only be provided from sources in Lebanon or Trans-Jordan, no water would have been available had the area been included in the Jewish province. Douglas Harris, the original author of the Plan, pointed out that in addition, both the arid Negev and the hill country of Galilee (which could not be irrigated) were considered incapable of supporting more people, and could be "dry farmed [or] developed by terracing as efficiently by the Arabs as by the Jews." He further noted that the Peel Commission's proposal to include Galilee in the Jewish state had "led immediately to an armed revolt throughout the area."[53]

With regard to finances, the Jewish Agency had suggested, as early as May, that the settlement of the 100,000 should be financed by German money as reparation for the victims of Nazism. The German reparation fund, however, amounted to only £7,500,000, and the Agency could not use its German mark assets outside Germany, since any goods required to be exported from Germany had, under the Quadripartite Agreement, to be paid for in dollars. In addition, the building materials needed to house the 100,000 in Palestine could not be purchased in Britain since there was an acute shortage of such materials there. The problem was eventually solved by the American Government and American Jewry which had to pay the lion's share in this project.[54]

Another question was what financial powers would devolve upon the Provincial Governments, since in most cases they were to have full control in their own financial matters. But because the budgetary analysis showed a surplus for the Jews and a deficit of over £2,000,000 per annum for the Arabs, the Central Government would have to balance the Arab budget, using its own surplus and a contribution from the Jewish province. On the assumption that the scheme would be accepted by both sides, no allowances were made for any increase in expenditures resulting from disorders and non-cooperation.[55]

Grady's endorsement of Provincial Autonomy was not, of course, his own idea; he was acting according to Presidential instruction. Prior to the establishment of the joint discussions to study the AAC Report, the State Department had tried to dispel the impression that another committee was about to go over the same ground as the AAC.[56] The Zionists apparently had caught the scent early on. With the establishment of the U.S. Cabinet Committee on Palestine, the American Zionists warned that

the ground is being prepared to enmesh the admission of the 100,000 into some recommendation concerning the future status of Palestine, so as to put the Jews before the alternative of either accepting a bad decision as a price for having the 100,000 admitted, or seeing [them] out of Palestine.[57]

In that same memo, the Zionists considered American readiness to negotiate with Britain "a negligent or deliberate maltreatment of the Palestine problem by Mr. Truman and Mr. Byrnes." And a week later, an Agency official summed up the forthcoming Brook–Grady discussion as follows:

They [the Americans] pretend that they have no instructions to separate the 100,000 from major policy. Somebody is double-crossing somebody ... this refers to the Boss [= Truman], Dean [Acheson], Dave [Niles] and ourselves. Hard to find out who are the victims of whom.[58]

The diary of Henry Wallace, then U.S. Secretary for Commerce, shows that Truman was in daily contact with his delegation and "the President says he has given them explicit instructions and they followed them exactly."[59] So, all in all, the evidence points to the fact that U.S. policy up to August 1946, at which point the United States decided to retreat from any involvement in Palestine, was far from pro-Zionist. The 100,000 was on the U.S. agenda for Palestine; Zionist aspirations were not. The British belief that American policy was motivated by a concern for the Jewish vote could not be substantiated in the summer of 1946.

NOTES

1. McDonald Papers, folder 187.
2. Cabinet meeting, 20 May 1946, CAB 128/5, No. CM(46)50.
3. Foreign Office to Washington, 26 May 1946, FO 371/52526/E4844.
4. Italy, India, Greece, Iran. Truman Library, Independence, holds the Grady Papers and ms. of his autobiography *Adventures in Diplomacy*.
5. See also Evan Wilson to Thames Television, 13 June 1977, SACMEC, Thames Television papers for the Palestine Mandate programme.
6. Ilan's version is that the appointment of a Cabinet committee was done to enable Truman "to hide behind the apron of others." See *America, Britain and Palestine*, p. 222.
7. Grady's autobiography, p. 159; Truman Library, Grady Papers. See details in this

chapter.

8. Evan Wilson's memo, 28 June 1946, USNA, RG 43, AAC, Box 13.
9. Washington to Foreign Office, 5 and 13 July 1946, CO 537/1736; State Dept. to Harriman, 23 June 1946, USNA, State Dept. Palestine Papers, Box 6756. On Grady's instructions to avoid military or political involvement, including participation as a trustee, see his autobiography, p. 157, Truman Library, Grady Papers.
10. FO 371/52530/E5627/G.
11. Minutes of the first meeting of the Anglo-U.S. Study of the Report, London, 17 June 1946, FO 371/52530/E5640.
12. Evan Wilson to Leslie Rood, London, 22 June 1946, USNA, RG 43, AAC, Box 13.
13. Report by Brook, undated, summarizing the June Conference, pp. 6-10, PREM 8/627 Pt. 2; record of the first meeting of the Brook–Harriman Conference, 17 June 1946, FO 371/52530/E5640. See also Agency estimate that reception of the 100,000 would not present a major problem: "65,000 were received in the single year 1935, when our economic base was much smaller than today," letter to Truman, 14 June 1946, CO 537/1765.
14. Memo by U.S. State Dept., Near Eastern Division, 27 Dec. 1946, FRUS 1946, vol. 7, p. 733; Sykes, *Crossroads to Israel*, p. 360.
15. Record of the Brook–Harriman Conference, 25 June 1946, FO 371/52533/E5981. Later a corrigendum was issued in which the word "freedom" was omitted, 28 June 1946, ibid.
16. Report of the sub-committee on Recommendation 1, 23 July 1946, CO 537/1765.
17. Note by the Foreign Office to the Anglo-U.S. Study of the Report, 15 June 1946, CO 537/2319.
18. Office of the British High Commissioner, Canberra, 27 July 1946, CO 537/2319. See also similar answers by Canada, South Africa and New Zealand, ibid; and memo by Refugee Dept., Foreign Office, 3 Jan. 1947, ibid.
19. Note on the meeting between Foreign and Colonial Office representatives, 23 Aug. 1945, CO 733/461 Pt. 2/75872, Pt. 3.
20. Comment by Wikeley, Foreign Office, Eastern Dept., 13 Jan. 1946, FO 371/52504/E389/G.
21. Cabinet meeting, 11 July 1946, CAB 128/6, No. CM(46)67.
22. C.O.S. Committee meeting, 12 July 1946, COS(46)109, FO 371/52539/E6629/G.
23. Army Council Secretariat (ACS), brief for War Secretary, No. ACS/B/2071, 11 July 1946, on C.O.S. attitudes towards the Report and Provincial Autonomy, WO 32/10260.
24. See note 22 above.
25. Attlee's note on the C.O.S. appreciation, 15 July 1946, PREM 8/627/Pt. 3.
26. Plan for Provincial Autonomy, note by the British delegation, 13 July 1946, p. 15, FO 371/51541/E6794/G. See also Hutcheson to C. in C. Middle East: "The precise amount of military force one solution or another will require is a matter for the military to decide based upon what we should decide to do, rather than for us to determine based on what the military tell us they think will happen." See page 156.
27. Cunningham to Hall, 9 July 1946, SACMEC, Cunningham Papers, Box 1, File 1.
28. In Shaw to Hall, 22 July 1946, CO 537/1767.
29. Scott (Palestine Secretariat, then in London) to Cunningham, in Hall to Cunningham, 5 July 1946, CO 537/1767.
30. Cabinet meeting, 11 July 1946, CAB 128/6, No. CM(46)67.
31. My emphasis. Norman Brook's note of points agreed with Bevin, Paris, 10 July 1946, PREM 8/627 Pt. 3. See also report by Brook to the Cabinet, 11 July 1946, CAB 128/6, No. CM(46)67.
32. Memo by Eastwood, Colonial Office, 30 June 1945, CO 733/463 Pt. 1, No. 75872/123.

33. Cabinet meeting, 11 July 1946, CAB 128/6, No. CM (46)67.
34. Cabinet meeting, 22 and 29 July 1946, CAB 128/6, No. CM(46)71 and CM(46)74. Kirk, *The Middle East, 1945–1950*, p. 233, reports that Bevin was ill.
35. Note by the Colonial Office on Recommendation 6: principle which should be observed in regulating future immigration, 3 July 1946, CO 537/1749.
36. Principles of government: no Arab, no Jewish state. Note by the British delegation, 11 July 1946, CO 537/1765; Appendix: Nature and Cost of the Services Recommended for the Benefit of the Arabs, ibid.
37. Cabinet meeting, 11 July 1946, CAB 128/6, No. CM(46)67. For the Colonial Secretary's Paper, see CAB 129/11, No. CP(46)258, 8 July 1946.
38. Ibid.
39. Hall to Cunningham, 13 July 1946, SACMEC, Cunningham Papers, Box 1, file 1.
40. Constitutional Development for Palestine, Note by the U.S. Delegation, 27 July 1946, CO 537/1765.
41. Record of meeting of the combined study of Report, 23 July 1946, FO 371/52546/E7274/G. On the initial British proposal of 4,000 a month, and the American proposal of 20,000, see respectively: report by Brook summarizing the Brook–Harriman Conference, undated, p. 8, PREM 8/627/Pt. 2; meeting of the Brook–Harriman Conference, 17 June 1946, FO 371/52530/E5640.
42. Howe to Orme Sargent (with Bevin in Paris), 22 July 1946, FO 371/52548/E7460/G.
43. Record of meeting, combined study of Report, 24 July 1946, FO 371/52546/E7257/G.
44. Beeley, 7 Aug. 1946, on comment in the *New York Times*, 4 Aug. 1946, about Grady's opposition to protests by his staff who wished to protect U.S. financial interests. Grady was also accused of not allowing documents to be sent to Washington during the negotiations, FO 371/52550/E7588.
45. Memo to Eliahu Epstein, 23 July 1946, CZA, Goldmann files, No. Z6, Bundle 5, file 20.
46. Record of meeting, combined study of Report, 13 July 1946, FO 371/52540/E6728.
47. Memo by Douglas Harris, 14 Aug. 1946, PREM 8/627, Pt. 4.
48. Minute by A. Winnifrith, 22 July 1946, T161/1251.
49. Brook to Attlee, 20 July 1946, PREM 8/627 Pt. 3. See also Cabinet meeting, 22 July 1946, CAB 128/6, No. CM(46)71.
50. Memo for Byrnes by Brook and the Colonial Office, 23 Nov. 1946, FO 371/52565/E11526/G. This enabled the administrative inclusion of Jaffa in the Arab province although surrounded by Jewish areas. See Scheme for Provincial Autonomy, Jan. 1946, FO 371/52504/E389/G.
51. Cabinet meeting, 22 July 1946, CAB 128/6, No. CM(46)71.
52. In the Autonomy proposal, the Negev was to be retained by the High Commissioner. Should investigation prove that development was possible, the area would be leased to the Jews. Should it be negative, the Negev would remain with the High Commissioner or be given to the Arabs. See Scheme for Provincial Autonomy, note by the British delegation, 13 July 1946, p. 14, FO 371/52541/E6794/G.
53. Memo by Douglas Harris, 13 Aug. 1946, PREM 8/627 Pt. 4. See also Scheme for Provincial Autonomy, note by the British delegation, 13 July 1946, p. 14: "On looking at a map, nothing is more striking than ... the areas in northern and central Palestine in which there is hardly a single Jew ... but which have been the seat for the most violent anti-Jewish outbreaks," FO 371/52541/E6794/G.
54. Brief for the Foreign Secretary's discussion with Byrnes, 7 May 1946, PREM 8/627 Pt. 2. See also Jewish Agency to Dept. of State, 12 June 1946, in note by the U.S. delegation to the joint talks over the Report, 18 June 1946, ibid.; report by financial sub-committee, 5 and 19 July 1946, CO 537/1765.

55. Report by financial sub-committee, 30 July 1946, pp. 5, 6, 8, CO 537/1765. See also report of financial sub-committee, 19 July 1946, p. 6, on the disagreement between the delegations on the possible financial losses resulting from political tension in the country, ibid.
56. Washington to Foreign Office, 13 June 1946, FO 371/52529/E5446.
57. AZEC file on the U.S. Cabinet Committee on Palestine, 28 June 1946, ZANY.
58. Letter to Epstein, London, 2 July 1946, CZA, Goldmann files, No. Z6, Bundle 5, file 20.
59. John Blum ed., *The Price of Vision: The Diary of Henry A. Wallace*, Boston, 1971, p. 604, 26 July 1946. See also William Phillips after a meeting in August 1946 with the Grady team: "The decision . . . was intended primarily to satisfy the President," *Ventures in Diplomacy*, p. 297.

14

Provincial Autonomy

On 31 July 1946 the House of Commons heard about the Provincial Autonomy Plan for the first time.[1] Since the White Paper of 1939, this was the first attempt of HMG to offer a comprehensive scheme for Palestine. The scheme envisaged the division of Palestine into four areas: an Arab province, a Jewish province, the district of Jerusalem and the district of the Negev. The population of these areas at the time was as follows:

	Arabs	*Jews*
Arab province	815,000	15,000
Jewish province	301,000	451,000
Jerusalem district	96,000	102,000
Negev district	–	–

The provincial governments would have the power of legislation and administration in municipal and village administration, agriculture, fisheries, forests, land sales and settlement, education, public health and other social services, trade, industry, irrigation, development and public works. They would also have the power to limit the number and determine the qualifications of persons taking up permanent residence in their territories, but they would not be allowed to impede free inter-territorial transit, trade or commerce. They could levy taxes, borrow within the province, and, with the consent of the Central Government, borrow abroad.

The Central Government would control foreign exchange, currency and the licensing of imports. Exclusive authority would rest with it in matters of defence, foreign relations, customs and excise, police, prisons, courts, railway facilities, the Haifa harbour, posts and telegraphs, civil aviation, broadcasting and antiquities. It would be empowered to examine and verify municipal and provincial accounts and to examine the budget estimates of the provinces. In general "all powers not expressly granted to the provincial governments will be reserved to the Central Government." Immigration

will be administered by the Central Government [which] will authorize the immigration desired by the respective provincial governments to the extent to which the economic absorptive capacity of the province will not thereby be exceeded. It shall not have the power to authorize immigration into either province in excess of any limitations imposed by the provincial governments.²

The administering authority would appoint a High Commissioner who would preside over the Central Government. An executive would be appointed in each province by the High Commissioner from among the members of the provincial Legislative Chambers. The Jerusalem and the Negev districts would be largely administered by the High Commissioner. The plan was seen as necessary for Jerusalem in particular. It was hoped it would narrow the gulf between the two communities which was "tending to promote the Jews into the position of an intelligentsia while relegating the Arabs into that of mere hewers of wood and drawers of water."³

Fifty million dollars would be granted by the U.S. Government to the Government of Palestine for development and, in case adequate finances from other sources, such as the International Bank, were not available, the United States would loan up to 250 million dollars for the development of the Arab Middle East, including Palestine.

During the first twelve months of the implementation of the plan, 100,000 DPs would be admitted into Palestine.

ON THE BRIGHT SIDE

These were the general lines of the scheme, and it was expected to succeed, inter alia, because a similar scheme had apparently succeeded in India and the situations of the two countries were considered to be analogous. It was expected that a Jewish province with a large Arab minority could be successfully created with the Arab minority selling their land and migrating to the Arab area. "A few successful settlement schemes would probably be a potent influence in inducing ... to migrate."⁴

The plan was presented in glowing terms; it accorded with the

UN Charter which called for self-governing institutions, and was thought to give the provinces sufficient freedom to encourage them to avoid central government interference.[5] It was also thought that it would prevent illegal immigration since the repercussions – unemployment, industrial unrest and financial embarrassment – would fall exclusively on the Jewish province.[6] With regard to finance, the Central Government would collect large revenues and spend them, not where they accrued, but where expenditure was most needed. In this way, deficits in the Arab province would be met from the revenues of Palestine as a whole.[7] It was thought that the plan could be implemented immediately without reference to the United Nations. This was seen as a great advantage because the Arab states could block any plan put before the Organization.[8] Above all, it was thought that autonomy would reduce violence and disorder in Palestine by segregating Jew and Arab; paradoxically, people believed that "unless a partial separation of the two antagonistic communities is made now, their eventual cooperation will become forever impossible."[9]

The plan seemed to offer the Palestinian Arabs something which they had hitherto lacked: it gave the majority of them their own political institutions in an Arab province, in addition to freedom from the fear of further Jewish immigration into that province. To the Jews it offered an opportunity to exercise a wide measure of control over immigration into one part of Palestine and to promote, in the Jewish province, the development of their National Home.[10] The plan also provided for the admission of 100,000 DPs at once, made future immigration subject only to their province's absorptive capacity and trebled the areas within which Jews could purchase land freely. Apparently the best land in Palestine was in the Jewish province, and the overwhelming majority of Jewish citrus farming was within it. Fifteen thousand Jews would be left in the Arab area, as against 300,000 Arabs in the Jewish province. Industry, ports, seaboard, railway and water supply were nearly all to be within the Jewish province.[11] If Jews now claimed that they had got the smaller province and it

is too small to absorb a considerable number of new immigrants ... [this] is easy to refute ... 82% of the[ir] population are living on an area of less than 90 square miles [and] it is difficult to argue that a province containing nearly 1,500 square miles affords ... no scope for substantial increase of population.[12]

Like the AAC Report, the Autonomy Plan sought to place Palestine under UN trusteeship, and the difficulties in application were apparent.

The UN Charter called for the promotion of self-government and the independence of dependent areas, as well as for the need to take into account the desires of the majority of the population in these areas. But the Autonomy Plan, like the AAC Report, contradicted the Charter both with regard to the indefinite continuation of the country's dependency and the recommendation to admit more Jewish immigrants. Furthermore, the Charter required that the states directly concerned be consulted, and it seemed unlikely that the Arab states would agree to trusteeship. It was, therefore, either the Report or the Autonomy Plan on the one hand, or the Charter trusteeship regulations on the other: the two could not go together.[13]

The Americans did not face these difficulties. For them the Mandate was the only state "directly concerned" and it "seemed to be news to Dr. Grady" that Britain expected the Arab states, as well as France and Russia, to be included in this definition.[14] In general, the United States did not consider that the Report had violated the Charter for the simple reason that the AAC had not functioned under UN auspices. The Americans, according to one British official, felt free

to persuade us to introduce ballot-box democracy into the terms of trusteeship for darkest Tanganyika [but] it was a little ironical to hear other State Department officials arguing that Article 76B did not necessarily mean that the "freely expressed wishes" of the advanced people of Palestine should be taken very seriously.[15]

At the Brook–Grady Conference, Britain and America differed in their interpretation of trusteeship. This had already been a source of controversy between Roosevelt and Churchill, with the latter viewing trusteeship as a mere cloak for American expansion, their "informal empire."[16] But in Britain itself, people disagreed about the results of trusteeship in Palestine. Bevin predicted that if trusteeship were accepted, Britain would probably have to move her forces out of Palestine.[17] On the other hand, in the Eastern Department of the Foreign Office, it was concluded that "we should merely be continuing the status-quo under another name."[18] The same idea – that trustees and trusteeship would not be effective enough to interfere with Britain's position in Palestine – perhaps lay behind the earlier view which stressed that if "it [trusteeship] cannot be exercised by the U.K. alone, then [it] should be in the hands of the widest possible group of states."[19] It seems, however, that neither this view nor Bevin's fear of Russian participation was shared by everybody in Whitehall, where some thought that

the more countries involved, the more impossible would our task become [but] we see ... that there might be disadvantages from the Foreign Office point of view to an interpretation which leaves Russia and China out of the picture.[20]

"A HUNDRED TIMES WORSE"

The Zionists believed that "trusteeship ... will be a hundred times worse than the old Mandate."[21] The Arabs, for their part, were expected to object to the extension of dependency more than to Jewish immigration.[22] Yet, Britain stayed on this track, deliberately avoiding the question of dual responsibility with America in Palestine.

"Our position as Mandatory would certainly be no easier after such implementation than it is today," said Hall, and rejected the AAC Report in favour of Provincial Autonomy.[23] Autonomy, however, was not chosen because it presented fewer difficulties: it was no more attractive to the Arabs than the Report, since, according to the former plan, part of Palestine was to be given to the Jews, and the promise of Autonomy in the Arab province was not a sufficient reward for this loss. In addition, the promised consultation with the Palestinians before implementation was not a novel idea. It was clear from Bevin's statement of November 1945 that the recommendations proposed by the AAC would be discussed with Jews and Arabs before being applied. Hence, if concern for Anglo-Arab relations led to the rejection of the Report, adoption of Autonomy would not make Britain's position any easier: the hint of partition in the plan was only one reason.

From the Jewish point of view, Autonomy did not give the "state within a state" anything new. In spite of the so-called pro-Jewish articles, the detailed plan was a greater blow to political Zionism than the Report, which at least left things in Palestine in a state of flux.

Britain's strange decision to adopt the Autonomy Plan did not, therefore, stem from the belief that it would be easier to implement than the AAC's recommendations.[24] It is possible that the main reason for adopting Autonomy in the summer of 1946, after having rejected it in autumn 1945, was in order to rectify an actual or potential devaluation of British authority in Palestine (in favour of America) conceived to exist in the AAC Report. This perhaps lay behind the C.O.S.'s opinion that because it was a good plan "it would be dangerous to hand over copies to the Americans."[25] It might also explain the view that "so long, therefore, as the Provincial Autonomy scheme remains in force, we shall continue to be solely responsible for defence."[26]

RESULT: AMERICAN WITHDRAWAL

The theoretical discussions over a plan for Palestine ended on 31 July 1946, with the announcement in London of the Autonomy Plan. There were some in Britain who expressed a true interest in the implementation of the scheme. America's subsequent rejection of what was seen as a "federal unity of Palestine," and her support for partition (see below) rather shocked one MP when he remembered that "the Americans themselves ... thought it worthwhile to fight a long ... civil war precisely in order to avoid American partition and to create ... federal unity."[27] Others – who faced Arab opposition – defended Autonomy in a way which had rarely been seen hitherto: the Minister in Beirut, for example, said that he would

be very grateful for any guidance you might be able to give as to the degree of pressure you would wish to exercise on the Lebanese and Syrian Governments in favour of acceptance of Palestine proposals. There is quite a lot of heat which we could ... turn on both.[28]

And a member of the Foreign Office suggested that "the Arabs, as always, want to interpose a buffer – HMG – between themselves and the Jews. It is time we stopped playing their game."[29]

The presentation of a detailed solution for Palestine brought out the contradictions and conflicting trends which existed among the various bodies dealing with the question, particularly in America. And following the U.S. rejection of Autonomy, the British began to have increasing doubts about the usefulness of involving them in the conflict at all. Beeley, for example, believed that "it would be unwise to take seriously into account the prospect of financial help from the U.S. in the framing of our Palestine policy."[30] Political support was not even mentioned. Similar doubts had emerged in the United States over American agreement to take part in the Committee at all, and in the subsequent June–July conferences. The Zionists also began to have second thoughts about the wisdom of pinning their hopes on America, and started to look towards London. In short, the aftermath of the AAC Inquiry – the Autonomy episode – was a crossroads in the Palestine conflict, perhaps the most important one. In the short run, it resulted in America's temporary withdrawal from the issue and, in the long run, in Truman's support for Jewish statehood.

America's hesitancy over the new plan resulted in Attlee's taking a hasty decision to go ahead with it, and signalled official British abandonment of the initative to involve the United States in Palestine.[31] A comparison between this act of the Prime Minister's and his speech of 1 May 1946, when he made implementation of the Report conditional upon the dispatch of U.S. troops, may suggest that he was now harbouring serious doubts about the wisdom of his Foreign Secretary's initiative. When HMG announced soon after that it would reconsider the British commitment to the figure of 100,000 – Truman's brainchild – the extent of Anglo-American disagreement was further revealed.[32]

Second thoughts were also being expressed by those who had initially supported Autonomy. According to Beeley,

all the arguments which [we] have been using to justify Provincial Autonomy as a means of safeguarding the position of the minority of 600,000 Jews in Palestine, could be used by the Arabs with equal force to justify a similar division of the Jewish area in the interests of the minority of 300,000 Arabs.[33]

In addition, important officials in the Middle East believed that the only workable solution was *partition* – for the sake of the Arabs, surprisingly, since they stood to lose a good deal if Autonomy were introduced. On the other hand, partition would give the Palestinian Arabs a chance to consolidate their position by uniting with one of the adjacent Arab states.[34]

ANGLO-JEWISH NEGOTIATIONS RESUMED

It was perhaps inevitable that the abortive attempt to come to an understanding with America over Palestine resulted in the resumption of British–Zionist negotiations in the late summer of 1946. It was the alliance of two parties who had been frustrated by the United States. Several signs point to an attempt to revive Anglo-Jewish understanding. Stephen Wise, one of the co-chairmen of the American Zionist Emergency Council, came out in support of the British loan.[35] On 14 November 1946, Bevin and the other co-chairman of AZEC, Abba Hillel Silver, met in New York, and although each reiterated his well-known position – Autonomy and Jewish statehood respectively – the very fact that the meeting took place was seen by both as a good omen.[36] In December 1946, Arthur Creech Jones, who had professed some favourable attitudes towards the Zionist movement, succeeded Hall as Colonial Secretary.[37] One of his first acts was to release the leaders of the Jewish Agency, arrested during Operation Agatha. In addition, during the Anglo-Arab London Conference, which assembled in September 1946 to discuss Autonomy, informal negotiations were held between HMG and the Jewish Agency.

This spirit of collaboration was based, however, on too narrow a footing – common disappointment with America – and could not revive the dying Anglo-Jewish understanding. Too many grievances had already accumulated. In addition, there were those in the United States, who, involved as they were in America's contradiction-ridden Palestine policy-making were no doubt opposed to a possible renewal of Anglo-Jewish understanding over Palestine with no say for America. This helps to explain Truman's statement of 4 October 1946 in favour of Jewish statehood, and Bevin's allegation that it had spoiled the Anglo-Zionist agreement which he was on the verge of concluding.

"CIVIL WAR ALONG THE POTOMAC"

The contradictions in American reactions to the Autonomy Plan made it almost impossible to ascertain what U.S. policy now was. Global, internal and Jewish factors, all expressed through intensive lobbying, made for confusion. The ultimate result was a temporary U.S. withdrawal from the Palestine problem.

Washington's initial reactions to Autonomy had been more than favourable. Byrnes was of the opinion that "the time has come when we should cease talking about a solution ... but determine upon a solution and carry it out." He cabled Truman from Paris to say that "the plan proposed is the best solution," adding that

I am convinced from what Mr. Attlee tells me that the consultations can be completed and the decision of HMG can be reached not later than September 15, and that the immigration will proceed as rapidly as the immigrants can be absorbed.[38]

He was so convinced that he allowed his views to become known in the press.[39] It is interesting here to compare Byrnes's impression with the minutes of the British Cabinet meeting:

The Prime Minister had made it plain that it would not be possible for HMG to agree to a firm date in advance of the acceptance of the plan ... as soon as the plan had been accepted, however, it would be possible to make a start with immigration.[40]

Truman's impression that the plan would provide a quick solution to immigration, and settle two other problems of a more global nature, apparently persuaded him at first to approve Autonomy.

Reports from Paris mentioned a deal between Attlee and Byrnes, in which Britain would agree to a unified Germany if America would agree to Autonomy.[41] In addition, the Americans must also have realized – as did Walter Smart in Cairo – that the 300 million dollars with which (according to the plan) Middle Eastern development was to be financed would "put practically the whole Middle East under American economic domination."[42] Thus, since the problems of immigration, Germany and the Near East were to be solved in the U.S. way, an anxious Zionist source cabled that the "decision reached by *Rosh* (= head [Truman]) and *Mazkir* (= secretary [Byrnes]) [is] to accept programme ... leave no stone unturned to express opposition."[43] This instruction to Epstein implied that America had not settled one aspect – political Zionism. This time it proved to be crucial since acceptance of Autonomy meant rejection of Jewish statehood. *The Washington Post*'s statement of 2 August 1946 that the plan

introduce[s] to Palestine the regime typical of British Crown Colonies

where native chieftains selected by a British adminstrator and removable
by him, preside over a "district" or "provinces" which are nominally "self-
governing,"

signalled the beginning of the lobbying to which the President was
to be subjected in August 1946. Truman, who described himself as
"the only fellow who suffers . . . the innocent bystander who tries to
help," had finally to give way.[44]

Pressure was put on the President from three sides: from the
Zionists, from the U.S. military authorities in Europe and from the
Treasury. The co-chairmen of AZEC, Wise and Silver, belonged
respectively to the Democratic and Republican parties. Neither
could afford to compromise, knowing that the other would derive
political benefit from it. As a result, they formed a united front in
opposition to Autonomy, and could easily manipulate anxious
Congressmen up for election in the autumn. So much so that
the President told one member of the New York Congressmen's
delegation which demanded the shelving of the scheme that he
already "knew all about Palestine [and] it was time someone came
to see him about a U.S. problem for a change."[45] A fortnight later,
Truman left Washington for two weeks, an act which the British
attributed to his desire "to evade Zionist importunities."[46]

The American military authorities in Germany, who carried the
main burden of the Jewish refugee problem, were another source
of pressure. The Brook–Grady insistence on consultations with the
Arabs before the admission of the 100,000 caused the U.S. Secretary of War to warn Truman that the delay could result in mass
suicides among the DPs.[47] But even stronger was the argument that
the acceptance of Autonomy would lay a heavy financial burden on
the United States: 50,000 DPs were to be admitted to the United
States; 50 million dollars were to be given to the Government of
Palestine to assist in the absorption of the 100,000; 250 million
dollars were to be loaned to the Arab states. These factors, when
taken together, considerably lessened the enthusiastic approval
initially given to Autonomy. U.S. officials were absolutely certain
that Congress would not approve it. According to a group of
Senators, it would be fought "every step of the way. British refusal
to cooperate with the wishes of the President . . . is daily inflicting
heavier burdens on American taxpayers."[48] In addition, meetings
between members of the AAC and officials in Washington and
quotations attributed to AAC members which appeared in the

U.S. press – all helped to discredit the Grady team and their plan. "The center of battle," wrote Acheson, "was moving from Israeli–British fighting in Palestine to civil war along the Potomac." He added:

Staff members of the Cabinet Committee were attacking the chairman; the American members of the AAC were attacking the Cabinet Committee ... A meeting was called to reconcile their views with me as Chairman. The Archangel Gabriel would have declined the assignment, but he had more latitude than Under Secretaries of State.[49]

With these protests and counter-protests, not much of the Autonomy Plan could survive.[50] In order to avoid a kind of "Donnybrook Fair," Truman decided to say nothing about the plan.[51] Support would provoke the Zionists; rejection would mean no 100,000. "Jesus Christ could not please them," he noted, "so how could anyone expect that I would have any luck."[52] This signalled American withdrawal from the Palestine question. As a result, as Evan Wilson wrote, "we are all rather depressed as far as our Palestine policy is concerned." And he added:

It seems unfortunate that after so much effort ... we should end up with ... complete bankruptcy ... I cannot see that we are any further along the way to a solution than we were ... before the appointment of the AAC ... We simply do not see what we can do ... Grady has gone to the Pacific coast for a more or less indefinite stay ... and his staff is being very considerably curtailed ... and the office is in the hands of Leslie Rood who has only a couple of girls to assist him ... The Cabinet Committee – in the present drifting phase of our Palestine policy, there is not very much for it to do.[53]

This was also the end of the attempt to achieve Anglo-American understanding over Palestine.

BRITAIN CARRIES ON

Britain was left alone to negotiate Autonomy with the Arabs and Jews. Anglo-Arab talks were held, as already noted, at the London Conference in September; Anglo-Zionist talks were held informally at this time, and again in January 1947, when they were resumed. For some people in Britain, this situation was preferable to joint responsibility with America: the success of the London Conference and the Anglo-Zionist talks could guarantee British authority in Palestine for the foreseeable future.

Arab reaction to the Autonomy Plan was summed up rather

tersely by Young, the British Minister in Beirut, in reporting his conversation with the Syrian Prime Minister:

I said ... that new remedies must be found for the new situations. He said that it was just this which worried him. In a few years there would be several million more Jews in Palestine and the British Government would say that this was a situation for which they must find a new remedy, and the Arabs would be let down again.[54]

So many past pledges had been broken and so many future developments might jeopardize the Arab cause in Palestine that outright rejection could only be expected.

There were other reasons for this, the chief one being the continuation of immigration and the hints of partition which they claimed the plan contained.[55] They also attacked the scheme for its so-called unfairness: Autonomy meant that there would be "three Jewish states and one Arab state, since obviously the Jews would ... get the whip hand in the Jerusalem–Bethlehem area and would settle in the Negev ... opening their mouth for more."[56] Similarly, a comparison of the cultivable land in the Arab province and its equivalent in the Jewish area showed one Arab farmer with eight dunams against one Jewish farmer with two hundred.[57]

An argument which recurred in reports coming from the Arab states was that the main merits of the plan from the Arab point of view – securing land in the Arab province and the denial of Jewish immigration into it – had already been assured to the Arabs in the 1937 Peel partition scheme which they had rejected. Similarly, the freeing of three-quarters of the Palestinian Arabs from the fear of Jewish domination had been suggested in the 1939 White Paper, which in fact gave the same freedom to the whole of the Arab sector. In addition, it was feared that Jewish colonies to the south and north of the Arab province might develop into a "Sudenten Jewry" which would attempt Jewish rescue missions.[58] Some Arabs were apprehensive about the possible development of clandestine Jewish activity which could intensify behind the frontiers of the Jewish province. The fear "that any corner ... that becomes effectively Jewish would be used as a base for preparation of all sorts of horrors (e.g., bacterial warfare) against the Arabs" was said to be stronger than the native resistance to the alienation of Palestinian territory.[59]

There were strong threats from the Arabs aimed at discouraging

HMG from implementing the scheme. The Iraqis warned of the disastrous effects on the Jews in the Middle East and in particular on the 150,000 Jews living in Iraq. "The fact that the economy of Iraq would be disastrously affected by such measures," wrote the British Embassy, "would not necessarily deter the Iraqi Government who are in a good mood to cut off noses to spite their faces."[60] Other threats were directed at Britain, which would be "committing slow suicide" as far as Anglo-Arab relations were concerned, should she implement Autonomy. Arabs would try to be reasonable and to help Britain, but, argued the Syrian Prime Minsiter, "if a friend asked him to cut off his right hand or to give his house to his worst enemy, he might or might not do it, but he could scarcely be expected to enjoy the process."[61]

The realization that any detailed scheme which came after the general AAC Report was bound to be more harmful to the Arab cause caused Azzam to propose the preservation of the status quo in the hope that after a few years some better solution might be found.[62] Although these arguments caused some Palestinian Arabs to demand their immediate right for independence, regardless of what the Arab states had promised the British, their voices did not change the basic style of Palestinian Arab politics.[63] The complacency which followed the crisis produced by the publication of the AAC Report was not particularly shaken by the announcement of Autonomy. In addition, because of Palestinian refusal to join the London Conference or to discuss the Autonomy Plan there, the Arab states were left as the only spokesmen for the Arab cause in the new Anglo-Arab discussions. This marked the completion of the expropriation of the Palestinian Arab case from the Palestinian Arabs themselves.

ZIONIST OBJECTIONS

Initial Zionist reaction to the Autonomy Plan can be seen in the Paris meeting of the Jewish Agency Executive in August, where it was decided, after all, to settle, however obliquely, for partition, and to pursue this policy in talks in London. Their attitudes towards Autonomy paralleled those of the Arabs in believing that any detailed solution presented after the AAC Report could only mean a further blow to Zionism. The AAC Report was considered a stepping-stone towards further achievements.[64] The new scheme made the immigration of the 100,000 dependent on the acceptance of Autonomy as a whole. Similarly, the AAC had given the Jews the right to immigrate and to settle in the whole of the country, whereas Brook–Grady had not confined such movement to a small area.[65] Opposition continued when the London talks were resumed in February 1947, on Bevin's amended autonomy proposals. By then Ben-Gurion found too many similarities between the 1939 White Paper and Bevin's proposals, and, in comparison, even the Brook–Grady scheme appeared more reasonable.[66] Furthermore, the Autonomy Plan precluded the idea of Jewish statehood, and since insistence on political independence was a position held by all sectors of the Zionist movement, there was no possibility of settling on the plan without dividing the movement.[67] General agreement could only be reached by the Zionists on the disadvantages of Autonomy, i.e., on what to reject. And here there were several points of criticism, which came out in the London talks of 11 February 1947. Open discrimination between the two provinces allowed the Arab Government to prohibit the entrance of Jews into its zone while the Jews were not free to admit people into theirs without the approval of the High Commissioner; Jews could only settle in their own province and their temporary exclusion from every other area of the country would become permanent as it had in Trans-Jordan (since the Mandate would still be valid, the Jews should have the right to settle in all of Palestine); the Jewish majority in Jerusalem would be converted into a minority by the administrative merger of Bethlehem and the surrounding Arab villages. With regard to the extent of autonomy granted, it was compared to the autonomous rights granted to primitive tribes in Central Africa.[68] It was noted that the "Crown Colonies of America in the eighteenth century, the humblest American township, or even the 'oppressed Philippine Commonwealth' of the 1920s had a far greater degree of self-government."[69]

The Jews would have to bear the deficits of the Arab province which treated them as enemies and denied them equality of rights in buying land and in immigration. The size of the Jewish province – only 15 per cent of Palestine thus made a "mockery" of their claims.[70] In addition, as Weizmann argued, the plan

appeared to be based on the mistaken idea that Palestine was to be primarily an industrial state, "the workshop of the Middle East." The Jews wished to reestablish themselves as agriculturalists and that required land.[71]

Finally, while both Jews and Arabs had claimed the Negev, "we have never heard that England too has any claim ... and it is difficult to explain in what respect it is either fair or reasonable for Great Britian itself to assume control ... of one-third of the area of Western Palestine."[72]

In general, Provincial Autonomy seemed to be "a sugar-coated putrefaction of the 1939 White Paper."[73] If the plan was conceived to allay Arab fears of Jewish domination, it was a failure since it would result in the complete opposite: "Arabs will be left with the fear that by growing in number in their own province, the Jews will become a majority of the country and ... the Arabs will come under Jewish domination."[74] And ironically enough, although the following statement was made to further the Jewish cause, such sentiments were never expressed by a delegate of an Arab state:

The Arabs of Palestine are at least as ready for self government as those of Egypt and the Lebanon. What justice is there in the position that the Arabs of Egypt and the Lebanon have sovereign Parliaments, while the Arabs of Palestine are offered only a puppet province run by a British High Commissioner?[75]

There were some Zionists, however, who saw merit in the plan, especially when they compared it to the still valid White Paper or evaluated the possible consequences of its rejection. Time was considered to be the enemy of Zionism, in light of what was regarded to be the almost inevitable confrontation between the Jews and the British Army, as well as the diminishing desire of DPs in Europe to emigrate to Palestine. This view urged "a speedy solution ... to avoid discussions of the problem of Palestine being resumed from scratch." It further noted that with the immigration of the 100,000, Autonomy ruled out the establishment of an Arab state in the whole of Palestine and set aside a larger area for Jewish settlement than the White Paper. Finally, it was argued that Zionism should strive for U.S. cooperation, so that "the present British proposals will be further whittled down."[76] This opinion, however, was very different from that held by the majority in the Zionist movement and which sought to exclude America from Palestine altogether.

Zionism had second thoughts about its American option. The

limited usefulness of the Jewish vote was apparent: "We have not got it in our pocket and the [U.S.] Government knows it. The Jewish vote might prove a great danger and we might kill ourselves with it."[77] The Movement, therefore, could not threaten the Presidency with election day. The disappointment with America was great and putting an end to Autonomy there, relatively easy: the Grady team was, after all, an initiative of the State Department, not of the President. London, therefore, was once again the Jewish option.

To enhance the chances of renewing the Anglo-Jewish understanding the Jewish Agency, as noted, had settled on partition as its policy, claimed by Goldmann to be a painful and tragic decision for Zionism.[78] And in order to make the introduction of such a solution easier for Britain, the Zionists were willing to enter "as a state into an Arab Federation as a protection against the Jews being used as a spearhead for any foreign policy." Though no agreement was achieved at this stage of the Anglo-Zionist discussions (in late summer 1946) the idea of a Jewish state within an Arab federation did appeal to Bevin.[79] The important thing was the change of spirit: for the moment, an Anglo-Jewish confrontation looked remote, largely owing to the common disappointment with America. But not for long: the U.S. was against British–Jewish rapprochement, and Britain could not afford to alienate America in a period of growing East–West tensions already felt in Germany, Greece, Turkey, Persia and China. This, together with the inherent controversies in the Palestine conflict, meant that the attempt to achieve an Anglo-Jewish understanding was bound to fail.

TRUMAN'S WITHDRAWAL WITHDRAWN

With the President's statement of 4 October 1946, supporting Jewish statehood, the United States was back in the Palestine arena. Truman's statement argued that the gap between the Jewish Agency's partition policy and HMG's Provincial Autonomy could be reconciled.[80] The American return could hardly have stemmed from Zionist pressures alone, or from American electoral considerations as several authors maintain.[81] The Jews at that time were against Provincial Autonomy, i.e., *they preferred no 100,000 rather than further U.S. involvement in the question:*

The [Brook–Grady] report should not be signed ... America should withdraw from the whole matter, which is better than the President signing the report.[82]

And:

The present tendency ... is to limit the American interest in the Palestine problem to its legal international aspect.[83]

The Jewish Agency was reported to have boycotted the London Conference and the discussions on the Provincial plan since it "was unwilling to be placed in a position where it might have to compromise between the Morrison–Grady proposals ... and its own partition plan."[84] And this was precisely the position of the President, his very words. It is, therefore, possible that the possibility of Anglo-Jewish rapprochement and an Anglo-Arab understanding over Palestine worried Washington.[85] This would create a situation in which Britain would, after all, be able to maintain the Mandate from a stronger position. This perhaps explains both Truman's statement of 4 October and Attlee's outraged and bitter reaction:

I asked you at least to postpone its issue for a few hours ... I have received with great regret your letter refusing even a few hours grace to the Prime Minister of the country which has the actual responsibility for the government of Palestine ... I am astonished that you did not wait to acquaint yourself with the reasons ... You do not seem to have been informed that ... conversations with leading Zionists ... were proceeding with good prospect of success. I shall await with interest to learn what were the imperative reasons which compelled this precipitancy.[86]

If the above failure is added to Bevin's repeated warnings that without an Anglo-U.S. understanding Britain would leave Palestine, and to America's concern that British withdrawal would force America into the position of having to look for bases and allies in the Near East, Truman's "precipitous" support for Jewish statehood in Palestine may thus be given a more logical context.[87]

NOTES

1. Statement of Policy: Plan for Provincial Autonomy, 26 July 1946, SACMEC, Cunningham Papers, Box 5, file 2 (hereafter PAP).
2. PAP, pp. 3, 4.
3. Note on PAP, Jan. 1946, FO 371/52504/E389/G.
4. Ibid.
5. Ibid.

6. Scheme for Autonomy, Note by the British Delegation, 13 July 1946, p. 5, FO 371/52541/E6794/G.
7. Memo for Byrnes, prepared by Brook and the Colonial Office, 23 Nov. 1946, FO 371/52565/E11526/G.
8. John Martin to Gater, 16 Sept. 1946, CO 537/1783.
9. Grady to Byrnes, 27 July 1946, FRUS, vol. 7, p. 659; Bevin to London Conference, 16 Sept. 1946, p. 5, FO 371/62544/E9178.
10. PAP, p. 5.
11. Advantages of the Autonomy Scheme for the Jews, undated and unsigned memo, USNA, RG 43, AAC, Box 2. Compare with 68% of Arabs' citrus and 70% of their irrigable plain to be in the Jewish province, undated and unsigned memo on the PAP, ibid. See also autobiography of Henry Grady, p. 161, Truman Library, Grady Papers, box 5.
12. Note on PAP, Jan. 1946, FO 371/52504/E389/G.
13. Application of the International Trusteeship to Palestine, note by the British delegation, 13 July 1946, p. 5, CO 537/1459.
14. Bennett, Colonial Office, to Ward, Foreign Office, 16 July 1946. Grady had been told in Washington that Britain too held the minimum interpretation for states directly concerned. Ibid., see also note 13 above.
15. Comment by Bennett, 22 Aug. 1946, CO 537/1459.
16. See Louis, *Imperialism at Bay*, passim.
17. See Henniker to Sargent, 8 July 1946, FO 371/52552/E7940/G. See similar appreciation by UN Dept., Foreign Office, Palestine and International Trusteeship, 26 Jan. 1946, article 21, CO 537/1459.
18. Comment by Howe, 10 July 1946, FO 371/52552/E7940/G. He reiterated, 17 Sept. 1946, that "there are no legal objections to our doing what we like with Palestine," FO 371/52559/E9509.
19. Trafford-Smith, Colonial Office, 5 Feb. 1946, CO 537/1459.
20. Eastwood, head of Colonial Office, Eastern Dept., to Baxter, 27 Sept. 1945, CO 733/411, Pt.2, No. 75872, Pt. 5.
21. Goldmann in AZEC meeting, 9 May 1946, CZA, AZEC files, No Z5/1172.
22. Wikeley, Foreign Office, Eastern Dept, 29 Sept. 1945, FO 371/45380/E7262/G.
23. Summary of the Colonial Secretary's paper, 8 July 1946, CAB, 129/11, No. CP (46) 258.
24. None of the numerous publications on Palestine has yet attempted to give an answer to the question of why the British took the decision they did.
25. See Chapter 13, p.238.
26. C.O.S., Note on Anglo-U.S. consultations, 24 July 1946, FO 371/52548/E7448/G. See also Monroe on the London Conference (with Arab states) where the Autonomy scheme was discussed: "[it] was the beginning of an abortive attempt to convince Arab states that Palestine should do better at British hands than at those of an international forum," "Mr. Bevin's Arab Policy," p. 30, in Hourani, ed., *Middle Eastern Affairs*, No. 2, 1961. See also Crossman, *Palestine Mission*, p. 208.
27. Captain Delargy, House of Commons, 31 July 1946, *Hansard*, vol. 426, p. 990.
28. Young to Foreign Office, 5 Aug. 1946, FO 371/52549/E7528/G. Beeley commented on it: "I am not at all sure that I understand this telegram," 6 Aug. 1946, ibid.
29. Wikeley, Foreign Office, Eastern Dept., 12 Aug. 1946, FO 371/52551/E7720.
30. Comment by Beeley on "Loan to Arab Nations," 16 Sept. 1946. FO 371/52559/E9506.
31. Attlee to Lord President of the Council and Colonial Secretary, in Paris to Foreign Office, 30 July 1946, FO 371/52546/E7318. His instructions were for the Parliamentary debate of 31 July 1946, and were based on the assumption that "no reply [from the U.S.] is received ... or that the reply is unfavourable."

32. Foreign Office to Washington, 7 Aug. 1946, FO 371/52548/E7458.
33. Beeley's comment, 17 Sept. 1946, FO 371/52559/E9509. See also Grady: "the same as Arabs could be a minority in a Jewish province, the same could the Yishuv in a Palestinian Arab state." To Byrnes, 24 July 1946, FRUS, 1946, vol. 7, p. 660.
34. Note by Brigadier Clayton, Aug. 1946, FO 371/52547/E7332/G. On Shaw's and Cunningham's support for partition, see Shaw to Hall, 22 July 1946, CO 537/1767; Cunningham to Hall, 9 July 1946.
35. See details in Washington to Foreign Office, 5 Aug. 1946, FO 371/52549/E7527.
36. For minutes of the meeting, see CO 537/1787. In anticipation of a second meeting, Inverchapel described Silver to Bevin as "vain ... and something of a megalomaniac, but he is susceptible to a friendly approach..if you turned a little of your charm on him, you could get him into your pocket ... do not ... coddle him. All he needs is to be smiled at and jollied a little, and be given the impression that he is being admitted to your confidence," 16 Nov. 1946, CO 537/1787.
37. On 28 Jan. 1945, Creech Jones addressed the New York Conference of the United Palestine Appeal and expressed strong support for the National Home. See text in *British Labour and Zionism*, published by the American Jewish Trade Union Committee for Palestine, 1946, Oxford, Rhodes House, Creech Jones Papers, Box 32.
38. Byrnes to Truman, text of statement for the President, in U.K. Delegation, Paris, to Foreign Office, 29 July 1946, PREM, 8/627 Pt. 3.
39. See David Niles, 4 Oct. 1946, on Truman's embarrassment following Byrnes's approach to the press, Weizmann Archives, Rehovot.
40. Cabinet meeting, 29 July 1946, CAB 128/6, No. CM(46)74.
41. In Washington to Foreign Office, 3 Aug. 1946, FO 371/52548/E7475.
42. Comment by Smart, 1 Aug. 1946, FO 141/1091, No. 101/343/46.
43. Wise and Goldmann to Epstein, 29 July 1946, Weizmann Archives.
44. Truman to Edwin W. Pauley, 22 Oct. 1946, Truman Library, President's Secretary's files.
45. Washington to Foreign Office, 1 Aug. 1946, FO 371/52548/E7419. On the Wise–Silver front see Washington to Britain's UN delegation, Paris, 31 July 1946, PREM 8/627, Pt.3.
46. Washington to Foreign Office, 14 Aug. 1946, FO 371/52552/E7998/G.
47. Heller, "From the 'Black Sabbath' to Partition," *Zion*, No. 3–4, 1978, p. 344. On the pressure of the military, see also Ben-Gurion to the Paris meeting of the Jewish Agency, 4 Aug. 1946, CZA.
48. Washington to Foreign Office, undated, FO 371/52552/E8008. See more on the financial concern in Donovan, *Truman's Presidency*, p. 322; Acheson to Inverchapel, 30 July 1946, FRUS 1946, vol. 7., pp. 673-674; memo to General Hilldring, 29 July 1946, USNA, RG 59, Herbert Fierst Papers, Box 6.
49. Dean Acheson, *Present at the Creation*, New York, 1969, p. 175.
50. See McDonald to Crum, 1 Aug. 1946, on "the stupidity of an American Committee getting itself involved in this sort of ghettoizing," McDonald Papers, file 93; Grady to the British Consul, San Francisco, on "Judge Hutcheson [who] has come to look upon his AAC's Report as his brainchild and could not bear to have any changes made," San Francisco to Washington Embassy, 7 Sept. 1946, FO 371/52558/E9379.
51. Inverchapel to Foreign Office, 31 July 1946, quoting Dean Acheson, FO 371/52546/E7316.
52. Donovan, *Truman's Presidency*, p. 319.
53. Wilson to Lowell Pinkerton, U.S. Consul General in Jerusalem, 26 Aug. 1946, Washington, State Dept. Building, Lot 54, D403, Box 9.
54. In Beirut to Foreign Office, 3 Aug. 1946, FO 371/52548/E7469/G.
55. See Azzam Pasha in London Conference, 12 Sept. 1946, p. 6, FO 371/52643/E9124.

56. See note 54 above.
57. Egyptian delegation presentation before the London Conference, 11 Sept. 1946, FO 371/52643/E9123.
58. See, e.g., Note by Brigadier Clayton, Aug. 1946, FO 371/52547/E7332/G., pp. 1, 4, 6.
59. Jeddah, Grafftey-Smith, 19 Aug. 1946, FO 371/52553/E8221.
60. Baghdad to Foreign Office, 7 Aug. 1946, FO 371/52551/E7753.
61. See note 54 above.
62. Azzam to Walter Smart, Cairo, 29 July 1946, FO 371/52551/E7720. See also Azzam to Glubb, acquiescing to another fifty years of British Mandate, memo by Glubb, Dec. 1946, p. 6, CO 537/1783.
63. See reactions by Ahmed Shukeiri and Musa Alami, in High Commissioner to Colonial Secretary, 3 Sept. 1946, FO 371/52559/E9089.
64. Report on Jewish reactions by General H.Q. Middle East Force, Weekly Military Intelligence Review, No. 58, 3 May 1946, WO 169/22882.
65. See paper by the Jewish Agency explaining the rejection of the Autonomy plan, p. 3, London, 4 Feb. 1947, CAB 133/85.
66. Paper by Ben-Gurion, London, 9 Feb. 1947, ZANY, Morrison–Grady file.
67. Goldmann to Proskauer, 8 Sept. 1946, AJC Archives, Proskauer Papers, Box 8; Bevin to Attlee and Hall on conversation with Goldmann, Paris, 29 Aug. 1946, CO 537/1772.
68. Agency's reason for rejecting Autonomy, London, 4 Feb. 1947, p. 9, CAB 133/85.
69. Zionist Office, London, on the Morrison–Grady plan, 26 July 1946, CZA, No. Z4/15440.
70. See note 68 above, pp. 6-10; also meetings between British and Agency delegations London, 3 and 6 Feb. 1947, CO 537/2326; reaction of Agency delegation when seeing the Autonomy map, London, 13 Feb. 1947, CO 537/2333.
71. Meeting with Hall, 2 Aug. 1946, CO 537/1785. See Douglas Harris, spiritual father of the Autonomy scheme, to the British Middle Eastern Ambassadors Conference, London, 6 Sept. 1945: "The future of the Jews in Palestine depended on industry rather than on agriculture," FO 371/45379/E6954.
72. Jewish Agency's reasons for rejecting the Autonomy scheme, London, 4 Feb. 1947, CAB 133/85.
73. The archaeologist Nelson Glueck to AJC, Jerusalem, 4 Aug. 1946, AJC archives, Federalization Plan files.
74. See note 69 above.
75. Zionist Office, London, comments on the Morrison–Grady plan, 26 July 1946, CZA, No. Z4/15440.
76. Paper on the Autonomy Plan signed by W.E. (probably Walter Ettinghausen, later Eytan, of the Zionist Office, London), Jerusalem, Aug. 1946, ZANY, Morrison–Grady file. On concern lest Zionists lose the DPs see also Stephen Wise, Jewish Agency Paris meeting, 4 Aug. 1946, CZA.
77. Rose Halperin, Agency's Paris meeting, 5 Aug. 1946, CZA. See also on Truman who "will attempt to pander to the Jewish vote by empty declarations which cost him nothing, without making any real effort to ram an unacceptable solution down the British throat," W.E. paper on Autonomy plan, Jerusalem, Aug. 1946, ZANY, Morrison–Grady file.
78. Goldmann to Inverchapel, in Washington to Foreign Office, 9 Aug. 1946, FO 371/52551/E7750/G.
79. Bevin to Attlee on conversation with Goldmann, Paris, 14 Aug. 1946, PREM 8/627, Pt. 4.
80. See text of the statement in Bevin (in Paris) to Attlee, 4 Oct. 1946, FO 371/52560/E9999/G.

81. See Ilan, *American, Britain and Palestine*, pp. 240-244; Bethell, *The Palestine Triangle*, pp. 282-283; Elath, *The Struggle for Statehood*, vol. 1, pp. 417-424.
82. H. Greenberg, Paris Jewish Agency Meeting, 5 Aug. 1946, CZA.
83. Epstein to Goldmann, 25 Sept. 1946, CZA, Goldmann files, No. Z6, Bundle 5, file 20; see also on Goldmann who appealed to Truman to make no more statements on Palestine, in Bevin to Attlee, Paris, 14 Aug. 1946, PREM 8/627, Pt. 4.
84. Conversation between State Dept., Near Eastern Division officials and Epstein, 5 Sept. 1946, FRUS, 1946, vol. 7, pp. 692-693. On Epstein's protest following Truman's call to bridge the gap between the proposals, see his *Struggle for Statehood*, vol. 1, p. 424.
85. See note of meeting between Bevin and Weizmann, 1 Oct. 1946, where some sort of agreement was about to appear about the transition stage of Autonomy in Palestine, FO 371/52560/E10030. See also Attlee to Truman, 4 Oct. 1946, FO 371/52561/E10164/G; Bevin–Goldmann meeting, Paris, 14 Aug. 1946, in Bevin to Attlee, 14 Aug. 1946, PREM 8/627, Pt. 4.
86. Attlee to Truman, 4 Oct. 1946, FRUS 1946, vol. 7, pp. 704-705.
87. On these warnings and concern see Bevin to Silver, New York, 14 Nov. 1946, CO 537/1787; Dean Acheson, *Present at the Creation*, p. 178; see also Washington, Mr. Balfour, to Foreign Office, 18 May 1946, FO 371/52524/E4561; U.S. Dept. of State's memo (undated) toward the 1947 "Pentagon Talks," FRUS 1947, vol. 5, p. 512.

15

In Conclusion

AAC's discussions should not be even partially suspended as regards the admission of the 100,000. To do so might lift the issue from one between the Mandatory and Jewish illegal organizations to one between HMG and the U.S. Government. This must at all costs be avoided.

Ernest Bevin[1]

The AAC was a step in the right direction; the negotiations which have taken place since are another favourable step, as was this scheme ... It is far more important that there should be agreement than there should be this or that variant of the scheme. I fully agree that the Government were right to labour with the United States; almost any solution in which the United States will join us would be made to work.

Winston Churchill[2]

Bevin's warning, like Churchill's words, accurately expressed the aims of the Labour Government's Foreign Secretary. Bevin, like Churchill, believed that without a British–American understanding, Britain should not – and could not – remain in Palestine. There were others, however, with power and influence in Britain who did not consider this understanding to be a prerequisite for their country's authority there, and did their utmost to frustrate the Foreign Secretary's policy, with success. They were wrong, however. Britain alone could not tackle the recrudescence of nationalism in the Middle East, especially as it was coupled with American determination not to let Britain follow its own course in Palestine. The result was the surrender of the Mandate.

AAC: BOUND TO FAIL

It was hardly possible for an initiative such as the AAC to survive the anxieties which enveloped Anglo-Arab, Anglo-Jewish, and Anglo-American relations and the post-war desire in Whitehall to maintain Britain's pre-war status as a Great Power. There were too many at cross purposes: the Military in Palestine held views which contradicted those of the C. in C. in Cairo and the C.O.S. in London; Bevin's concerns about Russia and UN involvement and his "American answer" to these concerns were not accepted by the Cabinet and Administration; their readiness to cooperate with the Americans was hamstrung by their fear that it would appear as if "we were working hand in glove with the American Government"; there were some in London who were ready to add to Britain's difficulties in Palestine for the sole purpose of excluding America from Palestine; for reasons of protocol Bevin's attempt to involve America had to be negotiated between Attlee and Truman, the two persons who, each for different reasons, were most strongly opposed to it. Stalemate was inevitable.

Nor did the AAC fulfil the hopes which led Bevin to propose it in the first place. It was itself a strange creature with no precedents save perhaps the Anglo-American Caribbean Commission, and under Hutcheson's guidance, the Committee torpedoed almost all the hopes invested in it. Those who expected the Inquiry to gain time for Britain were disappointed by the homesickness of the American judge for Houston: the Texan DP finished the Inquiry well within the allotted time. If there were expectations that the AAC would acknowledge Britain's difficulties in Palestine, thus recognizing the White Paper as the equitable solution, the Committee's recommendation to abolish the White Paper put an end to them. The same was true of the hopes that some political solution would come out of the Inquiry; they were laid to rest by the legalistic approach to the problem and by the fact that the Bench ruled out whatever was not strictly judicial and not within the terms of reference. It was only a year and a half later, in retrospect, that Hutcheson remarked: "In international relations many solutions must be accepted which fall short of doing justice."[3] His insistence during the Inquiry on admitting courtroom evidence only resulted in the non-consideration of a partition solution. The "secret trick" of the Jewish Agency in maintaining Biltmore as their official position vis-à-vis the Arab states, and suggesting partition only unofficially, contributed to the ultimate stalemate. A still greater frustration for Bevin was HMG's handling of the Report, which dismissed his search for a U.S. option, looking to the UN as the next stage: one of Bevin's reasons for the creation of the AAC had been – precisely – his reluctance to refer the problem to the UN.

The AAC was intended by Britain to fulfil one major function: involving the United States in Palestine by means of an Anglo-U.S. understanding. It failed in its main objective but succeeded in shifting some of the responsibility for the problem which had hitherto been exclusively British, to the United States. But Palestine was in any case likely to become a matter of U.S. interest, as were numerous other parts of the world. And Britain was bound to lose its position in the Middle East, as it lacked the resources and will to sustain it. Britain, however, was forced to pay a high price for its failure to come to terms with America over Palestine: the early and total loss of its position in the Middle East. Its success in securing an alliance with the United States in Europe and still maintaining some freedom of manoeuvre was possible only because the Russian threat in Europe was already visible even to the United States. In the Middle East, Soviet interest was not apparent enough to provide any incentive for Western co-operation. The result was that competition between the two powers impelled the peoples of the Middle East towards the far more powerful United States, which was that "most facinating of attractions – the untried devil."[4]

It should be added that the very existence of Anglo-American rivalry was, at the time, imperfectly recognized. For most historians, a direct line leads from the war-time alliance against Germany to the post-war alliance against the USSR. The relatively short period of struggle has been neglected, if not entirely overlooked. There may be a rather prosaic explanation for this: this rivalry is unemphasized in the available Cabinet Minutes at the Public Record Office: it is much more apparent in the less accessible sources.

The price for Britain was a Middle Eastern failure. Bevin believed that he might postpone the inevitable loss of the area by agreeing to whatever appeared to promote Anglo-U.S. understanding over Palestine, even to the point of agreeing to partition (i.e., *a Jewish state*) when it looked necessary in order to encourage HMG and the U.S. Government to settle on Provincial Autonomy. Whatever Bevin's chances of success may have been – and he almost certainly deceived himself in this matter – it was impossible to carry out his plan in the face of the opposition of several of his Cabinet colleagues, including the Prime Minister, as well as the most powerful officials in the Administration. The latter were convinced that they could manage without American assistance – all the time claiming that they were following Bevin's policy to the letter. Ironically the same British officials who emasculated HMG's decision-making process with regard to Palestine, excluding it even from the general Arab policy of their Foreign Secretary ("We cannot have it both ways"[5]) were continually complaining about America's total lack of policy. Very little of the AAC's work survived the handling of its recommendations by two frustrated administrations, both of which persistently opposed the Palestine moves of their chiefs, Bevin and Truman. However, in the infighting with his Administration, the American President proved to be more effective than the British Foreign Secretary.

AAC: A TURNING POINT FOR PALESTINE

The United States had an advantage over Great Britain in the Middle East. It had the ability to manipulate both the Arabs and the Jews, whereas Britain was limited by its Arab policy and the scarcity of its resources. However, America's position as a Superpower meant that even its simplest commercial acts were bound to develop into political involvement. Similarly, any small step, even taking part in the Inquiry, brought it into the Palestine conflict, despite Truman's desperate attempts to argue to the contrary. This, then, was the contribution of the AAC: it catalyzed a turning point in the history of the Palestine mission.

Insofar as it is possible to discern American policy lines for the Near East, there appear to have been important anti-British and anti-Zionist elements in it. For almost a year the United States pursued these lines until its attempt to dictate its terms to Britain failed. Apparently, Britain's reluctance to police the Middle East for America was what changed the course of the United States's Palestinian policy. From then on, a willing Zionist client replaced a reluctant Britain as America's policeman, and from the autumn of 1946, the United States gave its support to Jewish statehood.

Many scholars of Zionist history have tried to ascertain the reasons for the establishment of the State of Israel. The simple flow of events was too limited to explain such a revolution in the history of the Middle East and the Jewish people. Yehuda Bauer claims that the main reason was the Jewish DPs.[6] Joseph Heller argues that it was the Zionist decision to drop the Biltmore Programme in favour of partition.[7] Others believe that it was the force of Jewish armed resistance, while still others are convinced that it was the Zionist vote in America. None of these factors, however, was compelling enough to create such a phenomenon. Amitzur Ilan therefore decided that it was a miracle.[8] Anglo-American rivalry in the Middle East must be included as one of the more significant components in any evaluation of factors leading to the emergence of the state of Israel in 1948, whatever the relative weight of the others may be. It seems to me that the AAC, ended with the failure of America and Britain to come to terms over Palestine and the Middle East, turned the Jewish refugee problem into a political Zionist issue for Washington. On the back of Anglo-American rivalry, the State of Israel emerged.

The Arabs of Palestine themselves had no doubts regarding their right to, and qualifications for, self-determination or statehood. Yet not all of them envisaged a separate and independent Palestinian entity within the Arab world. Nor did the Arab states reveal much enthusiasm when it came to supporting their Palestinian brethren's right to independence. What they promised the AAC in 1946 they tried to fulfil in 1948: to crush any attempt at the creation of a Jewish state. There was, however, a difference between objection to Zionism, which the Arab states pursued vehemently, and support for Palestinian Arab independence, which they did not. The country was finally partitioned not between its Jews and Arabs, but between Israel and the Arab states.

NOTES

1. To Attlee, 20 June 1946, following Cunningham to Hall, 19 June 1946, to suspend the Anglo-U.S. discussions pending the release of five British officers kidnapped in Tel Aviv, FO 371/52530/E5668; FO 371/52531/E5747/G respectively. See also Cabinet Meeting, 20 June 1946, CAB 128/5, No. CM (46) 60.
2. In the House of Commons' debate on the Autonomy scheme, 1 Aug. 1946, *Hansard*, vol. 426, pp. 1254-1255.
3. See Chapter 4, p. 71.
4. See Chapter 2, p. 39.
5. Ibid., p.31.
6. *Flight and Rescue*, passim.
7. "From the 'Black Sabbath' to Partition," *Zion*, vol. 43, no. 3-4, 1978, passim.
8. *America, Britain and Palestine*, p. 9.

APPENDIX

Itinerary of Committee

1946

Jan. 4–17	Washington	Full Committee
Jan. 23–Feb. 4	London	Full Committee
Feb. 5–15	American Zone of Germany	Mr Crum
	Czechoslovakia	Sir Frederick Leggett
Feb. 5–22	Paris	Mr Phillips
	French Zone of Germany and Austria	Mr McDonald
Feb. 5–17	Berlin	Judge Hutcheson
		Sir John Singleton
		Lord Morrison
		Mr Buxton
		Mr Manningham-Buller
		Mr Crick
Feb. 7–13	Poland	Mr Buxton
		Mr Manningham-Buller
		Mr Crick
Feb. 8–11	British Zone of Germany	Judge Hutcheson
		Sir John Singleton
		Lord Morrison
Feb. 17–25	Vienna	Full Committee
Feb. 19–22	American Zone of Austria	Mr Buxton
		Mr Manningham-Buller
		Mr Crick
Feb. 25–26	British Zone of Austria	Mr Crum
		Mr Crossman
Feb. 25–27	Italy	Sir John Singleton
		Mr Phillips
		Mr McDonald
		Sir Frederick Leggett
Feb. 28–Mar. 5	Cairo	Full Committee
Mar. 6–28	Palestine	Full Committee
Mar. 15–20	Damascus; Beirut	Judge Hutcheson
		Lord Morrison
		Mr McDonald
Mar. 16–21	Baghdad; Riyadh	Sir John Singleton
		Mr Buxton
		Mr Manningham-Buller
Mar. 23–24	Amman	Lord Morrison

Mar. 29–Apr. 20 Lausanne

Mr Phillips
Sir Frederick Leggett
Full Committee

Bibliography

The AAC is mentioned in the historiography of the Palestine question mainly in relation to its Report. Very few authors describe the actual conduct of the Inquiry, and when they do, they concentrate on the Lausanne stage. For this they use the 1947 books of Bartley Crum and Richard Crossman, and later the Crossman papers at SACMEC. This book has already shown the discrepancies between Crossman's and Crum's accounts and the diaries of other members of the Committee. These diaries however, have seldom been used by researchers, nor have the extensive verbatim records of the Committee's public hearings: the only known work to have used them is Kirk, *The Middle East 1945–1950*, in which the Singleton–Ben-Gurion dialogue on the Jewish agency and the Hagana is quoted (see page 166). Much of the unpublished material listed below is, therefore, being used for the first time.

A. MANUSCRIPTS

1. Britain

Public Record Office, Kew

The titles refer either to the general names of these series or to the specific files quoted in the book and deposited in these series:

AIR 20	– Mediterranean and Middle East Policy.
BT 11	– Interdepartmental Committee to consider Anglo-American relations in the Middle East.
BT 60	– British Goodwill Trade Mission to the Levant
CAB 21	– Prime Minister's Minutes.
CAB 66	– Cabinet Papers (C.P.)
CAB 95	– Cabinet Committees.
CAB 120	– Cabinet Secretariat.
CAB 127	– Sir Edward Bridges' Papers.
CAB 128	– Cabinet Minutes and Conclusions (C.M.)
CAB 129	– Cabinet Papers.
CAB 133	– International Conferences.
CAB 134	– Interdepartmental Party to consider Anglo-American Relations in the Middle East.
CO 537	– Colonial Office, General.

CO 732 – Anglo-American Relations in the Middle East.
CO 733 – Palestine.
CO 814 – Palestine Executive Council.
FO 115 – British Embassy, Washington.
FO 141 – British Embassy, Cairo.
FO 181 – British Embassy, Moscow.
FO 366 – Foreign Office Chief Clerk/Staff.
FO 370 – Foreign Office Library.
FO 371 – Political Correspondence, General.
FO 624 – British Embassy, Iraq.
FO 816 – British Legation, Amman.
FO 921 – British Minister Resident, Cairo; British Middle East Office.
FO 924 – British Council, Jerusalem.
FO 939 – Confidential File, Special Reports, Cyprus.
FO 945 – Control Office, Germany and Austria.
FO 976 – United Nations San Francisco Conference.
PREM 4 – Prime Minister Office – Churchill.
PREM 8 – Prime Minister Office – Attlee.
T 161 – Treasury International – AAC.
T 220 – Treasury International – AAC.
T 236 – Economic Policy, Middle East.
T 247 – Lord Keynes Files.
WO 32 – Army Council Secretariat.
WO 106 – Middle East Strategy 1945.
WO 169 – War Diaries, British Units, Middle East.
WO 171 – Displaced Persons Assembly Camps Staff.
WO 201 – General Headquarters, Middle East Forces.
WO 216 – Chief of Imperial General Staff (C.I.G.S.).
WO 261 – Quarterly Historical Reports (succeeded the War Diaries).
WO 275 – 6th Airborne Division.

India Office Records, London

L/P & S/ – Weekly Political Summary, Washington.

Labour Party Archives, London

William Gillies Papers – Labour Party International Department, Advisory Committee on Imperial Questions.
National Executive Committee (NEC) – The International Sub-Committee.

London School of Economics – British Library of Economics & Political Science

Diaries of Hugh Dalton.

London, John Briance Papers

Head of Arab Section Palestine Police/C.I.D. With Mr Briance.

Oxford, Albert Hourani Papers

Arab Office – *The Problem of Palestine*, Jerusalem, March 1946. 3 Vols.
  With Mr Hourani.

Nuffield College, Oxford

Fabian Colonial Bureau – Minutes of International Colonial Bureau.

St. Antony's College, Oxford, Middle East Centre (SACMEC)

AAC Public Hearings – verbatim text.
Richard Crossman diary and papers.
Alan Cunningham papers.
Lt. General D'Arcy papers.
Jerusalem and East Mission papers.
Lord Killearn diaries – manuscript.
Elizabeth Monroe papers.
St. John Philby papers.
Edward Spears papers.
Thames Television interviews for the programme "Palestine Mandate."

Rhodes House, Oxford

Arthur Creech Jones papers, Box 32.
Fabian Colonial Bureau, Box 176 – Labour Party International Department Advisory Committee on Imperial Questions.

University College, Oxford

Attlee papers.

2. Israel

Jerusalem – Israel State Archives

Leo Kohn's papers.
Palestine Government, Chief Secretary Section.
Arab Higher Committee papers, Section 65.
Jewish Agency New York, series 93.03.

Jerusalem – Central Zionist Archives (CZA)

Jewish Agency Executive – minutes of meetings.
Jewish Agency Executive – Paris meeting.
S5 – Smaller Jewish Agency Executive.
S25 – Political Department.

Z4 – Zionist Office, London.
Z5 – U.S. Jewish Agency Offices; AZEC files; Elath files.
Z6 – Goldmann offices.

Jerusalem – Private Possession
David Ben-Gurion private diary. Paris, summer 1946.

Rehovot – Weizmann Archives
Papers and letters of President Weizmann.

3. United States

Cambridge, Harvard University, Houghton Library
Diary and papers of William Phillips.
Papers of William Yale, Counsellor at the State Department.

Houston, Texas
Papers of Judge Joseph Hutcheson. With Hutcheson family.

Independence, Missouri, President Truman Library
President's Secretary's files
Oral History: H.N. Howard, Chief of Research Branch, Near East
                        Division, State Department.
                        Loy Henderson, Chief, Near East African Section,
                        State Department.
Papers of Matthew J. Connally, Secretary to the President
President Truman's Official file No. 204 Misc.
Papers of Judge Rosenman, Assistant to the President.
Henry Grady papers.

New York – Archives of American Jewish Committee (AJC)
Judge Proskauer papers (President of AJC).
Federalization Plan for Palestine.

New York – Archives of American Joint Distribution Committee
James D. Rice Report.

New York – Columbia University, Lehman Library
Diary and papers of James McDonald.

*New York – United Nations Archives – UN Relief and Rehabilitation
   Agency, (UNRRA)*
German Mission, Legal Adviser, Classified file.
Austrian Mission No. B/JR/2.

New York Zionist Archives (ZANY)

AAC Confidential file.
AZEC file on the U.S. Cabinet Committee on Palestine.
James McDonald file.
Morrison–Grady file.
Captain Abraham Tulin papers (in charge on AZEC appearance before the AAC)

New York – Papers of Judge Simon Rifkind

Advisor on Jewish Affairs to U.S. Theater Commander. With Judge Rifkind.

Swarthmore College, Pennsylvania

Frank Aydelotte diary and papers.

Suitland Maryland – National Record Center (NRC)

RG (Record Group) 84 – Files of U.S. Legations and Embassies in Baghdad, Beirut, Cairo, Damascus, Jerusalem, London.
U.S. War Department – Strategic Service Unit reports (usually known as O.S.S. – Office of Strategic Services).

Washington D.C. – U.S. National Archives (USNA)

RG 43 – Material of the AAC, Boxes 1–15. (In Britain the papers of the AAC were destroyed. See minutes of Foreign Office Library, 26 Sept. 1968, FO 370/1337.)
RG 59 – State Department Palestine Papers 1946, Boxes 6753–6757.
U.S. War Department – Strategic Service Unit Reports.
RG 59 – Office of Near East Division, Palestine Affairs, Box 1; Herbert Fierst papers (Assistant to General Hilldring).

Washington D.C. – State Department Building – Material seen under Freedom of Information Act

Lot 54 D403 Papers of State Department Near East Division, Boxes 9, 1812, 1815.

Washington D.C. – Library of Congress

Justice Felix Frankfurter papers, container 40.

4. Official Publications

Palestine Royal Commission Report, London 1937, Cmd 5479.
The White Paper of May 1939, Cmd 6019.
British Parliamentary Delegation to Buchenwald Camp. London, April 1945. Cmd 6616.

AAC Report, London April 1946. Cmd 6806.
Government of Palestine – *A Survey of Palestine*, Jerusalem 1946, 3 Vols.
Parliamentary Debates 1945, 1946. *Hansard*, Vols. 419, 426.
United States, State Department – *Foreign Relations United States* (FRUS), Washington D.C.
  Year 1945 Vol. 8
  Year 1946 Vol. 7
  Year 1947 Vol. 5

5. Interviews

Harold Beeley, AAC Secretary. Oxford, Jan. 1980
John Briance, Head of Arab Section, Palestine Police/C.I.D. London, Jan. 1979.
Benjamin V. Cohen – Special Counsellor, U.S. State Department. Washington D.C., May 1979.
Albert Hourani, Arab Office, Jerusalem. Oxford, Summer and Fall 1979.
Frederick Leggett, member of AAC. Interviewed by Gabriel Cohen. London, 5 Dec. 1960 (by courtesy of Professor Cohen).

6. Unpublished Dissertations

Sister M.M. Lorimer, "America's Response to Europe DPs 1945–1952." Ph.D., Saint Louis University 1964.
M.J. Sage, "The Evolution of U.S. Policy Towards Europe DPs: World War II to June 25, 1948." M.A. thesis, Columbia University 1952.
E.B. Tripp, "DPs: the Legislative Controversy in the U.S. 1945–1950." M.A. thesis, Columbia University.

B. PRESS

Al-Ahram (Arabic), 1977
The Economist, 1946
Haaretz, (Hebrew), 1946
Jewish Telegraphic Agency, 1945–1946
The New York Times, 1946
The Observer, 1946
PALCOR News Agency (Palestine), 1945–1946
The Spectator, 1946
The Times, 1946
The Washington Post, 1946

C. PUBLISHED MATERIAL

Dean Acheson, *Present at the Creation*, New York, 1969.

Herbert Agar, *The Saving Remnant*, London, 1960.

American Jewish Yearbook, 1946/47, Philadelphia, 1946.

C. R. Attlee, *As It Happened*, London, 1954.

Frank Aydelotte, *The Vision of Cecil Rhodes*, Oxford, 1946.

Philip J. Baram, *The Department of State in the Middle East 1919–1945*, University of Pennsylvania, 1978.

Yehuda Bauer, *Flight and Rescue: Bricha*, New York, 1970.

Nicholas Bethell, *The Palestine Triangle*, London, 1979.

June Bingham, *Courage to Change: an Introduction to the Life and Thought of Reinhold Niebuhr*, New York, 1972.

Frances Blanshard, *Frank Aydelotte of Swarthmore*, Connecticut, Middletown, 1970.

Louis Blom-Cooper and Gavin Drewry, *Final Appeal: A Study of the House of Lords in its Judicial Capacity*, Oxford, 1972.

J. Blum, *The Price of Vision: The Diary of Henry A. Wallace*, Boston, 1971.

Alan Bullock, *The Life and Times of Ernest Bevin, Vol. I: Trade Union Leader 1881–1940*, London, 1960.

Alan Bullock, *The Life and Times of Ernest Bevin, Vol. II: 1940–1945 – Minister of Labour*, London, 1967.

Alan Bullock, *Ernest Bevin, Foreign Secretary, 1945–1951*, London, 1983.

Frank W. Buxton, "A Report in Retrospect," in *New Palestine*, Vol. 37, No. 20, 20 June 1947.

Chief Judge, U.S. Court of Appeals for 5th Circuit, *Joseph C. Hutcheson Jr.*, Washington, 1949.

Gavriel Cohen, *The British Cabinet and Palestine April–July 1943*, Tel-Aviv, 1976 (Hebrew).

Gavriel Cohen, *Churchill and Palestine, 1939–1942*, Jerusalem, 1976 (Hebrew).

Michael J. Cohen, *Palestine: Retreat from the Mandate – The Making of British Policy 1936–1945*, London, 1978.

Michael J. Cohen, *Palestine and the Great Powers, 1945–1948*, Princeton, 1982.

Richard Crossman, *Palestine Mission, A Personal Record*, London, 1947.

Richard Crossman, *Palestine Mission*, Merhavia, 1947 (Hebrew version).

Richard Crossman, *A Nation Reborn*, London, 1960.

Bartley C. Crum, *Behind the Silken Curtain*, New York, 1947.

Dictionary of National Bibliography 1951–1960 (DNB), Oxford, 1947.

L. Dinnerstein, "U.S. Army and the Jews: Policies Toward the DPs after World War II," *American Jewish History*, Vol. 68, No. 3, March, 1979.

Robert J. Donovan, *Conflict and Crisis: The Presidency of Harry Truman 1945–1948*, New York, 1977.

Eliahu Elath, *The Struggle for Statehood, Washington 1945–1948, Vol. I:*

1945–1946, Tel-Aviv, 1979 (Hebrew).

ESCO Foundation for Palestine, *Palestine: A Study of Jewish, Arab and British Policies*, Vol. 2, New Haven, 1947. Reprint, New York, 1970.

Michael Foot, *Aneurin Bevan – Biography, Vol. 2, 1945–1960*, London, 1973.

Joseph Frankel, *British Foreign Policy, 1945–1973*, Oxford, 1975.

Martin Gilbert, *Exile and Return*, London, 1978.

Joseph Gorny, *The British Labour Movement and Zionism 1917–1948*, London, 1983.

H. Greenberg, "Ten Recommendations: A Critique of the AAC Report," *Jewish Frontier*, May 1946.

P.S. Gupta, *Imperialism and the British Labour Movement, 1914–1964*, Cambridge, 1975.

Alfred F. Havinghurst, *Twentieth Century Britain*, Second edition, New York, 1962.

Anthony Howard, *The Crossman Diaries 1964–1970. Selections from the Diaries of a Cabinet Minister*, London, 1979.

Joseph Heller, "From the 'Black Sabbath' to Partition: Summer 1946 as a Turning Point in the History of Zionist Policy," *Zion*, Vol. 43, No. 3–4, Jerusalem, 1978 (Hebrew).

Joseph Heller, "The Anglo-American Commission of Inquiry on Palestine 1945–1946, The Zionist Reaction Reconsidered" (in typescript).

D. Horowitz, *State in the Making*, New York, 1953.

J.C. Hurewitz, *The Struggle for Palestine*, New York, 1950.

Joseph C. Hutcheson Jr., "The Judgement Intuitive: The Function of the 'Hunch' in Judicial Decision," *Cornell Law Quarterly*, Vol. 14, No. 3, April 1929.

Amitzur Ilan, *America, Britain and Palestine*, Jerusalem, 1979 (Hebrew).

Douglas Jay, *Change and Fortune*, London, 1980.

Jewish Agency, *The Jewish Case Before the AAC of Inquiry on Palestine as Presented by the Jewish Agency for Palestine*, Jeru-salem, 1947.

A. Karlibach, *The AAC of Inquiry on Palestine*, Tel-Aviv, 1946, 2 Vols. (Hebrew).

George Kirk, *Survey of International Affairs 1939–1946: the Middle East in the War*, Oxford, 1952.

George Kirk, *Survey of International Affairs: The Middle East 1945–1950*, London, 1954.

Roger Wm. Louis, *Imperialism at Bay: The United States and the De-colonization of the British Empire, 1941–1945*, Oxford, 1977.

Roger Wm. Louis, *The British Empire in the Middle East, 1945–1951*, Oxford, 1984.

Walter Clay Lowdermilk, *Palestine – Land of Promise*, London, 1944.

Nicholas Mansergh and Penderel Moon, eds., *India – The Transfer of Power 1942–1947*, vol. 7, London, 1977.

Frank E. Manuel, *The Realities of American–Palestine Relations*, Washington, 1949.

W. N. Medlicott, *Contemporary England 1914–1964*, London, 1967.

Walter Millis, ed., *The Forrestal Diaries*, New York, 1951.

Elizabeth Monroe, "Mr. Bevin's Arab Policy," in A. Hourani, ed., *Middle Eastern Affairs*, No. 2, St. Antony's Papers, No. 11, London, 1961.

Elizabeth Monroe, *Britain's Moment in the Middle East 1914–1956*, London, 1963.

B. L. Montgomery, *The Memoirs of Field Marshal the Viscount Montgomery of Alamein*, London, 1958.

Lord Morrison, *Herbert Morrison: an Autobiography*, London, 1960.

Joseph Nevo, *Abdullah and the Arabs of Palestine*, Tel-Aviv, 1975 (Hebrew).

William Phillips, *Ventures in Diplomacy*, Boston, 1952.

N. A. Rose, *Baffy: The Diaries of Blanche Dugdale*, London, 1973.

Harry Sacher, *Israel, the Establishment of a State*, London, 1952.

A. Shlaim, P. Jones and K. Sainsbury, *British Foreign Secretaries Since 1945*, London, 1977.

Ahmaad Al-Shuqairi, *Forty Years in Arabic and International Life*, Beirut, 1969 (Arabic).

J. E. Singleton, *Conduct at the Bar*, London, 1933.

Richard P. Stevens, *American Zionism and U.S. Foreign Policy 1942–1947*, New York, 1962.

Christopher Sykes, *Crossroads to Israel*, London, 1965.

Harry S. Truman, *Memoirs, Vol. II: Years of Trial and Hope 1946–1953*, New York, 1956.

Margaret Truman, *Harry S. Truman*, New York, 1973.

Carl H. Voss, "The American Christian Palestine Committee: the Mid 1940's in Retrospect," *Midstream*, June–July, 1979.

Bernard Washerstein, "Richard Crossman and the New Jerusalem," *Midstream*, April, 1975.

Bernard Wasserstein, *Britain and the Jews of Europe 1939–1945*, Oxford, 1979.

Francis Williams, *Ernest Bevin: Portrait of a Great Englishman*, London, 1952.

Evan Wilson, *Jerusalem, Key to Peace*, Washington, D.C., 1970.

Evan Wilson, *Decision on Palestine*, Stanford, California, 1979.

Index